In the infancy of heaven and earth, there were no names.
It is naming that gave birth to the myriad things.

– Tao Te Ching, Verse 1

Nouns and Verbs in Chinese I

As the first volume of a two-volume set that re-examines nouns and verbs in Chinese, this book proposes the verbs-as-nouns theory, corroborated by discussions of the nature and relationship between nouns and verbs in Chinese.

Seeking to break free from the shackles of Western linguistic paradigms largely based on Indo-European languages and to a great extent inappropriate for Chinese, this two-volume study revisits the nature of nouns and verbs and relevant linguistic categories in Chinese to unravel the different relationships between nouns and verbs in Chinese, English, and other languages. It argues that Chinese nouns and verbs are related inclusively rather than in the oppositional pattern found in Indo-European languages, with verbs included in nouns as a subcategory. Preliminary to the core discussion on the verbs-as-nouns framework, the author critically engages with the issues of word classes and nominalization, as well as problems with the analysis of Chinese grammar due to the noun-verb distinction. Through linguistic comparisons, the following chapters look into noticeable differences between Chinese and English, the referential and predicative natures of nouns and verbs, the asymmetry of the two, and the referentiality of predicates in Chinese.

The volume will be a must-read for linguists and students studying Chinese linguistics, Chinese grammar, and contrastive linguistics.

Shen Jiaxuan is Professor of Linguistics at Institute of Linguistics, Chinese Academy of Social Sciences. His main research interests include contrastive studies between Chinese and English and grammatical theories.

Chinese Linguistics

Chinese Linguistics series selects representative and frontier works in linguistic disciplines including lexicology, grammar, phonetics, dialectology, philology and rhetoric. Mostly published in Chinese before, the selection has had far-reaching influence on China's linguistics and offered inspiration and reference for the world's linguistics. The aim of this series is to reflect the general level and latest development of Chinese linguistics from an overall and objective view.

Titles in this series currently include:

A Brief History of the Chinese Language VI
Middle Chinese Lexicon 2
Xi Xiang

A Brief History of the Chinese Language VII
Modern Chinese Lexicon 1
Xi Xiang

A Brief History of the Chinese Language VIII
Modern Chinese Lexicon 2
Xi Xiang

Modern Chinese Complex Sentences III
Adversative Type
XING Fuyi

Modern Chinese Complex Sentences IV
General Review
XING Fuyi

Nouns and Verbs in Chinese I
Facts and Theories
Shen Jiaxuan

For more information, please visit: www.routledge.com/Chinese-Linguistics/book-series/CL

Nouns and Verbs in Chinese I
Facts and Theories

Shen Jiaxuan

LONDON AND NEW YORK

This book is published with financial support from the Chinese Fund for the Humanities and Social Sciences (20WYYB010)

First published in English 2024
by Routledge
4 Park Square, Milton Park, Abingdon, Oxon OX14 4RN

and by Routledge
605 Third Avenue, New York, NY 10158

Routledge is an imprint of the Taylor & Francis Group, an informa business

© 2024 Shen Jiaxuan

Translated by Zheng Lianzhong and Louis Mangione

The right of Shen Jiaxuan to be identified as author of this work has been asserted in accordance with sections 77 and 78 of the Copyright, Designs and Patents Act 1988.

All rights reserved. No part of this book may be reprinted or reproduced or utilised in any form or by any electronic, mechanical, or other means, now known or hereafter invented, including photocopying and recording, or in any information storage or retrieval system, without permission in writing from the publishers.

Trademark notice: Product or corporate names may be trademarks or registered trademarks, and are used only for identification and explanation without intent to infringe.

English Version by permission of The Commercial Press.

British Library Cataloguing-in-Publication Data
A catalogue record for this book is available from the British Library

Library of Congress Cataloging-in-Publication Data
Names: Shen, Jiaxuan, author.
Title: Nouns and verbs in Chinese / Shen Jiaxuan. Other titles: Mingci yu dongci. English
Description: Abingdon, Oxon ; New York, NY : Routledge, 2023– |
   Series: Chinese linguistics | Includes bibliographical references and indexes. | Contents: v. 1. Facts and theories
Identifiers: LCCN 2022056058 (print) | LCCN 2022056059 (ebook) |
   ISBN 9781032473376 (v. 1 ; hardback) | ISBN 9781032480886
   (v. 1 ; paperback) | ISBN 9781003385899 (v. 1 ; ebook)
Subjects: LCSH: Chinese language—Noun. | Chinese language—Verb.
Classification: LCC PL1232 .S5413 2023 (print) | LCC PL1232 (ebook) |
   DDC 495.15—dc23/eng/20230222
LC record available at https://lccn.loc.gov/2022056058
LC ebook record available at https://lccn.loc.gov/2022056059

ISBN: 978-1-032-47337-6 (hbk)
ISBN: 978-1-032-48088-6 (pbk)
ISBN: 978-1-003-38589-9 (ebk)

DOI: 10.4324/9781003385899

Typeset in Times New Roman
by Apex CoVantage, LLC

Contents

List of figures	*viii*
List of tables	*ix*
List of abbreviations	*x*
Preface	*xi*

Introduction: Between discarding and recovering		1
1	Breaking with earlier assumptions	14
2	The problems	51
3	The verbs-as-nouns framework in Chinese	90
4	Realizational relations and constitutive relations	138
5	The asymmetry between nouns and verbs	176
6	The referentiality of predicates	203
	Subject index	*277*
	Index of languages and dialects	*285*

Figures

0.1 The relationship between noun-verb categories and referring-predicative categories in Indo-European languages and in Chinese 2

0.2 The relationship between nouns and verbs in Indo-European languages and Chinese 2

2.1 Nouny verbs 60

2.2 DP analysis of *Shāngwù zhè běn shū de chūbǎn* and IP analysis of *Shāngwù chūbǎn le zhè běn shū* 68

3.1 The skewed distribution between nouns and verbs 101

3.2 One-to-one correspondence vs. skewed correspondence 104

4.1 Realizational metaphors and constitutive metaphors 139

4.2 The tree diagram of *The play, John saw yesterday* 156

4.3 Syntactic topic 157

4.4 The tree diagram of *Zhè běn shū wǒ bù dǎsuàn xiě le* 158

4.5 The inclusion of subject in topic in Chinese 159

4.6 The relationship between usage and grammar in Indo-European languages and in Chinese 169

4.7 Grammaticalization of usage 170

5.1 The relationship between nouns/verbs and syntactic constituents in Chinese 183

6.1 The difference between progressive tense and expanded tense 262

Tables

1.1	The form classes of verbs in the traditional English grammatical system	33
1.2	Six form classes of verbs in English	33
4.1	English and Chinese "sentence", "subject/predicate", and "noun/verb" in terms of realizational and constitutive relations	159
5.1	Comparison between English and Chinese at three levels of using nouns as verbs and verbs as nouns	181

Abbreviations

ACC	accusative case
ADV	adverbial
ATT	attributive
AV	actor voice
BEG	begun aspect
CL	classifier
CSC	complex stative construction
CV	conveyance voice
DIR	directional verb
DUP	duplicative
DUR	durative aspect
EMPH	emphasis
EXP	experiential aspect
FACT	factual mood
GEN	genitive case
INT	interjection
LIM	limitative
LNK	linker
LV	locative voice
MM	marker of modification
MNN	manner
MP	modal particle
NOM	nominative (default) case
NSF	noun suffix
OBL	oblique case
PL	plural
PSP	presentative status particle
PUNC	punctual aspect
PV	patient voice
S	singular
SEP	separable verb compound
TAM	tense-aspect marker
TOP	topic
trs	translators' note

Preface

Since 2007 I have published a series of articles adopting a new perspective on the relationship of nouns to verbs in Chinese. This in turn brought forth some new thinking on related issues. These publications, which come to about ten articles, are scattered in different journals and collections, making them hard to find, a situation not conducive to a comprehensive understanding of my argument. Thus, a lot of readers suggested that I should elaborate my argument and work the separate articles into a book. Moreover, my understanding of this issue has also undergone a process of continuous deepening. What is emphasized in later discussions is different from what earlier ones emphasized. Some ideas have even been partially revised. This again highlights the need to systematize my discussion.

Although the Commercial Press requested that I write such a book long ago, even after more than two years of planning, writing, repeatedly revising and adjusting, I continued to feel that there were still places that needed to be fixed or improved. Therefore, I kept delaying the submission of my manuscript. However, upon reflection, I accepted that in going about writing the book in this way, the task would never end. Besides, the earlier I got the manuscript published, the sooner I could benefit from various readers' responses.

During the past seven or eight years, I have received a lot of feedback on my new argument, both from those who agree and from those who disagree and from those who understand the argument and from those who do not. Most of the comments have been very helpful in prompting me to think and reflect further. Accordingly, I have adjusted the focus of my argument and improved the way it is presented. In the book I have also responded as much as possible to the criticisms I have received.

Unless it affects the understanding of the text, in keeping with this book's argument and to avoid the occasional trouble of choosing between attributive-*de* and adverbial-*de*, occurrences of the particle are always written as *de*, except in examples and quotations.

Shen Jiaxuan
Beijing
October 21, 2014

* * *

xii *Preface*

The following published articles that the book is based on are generally not cited in the text. Where inconsistencies arise between content in the earlier articles and in the book, the latter should be followed.

Chen, Gang and Jiaxuan Shen (2012) 'Cong biaoji diandao kan yunlu he yufa de xiangsi guanxi' ('Markedness Reversal: The Iconicity of Prosody and Syntax in Chinese'), *Foreign Language Teaching and Research* 4: 483–495.

Shen, Jianxuan (2007) 'Hanyu li de mingci he dongci' ('Nouns and Verbs in Chinese'), *Journal of Sino-Tibetan Linguistics* 1: 27–47.

Shen, Jiaxuan (2009a) 'Wo kan hanyu de cilei' ('My View of Word Classes in Chinese'), *Linguistic Sciences* 1: 1–12.

Shen, Jiaxuan (2009b) 'Wo zhishi jiezhe xiangqian kuale banbu: zaitan hanyu de mingci he dongci' ('Just a Small Step Forward: Further Remarks on Nouns and Verbs in Chinese'), *Essays on Linguistics* 40: 3–22.

Shen, Jiaxuan (2010a) 'Cong *yanyuan shi ge dongci* shuoqi: mingci dongyong he dongci mingyong de buduicheng' ('The Asymmetry in the Use of Verbs as Nouns and Nouns as Verbs as Seen from *Yanyuan Shi Ge Dongci*'), *Contemporary Rhetoric* 1: 1–12.

Shen, Jiaxuan (2010b) 'Bingdu he mingci' ('Viruses and Nouns'), *Journal of Chinese Linguistics* 14: 1–13.

Shen, Jiaxuan (2010c) 'Yinghan foudingci de fenhe he mingdong fenhe' ('Division of Negatives and Noun/Verb Division in English and Chinese'), *Studies of the Chinese Language* 5: 387–399.

Shen, Jiaxuan (2010d) 'Ruhe jiejue buyu wenti' ('How to Solve the *Buyu* Problem'), *Chinese Teaching in the World* 4: 435–445.

Shen, Jiaxuan (2011a) 'Nouns and Verbs in Chinese: Cognitive, Philosophical, and Typological Perspectives', Keynote speech at the 11th International Cognitive Linguistics Conference (Xi'an).

Shen, Jiaxuan (2011b) 'Zhudexi xiansheng zui zhongyao de xueshu yichan' ('The Most Valuable Legacy of Zhu Dexi's Grammatical Theory'), *Language Teaching and Linguistic Studies* 4: 7–19.

Shen, Jiaxuan (2011c) 'Cong youya zhunze kan liangzhong dongdan mingshuang shuo' ('Two Views on Monosyllabic Verbs and Disyllabic Nouns as Seen from the Principle of Elegance'), Paper presented at the Third Cross-Strait Mini-Symposium on Modern Chinese Syntax and Semantics for the Mainland, Taiwan, Hong Kong and Macau.

Shen, Jiaxuan (2011d) 'Cong yunlü jiegou kan xingrongci' ('Rhythmic Structures and Adjectives in Chinese'), *Chinese Language Learning* 3: 3–10.

Shen, Jiaxuan (2012a) 'Guanyu xianqin hanyu de mingci he dongci' ('On Nouns and Verbs in Pre-Qin Chinese'), *Journal of Chinese Linguistics* 15: 100–113.

Shen, Jiaxuan (2012b) 'Mingdongci de fansi: wenti he duice' ('Reflections on Nouny Verbs: Problems and Solutions'), *Chinese Teaching in the World* 1: 3–17.

Shen, Jiaxuan (2012c) 'Zenyang duibi caiyou shuofuli: yi yinghan mingdong duibi weili' ('How to Make Contrastive Studies More Convincing: Nouns and Verbs in English and Chinese'), *Modern Foreign Languages* 1: 1–13.

Shen, Jiaxuan (2012d) 'Lingju he liushuiju: wei Zhaoyuanren xiansheng danchen 120 zhounian erzuo' ('On Minor Sentences and Flowing Sentences in Chinese: In Commemoration of the 120th Anniversary of the Birth of Yuen Ren Chao'), *Studies of the Chinese Language* 5: 403–415.

Shen, Jiaxuan (2012e) 'Mingci he dongci: hanyu tangjiayu ladingyu' ('Nouns and Verbs: Chinese, Tongan, Latin'), *Contemporary Research in Modern Chinese* (Japan) 14: 1–14.

Shen, Jiaxuan (2012f) 'Lun xushi xiangsi yuanli: yunlü he yufa zhijian de niuqu duiying' ('On the Principle of Fullness Iconicity: The Skewed Correspondence Between Prosody and Grammar'), *CASLAR* (*Chinese as a Second Language and Research*) 1(1): 89–103, Berlin: De Gruyter Mouton.

Shen, Jiaxuan (2012g) 'Yuyan gongxing hechu qiu' ('Where to Seek Language Universals'), *Chinese Social Sciences Today*, July 2, B-03.

Shen, Jiaxuan (2013a) 'Weiyu de zhichengxing' ('Can Predicates Be Nominals?'), *Foreign Studies* 1: 1–13.

Shen, Jiaxuan (2013b) 'Nouns and Verbs: Evolution of Grammatical Forms', Keynote speech at the 5th International Conference in Evolutionary Linguistics (CIEL-5), The Chinese University of Hong Kong.

Shen, Jiaxuan (2013c) 'Danshuang qufen zai hanyu zhong de diwei he zuoyong' ('The Status and Role of the Mono- vs. Disyllabic Distinction in Chinese'), Keynote Speech at the 63rd Annual Meeting of the Chinese Linguistic Society of Japan (Tokyo).

Shen, Jiaxuan (2013d) 'Kesi xueshuo dui yuyanxue de qishi' ('Implications of Coase Theorem for Linguistics'), *Nankai Linguistics* 2: 1–5.

Shen, Jiaxuan (2014a) 'Ruhe jiejue zhuangyu wenti' ('How to Solve the Problem of Adverbials'), *Yufa Yanjiu yu Tansuo* (*Studies and Explorations on Grammar*) 17: 1–22.

Shen, Jiaxuan (2014b) 'Hanyu de luoji zhegeyang, hanyu shi zheyang de: wei Zhaoyuanren xiansheng danchen 120 zhounian erzuo zhi er' ('A Review of Yuen Ren Chao's Two Articles on Chinese Grammar and Logic: In Commemoration of the 120th Anniversary of the Birth of Yuen Ren Chao (II)'), Paper presented at the Sixth International Symposium on Grammar of Chinese Dialects, Mianyang, also in *Language Teaching and Linguistic Studies*, 2: 1–10.

Shen, Jiaxuan (2014c) 'Hanyu mingdong baohan shuo' ('The Super-Noun Category in Chinese'), *Yinghan Duibi yu Fanyi* (*Contrastive and Translation Studies of English and Chinese*) 2: 1–28.

Shen, Jiaxuan (2015a) 'Xingshilei de fenyuhe' ('On Division of Form Classes'), *Modern Foreign Languages* 1: 1–14.

Shen, Jiaxuan (2015b) 'Zouchu *dou* de lianghua mitu: xiangyou bu xiangzuo' ('Leftward or Rightward? The Quantifying Direction of *Dou*'), *Studies of the Chinese Language* 1: 3–17.

Shen, Jiaxuan (2015c) 'Cilei de leixingxue he hanyu de cilei' ('Word Class Typology and the Chinese Nominalism'), *Contemporary Linguistics* 2: 127–145.

Shen, Jiaxuan (2015d) 'Hanyu cilei de zhuguanxing' ('On Subjectivity in Chinese Word Classes'), F*oreign Language Teaching and Research* 5: 643–658.

Shen, Jiaxuan and Hang Ke (2014) 'Hanyu de jiezou shi songjin kongzhi qingzhong' ('Chinese Rhythm Is Syllable-timed, Not Stress-timed'), *Essays on Linguistics* 50: 47–72.

Shen, Jiaxuan and Jiangzhi Zhang (2013) 'Yetan xingshi dongci de gongneng' ('On the Grammatical Function of Dummy Verbs in Chinese'), *TCSOL Studies* 2: 8–17.

Shen, Jiaxuan and Quan Wan (2009) 'Yetan *zhi* zi jiegou he *zhi* zi de gongneng' ('A Further Study on the *Zhi*-Construction and the Function of *Zhi* in Pre-Qin Chinese'), *Studies in Language and Linguistics* 2: 1–12.

Shen, Jiaxuan and Yao Yue (2013) 'Cilei de shiyan yanjiu huhuan yufa lilun de gengxin' ('Explaining Experiment Results on Word Classes: Toward an Updated Grammatical Theory'), *Contemporary Linguistics* 3: 253–267.

xiv *Preface*

Wan, Quan and Jiaxuan Shen (2010) 'Kua yuyan cilei bijiao de amusitedan moxing' ('Kees Hengeveld's Cross-linguistic Model for Word Class Systems Comparison'), *Minority Languages of China* 3: 4–17.

Wang, Wei and Jiaxuan Shen (2011) 'Hanyu weishenme meiyou zhenzheng de weiyu: mingdong de zhicheng/shuwei buduicheng' ('Why There Is No Real Predicate in Chinese: The Reference/Predication Asymmetry of Nouns and Verbs'), Paper presented at the Third Cross-Strait Mini-Symposium on Modern Chinese Syntax and Semantics for the Mainland, Taiwan, Hong Kong and Macau.

Introduction

Between discarding and recovering

0.1 The essentials of the verbs-as-nouns theory

This book argues that Chinese nouns and verbs are different from their Indo-European counterparts both in terms of their nature and the way they are related. In terms of nature, Indo-European nouns and verbs fall into grammatical categories that are not the same as the pragmatic categories "referring expressions" and "predicative expressions", whereas Chinese nouns and verbs belong to both grammatical and pragmatic categories, i.e. they are referring and predicative expressions, respectively. In Chinese, the pragmatic categories of referring expressions and predicative expressions include the grammatical categories of nouns and verbs, as depicted in Figure 0.1.

The intersection between the two kinds of categories on the left side of Figure 0.1 shows the so-called interface between grammar and usage in Indo-European languages. In contrast, there is no such interface in Chinese. If we consider grammar as the "structure" of language, the inclusion pattern in Chinese can be called "the inclusion of structure in use", where "use" includes "structure". In this inclusion pattern, nouns and verbs serve as referring and predicative expressions respectively, but not all referring expressions are nouns and not all predicative expressions are verbs. In Indo-European languages nouns and verbs undergo a process to be *realized* as referring and predicative expressions. Chinese has no such process. Its nouns and verbs are *constituted* by referring and predicative expressions.

In terms of relationship, Indo-European nouns and verbs are in an oppositional pattern, whereas Chinese nouns and verbs follow an inclusion pattern, with verbs included in nouns as a type of dynamic nouns, though not all nouns are verbs. Logically speaking, the inclusion relationship is that of class and type or that of superordinate and subordinate, as depicted in Figure 0.2.

In the oppositional pattern of Indo-European languages, the relationship between nouns and verbs is similar to that between males and females: Being male excludes being female; being female excludes being male. Analogously, Indo-European nouns and verbs fall in discrete categories with very little overlap; some nouns can be converted into verbs and some verbs into nouns. In contrast, in the inclusion pattern of Chinese, the relationship between nouns and verbs is like that between *man* (human beings; males) and *woman* in English, where women are also

DOI: 10.4324/9781003385899-1

2 Introduction

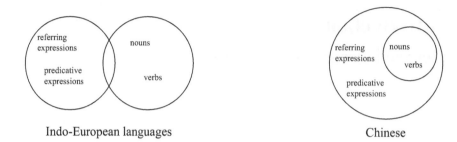

Figure 0.1 The relationship between noun-verb categories and referring-predicative categories in Indo-European languages and in Chinese

Figure 0.2 The relationship between nouns and verbs in Indo-European languages and Chinese

included in the category *man* in the sense of human beings. In Chinese there is no such thing as nouns converting into verbs or verbs into nouns because all verbs are included in nouns as dynamic nouns. Given that nouns and verbs in the inclusion pattern in Chinese stand in the relationship of class to type, they are different in one way and similar in another. Thus, on the one hand, they are conceptually distinct from each other, as nouns do not consist entirely of verbs. On the other hand, they are not distinguished from each other, for verbs are included in nouns as a type of dynamic nouns. As to the question of whether there is a word class of verbs in Chinese, the answer is both yes and no. The affirmative answer is based on the fact that verbs exist as a special type of dynamic noun in Chinese. The negative answer is given on account of the lack of a separate word class for verbs in Chinese. As said earlier, nouns and verbs in Chinese can serve directly as referring and predicative expressions, and thus the inclusion of verbs in nouns is essentially the inclusion of predicative expressions in referring expressions. Nouns and verbs in the inclusion pattern entail both a relationship of class and type and that of part and whole. These are the essentials of the verbs-as-nouns theory, which will be discussed in detail in Chapters 3 and 4.

It is a controversial question among linguists whether word classes, especially nouns and verbs, are universal. Generative linguists answer in the affirmative. Nouns have the [+ N] feature, and verbs have the [+ V] feature. This is hypothesized to be part of humanity's innate linguistic knowledge. Linguistic typologists are divided over whether nouns and verbs are universal in human languages (see Vogel & Comrie 2000). We argue in this book that it is important to divide the question into two: Whether there is a distinction between nouns and verbs and how to make a distinction between them. The distinction between nouns and verbs is made on the basis of the conceptual distinction between things and actions and thus can be assumed to be universal in human languages. However, the way of distinguishing between nouns and verbs varies from language to language and can be divided into at least two types: the Indo-European oppositional pattern and the Chinese inclusion pattern. This results from the difference or different tendencies in perceiving and construing the relationship between things and actions. To say that there are different ways of distinguishing is not equivalent to saying that they are unlimited. This book hypothesizes that for the inclusion pattern there is only the type of verbs included in nouns. It would be inconceivable for there to be a type in which nouns were included in verbs. The reason for this lies in the asymmetrical cognitive construal of things and actions, which will be elaborated on in Chapter 5. It is a misconception that the verbs-as-nouns theory makes no distinction between nouns and verbs and that it treats nouns as predicate verbs. On the contrary, these are exactly what the verbs-as-nouns theory is against. This misconception presupposes that nouns and verbs are either separate or united.

Evidence from the entire range of linguistic facts converges to support the verbs-as-nouns framework in Chinese. The inclusion of verbs in nouns is not a way of dealing with word classes on an ad hoc basis. Instead it is vital to the construction of the word class system in Chinese or even of Chinese grammar as a whole. It has important implications not only for the study of Chinese but also for the study of other languages and for theory building in general linguistics.

Some people may ask, "since Chinese nouns and verbs are so radically different from those in Indo-European languages, why not use different terms for Chinese nouns and verbs?" The reason for not using different terms is to conform to established conventions and to facilitate comparisons with other languages. After all, the word classes in Chinese should be investigated with reference to the world's other languages. Where confusion may arise, we call the nouns that include verbs (i.e. dynamic nouns) "super-nouns" and those nouns other than dynamic nouns "small nouns", "static nouns", or "general nouns". In most cases, I abide by the conventional use of nouns and verbs, for context can remove possible misunderstandings. In so doing, some degree of redundancy can be avoided in writing. What readers need to keep in mind is that the distinction between static and dynamic nouns is based on the inclusion pattern, and the inclusion of verbs in nouns is essentially the inclusion of predicative expressions in referring expressions.

0.2 The principle of simplicity

The purpose of distinguishing word classes is to facilitate the explanation of a language's grammar by grouping words of the same kind together. After determining

4   *Introduction*

a language's word class system, we can evaluate its strengths and weaknesses to see whether it is effective in explaining a language's grammar. There are two main criteria for evaluating a theoretical system, consistency and simplicity. Consistency refers to there being no contradictions or circular argumentation. Simplicity entails rejecting unnecessary complexities. When a simpler account is possible, it should be preferred. Consistency has been accepted as a criterion, requiring no further explanation, whereas there seems to be no agreement on what constitutes the simplicity criterion.

Some do not have a proper understanding of the criterion of simplicity. They contend that a grammar should be treated as a coherent whole. If one part of the grammar is simple, another part must be complex. For example, if the syntax component is simple, the lexical component must be complex. This is like a verbose person defending himself by arguing that by making complicated statements here, he is enabled to speak more concisely elsewhere. However, this is both a misunderstanding and a distortion of the criterion of simplicity. The opposite of simplicity is redundancy and unnecessary complexity.

Others ask, "How can we judge something to be concise or not?" This question implies that simplicity is hard to measure. It's like a verbose person who responds rhetorically to criticism by asking, "On what basis do you say that I am a verbose person?" However, simplicity is easy to measure in that there is no need to create two categories if one is enough to cover the same linguistic facts. This same reasoning holds for rules, assumptions, and levels of analysis.

There are still others who propose the criterion of comprehensiveness in addition to the criteria of consistency and simplicity when evaluating a theory. They treat simplicity and comprehensiveness as mutually incompatible arguing that the two cannot be satisfied at the same time. Again, this is a defense of unnecessary complexity. Indeed, the criterion of comprehensiveness can be subsumed into that of simplicity. A theoretical system is more concise because it is more thorough and thus should be considered to be a better account of the same facts. Needless to say, to deliberately avoid some linguistic facts for the sake of simplicity is not to observe but to abuse the criterion of simplicity. Inconsistency and lack of simplicity are a pair of bad twin brothers. The former is bound to bring about the latter, and the latter usually entails the former.

Many talented physicists view "elegance"[1] as the highest standard in theory construction. For example, the discovery of antimatter is the result of taking elegance as the highest standard. This discovery derives its origin from Paul Dirac (1902–1984) and his relativistic quantum mechanics. As one of the greatest physicists of the 20th century, Dirac had insights into physics that left many of his gifted contemporaries in awe. The Dirac equation that he created is not only extremely important in physics but also has had an immeasurable impact on chemistry and many new widely applied technologies.

When Dirac applied his equation to electrons, he found an amazing fact: There were not only solutions that could describe the properties of electrons with accuracy but also solutions corresponding to negative energy states. Before that, we all know energy can only be positive in the real world. Faced with similar situations, the ordinary physicists would suspect that the equation itself is flawed or just ignore the negative energy by dismissing it as a kind of purely mathematical non-physical solution.

Dirac, however, was an extraordinary physicist. In determining whether a theory in physics was true or not, Dirac, like Einstein, took "elegance" as the highest standard. According to Einstein, theories should be "as simple as possible, but not simpler". Because the Dirac equation was so elegant, Dirac was confident about its correctness, and he believed that the negative energy solution was sure to have profound implications. After carefully thinking through the implications, Dirac asserted in 1931 that the negative energy solution actually corresponded to another type of particle as opposed to electrons. In the real world, this particle seemed to be an antiparticle with positive energy or a positively charged antielectron, which was later renamed a positron.

This bold prediction immediately set off an uproar in the physics community. Most people were skeptical about it and some even treated this antiparticle theory as the object of jokes and ridicule. However, to everyone's surprise, just one year later, positrons were discovered while studying cosmic rays! Based on this discovery, Dirac further predicted that all elementary particles have corresponding antiparticles. For example, if there are protons, there should be anti-protons. Anti-protons were indeed discovered and confirmed in 1955. The recognition of the existence of antimatter was a major step forward in the understanding of the physical world. Chen Ning Yang (2013: 176) likened Dirac's bold and original prediction "to the first introduction of negative numbers, an introduction that enlarged and completed our understanding of the integers which lie at the foundation of all mathematics". Dirac's prediction expanded our understanding of field theory and laid the foundation for quantum electric field theory. (All of the previous discussion concerning antimatter is based on Tang Shuang 2011).

The standard of elegance is in fact the principle of Occam's razor, which posits that entities are not to be multiplied beyond necessity. According to this principle, the theory that assumes less should be favored if there are two theories capable of explaining the same range of facts. For example, the statements that "the earth is originally square, but it appears to be round when observed" and that "the earth is originally round" describe the same fact. The former statement, however, is not credible as it introduces an inexplicable and unnecessary assumption.

As Lao Tzu said, "With less you gain; having excess leads you astray". For many distinguished scientists, this is not only one of their beliefs about science but also one of their guiding principles in exploring the physical world and one of their methodological considerations in doing research (Zhang & Zhang 2012). Those who regard linguistics as a branch of science should see the importance of the principle of simplicity, even if they do not accept simplicity as the highest standard. Zhu Dexi treats simplicity as an important evaluative criterion in his construction of a phrase-based grammatical system for Chinese. He addresses the

6   *Introduction*

importance of simplicity in at least three places in his *Answering Questions about Chinese Grammar* (1985).

> In short, many contradictions in a sentence-based grammatical system arise from the incompatibility between basic concepts such as phrases, sentence constituents, and head words. To resolve these contradictions, terms like phrasal "fusion" and word class conversion are thought up. When these terms lose their explanatory power, exceptions to general rules have to be listed. Consequently, the grammatical system becomes more and more complicated. From this, it can be seen that the sentence-based grammatical system is by no means a good one because it lacks both rigorousness due to internal contradictions and simplicity.
>
> (pp. 72–73)

> When evaluating a theory or a system, both simplicity and rigorousness are very important criteria.
>
> (p. 77)

> A phrase-based grammatical system is both concise and natural as it conforms to the actual Chinese language. In contrast, a sentence-based grammatical system is both redundant and barely adequate because it forces incompatible Indo-European grammatical constructs onto the Chinese language.
>
> (p. 78)

These three quotations can be summarized as follows: 1) simplicity and rigorousness are equally important, redundancy should be avoided, and systems cannot be allowed to become ever more complex; 2) the system should be natural, it cannot be barely adequate, and it should conform to the actual Chinese language; 3) simplicity and naturalness are inherently connected, and the grammatical system that captures the actual Chinese language must be a system that is both concise and natural. It is this principle of simplicity that prompts Zhu Dexi to insist that Chinese verbs functioning as subjects and objects do not undergo "nominalization" and are thus still verbs. In Chinese, for example, the verb *kāi* 'fly' is morphologically the same whether in the predicate position as in *Tā kāi fēijī* 'He flies airplanes' or in the subject position as in *Kāi fēijī róngyì* 'To fly a plane is easy'. However, the corresponding verb 'to fly' in English should be changed to its finite form when it serves as a predicate verb, and to an infinitive, a present participle, or a past participle when it is used as a subject. It is typical for Chinese verbs to be used as subjects and objects without undergoing any morphological changes. This is true for both classical and modern Chinese. To explain this fact, two theories are proposed. One is a traditional theory with two assumptions: 1) verbs can serve as predicates and they cannot be used as subjects and objects; 2) what appear to be verbs serving as subjects and objects are forms that have been changed into nouns. The other theory is proposed by Zhu Dexi, which has only one assumption that verbs, given their basic properties, can be used both as predicates and as subjects and objects. The latter

Introduction 7

theory is certainly simpler as it has one less assumption and so should be more credible. By using Occam's razor, Zhu Dexi removes an unnecessary assumption as well as the assumption that phrases "fuse" into sentential constituents when occurring in sentences. In so doing he builds the phrase-based grammatical system that is simpler and more elegant than the traditional sentence-based grammatical system. See Chapter 1 for details.

In short, this book is based on the idea that simplicity and consistency are equally important in linguistics as a science and that both of them, instead of some a priori assumption (e.g., "the noun-verb distinction"), should be regarded as the highest criteria. The principle of simplicity overrides the different schools of linguistics.[2]

0.3 Breaking free from Indo-European conceptual shackles

The inclusion of verbs in nouns is not something imaginary or something emerging from nowhere. Rather, it continues the long-standing efforts of Chinese grammarians to break free from the Indo-European conceptual shackles. Zhu Dexi (1985) made the following remarks in his preface to the Japanese translation of *Answering Questions about Chinese Grammar*:

> From the very beginning, the study of Chinese grammar has been deeply influenced by the grammars of Indo-European languages. Most of the early works on Chinese grammar are imitative of grammars for Indo-European languages. It is not until the 1940s that some scholars began to try to break free from the Indo-European framework and explore Chinese-specific grammar rules. Despite the valuable work they have done since then, it is still difficult to eliminate the long-standing negative influence of Indo-European grammatical concepts on the study of Chinese. This influence is mainly manifested in viewing Chinese through the lens of Indo-European languages and imposing on Chinese features that Indo-European languages possess but Chinese lacks.
>
> Chinese has an idiom "first impressions are strongest." Its meaning is that the preconceptions are enormously powerful. We are now criticizing certain traditional concepts here, but very likely we ourselves have unknowingly fallen under the influence of these very concepts. Doubtless our inadequacies can only be overcome by others in the future. This is a typical example of the truism that "the future views the present as the present views the past."

Among the Chinese-specific grammar rules, one that cannot be underestimated is that Chinese verbs serving as subjects and objects do not undergo any process of nominalization, a process that is found in Indo-European languages but not in Chinese. The verbs-as-nouns theory takes this one step further by challenging the deep-rooted traditional idea that nouns and verbs are distinct. It goes on to argue that this distinction is found in Indo-European languages but not in Chinese. The logic herein is quite simple: The reason why Chinese does not have the kind of

8   Introduction

nominalization processes found in Indo-European languages is that Chinese verbs, by their very nature, are nouns.

Following are some of the most important views on Chinese grammar from the precursors of the verbs-as-nouns theory:

Yuen Ren Chao argues that 1) minor sentences can be free standing, are the basic grammatical unit, and can compose full sentences; 2) subjects are actually topics; 3) subject-predicate phrases can serve as the predicates; 4) nouns can be predicates, and the types of predicates cannot be divided into nouns, verbs, and adjectives; 5) there are no adjectives equivalent to the English adjectives *no, all, some*.

Lü Shuxiang argues that 1) with respect to changes in word class, if all the members of a word class can be used in a given structure, their use in that structure cannot be accounted for by having them changed into derived members of another word class; 2) Chinese nouns themselves are not subject to negation; 3) Chinese distinguishes *shì* 'be' from *yǒu* 'have/there be'; *shì* concerns yes-no questions; *yǒu* concerns question of having and not having; 4) the pattern of narrative sentences is "subjects—verbs—objects", whereas the pattern of judgment sentences is "subjects—predicates" where predicates themselves can be subject-predicate phrases; 5) structural relations are closely related to the pairing of monosyllabic and disyllabic words, with most sequences of a disyllabic word followed by a monosyllabic word [2 + 1] being attribute-head phrases and most monosyllabic-disyllabic word sequences [1 + 2] being verb-object types.

Zhu Dexi argues that 1) verbs serving as subjects and objects are still verbs without undergoing a process of nominalization; 2) subject-predicate constructions are also a type of phrase, functioning in a similar manner to other types of phrases; 3) the relationship that holds between phrases and sentences is not constitutive but realizational, a relationship of the abstract being realized in the concrete; 4) Chinese nouns can only be negatively defined, that is, nouns cannot serve as predicates without any constraints; 5) nouns can be modified by all types of nouns, and *de* constructions should be considered nominal grammatical units, as in *bái de zhǐ* 'white paper', *dǒng de rén* 'people who understand', and *zuótiān de bào* 'yesterday's newspaper'.

In this book, the previous points are fully accepted and quoted when arguing for the verbs-as-nouns theory. In particular, Zhu's proposition that "Chinese nouns can only be negatively defined" can be said to have already called forth the verbs-as-nouns framework to emerge. The theory is only a small step forward on the road to breaking out of the constraints imposed by the Indo-European framework. Chapter 1 will examine Zhu's scholarly legacy and clarify some misconceptions.

Given that preconceptions are enormously powerful, some will consider it a sudden, if not crazy, change for the noun-verb distinction in Chinese to give place to the verbs-as-nouns framework. This brings to mind what the brilliant quantum physicist Niels Bohr once said, "We are all agreed that your theory is crazy. The question which divides us is whether it is crazy enough to have a chance of being correct" (https://en.wikiquote.org/wiki/Niels_Bohr). Scientific breakthroughs dispel myths, challenge preconceived ideas, and sometimes require a tremendous

Introduction 9

amount of craziness. To presuppose that the noun-verb distinction is fundamental both in Chinese and in Indo-European languages is the very myth and preconceived idea this book is intended to dispel and challenge. In his later years, Lü Shuxiang made the following remarks in his article "Arguments and refutations in grammatical studies" (2002: 402, 404):

> It takes courage to unlearn. . . . Discard terms like *word, verb, adjective, subject,* and *object* for the time being. Though they might be taken up again later, there will be significant changes between when they are discarded and when they are recovering. The significant changes will consist of the differences in their meanings and value, thereby creating the possibility of daring to push against constraints now considered untouchable.
>
> Though terms are indispensable in exploring regularities, they and their terminological system are created to serve the description of regularities. We made these terms, and we use them. We should control them. We cannot let them control us.

This book's arguments for the verbs-as-nouns framework are essentially the type of work that falls between discarding terms and recovering them.

0.4 Chinese in the world's languages

When Chinese is examined without reference to other languages, its true features can hardly be revealed; it is even more so the case for the features of languages other than Chinese. This is like the situation described by Su Shi in a poem in which you cannot tell the true shape of the Lushan mountain because you yourself are in the mountain. When a native speaker of Chinese looks out into the world of other languages, his or her horizons will be broadened. However, for historical reasons, his or her attention will be easily drawn to Indo-European languages, thereby imposing on Chinese features that Indo-European languages possess but Chinese lacks. It is equally likely that Chinese-specific features will be easily overstated and features it shares with other languages will be ignored. When Chinese is viewed as a member of the world's languages or placed within the map of languages in the world, this broader perspective enables a clearer understanding of the Chinese language and its true features with respect to other languages. This will in turn facilitate a deeper understanding of other languages and the nature of human language.

The focus of linguistic typology shifted from morphology to word order in the 20th century. In recent years, its scope has been extended to types of word classes. This extension is a matter of course because the grammatical categories S (subject), O (object), V (verb), N (noun), and A (adjective) in the word order types such as SVO, SOV, AN, NA are found to vary considerably across languages and thus defy sweeping generalizations. The word class systems of different languages are found to be typologically very different as well. Ignoring these typological differences is arguably an inherent deficiency of word order typology. Therefore, some linguistic typologists (e.g. Hengeveld 1992, 2013; Himmelmann 2007) have begun to build

10   *Introduction*

word class models for cross-linguistic comparison. They point out that the four-way word class system of nouns, verbs, adjective, and adverbs in English is not universal. In fact, it is relatively rare among human languages. Moreover, the word class systems of human languages are not only not identical but also vary considerably. Linguistic typologists who work on the typology of word classes are exploring the possibility that different groupings of word classes constitute one of the root causes for language variation and that the parameters for grouping word classes are an important type of parameter that determines the typological differences among human languages (see Wan & Shen 2010). Based on a field survey of Tongan, a Polynesian language, Broschart (1997) argues in his paper in the inaugural issue of *Linguistic Typology* that unlike Indo-European noun/verb-languages, Tongan is a type/token-language. In the framework of generative grammar, through comparisons of the particle *de* in Chinese and the corresponding *Ezafe* in Iranian languages, Larson (2009) argues that the nouns in both Chinese and Iranian languages belong to a super-noun category that includes verbs and adjectives. According to Kaufman (2009), who also works in the generative framework, all verbs and verb roots in Tagalog should be reanalyzed as nouns and noun roots. (See Sections 6 and 7 of Chapter 3 in this volume and Chapter 2 in Volume II for details.) Based on the facts found in a large amount of languages, especially African languages, the historical linguists Heine and Kuteva (2002) conclude that in terms of the evolution of word classes, nouns and verbs are not on the same level and that verbs are derived from nouns. What this book intends to do between discarding and restoring of word classes is to draw on the latest findings in the typology of word classes and show how the Chinese verbs-as-nouns framework contributes to the understanding of the typology of word classes in the languages of the world. In particular, it will provide insights into the typological evolution of word class systems. (See Section 6 of Chapter 2 in Volume II.) This book will demonstrate that a deeper understanding of the grammars of other languages can be achieved from the standpoint of Chinese-specific word class features. (See Section 5 of Chapter 6 in this volume and Section 5.3 of Chapter 3 in Volume II).

The verbs-as-nouns theory has been informed by markedness theory. It will in turn deepen and refine markedness theory. The studies on markedness theory, including my book *Asymmetry and Markedness Theory* (1999), fail to attach sufficient importance to the distinction between "unmarked" and "non-marked". The importance of this distinction can be seen in the context of the verbs-as-nouns theory. (See Chapter 3, Section 3.) Moreover, the markedness reversal theory as a later development in markedness theory corroborates the position of the verbs-as-nouns theory. (See Chapter 5 in Volume II.)

The verbs-as-nouns theory critically reflects on the three-way division of syntax, semantics, and pragmatics in mainstream linguistics. It also contributes to theory construction in cognitive linguistics. (See Section 4 of Chapter 4 in this volume and Section 6 of Chapter 4 in Volume II.) We also discuss the theory in a broader context outside of linguistics. Chapter 4's discussion of realizational and constitutive relations is an example of this interdisciplinary approach. Grammatical theories without philosophical foundations lack depth. Section 6 of Chapter 3 and Section

Introduction   11

3 of Concluding Remarks in Volume II will respectively discuss the philosophical background of the noun-verb distinction and that of the inclusion of verbs in nouns. In addition, the theory developed in this book helps to facilitate communication between linguistics and other disciplines at the frontiers of research.

0.5   The explanatory power of the verbs-as-nouns theory

After "discarding and recovering" earlier constructs, our understanding of Chinese nouns and verbs shift from an oppositional pattern to an inclusion pattern. This conceptual change will bring considerable benefits to the building of a Chinese grammatical system. Those who do not understand the inclusion pattern may ask, "What are the benefits of this change?" The implication is that there are no benefits to be seen. This disagreement over this change lies primarily in the perception of what "benefits" are. As discussed in Section 2, eliminating the problems of inconsistency and unnecessary complexity counts as a greatest benefit. There is no need for more linguistic facts to show that a system that is neither consistent nor concise has problems and is nowhere near being an optimal grammar. Chapter 2 will analyze the problems with the current word class system, including the definition of nouns, the nature of nouny verbs, the violation of the head feature convention and the coordination test, the indeterminate syntactic functions of word classes, and the multi-class words. Along with the establishment of the verbs-as-nouns framework, the problems that will be solved include the nature of nominal predicates (Chapters 5 and 6), the demarcation of complements and adverbials (Volume II, Chapter 1), and the function of dummy verbs (Chapter 6, Section 4). Some long-debated specific problems will be solved to a reasonable extent, such as the analysis of the "N *ér* V" structure as in *rén ér wú xìn* 'people without integrity'. (Chapter 6, Section 3.4) The verbs-as-nouns framework will also help to answer some of the important questions: Why are there so many flowing sentences in Chinese (Chapter 6, Section 3.3)? Why is the Chinese way of responding to yes-no questions different from English (Chapter 4, Section 4.2)? The answers to these questions will deepen our understanding of the Chinese language as well as of other languages. As pointed out in the last section, establishing the verbs-as-nouns framework in Chinese is conducive to reviewing other languages from the perspective of this framework and thereby enhancing the development of linguistic typology.

Innovation requires a break with tradition. In the verbs-as-nouns framework for Chinese, despite some differences between nouns and verbs, these differences are not as significant as they are in Indo-European languages. Chinese grammar should have its own way to differentiate the two. Linguistic typology is not only about investigating what each language's main categories are. It is also about investigating the important distinctions each language makes. Chapter 3 in Volume II argues that the distinction between the sentence types "assertion" and "narration" marked by *shì* 'be' and *yǒu* 'have/there be' respectively and the distinction between the indicative and non-indicative moods are important categorical distinctions in Chinese. The difference between being depictive or non-depictive is a primary way

12 *Introduction*

in which words and phrases are differentiated and reduplication is an important morphological process in Chinese that has a significant role in establishing this difference (Chapter 3, Section 5). Chapter 4 in Volume II argues that the monosyllabic vs. disyllabic opposition and the related prosodic [2 + 1] vs. [1 + 2] distinctions in syllable alignment are important morphosyntactic means. Moreover, the distinctions between "function" and "content" cut across rhythm, grammar, semantics, and pragmatics and play a very important role in Chinese. Chapter 5 in Volume II goes on to argue that the difference between adjectives and nouns/verbs is greater than that between nouns and verbs. Finally, in the Concluding Remarks of Volume II, the author brings together all these new understandings, formulates the idea of rewriting Chinese grammar with a new word class system, and calls for the necessity to respect language diversity in linguistics. The verbs-as-nouns framework, built on linguistic facts rather than presupposed theories, also provides a solid frame of reference for exploring the differences between Chinese and Western views of categories (i.e. "distinction" and "opposition").

Notes

1 The *Oxford English Dictionary* defines *elegance* as "ingenious simplicity". Coincidentally, "simplicity and elegance blend together" in traditional Chinese aesthetics (Wu 1986: 368).
2 Though the noun-verb distinction is taken as a theoretical presupposition in the prominent generative grammar school of linguistics, this presupposition can be revised to comply with the principle of simplicity. See Sections 6 and 7 of Chapter 3 for details.

References

Broschart, J. (1997) 'Why Tongan Does It Differently: Categorial Distinctions in a Language without Nouns and Verbs', *Linguistic Typology* 1: 123–165.
Heine, B. and T. Kuteva (2002) 'On the Evolution of Grammatical Forms', in Alison Wray (ed) *The Transition to Language*, Oxford: Oxford University Press, 376–397.
Hengeveld, K. (1992) 'Parts of Speech', in M. Fortescue, P. Harder and L. Kristoffersen (eds) *Layered Structure and Reference in a Functional Perspective*, Amsterdam: John Benjamins, 29–55.
Hengeveld, K. (2013) 'Parts-of-Speech Systems as a Basic Typological Determinant', in J. Rijkhoff and E. van Lier (eds) *Flexible Word Classes*, Oxford: Oxford University Press, 31–55.
Himmelmann, N. (2007) 'Lexical Categories and Voice in Tagalog', in P. K. Austin and S. Musgrave (eds) *Voice and Grammatical Functions in Austronesian Languages*, Stanford: CSLI.
Kaufman, Daniel (2009) 'Austronesian Nominalism and Its Consequences: A Tagalog Case Study', *Theoretical Linguistics* 35(1): 1–49.
Larson, R. K. (2009) 'Chinese as a Reverse *Ezafe* Language', *Essays on Linguistics* 39: 30–85.
Lü, Shuxiang (2002) 'Yufa yanjiu zhong de po yu li' ('Arguments and Refutations in Grammatical Studies'), in *Lü Shuxiang Quanji* (*The Complete Works of Lü Shuxiang*), vol. 13, Beijing: The Commercial Press, 402–404.

Shen, Jiaxuan (1999) *Bu duicheng he Biaoji lun* (*Asymmetry and Markedness Theory*), Nanchang: Jiangxi Education Publishing House, Reprinted in Beijing: The Commercial Press, 2015.

Tang, Shuang (2011) 'Fan wuzhi zhi mi' ('The Puzzle of Antimatter'), *Dushu Magazine* 2: 64–69.

Vogel, P. M. and B. Comrie (eds) (2000) *Approaches to the Typology of Word Classes*, Berlin and New York: Mouton de Gruyter.

Wan, Quan and Jiaxuan Shen (2010) 'Kua yuyan cilei bijiao de amusitedan moxing' ('Kees Hengeveld's Cross-linguistic Model for Comparing Word Class Systems'), *Minority Languages of China* 3: 4–17.

Wu, Lifu (1986) *Wu Lifu Yishu Meixue Wenji* (*Wu Lifu's Essays on the Aesthetics of Art*), Shanghai: Fudan University Press.

Yang, Chen Ning (2013) *Selected Papers II with Commentaries*, Singapore: World Scientific.

Zhang, Yiming and Zengyi Zhang (2012) 'Lun Aiyinsitan luoji jiandanxing sixiang jiqi yuanyuan' ('On Einstein's Thought of Logical Simplicity and Its Origin'), *Studies in Dialectics of Nature* 28(9): 112–116.

Zhu, Dexi (1985) *Yufa Dawen* (*Answering Questions about Chinese Grammar*), Beijing: The Commercial Press.

1 Breaking with earlier assumptions

1.1 An important step in casting off Indo-European shackles

In the history of studies on Chinese grammar, the greatest significance of *Ma's Grammar* lies in its introduction of detailed analyses of grammar from the West. This changed the whole approach to Chinese grammatical studies. The author, Ma Jianzhong, felt that traditional research on grammar failed to differentiate between word classes. It was according to him satisfied with elucidating the main thrust of an entire sentence. He criticized this approach as not seeking the underlying reasons for why a sentence's meaning was what it was:

> As for the differentiation of word/character classes and the grammar rules for how they collocate to form sentences . . . everyone says that these can only be sensed through intuition and not explained in words/characters. Alas! This is certainly an instance of taking things for granted and not seeking their underlying mechanisms!
>
> (Preface to *Ma's Grammar*)

Ma believes that it is an unchanging principle for all languages that words belong to classes and sentences determine the choice of words. Thus he adopts Western analytical methods to analyze Chinese into units, word classes, syntactic constituents, and levels of syntactic structure. This kind of "detailed analysis of each and every paragraph, sentence and word" follows exactly in "the thousand-year tradition of the thousand-year tradition of how grammar has been taught in the west" (Xu 1991: 92). For more than a century, Chinese grammar has closely followed the path offset out by *Ma's Grammar*, constantly borrowing Western analytical methods. Grammatical analysis has thus become almost synonymous with grammatical research. Some major debates on Chinese grammar have arisen from questions about what can be divided and how. First to arise have been debates over how to divide the language into units like morphemes, words, and phrases, or how to distinguish simple sentences from complex sentences. Then came questions regarding the classification of the resulting units: Can content words in Chinese be categorized? If so, how? What is the appropriate number of types for syntactic constituents? How are subjects distinguished from objects? Besides, there are a number of

DOI: 10.4324/9781003385899-2

analytical methods such as hierarchical analysis, isomorphic analysis, transformational analysis, semantic component analysis, and three-plane analysis. One category is divided into several subcategories. The particle *de* 'marker of modification', for example, has been divided into three particles. In short, our grammatical research over the past century has been "analysis followed by analysis leading to more analysis". Its progress consists largely in the extension of the breadth and depth of analysis and the improvement of analytical methods. The introduction of analytical methods has greatly deepened our understanding of Chinese grammatical structures. Through different types of analysis, we have discovered the differences between components. This has indeed contributed to our understanding of the properties of the whole.

Even while recognizing its contributions, the negative impact *Ma's Grammar* has had on the study of Chinese cannot be underestimated. It highlighted some unique characteristics of Chinese grammar. However, its entire system of divisions and classification was established by modeling on the Indo-European framework. It is undeniable that many difficulties and problems have arisen whenever the Western analytical framework, one primarily focused on Indo-European languages, has been applied to Chinese. First, there are many situations in which the classifications are unclear and possible differentiations are never ending. Because Chinese lacks a full-fledged morphology, many grammatical phenomena change gradually rather than abruptly. This results in there being a wide range of easily identified "intermediate states" in Chinese grammar. To this needs to be added the difficulty of using a single uniform approach to draw the boundaries between words and phrases, between word classes, and between syntactic constituents.[1] An even knottier problem is the tools the West relies on to build grammars. Using the basic grammatical categories the West has defined and the basic grammatical laws it has elaborated to describe Chinese is like putting a square peg into a round hole.

In the 1950s, there were three wide-ranging discussions among Chinese linguists on word classes, subjects and objects, simple and complex sentences. Debates on these topics have continued unabated ever since. This controversy shows the seriousness of the problem because "these debates for the most part are caused by the influence of traditional Indo-European grammatical notions/concepts that prevent linguists from seeing Chinese grammar as it is" (Zhu 1985: iii). Immediately after the rise of transformational-generative grammar in the West, Zhu Dexi perceptively pointed out that its two most basic rewrite rules, S→NP + VP and VP→V + NP, "are not applicable in Chinese" (Zhu 1985: 64). With respect to Western grammatical influences, Lü Shuxiang commented late in life that research on Chinese grammar needs to get rid of its current approaches and dare to push against the existing constraints, even going so far as to "temporarily discard" Western grammar's technical vocabulary (Lü 2002).

Looking back on the path taken over the past hundred years, Chinese grammarians have never ceased in their efforts to break free from the shackles of traditional concepts derived from Indo-European languages. Among these efforts, the most important step was taken by Zhu Dexi, though he himself described it as "a very small step". Zhu's new ideas are fully put into practice in his *Lectures on Chinese*

16 *Breaking with earlier assumptions*

Grammar in 1982. In his *Answering Questions about Chinese Grammar* published in 1985, he intends to "analyze and comment on some basic concepts and ideas that often cause controversy". Although it is only a short book, it presents a robust, explicit, and systematic exposition of the characteristics of Chinese grammar and of an appropriate grammatical system for Chinese. This is something no previous works on grammar have achieved. To build on our predecessors' foundations, we should first make an inventory of and inherit Zhu's important academic legacy.

What is the content/substance of Zhu's important step forward? It is that he explicitly and correctly put forward the two global features of Chinese grammar. He states them as follows in *Answering Questions about Chinese Grammar*:

> [W]hat are the true/real/actual characteristics of Chinese grammar? If you reject nothing, you can enumerate many. If you focus on what is globally important, there are only two. One is that there is no one-to-one correspondence between Chinese word classes and syntactic constituents (commonly known as sentence constituents). The other is that the rules for constructing sentences in Chinese are basically the same as those for constructing phrases.
>
> (p. 4)

Zhu summarizes the first feature as follows: Apart from being predicates, verbs can serve as subjects and objects; apart from being subjects and objects, nouns can be generally attributive and, under certain conditions, predicative; apart from being attributes, adjectives can be predicates and adverbials. Especially with respect to verbs functioning as subjects and objects, Zhu offers the following explanation:

> Chinese verbs and adjectives remain the same, whether they are used as predicates or as subjects and objects. Chinese grammar works traditionally treat verbs and adjectives in the subject and object positions as having been nominalized. This is to view Chinese from the perspective of Indo-European languages. In fact, Chinese verbs and adjectives can serve both as predicates and as subjects and objects. When they serve as subjects and objects, they are still verbs or adjectives, without undergoing any changes to their grammatical properties. This is a very important feature that distinguishes Chinese from Indo-European languages. It is important in the sense that it not only affects our understanding of the entire question of word classes, but also relates closely to our understanding of syntactic structure.
>
> (p. 5)

Zhu's position is consistent throughout. He establishes "gerunds" as a class whose members are simultaneously nouns and verbs. However, he does not posit gerunds to negate or modify this important position. The syntactic behavior of Chinese verbs and adjectives functioning as predicates, subjects, and objects is, of course, true for the vast majority of them. In his *Lectures on Chinese Grammar*, Zhu states that "in fact the vast majority of verbs and adjectives can serve both as subjects and as objects" (p. 101); in his *Answering Questions about Chinese*

Grammar, he contends that "eighty to ninety percent of verbs and adjectives can serve as subjects and objects" (p. 7). If this syntactic behavior did not account for "the vast majority" or "eighty to ninety percent" of the verbs and adjectives in Chinese, the position that their grammatical properties did not undergo changes when functioning as subjects and objects would simply not hold water.

Why is this feature said to be "very important"? It is because it "not only affects our understanding of the entire question of word classes, but also relates closely to our understanding of syntactic structure". It is also inherently connected with the second feature, which Zhu explains as follows (example sentences are numbered according to the original text):

> "(In English), there is one set of structural principles for sentences and clauses and another for phrases. For example:
>
> (11) He flies a plane.
> (12) To fly a plane is easy.
> (13) Flying a plane is easy.
>
> In English, *flies* acts as a predicate in its finite form in (11); *to fly a plane* and *flying a plane* in the subject positions of (12) and (13) take the form of an infinitive and that of an -ing participle respectively. The situation is different in Chinese. No matter where verbs and verb structures appear in a sentence, their forms remain the same. In (11) to (13), *flies a plane*, *to fly a plane*, and *flying a plane* are all rendered as kāi fēijīin Chinese.
>
> (p. 7)

The point often overlooked seems to be that it is not just verbs that do not change form when functioning in various syntactic roles, but it is also true of verb structures that they maintain the form regardless of their syntactic function. Zhu continues:

> In Chinese, sentences and phrases share a single set of structural principles. This is particularly evident in the subject-predicate structure. Chinese subject-predicate structures are equivalent to English sentences when they are free-standing and to English clauses when they are not. From the perspective of English grammar, subject-predicate structures are opposed to phrases. However, in Chinese they are in fact a type of phrase. Like other types of phrases, they can be used as a full sentence or as a sentential constituent. . . . When compared to Indo-European languages, it is an obvious special feature of Chinese grammar that its subject-predicate structures can function as predicates.
>
> (p. 8)

Zhu Dexi's position is consistent with Yuen Ren Chao's earlier position (1968: 57)[2] that full sentences (S-P) can serve as predicates. Both of their positions are

18 *Breaking with earlier assumptions*

based on keen observations of how Chinese is actually used. On the one hand, a Chinese subject-predicate structure can be the predicate of a sentence as can verb-object structures, verb-adverbial structures, and serial verb constructions. On the other hand, "subjectless sentences are as independent and complete as sentences with subjects" (Zhu 1987). Accordingly, Chinese subject-predicate structures are functionally equivalent to other types of structures. This echoes Lü Shuxiang's remarks (1979: 31), "The distinction between sentences and phrases does not lie in the subject-predicate relation as a sentence is not necessarily bipartite with a subject and predicate, and a phrase can also be formed from a subject-predicate structure". Zhu's contribution is that he clearly shows that the ability of subject-predicate structures to function as predicates is an especially important demonstration that the same construction principles govern the formation of sentences and phrases. Therefore, if you accept the view that subject-predicate structures can be used as predicates (as have most Chinese grammarians as is evident in their writings). It follows that you accept that the construction principles governing Chinese sentence formation are the same as those for phrases. Building on this fact, Zhu proposes a "phrase-based" Chinese grammatical system. His argument is developed as follows:

> Because the construction principles are the same for sentences and phrases, it is possible for us to describe syntactic rules based on phrases and thereby establish a phrase-based grammatical system. . . . If our description of the structure and function of various types of phrases is sufficiently detailed and clear, the structure of sentences will have been clearly described because sentences are actually free-standing phrases.
>
> (p. 74)

Zhu effectively argues for his proposed "phrase-based grammar" in *Lectures on Chinese Grammar*. His approach departs radically from traditional sentence-based approaches to Chinese grammar. Its influence has been profound and far-reaching.

Currently, some people only contend that both "phrase-based" and "sentence-based" approaches have their own strengths and weaknesses. They treat the two approaches as equivalent in value given their weaknesses. What they have overlooked is that Zhu's proposed "phrase-based" approach is an important step forward in our ongoing efforts to break free from the shackles imposed by traditional concepts derived from Indo-European languages. Whether the "phrase-based" approach is right or wrong, it cannot be dismissed lightly.

Regarding the intrinsic connections between the two features of Chinese mentioned earlier, Zhu explains,

> The root cause for both of these features lies in the fact that Chinese word classes are not morphologically marked. In English, when verbs and adjectives are used as subjects and objects, they are either nominalized by adding suffixes like *-ness*, *-ation*, *-ment*, *-ity*, or turned into an infinitive or a participle. However, Chinese lacks morphological markers for word classes.

Breaking with earlier assumptions 19

Chinese words remain morphologically the same no matter what syntactic positions they appear in, hence the multifunctionality of word classes in Chinese. Moreover, there is no distinction between the finite and non-finite forms (i.e. infinitives and participles) of Chinese verbs. This, in turn, brings about the structural uniformity found in phrases and sentences.

(p. 9)

It can be seen that Zhu's discussion on the characteristics of Chinese is systematic, and the underlying reason for both features lies in the well-known fact that Chinese lacks morphological changes. Zhu, however, elucidates the profound implications arising from this fact. Indeed, these two features are inseparably connected. If you accept the first feature, you have to accept the second, and vice versa. Conversely, if you reject one of them, the other is also rejected. With this inseparable connection in mind, we can understand why when Zhu discusses the ability of verbs and adjectives to function as subjects and objects, he observes that this fact not only affects our understanding of word classes as a whole but also relates closely to our understanding of syntactic structure. Some current Chinese grammar books affirm that subject-predicate structures in Chinese can be used as a predicate, but they nevertheless take the sentence-based approach. Some agree that the construction principles governing sentence formation are basically the same as those for phrases but still claim that Chinese verbs only occur as subjects and objects under highly restricted conditions. It must be noted/acknowledged that such statements are inconsistent and incongruous.

1.2 Preliminary issues

1.2.1 On verbs functioning as subjects and objects

Zhu insists that Chinese verbs that function as subjects and objects remain verbs; they are not nominalized. This obviously adheres to the principle of simplicity (see Section 2 of Introduction). Since the vast majority of verbs can serve as subjects and objects, it is a totally unnecessary move to argue that verbs functioning as subjects and objects are turned into nouns. However, many scholars are trying to revise Zhu's position. Generative grammarians think that verbs must have been nominalized when they are used as subjects and objects. Even the most faithful followers of Zhu retreat from his theory, saying that it is still necessary to admit to there being nominalization to a certain extent. This is by no means a trivial matter. Naturally previous theories like Zhu's can be revised by later generations, but the prerequisite for revision should be a correct understanding of Zhu's position and his original intention.

There are quite a few people who rely on statistics to assert that it is not the case that the vast majority of Chinese verbs can be used as subjects and objects. Some contend that the usage of a single verb functioning as the subject or the object without a modifier or taking its own object is rare and severely restricted.

20 *Breaking with earlier assumptions*

For example, according to Guo Rui's statistics (2002: 185, 189), the verbs that can, by themselves, be used as subjects and objects only account for 46% of all verbs. Some argue that there are many constraints on the entry of monosyllabic verbs into the "N *de* V" structure. For example, according to Zhan Weidong's statistics (1998), of the 1,316 monosyllabic verbs in *A Dictionary of Chinese Verb Usage*, only the four monosyllabic verbs *ài* 'to love', *kǔ* 'to suffer', *sǐ* 'to die', *xiào* 'to smile or laugh' can go into the structure, accounting for only 0.3% of all monosyllabic verbs. Wu Chang'an (2012) also believes that the capability of monosyllabic verbs going into the structure is remarkably limited. Yuan Yulin (2010a, 2010b) claims that expressions in the "N *de* VP" structure (as in *túshū de chūbǎn* 'the publication of a book') are literal translations of English corresponding expressions, and their usage is strictly limited to written language and far from being colloquial. There are still others who contend that the predicate verbs are heavily restricted when monosyllabic verbs function as subjects and objects. After examining all the monosyllabic verbs, Piao Chongkui (2003) concludes that only the sentences that use the modal verb *kěyǐ* 'may, might' as predicates can take monosyllabic verbs as subjects, as in *qù kěyǐ* '(you) may go', *kàn kěyǐ* '(you) may have a look'. Fan Xiao (1992) also says that there are constraints on the types of predicates in the sentences with their subjects being a VP. Even I myself (Shen 1999: 274–282) enumerate the conditions for verbs acting as subjects and objects. Shi Youwei (2014) also emphasizes that not all verbs can serve as subjects and objects.

Before spending a lot of time and energy producing such statistics, it is better to take a look at how Zhu argues. Consider the seven examples used in his *Answering Questions about Chinese Grammar* when demonstrating that Chinese verbs are not nominalized in the positions of subjects and objects (p. 23):

(1) *Qù   shì   yǒu   dàolǐ   de.*
    go   be   have   reason   MP
    'Going makes sense.'

(2) *Bú   qù   shì   yǒu   dàolǐ   de.*
    not   go   be   have   reason   MP
    'Not going makes sense.'

(3) *Zànshí   bú   qù   shì   yǒu   dàolǐ   de.*
    temporary   not   go   be   have   reason   MP
    'Not going for now makes sense.'

(4) *Tā   zànshí   bú   qù   shì   yǒu   dàolǐ   de.*
    he   temporary   not   go   be   have   reason   MP
    'It makes sense for him not to go for now.'

(5) *Tā   de   qù   shì   yǒu   dàolǐ   de.*
    he   MM   go   be   have   reason   MP
    'His going makes sense.'

(6)   *Tā   de   bú   qù   shì   yǒu   dàolǐ   de.*
      he   MM   not   go   be   have   reason   MP
      'His not going makes sense.'

(7)   *Tā   de   zànshí   bú   qù   shì   yǒu   dàolǐ   de.*
      he   MM   temporary   not   go   be   have   reason   MP
      'His not going for now makes sense.'

First, it is monosyllabic verbs rather than disyllabic ones that Zhu use as examples to illustrate his point, and *qù* 'go' is beyond the scope of the four monosyllabic verbs *ài* 'love', *kǔ* 'suffer', *sǐ* 'die', *xiào* 'smile or laugh'. Second, the examples include both free-standing V and 'N *de* V' phrases, neither of which are said to be nominalized. Third, the examples show that the verb V and the verb phrases VP remain morphologically the same no matter what syntactic positions they occupy, and there is no need to say that the nature of the word *qù* 'go' and the phrases *bú qù* 'not to go', *zànshí bú qù* 'not to go for the time being' are changed to and fro.

If you look in a corpus, you will probably find none or very few of these sentences, not to mention the faint possibility of an ordinary dictionary of verb usage including such examples. However, the fact that such sentences can hardly be found in corpora or dictionaries does not amount to denying the validity of Zhu's examples, because according to Zhu these sentences are natural-sounding to native speakers of Chinese and thus they are naturally in accordance with the rules of Chinese grammar. The verb *qù* 'go' can be replaced by other monosyllabic verbs, and in fact monosyllabic verbs functioning as subjects and objects (either alone or as the head of a phrase) are perfectly normal in Chinese. This can be easily seen in classical Chinese, and numerous excellent examples are idioms originating from classical Chinese such as *juéchùféngshēng* 'be unexpectedly rescued from desperate situation', *jiànyìsīqiān* 'change one's mind the moment one sees something new', *chánggēdāngkū* 'vent somber song instead of crying', and *shēngbùrúsǐ* 'to live is worse than to die'. Similar examples can also be easily found in modern Chinese:

Dǎ   shì   téng,   mà   shì   ài.
beat   be   pain   scold   be   love
'Beating causes pain, and scolding shows love.'

Chī   yǒu   chī   xiàng,   zhàn   yǒu   zhàn   xiàng.
eat   have   eat   manners   stand   have   stand   manners
'There are manners of eating and standing.'

Búyào   lǐcǎi   tā   de   dà   kū   dà   nào.
don't   pay attention to   her   MM   big   cry   big   fuss
'Ignore her fussing and crying.'

Tā   de   kuài   chī   hé   cháng   shuì   dōu   shì   bān   lǐ   dìyī.
he   MM   fast   eat   and   long   sleep   both   be   class   in   first
'His eating fast and sleeping long are the first in the class.'

22   *Breaking with earlier assumptions*

In colloquial Chinese, verbs functioning as subjects and objects tend to be monosyllabic rather than disyllabic. Consider the following examples:

Mài   háishì   zū   nǐ   yào   xiān   xiǎng   hǎo.
Sell   or   rent   you   should first   think   well
'To sell or to rent, you should first think it over.'

(*Mài* and *zū* can be changed into disyllabic *chūmài* and *chūzū* respectively without changing the basic meanings.)

Wǒ   bú   pà   bǐ,   bǐ   jiù   bǐ.
I   not   fear   compete   compete   then   compete
'I don't fear to compete; if you want, bring it on.'

(A change of *bǐ* into disyllabic *bǐshì* would render the second clause colloquially awkward.)

Zhèzhǒng   xínghào   de   kèjī   guòqù   cónglái   méiyǒu   shī   guò   lián.
this   type   MM   airliner   past   never   not   lose   EXP   connect
'This type of airliners have never lost their connections in the past.'

Nǐ   zhǎo   lǎopo   shì   zhǎo   mā   háishì   zhǎo   chou?
you   find   wife   be   find   mother   or   find   whip
'Are you looking for a motherly wife or a good whipping?'

Chōu   nǐ   méi   shāngliàng.
whip   you   not   negotiate
'Whipping you is not negotiable.'

The list of examples could go on endlessly. There are very few verbs that cannot really function as subjects and verbs; even abstract verbs such as *shì* 'be', *yǒu* 'have/there be', *zhí* 'be worth', *xìng* 'surname (used as a verb)', *xiàn* (*yuánxíng*) 'reveal (original form)', and *rènwéi* 'think' are no exception.

Wǒ   xiǎng   shì,   tā   yīdìng   líhún   le.   Shì   yě   hǎo.
I   think   yes   he   must   divorce   PSP   yes   also good
'I think so. He must have divorced. And it's not a bad thing.'

Yǒu   zǒng   bǐ   méiyǒu   hǎo,   dàjiā   háishì   xiǎng   yǒu.
Something   always   than   nothing   better   Everyone   still   want   something
'Something is better than nothing. People still want to own something.'

Zhí   jiù   mǎi,   bù   zhí   jiù   bù   mǎi.
be worth   then   buy   not   be worth   then   not   buy
'Buy it if it's worthy; if not, then don't.'

Nǐ xiǎng bù xiǎng xìng nǐ mǔqīn de xìng?
You want not want surname v. your mother MM surname
'Do you want to follow your mother's surname?'

Wǒ xiǎng <u>xìng</u>, <u>xìng</u> yě méi guanxi.
I want surname v. surname v. also not matter
'I would like to follow, and it's no big deal.'

Xiàn le yuánxíng méiyǒu?
reveal PSP original form not
'Is its original form revealed?

—*<u>Xiàn</u> zěnmeyàng, bú <u>xiàn</u> yòu zěnmeyàng?*
reveal how not reveal again how
—What if it is? And what if it is not?'

Nǐ zěnme huì jiānchí zhème <u>rènwéi?</u>
you how can insist so think
'What makes you insist on thinking so?'

The substitute words used in the predicate are by no means limited to *kěyǐ* 'can'. Consider the following examples with *qù* 'go' functioning as subjects:

Qù yǒu nánchù, bú qù yě yǒu nánchù.
go have difficulty not go also have difficulty
'There are difficulties in both going and not going.'

Qù zěnmeyàng, bú qù yòu zěnmeyàng.
go how not go also how
'What if I go, and what if I don't?'

Qù yǒu hǎochù, bú qù yě bú yàojǐn.
go have benefit not go also not matter
'There are benefits if you go and it doesn't matter if you don't.'

Qù bú duì, bú qù yě bú duì.
go not right not go also not right
'It's not right whether you go or not.'

Qù áimà, bú qù yě áimà.
go be scolded not go also be scolded
'You will be scolded whether you go or not.'

Qù jiù qù, bú qù jiù bú qù.
go then go not go then not go
'If you decide to go, then go. If not, then don't.'

24   *Breaking with earlier assumptions*

Qù   zài   wǔ   tiān   qián,   huí   zài   liǎng   tiān   hòu.
go   at   five   days   ago   come back   at   two   days   later
'We went there five days ago and returned two days later.'

Qù   tuōtuōlālā,   bú   qù   yòu   yóuyùbúdìng.
go   procrastinate   not   go   also   hesitate
'You procrastinate when we decide to go, but you also hesitate when we decide
not to go.'

Some argue that monosyllabic verbs functioning as subjects act as a quote of
the previous utterance or only appear in response expressions, and therefore it is a
special reference and is not representative (Wu 2012). Both *qù* in *qù zěnmeyàng, bú
qù yòu zěnmeyàng* 'Go and what will happen; don't go and what else will happen'
are like a quoted expression, but both *qù* in *qù tuōtuōlālā, bú qù yòu yóuyùbúdìng*
'you drag your feet after we decided to go; but you hesitate when we once decided
not to go' are not. And the questioning expressions that elicit response expressions
often use monosyllabic verbs as subjects as in *Qù zěnmeyàng?* 'As for going there,
how's that?' and *Kàn yīxià kěyǐ ma?* 'As for having a look, is it allowed?'. The subject used as the topic is often a quoted expression of the previous utterance, which
has little to do with whether it is a verb.

Some claim that verbs or verb phrases functioning as subjects are mainly limited to assertive sentences. It is not a convincing reason, because most of abstract
nouns functioning as subjects also appear in assertive sentences. Moreover, narrative sentences should not be excluded, as verbs or verb phrases functioning as
subjects exist in classical Chinese. Consider the following examples:[3]

Xíng   zhī   shí   nián,   qín   mín   dà   yuè.
enforce   them (the laws)   ten   year   Qin   people   extremely   pleased
'By the time the laws had been enforced for ten years, the people of Qin were
overjoyed.'

(from The Biography of Lord Shang, *Records of the Grand Historian*)
(*Xíngzhī* functions as the subject of *shínián*; taken together, *Xíngzhī shínián* functions as the subject of *qínmíndàyuè*.)

Zǐlù   wén   zhī   xǐ.
Zilu   hear   this   happy
'Zilu, on hearing this, was happy.'

(from GongYechang, *The Analects of Confucius*)
(*Wénzhī* can be analyzed as the subject of *xǐ*.)

Verbs functioning as objects are even less restricted in narrative sentences.
To argue that the semantic types of predicates are limited is not a cogent reason
either, because when abstract nouns such as *xìnxīn* 'confidence', *bēiqíng* 'sadness',

nèiróng 'content', *kōngjiān* 'space', *mìngtí* 'proposition' function as subjects and objects, the semantic types of predicates are also restricted.

In order to prove the strict restrictions of VP modified by *de* phrases, Yuan Yulin (2010a, 2010b) gives the following examples:

* duì   shēntǐ hěn   yǒu   hǎochù   de   yóuyǒng
  for   body   very have benefit   MM   swim
  'the swimming that is beneficial to our body'

* xīwàng   de   zànhuǎn
  hope   MM   temporarily delay
  'the temporary delay of hope'

* xǐhuān   de   qí   mǎ
  love   MM   ride horse
  'the horse riding that (I) love'

* kāishǐ   de   xiě   shī
  start   MM   write poem
  'the poem writing that is started'

* kàn   de   xià   xiàngqí
  watch MM   play chess
  'the chess playing that (I) watch'

* bú   róngyì   de   jiāo   gāozhōng   bìyè   bān
  not   easy   MM   teach senior high school graduate class
  'the teaching of graduating classes in a senior high school that is not easy'

* bǐjiào   hǎo   de   shuìjiào qián   hē   niúnǎi
  comparatively   good MM   sleep   before drink milk
  'the drinking of milk before going to sleep that is relatively good'

Apart from the first two examples that are highly acceptable and thus should not be asterisked, some examples become natural by simply adding a few modifiers while retaining the basic structure; for example, the insertion of *shífēn* 'completely' to the front of *xǐhuān* 'love', the addition of *bùjiǔ* 'not long' to the end of *kāishǐ* 'start', and the insertion of *liánzhe* 'continuous' to kàn 'watch' all render the original examples acceptable. All these changes prove nothing but show that the semantic content of modifiers should be adequate. The last two examples do make sense when they are contextualized in some way. They are not so acceptable probably because the heads are too long. In short, these restrictions also need to be studied, but they cannot be used to argue against Zhu's statement that both V and VP can function as subjects and objects.

Yuan (2010b) devotes a large space to explain that expressions such as *túshū de chūbǎn* 'the publication of the book' and *àomàn yǔ piānjiàn* 'pride and prejudice'

26 *Breaking with earlier assumptions*

are literal translations from English. This statement is highly confusing. In English, *publish* and *proud* are nominalized into *publication* and *pride* by adding a *-tion* suffix and applying a form of suppletion ([au]/[ai]) respectively. If we follow strictly these nominalization processes, we are exactly caught in a trap of literal translations from English. Nonetheless, *túshū de chūbǎn* and *àomàn yǔ piānjiàn* are perfectly natural expressions in Chinese.

As for corpora, the following examples found in a child language corpus[4] use verbs and verb phrases as the object of the predicate verb *pà* 'be afraid of.'

Pà   diū   le.
be afraid of   lose   PSP
'I'm afraid of losing it.'

Pà   dǎ   pìgu
be afraid of   beat   buttock
'I'm afraid of being spanked.'

Wǒ   pà   dǎo.
I   be afraid of   fall
'I'm afraid it's going to fall.'

Wǒ   pà   shuō   wǒ.
I   be afraid of   tell   me
'I'm afraid of being told off.'

Wǒ   pà   diào   xiàqù.
I   be afraid of   fall   down
'I'm afraid of falling down.'

Wǒ   pà   bù   chūlái   jiē   wǒ.
I   be afraid of   not   come out   pick up   me
'I'm afraid they won't come out to pick me up.'

Wǒ   pà   guòlái   tōu   wǒde.
I   be afraid of   come over   steal   mine
'I'm afraid they will come over to steal mine.'

Despite the usefulness of corpora as an important source of reference, we still think that we must not rely heavily on corpora, let alone entirely trust them.[5] To prove the existence of syntactic structure, Chomsky relies on his own intuition to create the famous non-existent sentence *Colorless green ideas sleep furiously*. His argument cannot be dismissed because we fail to find the sentence in corpora. If a sentence cannot be found in corpora for the time being, it does not necessarily mean that it will not be found in the future. Grammar rules must be able to generate not only existing grammatical sentences but also possible grammatical ones. This is one of the tenets of generative grammar.

Breaking with earlier assumptions 27

In short, when Zhu states that in Chinese, "the vast majority of verbs and adjectives *can* be actually used as subjects and objects" (1982: 101; emphasis mine) and "eighty to ninety percent of verbs and adjectives *can* be used as subjects and objects" (1985: 7; emphasis mine), he is not reporting how many verbs and adjectives are actually used as subjects and objects. His statements apply to both monosyllabic and disyllabic verbs, to both free-standing verbs and the verbs in "N *de* V" phrases, and to verbs and verb phrases. Zhu himself is Chinese and speaks Chinese, and thus he is reasonably capable of determining whether his own example sentences are grammatical or not in Chinese. Those who try to prove that it is not the case that the vast majority of verbs can serve as subjects and objects should instead reflect on whether they are controlled by preconceived traditional ideas and have lost their sensitivity towards the global features of Chinese.

There are still others who argue that verbs functioning as subjects and objects are not an exclusive feature of Chinese, and it is the same with English verbs, except that English verbs need to be morphologically marked and Chinese verbs undergo "zero derivation" as in *work* and *play* in English (Lu 2013). Zero derivation works only for a limited number of Chinese verbs; if the vast majority of Chinese verbs need to undergo zero derivation before functioning as subjects and objects, it would be an unnecessary move like asserting that the vast majority of Chinese verbs are nominalized in the positions of subjects and objects.[6] As Zhu Dexi (1983) declares, the so-called zero-form nominalization is only a theoretical construct that is incapable of capturing the linguistic facts of Chinese.

1.2.2 On phrases as basic units

The second issue that needs to be clarified is whether phrases can be used as full sentences or not. As to the second feature and the idea of "phrases as basic units" proposed by Zhu, some people now comment that phrases and sentences are not the same after all, and some phrases cannot be used as full sentences. According to them, subject-predicate structures such as *tā kāi fēijī* 'he flies a plane' can only be used independently when making responses (as an answer to *Tā shì gàn shénme de* 'What does he do?'),; otherwise they have to be expressed antithetically (as in *Wǒ kāi huǒchē, tā kāi fēijī* 'I drive a train; he flies a plane'). This criticism also fails to correctly understand the intended meaning of Zhu, and this was already addressed in *Answering Questions about Chinese Grammar*. In proposing the establishment of a phrase-based grammatical system, Zhu makes the following remarks:

> This means that we can use every type of phrases (subject-predicate, predicate-object, predicate-complement, modifier-head, coordinate, serial verbs, prepositional, and phrases characterized by function words such as *de* 'of') as abstract syntactic patterns to describe their internal structures and the distribution of each type of phrases as a whole within larger phrases, *rather than rushing to* relate them to concrete sentences, and especially without nailing them to a particular element of a sentence.
>
> (1985: 74; emphasis mine)

28 *Breaking with earlier assumptions*

As to the questions whether sentences have no important role in a phrase-based grammatical system and whether it means there is no need for us to talk about sentences after phrases are studied, Zhu explains as follows:

> I'm just *emphasizing* that the construction principles of sentences are consistent with those of phrases in Chinese. The structure of sentences is actually the same as the structure of phrases.
>
> (1985: 78, emphasis mine)

Both *rather than rushing to* and *emphasizing* show how Zhu thinks about this issue. Taking the grammatical system as a whole, we have to identify priorities so that we can concentrate on the essentials. To identify priorities, we need to *emphasize* some facts while downplaying others and decide which problems we *don't rush to* solve while highlighting central problems. In establishing the "grammatical framework", Zhu downplays the fact that some phrases cannot stand alone as full sentences because it is mainly related to how it is expressed. It can be easily seen from Zhu's answer that we cannot deny the same set of construction principles sentences and phrases share because there are some phrases that cannot stand alone as full sentences. The reason is simple, because the idea that sentences and phrases share the same set of construction principles is fundamental to a grammatical system, and it is an important aspect of the overall grammatical system. Therefore, it is necessary to be *emphasized* and dealt with first (the contrary of *rather than rushing*). Contrariwise, critics of Zhu should reflect on whether they are trying to attend to big and small matters all at once or simply pennywise and pound foolish.

Zhu does say that "sentences and phrases are two different things after all and they should not be mixed up" (1985: 78). Based on this, some people think that Zhu intends that phrases and sentences are only structurally consistent and the consistency has nothing to do with the "specific utterances". This is a case of knowing only one thing but not the other: One thing is that some phrases cannot be full sentences on their own, and the other is that the vast majority of phrases can be full sentences as long as they are properly contextualized. From Zhu's viewpoint, this "one thing" is a fact that should be acknowledged and needs to be clarified, while "the other thing" is a default fact that needs no explanation. When it comes to some phrases that cannot be full sentences on their own, Zhu cites the frequently mentioned examples: V + *le* + O (*chī le fàn* 'ate a meal', *dǎ le diànhuà* 'made a phone call') and V + C + O (*chī wán fàn* 'finish eating', *ná chū yī běn shū* 'take out a book'). The reason why such phrases cannot be full sentences on their own is simply that they are usually used in responses or in juxtaposed expressions, e.g.

—*Zǒu,*	*sànbù*	*qù!*				
go	walk	go				

'Go, go for a walk!'

—*Chī*	*le/wán*	*fàn.*	*Zháo*	*shénme*	*jí*	*yā!*
eat	PSP/TAM	rice	hurry-SEP	what	hurry-SEP	MP

'Wait until the meal is finished. What's the hurry!'

Dǎ   le   diànhuà,   lái   le   jǐngchá.
make   PSP   call   come   PSP   police
'(Someone) made a phone call and the police came.'

—*Tā   ná   chū   le   shénme?*
he   take   out   PSP   what
'What did he take out?'

—*Ná   chū   yī   běn   shū.*
take   out   one   CL   book
'He took out a book.'

Ná   chū   yī   běn   shū,   fàng   jìn   yī   jiàn   yīfú.
take   out   one   CL   book   put   in   one   CL   clothes
'Take out a book and put in a piece of clothing.'

What makes *tā kāi fēijī* 'he flies a plane' different from *tā kāi guò fēijī* 'he flew a plane' is also that the former is only used either in responses or in juxtaposed expressions. Consider the following examples:

—*Tā   gàn   shénme   de?*
he   do   what   MP
'What does he do?'

—*Tā   kāi   fēijī.*
he   fly   plane
'He flies a plane.'

Wǒ   kāi   huǒchē,   tā   kāi   fēijī.
I   drive   train   he   fly   plane
'I drive a train and he flies a plane.'

However, in arguing that phrases and sentences in Chinese share a single set of construction principles, Zhu's whole argumentation starts precisely from the comparison between *tā kāi fēijī* 'he flies a plane' and the English counterpart *He flies a plane*. Zhu does not use *tā kāi guò fēijī* 'he flew a plane', because the difference between *tā kāi fēijī* 'he flies a plane' and *tā kāi guò fēijī* 'he flew a plane' in Chinese is not as important as the difference between *He fly a plane* and *He flied a plane* in English and because the nature of *He fly a plane* in English is totally different from that of *tā kāi fēijī* 'he flies a plane' in Chinese, the former being ungrammatical and the latter being grammatical. It can be seen that what Zhu intends to argue is that the vast majority of Chinese phrases can become full sentences as long as they are properly contextualized. But which sentence (including *tā kāi guò fēijī* 'he flew a plane') is not actually an "utterance" in a certain context? Undoubtedly there are

30 *Breaking with earlier assumptions*

differences between *chī wán fàn* 'finish eating' and *chī wán fàn le* 'finished eating', *ná chū yī běn shū* 'take out a book' and *ná chū le yīběn shū* 'took out a book', *tā kāi fēijī* 'he flies a plane' and *tā kāi guò fēijī* 'he flew a plane', and the extent of being freestanding is not the same, which is also admitted by Zhu. However, as shown in the argumentation of *Answering Questions about Chinese Grammar*, to admit this "one thing" is definitely not to deny the default[7] "other thing".

Zhu not only insists that phrases and sentences share the same set of construction principles in Chinese but further proposes that the relationship between phrases and sentences is compositional in Indo-European languages but realizational in Chinese. His detailed explanation of these two relationships goes as follows:

> This grammatical system regards phrases as something abstract and general and sentences (wholly or partially) as something concrete and particular. When describing the internal structure and grammatical function of a phrase, it is not considered whether it is a sentence or a constituent part of a sentence, treating it only as an abstract syntactic structure. Nevertheless, a phrase enjoys the freedom of being used as a full sentence or as a constituent part of a sentence. This is a process of an abstract phrase 'realized' into a concrete sentence or a constituent part of a sentence. According to this view, the relationship between a phrase and a sentence is not that between part and whole, but that between the abstract grammatical structure and the concrete utterance.
>
> (1985: 75)

The compositional relationship is that between part and whole, whereas the realizational relationship is that between the abstract and the concrete. The proposal of this pair of concepts indicates that Zhu's generalization of the features of the Chinese grammatical system has risen to a theoretical level, and only later did linguistic typologists begin to realize this when comparing the word class systems of different languages.[8] It is very unfortunate that we ourselves dwell so much on the partial and secondary phenomenon that some phrases cannot be full sentences on their own, that we cannot see the wood for the trees and thereby ignore Zhu's important contribution in this regard. Some people argue that Zhu's assertion is just a "shortcut", sacrificing rigorousness for readability since both phrases and sentences have different levels of abstraction (Yuan 2010b). If so, why cannot the relationship between phrases and sentences be the one between abstract grammatical structures and concrete utterances? We do not see the logic of this statement but rather feel that it underestimates the importance Zhu attaches to rigorousness and ignores his careful analysis and comparison of linguistic facts.

1.2.3 On the noun-verb continuum

The third issue that needs to be clarified is how to have a proper understanding of the noun-verb continuum. According to functionalists, there is a continuum between nouns and verbs, and on the continuum are varying degrees of strength in terms of

Breaking with earlier assumptions 31

nouniness or verbiness. However, it is important to know that word classes are both continuous and discrete. Observed from different angles or in different ways, the same thing may produce different results. In quantum physics, Bohr proposed the "complementarity principle": Light, by its very nature, has wave-particle duality; it is a discrete particle in one way of observation and is a continuous wave in another way of observation, but we cannot see light both as a particle and as a wave at the same time, and the two observation results can only be "complementary" to form a whole (Cao 2006: 168). Therefore, continuity cannot be denied by discreteness and vice versa.[9] When a verb functions as the subject or the object, you still have to determine whether it becomes a noun or remains a verb. It is unacceptable to say that 60% of it becomes a noun and 40% of it remains a verb or vice versa. Similarly, when you took a dog onto a train, your dog either got aboard the train or failed to, and you can hardly claim that 60% of your dog got aboard.

Some people argue that *chūbǎn* 'publishing' in the noun phrase *túshū chūbǎn* 'book publishing' is directly modified by a noun *túshū* 'book'; it can no longer be modified by an adverb or take an object, and it loses its main function as a verb, so at least *chūbǎn* in this position should be distinguished from *chūbǎn* in other positions and acknowledged as a real noun.[10] That is, it has been nominalized. According to this logic, since *cāngkù* 'warehouse' in *túshū cāngkù* 'book warehouse' and *mùtou* 'wood' in *mùtou fángzi* 'wooden house' can no longer be modified by numerals and classifiers, does it amount to saying that *cāngkù* and *mùtou* have been "de-nominalized"? Lu Jianming (2003) points out that the class properties of a word is one thing, and the realization of these class properties in a specific utterance is quite another, and there is no reason to require that all the class properties of a word be realized in specific syntactic positions. By way of illustration, he contends that the transitive verb *chī* 'eat' in verb-complement phrases (as in *chī kuài le* 'eat quickly', *chī dé hěn bǎo* 'eat very much', *chī bù wán* 'cannot eat up') can no longer take an object or an aspect marker or be modified by *bù* 'not', but no one would think that the verbiness of *chī* 'eat' therein is weakened, and still fewer would think that it has been nominalized. Lu's view is in fact consistent with Zhu's view that the grammatical properties of a word class cannot be fully realized in one position.

Some people maintain that to fully understand an object, one must observe it as closely as possible, and it is necessary to distinguish the varying degrees of nouniness of verbs in subject or object positions. Some even claim that a theory is evaluated by how perfectly it captures the distinctions that exist in linguistic facts (Zhan 2012). But the truth is quite the opposite; it is not the case that the more distinctions are made in a grammar, the better it is. The reason is quite simple. For example, of the two close-up digital photos of comedians I send you, I ask you to tell which is a photo of Guo Degang and which is of Zhou Libo. If you zoom in to the highest resolution, all you will see are only blocks of different colors, and there seems to be no big difference between the two photos. Only when the resolution is changed "low" enough or you step back far enough are these color blocks blurred and you can see the entire composition and thus effectively distinguish between the two photos. Although the reason is simple, there are still many people who cannot

32 *Breaking with earlier assumptions*

figure it out. It will be further explained in the next section from the theoretical perspective of dividing form classes.

1.3 The division of form classes

1.3.1 *The principle of syncretism*

Those who are obsessed with nominalization are trying to find some formal criteria in Chinese to prove that some verbs in some positions have become real nouns. This problem, which is related to the principle of the division of form classes, has received little sufficient theoretical attention so far. According to Crystal (1997: 155), a set of forms that display "similar or identical grammatical features" is said to constitute a form class. The "grammatical features" in this definition refer to morphological features and syntactic distribution. Since a set of forms with different morphological features must be different in syntactic distribution, Yuen Ren Chao (1968: 5) defines a form class only in terms of syntactic distribution: "Grammar is the study of groups or classes of forms as regards their occurrence in frames or slots constituted by other classes. All forms which behave alike in this respect are members of a form class". His examples are as follows:

chī   le   fàn
eat   PSP   rice
'have eaten (one's) meal'

dǎ   guò   qiú
play   EXP   ball
'have played ball'

qí   zhe   mǎ
ride   DUR   horse
'riding a horse'

All three forms are all of the class of verbal expressions, and within each of them, *chī, dǎ,* and *qí* are all of the class of verbs; *le, guò,* and *zhe* are all of the class of verbal suffixes; and *fàn, qiú,* and *mǎ* are all of the class of nouns, "which, among other things, can fill the frame or slot of objects after verbs" (1968: 5).

A proper extent needs to be maintained in distinguishing between form classes according to some principles. We should not keep dividing all the way down. Some form classes should instead be grouped together when necessary. The practice English grammarians adopt in this respect gives us useful insights. The following is an introduction to the division of English verb forms and V-ing forms, starting with the form class of verbs. The traditional English grammatical system divides verbs into no less than 30 form classes (excluding 2—*will take* and *has taken*).

Breaking with earlier assumptions 33

Table 1.1 The form classes of verbs in the traditional English grammatical system

FINITE	*Indicative*		*Subjunctive*		*Imperative*	*NON-FINITE*	
	Past	*Pres*	*Past*	*Pres*	*Pres*		
1st sg	took	take	took	take		Infinitive	take
2nd sg	took	take	took	take	take	Gerund	taking
3rd sg	took	takes	took	take		Present participle	taking
1st pl	took	take	took	take		Past participle	taken
2nd pl	took	take	took	take	take		
3rd pl	took	take	took	take			

(Huddleston & Pullum 2002: 76)

Table 1.2 Six form classes of verbs in English

			take	*want*	*hit*
Primary	⌠preterite		*took*	*wanted*	*hit*
	{	{ 3rd sg	*takes*	*wants*	*hits*
	⌊present tense	⌊ plain	*take*	*want*	*hit*
Secondary	⌠plain form		*take*	*want*	*hit*
	{ gerund-participle		*taking*	*wanting*	*hitting*
	⌊past participle		*taken*	*wanted*	*hit*

(Huddleston & Pullum 2002: 74)

It is necessary to create this many classes for languages with a rich morphology of verbs such as Latin, but it is cumbersome and disturbing to do the same for contemporary English, as it will cause serious misinterpretation of the current state of English, and the inflectional paradigm of verbs has become quite simple in contemporary English after a long history of evolution. *The Cambridge Grammar of the English Language*[11] (Huddleston & Pullum 2002) carries out syncretism, dividing verbs into only six form classes, as illustrated in the following table.

The form classes of auxiliary verbs and *be* are a little different from this table, with a bit more variation in form, but the six form classes remain the same. According to Huddleston and Pullum (2002: 76), there are two principles of syncretism:

i. An inflectional distinction is accepted between two forms only if there is at least one lexeme with an overt and stable contrast in realization between those two forms;
ii. Inflectional distinctions involving agreement properties are not generalized from one lexeme to another.

For example, the difference in form between *took* and *taken* reflects the syntactic difference between preterite and past participle, as illustrated here:

She *wanted* the car.　　She *took*/*taken the car.
She had *wanted* the car.　　She had *taken*/*took the car.

34   *Breaking with earlier assumptions*

Moreover, this contrast in form is realized, overt, and stable, is morphosyntactic in nature, and therefore these two lexemes are grouped into different form classes. On the contrary, if a syntactic difference is never marked by realized, overt, and stable morphosyntactic means, there is no reason to assign the two lexemes to different form classes. Consider, for example:

I'm warning you, [<u>take</u> careful note of what they say].   [imperative]
It is essential [that he <u>take</u> careful note of what they say].   [subjunctive]

There is a syntactic difference between the bracketed parts of the two sentences, one imperative and the other subjunctive, but the form of the verb is always the same no matter what word is used to replace *take*. This is true even with the verb *be*, which enjoys more distinctions of form than any other verb; compare *<u>Be</u> patient* and *It is essential [that he <u>be</u> patient]*. Therefore it cannot be said that the two lexemes of *take* in these two different sentence patterns belong to two different form classes. This is an illustration of the first principle of syncretism.

The second principle is only for the agreement properties. When the sentence is in the past tense, the agreement between the verb and the subject is found only with the verb *be* but not with other verbs such as *look*:

She <u>was</u> ill.   *They <u>were</u> ill.*   [verb agrees with subject]
She <u>looked</u> ill.   *They <u>looked</u> ill.*   [no agreement]

It is true that there are two form classes of *be*, singular *was* and plural *were*, in exhibiting agreement properties, but one cannot extend this to other verbs and say that *looked* has also two form classes that distinguish between singular and plural.

In other words, the first principle is that one should not distinguish between different form classes if there are no morphological differences, and the second one is that individual distinctions of form should not be extended to the whole. The division of form classes should adhere to these two principles in order to ensure the usefulness of grammar. Accordingly, if the various syntactic distinctions of lexemes are not made by realized, overt, and stable morphological markers, they should not be grouped into different form classes. The improper division would lead to the loss of generality in grammar, which runs counter to the original purpose of division—that is to cope with complexity through simplicity, thus bringing about redundancy and interference.

1.3.2   The division of V-ing forms in English

V-ing forms in English are discussed in the section of "The noun phrase" in *A Comprehensive Grammar of the English Language* (Quirk et al. 1985: 1290–1292), and in the section of verb phrases in *The Cambridge Grammar of the English Language* (Huddleston & Pullum 2002: 74–83, 1220–1222). From this, the duality of V-ing forms, nouniness and verbiness, can be seen. The gradience of nouniness and verbiness of V-ing forms constitutes a continuum, and Quirk et al. (1985: 1290–1291)

Breaking with earlier assumptions 35

list fourteen examples of the word *painting* in the order of nouniness, from strongest to weakest:

    i. *Some paintings of Brown's*
    ii. *Brown's paintings of his daughter*
    iii. *The painting of Brown* is as skillful as that of Gainsborough.
    iv. *Brown's deft painting of his daughter* is a delight to watch.
    v. *Brown's deftly painting his daughter* is a delight to watch.
    vi. I dislike *Brown's painting his daughter*.
    vii. I dislike *Brown painting his daughter*.
    viii. I watched *Brown painting his daughter*.
    ix. *Brown deftly painting his daughter* is a delight to watch.
    x. *Painting his daughter*, Brown noticed that his hand was shaking.
    xi. *Brown painting his daughter* that day, I decided to go for a walk.
    xii. *The man painting the girl* is Brown.
    xiii. *The silently painting man* is Brown.
    xiv. Brown *is painting* his daughter.

    Forms like *paintings* with a plural ending *-s* in i. and ii. are deverbal nouns; forms like *painting* in iii. and iv. are verbal nouns, and all the *-ing* items in v. to xiv. are terminologically classed as participles.

    Unlike this three-way classification, traditional English grammar divides these *-ing* items into four categories, with the *-ing* items in v. and vi. being classed as gerunds in view of the fact that both of them are modified by genitives. However, Quirk et al. (1985: 1292) "do not find it useful to distinguish a gerund from a participle", and they seek to represent more satisfactorily the complexity of the different participial expressions by "avoiding the binary distinction of gerund and participle". The differences between examples from v. to xiv. are so complicated that it is utterly impossible to solve the problem by dividing them into two or three categories. For example, the traditional grammar says that *painting* is a gerund when it functions as a subject and it becomes a participle when it functions as an adverbial:

Painting a child is difficult.   (gerund)
Painting a child that morning, I quite forgot the time.   (participle)

However, there is no distinction between the overt forms of *painting* in these two examples. It is unnecessary to divide them into two categories if an infinitive *to paint* is used instead in both:

To paint a child is difficult.
To paint a child, I bought a new canvas.

The motivation for dividing V-ing forms but not dividing infinitives is primarily historical: Historically gerunds and participles have different historical sources. But a grammar of contemporary English should respect the current state of English

36 *Breaking with earlier assumptions*

that there are no overt distinctions of form between V-ing as a gerund and as a participle.

The Cambridge Grammar of the English Language also holds that the distinction between gerunds and participles cannot be maintained in English though it may be in other languages. In English they can only be grouped together under the name "gerund-participle", because it is not possible to distinguish between the primary and the secondary. The reason for grouping instead of dividing is that, according to the first principle of syncretism, no realized, overt, and stable morphological distinction can be found in modern English with a gerund-participle, even with *being*. *The Cambridge Grammar of the English Language* not only argues that no viable morphological distinction can be drawn between gerunds and participles but also holds that if there is no morphological distinction, it is also difficult to distinguish them based on syntactic distribution, which is largely manifested in morphological distinctions. Finally, the semantic distinction between gerunds and participles is equally unworkable. (See Shen 2015 for details.)

Note that the fourteen examples listed previously cannot fully reflect the differences in the gradience of nouniness or verbiness of *painting*. Quirk et al. (1985: 1291) point out that v. has two meanings, 'Brown's action of deft painting his daughter is a delight to watch' and 'It is a delight to watch while Brown deftly paints his daughter'. When the latter meaning is intended, *painting* is verby and close to a participle. *Brown's painting his daughter* in vi. can also be understood as either the fact or the way that Brown paints his daughter. When the latter meaning is intended, *painting* is more verby and close to a participle. Besides, there is a distinction whether the gerund carries modal meanings or not:

There was *no shouting, no merry-making, no waving of flags*.
"No shouting, merry-making, or waving of flags took place".

There was *no mistaking that scream*.
"No one could mistake that scream".

The second sentence carries a modal meaning that the first does not, and the V-ing is more verby and close to a participle. Furthermore, it is difficult to distinguish gerunds from deverbal nouns. Consider the example:

There's no writing on the blackboard today.

If it means "we are not going to write on the blackboard today (since all our work is going to be oral)", *writing* is a nonmodal gerund. If it means "we can't write on the blackboard today (because we have no chalk)", *writing* is a modal gerund that is close to a participle. If it means "there's nothing written on the blackboard today (because we haven't used this classroom)", *writing* is a nonmodal deverbal noun.

There is also a difference in the strength of verbiness within the verbal nouns. For example, *painting* in iii. with an *of*-phrase postmodifier tends to refer to the way a famous painter paints; if the modifier is changed to a genitive premodifier, as in *Brown's painting is nearly as good as his wife*, then the verbiness of *painting* becomes stronger and tends to refer to the specific action of painting, which is similar to iv. Verbal nouns can denote not only activity that is in process but also completed activity. For example, in *His exploring of the mountain is taking a long time/took three weeks*, when completed activity (lasting three weeks) is intended, *exploring* is more nouny and thus should better be replaced by *exploration*.

The distinction between verbal nouns and deverbal nouns is not very important, because almost all deverbal nouns (with plural forms) can be preceded by articles and thus are also verbal nouns. It is ambiguous whether a plural suffix can be added to some forms. As Quirk et al. (1985: 1290) point out, there are two meanings of *painting* in ii.: 'paintings depicting his daughter and painted by him' and 'paintings depicting his daughter and painted by someone else but owned by him', and when the latter meaning is intended, it borders on a verbal noun. In *The Cambridge Grammar of the English Language* no distinction is made between verbal nouns and deverbal nouns, but they are grouped together as "gerundial nouns".[12]

It is because all these differences are continuous and very complicated that many English grammar books now simply use the term "V-ing forms". It is not meaningless but makes little sense to spend effort on their internal distinctions. On the contrary, it brings unmotivated complication to English grammar. Linguists are of course sensitive to differences in the nominal strength of verbs, and they try to explain that these differences make sense, as they can be used as evidence to justify some tendency laws. And we have been trying to do so,[13] but describing these subtle differences does not mean dividing them into different form classes.

In sum, from traditional grammar to *A Comprehensive Grammar of the English Language* and *The Cambridge Grammar of the English Language*, the tendency is to shift from a focus on "separation" to a focus on "unification" in the division of V-ing forms, just as in the division of verb forms. The rationale lies in the principle of simplicity. It is good not to divide if possible, rather than to divide as much as possible, and sometimes no division can "more satisfactorily" represent the complexity of different examples. The superfluous divisions in traditional grammar introduce unmotivated complication into English grammar, and therefore they should be examined and discarded.

1.3.3   The division of "gerunds" in Chinese

As discussed in Section 1 of the Introduction and Chapter 3, all Chinese verbs are actually "gerunds" (or "dynamic nouns"), which exhibit both verbal and nominal characteristics. According to Yuen Ren Chao (1968: 5), which has been quoted earlier, one function of nouns is that they "can fill the frame or slot of objects after verbs". In fact, for Chinese, verbs can also fill this frame or slot:

Wǒ   xiǎng   jiā,   hái   xiǎng   chī.
I   miss   home   also   want   eat
'I'm homesick and want to eat.'

38 *Breaking with earlier assumptions*

Wǒ   pà   bà,   shì   pà   dǎ.
I   be afraid of dad   be   be afraid of   beat
'I'm afraid of Dad because I'm afraid of beating.'

Tā   ài   mǎ,   yě   ài   qí.
he   love horse also love ride
'He loves horses and riding.'

Of course, there is a difference in the strength of nouniness and verbiness within Chinese "gerunds", but this difference in strength is also indistinguishable and inexhaustible. Taking the word *qù* 'go' for example, it is easy to list fourteen examples like English *painting*, roughly in the order of decreasing nouniness:[14]

i. *Tā   yī   xīn   xiǎng   zhe   gè   qù.*
   he   one   heart   want   DUR   CL   go
   'He had his heart set on going.'

ii. *Sān   qù   sān   huí   shì   yǒu   dàolǐ   de.*
    three   go   three   return   be   have   reason   MP
    'Three goings with three returns make sense.'

iii. *Tā   de   qù   shì   yǒu   dàolǐ   de.*
     he   MM   go   be   have   reason   MP
     'His going makes sense.'

iv. *Qù   shì   yǒu   dàolǐ   de.*
    go   be   have   reason   MP
    'Going makes sense.'

v. *Qù   hé   bú   qù   dōu   yǒu   dàolǐ.*
   go   and   not   go   all   have   reason
   'Both going and not going make sense.'

vi. *Gěi   tā   lái   gè   tuōyán   shì   bú   qù.*
    give   he   come   CL   delay   mode   not   go
    'Give him a delayed not-going.'

vii. *Tā   de   tuōyán   shì   bú   qù   shì   yǒu   dàolǐ   de.*
     he   MM   delay   mode   not   go   be   have   reason   MP
     'His delayed not-going makes sense.'

viii. *Tā   de   bú   qù   shì   yǒu   dàolǐ   de.*
      he   MM   not   go   be   have   reason   MP
      'His not going makes sense.'

Breaking with earlier assumptions 39

ix. *Tā   de   zànshí   bú   qù   shì   yǒu   dàolǐ   de.*
    he   MM   temporary   not   go   be   have   reason   MP
    'His not going for now makes sense.'

x. *Zànshí   bú   qù   shì   yǒu   dàolǐ   de.*
    temporary   not   go   be   have   reason   MP
    'Not going for now makes sense.'

xi. *Bú   qù   máolú   shì   yǒu   dàolǐ   de.*
    not   go   thatched cottage   be   have   reason   MP
    'It makes sense not to go to the thatched cottage.'

xii. *Qù   guò   máolú   sān   cì   shì   yǒu   dàolǐ   de.*
    go   EXP   thatched cottage   three   CL   be   have   reason   MP
    'It makes sense to have visited the thatched cottage three times.'

xiii. *Tā   zànshí   bú   qù   máolú   shì   yǒu   dàolǐ   de.*
    he   temporary   not   go   thatched cottage   be   have   reason   MP
    'It makes sense for him not to go to the thatched cottage for now.'

xiv. *Tā   rúguǒ   qù   máolú,   shì   yǒu   dàolǐ   de.*
    he   if   go   thatched cottage   be   have   reason   MP
    'If he goes to the thatched cottage, it makes sense.'

Seven of these fourteen examples are already used by Zhu (see Section 1.2.1), who insists on the same verb *qù* 'go' according to the principle of simplicity and tries his best to object that *qù* 'go' in some examples have been nominalized. Nowadays, many Chinese grammarians want to group these examples of *qù* 'go' into different form classes. They do not understand that Quirk et al.'s (1985) intention in listing fourteen examples of *painting* is to emphasize that the V-ing forms are indistinguishable and inexhaustible, and they should be unified rather than divided whenever possible. Some people argue that *qù* 'go' in i. and ii. (modified by quantifiers) and perhaps iii. (preceded by a genitive) has been changed from a verb to a real noun, similar to a deverbal noun or a verbal noun in English. It is important to know that there is a reliable standard of form in English to distinguish a deverbal noun and a verbal noun, namely the plural marker and articles, both of which define positively the form class of nouns. Without these, they would certainly be not divided as participles and gerunds are not distinguished. However, Chinese has no plural suffixes or articles, and modification by a quantifier or by a *de* genitive is not a grammatical property only possessed by Chinese nouns—Chinese verbs also have this grammatical property.

According to Zhu Dexi (1985: 16), traditionally Chinese nouns are in fact defined negatively; that is, they cannot generally function as a predicate. As for English with overt form markers, Quirk et al. (1985) still think that it is not important to distinguish a deverbal noun from a verbal noun and thus division can be avoided. For Chinese

40   *Breaking with earlier assumptions*

with no such form markers, some still insist on divisions. This contrast deserves our serious reflection. In English the traditional distinction between gerunds and participles is somewhat justified because there is a clear distinction between subjects and adverbials, with gerunds tending to be subjects and participles adverbials. But in Chinese it is difficult to make a clear distinction between subjects and adverbials, and most adverbials can be analyzed as subjects or topics. For example, Yuen Ren Chao (1968: 52) analyzes the conditional clause in xiv. as the subject, and for another example, *jīntiān* 'today' in *Jīntiān bù xiūxī* 'No rest today' is almost always recognized as the subject. For subjects and adverbials much clearly differentiated in English, English grammarians still believe that no distinction should be made between gerunds and participles, but for subjects and gerunds vaguely distinguished in Chinese, some Chinese grammarians insist on divisions. This should also stimulate our further thinking.[15]

Such a division can only bring unmotivated complication to Chinese grammar and even bring about redundancy and interference. If it is judged as a noun as long as it is modified by a quantifier, e.g. *fēn* 'division' in *fēn hěn zhòngyào* 'division is important' is a verb, and *fēn* 'division' in *sānfēn hěn zhòngyào* 'three-way classification is important' becomes a noun, then how can we explain why the *dǎ* 'hit' of *sān dǎ Zhùjiāzhuāng* 'three attacks on Zhujiazhuang (place name)' has an object, and the *tán* 'talk' of *duìfāng tíchū sān bù tán* 'the other side proposed three no-talkings' is modified by *bù* 'not'? Those words that can directly take modifiers of nouns or differentiating words, for example, *gǎigé* 'reform' in *zhèngtǐ gǎigé* 'reform of political system', must be nouns, but in fact such a combination of attribute and noun still have some properties of verbs. Consider the following examples:

Wǒmen   bú   zhèngtǐ   gǎigé   Dehuà ......
We   not   political system reform   if
'If we don't reform the political system ......'

(*zhèngtǐgǎigé* is modified by the adverb *bù* 'not')

Tā   dǎsuàn   zài   xiànchǎng   xuèxíng   jiàndìng.
he   plan   on   spot   blood type test
'He planned to take the blood type test on the spot.'

(*zài xiànchǎng xuèxíng jiàndìng* functions as the object of the verb *dǎsuàn* 'plan')

Dìfāng   zhèngfǔ   kěyǐ   jiēdào   gǎizào.
local   government can   street   transform
'The local government can make street improvements.'

(*jiēdào gǎizào* can be preceded by the auxiliary verb *kěyǐ* 'can')

Tā   yǐjīng   yàowù   jiǎnyàn   guò   le.
he   already   drug   test   EXP   MP
'He has already been drug-tested.'

(*yàowù jiǎnyàn* is modified by an adverb *yǐjīng*, followed by *guò* and *le*)

Jìnxíng   wūshuǐ   jíshí   chǔlǐ.
carry out   sewage   in time treat
'Treat the sewage promptly.'

(*wūshuǐ chǔlǐ* functions as the object of a dummy verb *Jìnxíng*, with an adverb *jíshí* inserted in between)[16]

Some people say what is modified by an attributive *de* 'of' must be a noun, e.g. *qù* 'go' in *tā de qù* 'his going', because we cannot add *le* to *tā de qù*. According to this logic, *mùtou* 'wood' in *mùtou fángzi* 'wooden house' cannot be preceded by a numeral-classifier modifier, and *yīgēn mùtou fángzi* is not acceptable, so can we say *mùtou* has become an adjective in *mùtou fángzi*? Similarly, *fángzi* 'house' cannot be preceded by a numeral-classifier modifier and *mùtou yīzhuàng fángzi* is not acceptable, so can we say *fángzi* has lost its nominal property in *mùtou fángzi*? And how can we explain *tā de qù le yòu qù* 'his going again and again'? It is also difficult to deal with *tā de qù guò sān cì* 'his being there three times', *tā de qù hé bú qù* 'his going and not going', *tā de tuōyán shì bú qù* 'his delayed not-going', and the like.

Some people classify *qiānxū* 'modesty' in the following two sentences into different categories: (Lu 2014; Li 2014)

Qiānxū   shì   yī   zhǒng   měidé.
modesty   be   one   CL   virtue
'Modesty is a virtue.'

Qiānxū   cái   néng   yíngdé   rénmen   de   zūnzhòng.
modesty   only   can   win   people   MM   respect
'Only modesty can win others' respect.'

They say that *qiānxū* 'modesty' in the first sentence refers to a virtue in general and has been nominalized, whereas *qiānxū* 'modesty' in the second sentence is a subjectless clause that can be recovered as *Tàidù qiānxū cái néng yíngdé rénmen de zūnzhòng* 'only a modest attitude can win others' respect'. The first *qiānxū* 'modesty' is strong towards the end of nouniness while the second *qiānxū* 'modesty' is strong towards the end of verbiness. This subtle difference does exist, but it is almost indistinguishable and inexhaustible, because the first sentence can also go like *Tàidù qiānxū shì yīzhǒng měidé* 'Modesty in attitude is a virtue', and *qiānxū* in the second sentence also refers to a virtue. Following this division, should we say that *bù qiānxū* in *Bù qiānxū shì yīzhǒng máobìng* 'Not being modest is a fault' has also been nominalized? Is *qiānxū* in *Qiānxū hěn zhòngyào* 'Modesty is important' nominalized or a condensed clause? Different opinions may arise and lead to endless arguments. Again, what about the sentence *Qiānxū shì yīzhǒng měidé, néng yíngdé rénmen de zūnzhòng* 'Modesty is a virtue that can win others' respect'?

According to this logic, *mùtou* 'wood' in *Zhè shì zhuàng mùtou fángzi* 'This is a wooden house' represents the nature of the material, and *mùtou* in *Gài fángzi yào yòng hěn duō mùtou* 'It takes a lot of wood to build a house' represents the specific

42   *Breaking with earlier assumptions*

materials. Does it follow that *mùtou* should also be divided into two form classes? This is not something new. Long ago Zhu Dexi (1985: 19) made critical remarks that in the early Chinese grammar works the nouns used as attributes are regarded as adjectives only because they semantically indicate the nature of the head. These controversies are the inevitable result of dividing what should not be divided, and "such circuitous argument not only lacks theoretical basis, but is also difficult for learners to understand and master" (ibid.: 23).

It is of great significance to borrow and learn from international theories and methods, but we need to recognize the nature and grasp the essentials. For the division of verb forms and V-ing forms, English grammarians start with the principle of avoiding unmotivated complication and gradually shift from "dividing as much as possible" to "not dividing whenever possible". This is a case of the nature and the essentials. Conversely, the practice of trying to solve the long-standing problem of nominalization in Chinese grammar with reference to the internal distinction of V-ing forms in English, which English grammarians themselves do not attach much importance to, is not a useful reference but an act of mechanical copying. Some may complain that Chinese lacks the kind of realized, overt, and stable morphological markers of Indo-European languages, and we have no choice but to make similar divisions. We sympathize but disagree with this argument. We should not just talk about what Chinese lacks; instead we should ask what features Chinese has. Each language should have its own important distinctions and its own means of distinguishing. To investigate the grammar of a language, it is important to find out what distinctions it values, rather than to look for all the distinctions of the language we happen to be familiar with. This requires that we continue to break free from the conceptual shackles of traditional ideas and even to make strategic breakthroughs by discarding current terminology for the time being. The distinction between monosyllabic and disyllabic words (and the way they are grouped) discussed in Chapters 4 and 5 in Volume II is a morphological device of Chinese itself, which is different from that of Indo-European languages, and its status and importance are equal to or even greater than the morphological distinctions between verbs and V-ing forms in English.

1.4   On the new three-tier system

Unnecessary distinctions lead to interference and redundancy. The distinction between word classes at the lexical and syntactic levels has been used to bridge the gap between word classes and sentence elements in Chinese.

Shi Dingxu (2011: 4–10) reintroduces the idea that "words should be classified according to semantic criteria", and he argues that sentences make content words gain an external nature, i.e. syntactic function. This is actually a three-tier system of "lexical-level word classes vs. syntactic-function-level word classes vs. syntactic constituents" by distinguishing between word classes at the lexical level and at the syntactic function level. The so-called word classes at the lexical level are determined on the basis of semantic criteria, which are the characteristic of the words themselves. This is actually the belief that the characteristics of the words themselves deserve classification and need to be classified. However, Lü Shuxiang (1979: 32) has long pointed out that this may be true for languages with well-developed morphology but not for Chinese, because the characteristics of the words themselves actually refer to morphological changes. Even in those morphologically developed languages, word classes are ultimately determined by the syntactic functions of the words, because only when words are used in utterances do they have various forms, and words in isolation or in a dictionary take the basic forms abstracted from the many forms of the words, and there is no need to know their morphological changes until they are used in utterances. *The Contemporary Chinese Dictionary* (5th ed.) labels words with their word class properties based on the principle that "word classes are grammatical classifications of words that can describe their functions and usage in general" (Xu & Tan 2006). It is noteworthy that this dictionary does not label words with their word class properties in its previous editions, and instead the word classes are revealed by the example sentences in which the words are used. Shi (2011: 6) says that the difference between *zhànzhēng* 'war' and *zhàndòu* 'battle' is that semantically *zhànzhēng* can only be a noun because when it is put into a specific sentence it is always used to describe an event instead of an action. From this we can see that when he determines the word class of a word based on semantic criteria, he still depends on the specific sentence in which the word appears.

Determining word classes on the basis of semantic criteria, as Zhu (1985: 10) has long pointed out, is unworkable and would not only be a matter of opinion but also a circular argument. For example, in determining that words such as *zhēnlǐ* 'truth', *diàn* 'electricity' and *liángxīn* 'conscience' are nouns, they are said to denote the names of things, but the only reason for saying so is that they have been previously determined to be nouns. Lyons (1968: 147) criticizes the traditional theory of word classes, pointing out that it confuses two issues of a different nature, i.e. the basis for classifying word classes and the naming of classified word classes. The basis for classifying word classes should be the grammatical functions of the words, and classified word classes should be appropriately named by virtue of meaning. For a word class X that is distinguished according to the grammatical function of the words, its members may include *nánhái* 'boy', *nǚrén* 'woman', *cǎo* 'grass', *yuánzǐ* 'atom', *shù* 'tree', *niú* 'cow', *zhēnlǐ* 'truth', *diàn* 'electricity', *liángxīn* 'conscience', etc. Although it cannot be said that all members represent things, it can be said conversely that everything that represents things belongs to the class X. Therefore, the class X can be called the 'noun' class. After nearly a century of exploration, from *Ma's Grammar* to *Answering Questions about Chinese Grammar*, we have managed to get rid of the semantically based view of word classes, but now if we follow Shi, we have to backtrack.[17] After distinguishing between two levels of word classes, Shi (2011: 45) distinguishes three form classes of verbs in the positions of subjects and objects. For example, the word *qiúdù* 'swim across' is still a verb in *wǒmen bù dǎsuàn qiúdù* 'we do not plan to swim across'; it has become a noun in *wǒmen bù shúxī qiúdù* 'we are not familiar with swimming across'; in *wǒmen bú zànchéng qiúdù* 'we do not approve of swimming across', it is only semantically nominalized but not syntactically. This trichotomy is based on

44   *Breaking with earlier assumptions*

the different degrees of domination over the object from *dǎsuàn* 'plan', *shúxī* 'be familiar with', and *zànchéng* 'approve of'. But as the previous section has shown, it is impossible to distinguish between the nominal strengths of verbs, and insisting on this would create an infinite number of types.

Guo Rui (2002: 89–90) also argues that the inherent word classes of words at the lexical level need to be indicated in a dictionary. He also proposes a syntactic level for word classes and establishes another three-tier system. What distinguishes Guo (2002) from Shi (2011) is that Guo argues that word classes are based not on semantic criteria but on the denotational functions such as reference and predication.[18] He makes a distinction between intrinsic and extrinsic denotational functions, the former being word classes at the lexical level and the latter being word classes at the syntactic level, and thus the change in the denotational function results in the change of word classes. For example, at the lexical level *chūbǎn* in *zhè běn shū de chūbǎn* 'the publication of this book' is a verb whose intrinsic denotation function is predicative; at the syntactic level, it is transformed into a noun whose function is changed from being predicative to being referential. The *huáng tóufà* 'yellow hair' in *xiǎowáng huáng tóufà* 'Xiao Wang has yellow hair' is a referring expression used as a predicative expression, that is, a noun phrase used as a verb one.

The new three-tier system is not fundamentally different from the old three-tier system in Otto Jespersen's theory of three ranks, and the so-called word classes at the syntactic level are equivalent to the ranks in the theory of ranks that also hold between word classes and syntactic constituents. The ranks are of three kinds: Primary, secondary, and tertiary. When verbs function as subjects and objects, they change from secondary to primary; when nouns function as attributes, they change from primary to secondary; when adjectives function as adverbials, they change from secondary to tertiary. In his preface to the revised edition of *The Essentials of Chinese Grammar* (1956), Lü Shuxiang claims that the relationship between word classes and sentence elements in Chinese is so intricate and complex that it cannot be dealt with by adding a rank, for almost any word can have different ranks, and they still need functional shifts among word classes, which does not solve the problem. In his note to the new printing of the book (1982), he restates that doing so does not solve the problem. It is against the principle of simplicity to add a level of analysis without solving the problem, so Lü later determined to remove this level. Wang Li (1954) also declared in his preface to the new edition of *The Theory of Chinese Grammar* that he would do away with the theory of ranks.

The new three-tier system is even more complicated than the theory of ranks. For example, Guo (2002) says that the intrinsic and extrinsic denotational functions are actually the word classes at the lexical and syntactic levels respectively and that the shifts of denotational functions are functional shifts of word classes. Since they refer to the same things, why do we bother to use two sets of terms? It is further complicated by his view that the words classed as nouns and verbs like *chūbǎn* 'publish' fall into two classes at the lexical level, one being verbal as in *zhè běn shū de chūbǎn* 'the publication of this book' and one being nominal as in *túshū chūbǎn* 'book publishing'. The former is converted from verbal to nominal when it enters the syntactic level, while the latter is converted from verbal to nominal at the lexical level. These two types of class conversion are considered to be 'grammatical and lexical respectively' (Guo 2002: 101), which adds another layer of distinction to class conversion. This treatment leads to both interference and redundancy. For a coordinate phrase like *bǎnquán bǎohù hé tèbié bǎohù* 'copyright protection and special protection', this treatment will render the first *bǎohù* as a noun and the second *bǎohù* as a verb, and these two instances of *bǎohù* undergo nominalization at the lexical and syntactic levels, respectively. In the case of *túshū de chūbǎn yǔ bù chūbǎn* 'the publishing and not publishing of books', if the first *chūbǎn* is considered to be nominalized at the syntactic level, then the juxtaposed second *chūbǎn* (modified by the adverb *bù* 'not') cannot be nominalized at the syntactic level. How can *bù chūbǎn* 'not publishing' be nominalized at the lexical level in phrases like *tuōyán shì bù chūbǎn* 'not publishing through delaying' and *gěi tā lái yī gè bù chūbǎn* 'give him a not-publishing'?

The new three-tier system is not only more complicated than the theory of ranks, but also it does not make the distinction where it should, as the theory of ranks does. For class conversion in English, the theory of ranks (Jespersen 1924: 62) holds that verbs used as subjects or objects are cases of class conversion from secondary to primary, whereas nouns used as predicates are not cases of class conversion from primary to secondary but become real verbs. This is an important distinction, and Zhu Dexi sees the importance of this distinction, saying that verbs can be used as subjects and objects but nouns cannot be generally used as predicates. This asymmetry between nouns and verbs exists both in English and in Chinese (see Chapter 5). Nevertheless, the new three-tier system makes no such distinction.

1.5   Overriding rather than overthrowing

The practice of adding a level of analysis between word classes and syntactic constituents, which fails to solve the problem and violates the principle of simplicity, has been abandoned by the two well respected predecessors, Lü Shuxiang and Wang Li. But there are some people who want to roll back and adopt this practice again. This is because they don't understand the reason why the two predecessors gave up on it. They disregard the principle of simplicity and don't know much about the division of form classes. To make the studies of Chinese grammar more scientific, Zhu seriously proposes that simplicity and rigorousness are equally important in establishing the Chinese grammatical system. In implementing these principles, he first proposed that verbs functioning as subjects and objects do not undergo any process of nominalization, which is a very important feature that distinguishes Chinese from Indo-European languages and is inextricably related to our comprehensive understanding of word classes and syntactic structures in Chinese. The syntactic multifunctionality of Chinese word classes and the consistency of phrase structures and sentence structures are both inseparable from this feature.

Nowadays, many people like to raise a rumpus about some side issues, treating secondary phenomena as primary phenomena and special phenomena as general phenomena. In so doing they try to revise Zhu's view by reverting to the semantic

46 *Breaking with earlier assumptions*

division of word classes and reintroducing the concept of nominalization. They argue that "the knot cannot be untied without assuming a certain procedure of nominalization" and that "English imposes nominalization on Chinese verbs" (Yuan 2010b).[19] They believe that if there is no nominalization at the lexical level, then it should be assumed at the syntactic level, and that it is necessary to reintroduce the concept of zero nominalization. The consequences of doing so are serious, for denying this feature is tantamount to pulling the carpet from under someone, and the whole phrase-based grammatical system established by Zhu will basically collapse, and there will be no more of Zhu's scholarly contributions worthy of discussion. It is intended be a partial revision of Zhu's system, but it turns out to be the overthrow of Zhu's entire theoretical system. Big truths should govern and account for small truths. There is no denying the need to study the side issues or the importance of corpus statistics, but it is more important to have an accurate grasp of the big picture of the Chinese grammatical system. Lack of prioritization and attending to trifles but neglecting essentials can lead not only to bad consequences but also to a misinterpretation of Zhu's original intention, which is grossly unfair to him.

To realize that Chinese verbs are not nominalized when they are used as subjects and objects is to reach a higher level in the century-long effort to break free from the analytical framework of Indo-European languages and search for the Chinese-specific characteristics. Naturally there are still many problems with the current Chinese grammatical system (see the next chapter). To solve them, we should fulfil Zhu's expectations and continue to break free from traditional ideas rather than retreating from the frontier we have reached, for reversion is not feasible. We appreciate the process of scientific development in which new theories override rather than overthrow old ones, just as Einstein's theory of relativity overrides rather than overthrows Newton's theory of classical physics. When we take stock of Zhu's academic legacy, we must not underestimate and dispose of the most valuable parts, otherwise it will turn out to be like throwing the baby out with the bathwater.

The good thing is that Zhu's works have provided a direction for moving forward. In arguing that Chinese verbs in the positions of subjects and objects do not undergo nominalization, he also proposes that, unlike Indo-European nouns, Chinese nouns are negatively defined. This book will further argue that only in the verbs-as-nouns framework can Chinese nouns in the traditional sense be negatively defined and that the reason why Chinese verbs are not nominalized in the positions of subjects and objects is that Chinese verbs are, by their very nature, a type of nouns.[20] The verbs-as-nouns theory is put forward to override rather than overthrow Zhu's theory.

Notes

1 This does not amount to saying that everything in Chinese is fully integrated, and there are no distinctions at all. See Lü (1979: 11–12). Or "This does not mean that everything in Chinese is blended together into a single mass without distinctions among its parts".
2 Citations of Yuen Ren Chao (1968) in this book are based on Lü Shuxiang's translation (1979), unless otherwise noted.

3 These examples are cited from Li Zuofeng (2004), in which he contends that verbs functioning as subjects are mainly limited to assertive sentences.
4 The examples are provided by Zhang Yunqiu from her collection of child language data.
5 The movie *The Hunt for Bin Laden* is fascinating because it does not focus on the killing operation, but it details the tortuous process of how the protagonist, a female agent, locates Bin Laden's hideout. The twists and turns are that the female agent's immediate supervisor only trusts the data collected instead of her intuitive judgment, but the data indicates the probability of Bin Laden hiding in that house is no more than 60%.
6 English morphology is on the decline. Although it is true that quite a few verbs can be used as nouns like *work* and *play* without any morphological changes, they only account for a small part of verbs in English. Therefore, they defy generalization.
7 The term *default* is sometimes phonetically transliterated into Chinese as *dǐfú de* 'underlying', which better expresses the fundamental nature of default rules.
8 Broschart (1997), for example, realizes that the word class system of Tongan is very different from that of Indo-European languages, in that it does not distinguish between nouns and verbs in the first place but rather distinguishes between types and tokens, valuing the distinction between abstract and concrete units. (See Chapter 2 in Volume II for details.)
9 Both Yuan Yulin (1995) and Shen Jiaxuan (1999) view Chinese word classes from the perspective of continuity, which has its own value, but it cannot completely replace the perspective of discreteness.
10 Following Lü Shuxiang (1979: 47), it must be acknowledged that *pīpíng* 'criticism' in *wényì pīpíng* 'literary criticism' has been turned into a real noun.
11 *The Cambridge Grammar of the English Language* offers new insights of many distinguished linguists into English grammar and serves to bridge the gap that exists between traditional grammar and modern linguistics. (See its Preface.)
12 *The Cambridge Grammar of the English Language* establishes a form class of "participial adjective", which refers to V-ing forms functioning as adjectival predicates, as in *The show was entertaining*. This type of usage is not included in *Quirk et al*'s fourteen examples, because it is not a noun phrase. It makes sense to identify this form class, because in English adjectives are significantly different from verbs in that they cannot function directly as predicates as verbs do.
13 For example, Shen Jiaxuan (1999: Chapter 10) uses these to justify that there is a general "correlated markedness pattern" between word classes and syntactic constituents, and Wang (2001: Chapter 5) uses these to prove that there is a covariation pattern of predication and reference between verbs and objects (also called "noun-verb covariation"). In addition, Lu Bingfu (2005) uses these to demonstrate the enormous influence of "identifiability" on word order.
14 It is only a rough order. In fact, it is no easy job to give an exact order because the varying strengths of nouniness are difficult to distinguish.
15 In English *exploring* (V-ing) is distinguished from *to explore* (infinitive) in terms of form, which is taken for granted, for there are differences in the strength of nouniness or verbiness.
16 The examples are provided by Zeng Qian. If I were a self-important literary theorist, I would say, '*Nǐ yě wényì pīpíng, tā yě wényì pīpíng, hǎoxiàng ā gǒu ā māo dōu néng wényì pīpíng sì de*'. (You work on literary criticism, and he works on literary criticism, as if every dog and every cat can work on literary criticism.)
17 Scholars working on the emerging 'cognitive grammar' like Langacker (1987) define all grammatical categories in terms of cognitive semantics. This practice at least maintains theoretical consistency and is formally justified, but advocates of backtracking lack such theoretical consistency.
18 It should be admitted that this view is much more insightful than a semantic-based view of word classes (see Chapter 4, Section 1).

48 *Breaking with earlier assumptions*

19 In fact, it is not that 'English imposes nominalization on Chinese verbs' but that the traditional ideas derived from English drive them to find nominalization for verbs in Chinese.
20 Guo Rui (2011) says that the verbs-as-nouns theory is more thoroughgoing in terms of nominalization, but I declare that, on the contrary, it is actually more thoroughgoing in terms of anti-nominalization. How can we confuse nominalization with nouns as they are?

References

Broschart, J. (1997) 'Why Tongan Does It Differently: Categorial Distinctions in a Language without Nouns and Verbs', *Linguistic Typology* 1: 123–165.
Cao, Tianyuan (2006) *Shangdi Zhi Touzi Ma: Liangzi Wuli Shihua* (*Does God Roll the Dice: History of Quantum Physics*), Shenyang: Liaoning Education Press.
Chao, Yuen Ren (1968) *A Grammar of Spoken Chinese*, Berkeley and Los Angeles: University of California Press. Translated as *Hanyu Kouyu Yufa* by Lü Shuxiang in 1979, Beijing: The Commercial Press, and as *Zhongguohua de Wenfa* (Revised edition) by Pang-hsin Ting in 2002, Hong Kong: The Chinese University of Hong Kong Press.
Crystal, David (1997) *A Dictionary of Linguistics and Phonetics*, 4th ed., Oxford: Blackwell Publishers Ltd.
Fan, Xiao (1992) 'VP zhuyuju: jianlun N *de* V zuo zhuyu' ('The Sentences with VP Subjects, with Remarks on N *de* V Functioning as Subjects'), in *Yufa Yanjiu he Tansuo* (*Studies and Explorations on Grammar*) 6: 176–189.
Guo, Rui (2002) *Xiandai Hanyu Cilei Yanjiu* (*A Study of Word Classes in Modern Chinese*), Beijing: The Commercial Press.
Guo, Rui (2011) 'Zhu Dexi xiansheng de hanyu cilei yanjiu' ('Zhu Dexi's Study on Parts of Speech in Chinese'), *Chinese Language Learning* 5: 14–26.
Huddleston, R. and G. K. Pullum (2002) *The Cambridge Grammar of the English Language*, Cambridge: Cambridge University Press.
Jespersen, Otto (1924) *The Philosophy of Grammar*, London: George Allen & Unwin Ltd.
Langacker, R. (1987/1991) *Foundations of Cognitive Grammar*, vols. 1 & 2, Stanford: Stanford University Press.
Li, Baojia (2014) 'Quzheyu cilei huafen de beijing ji dui Shen Jiaxuan *wo kan hanyu de cilei* de zhiyi' ('The Background of Word Class of Inflected Languages and the Questions in Shen Jiaxuan's "*My View of Word Classes in Chinese*"'), in *Yinghan Duibi yu Fanyi* (*Contrastive and Translation Studies of English and Chinese*), vol. 2, Shanghai: Shanghai Foreign Language Education Press, 84–99.
Li, Zuofeng (2004) *Gudai Hanyu Yufaxue* (*A Grammar of Ancient Chinese*), Beijing: The Commercial Press.
Lu, Bingfu (2005) 'Yuxu youshi de renzhi jieshi: lun kebiedu dui yuxu de pubian yingxiang' ('Word Order Dominance and Its Cognitive Explanation: The Pervasive Influence of Identifiability on Word Order'), *Contemporary Linguistics* 1: 1–15, 2: 132–138.
Lu, Jianming (2003) 'Dui NP+de+VP jiegou de chongxin renshi' ('A New Understanding of the NP+*de*+VP Structure'), *Studies of the Chinese Language* 5: 387–391.
Lu, Jianming (2013) 'Qianyi hanyu mingdongxing cengceng baohan cileiguan ji qita' ('A Discussion on Hierarchical Inclusion of Chinese Nouns, Verbs and Adjectives and Other Things'), *Journal of Sino-Tibetan Linguistics* 7: 137–146.
Lu, Jianming (2014) 'Zenme renshi hanyu zai cilei shang de tedian?' ('How to Discern the True Features of Word Classes in Chinese?'), in *Yinghan Duibi yu Fanyi* (*Contrastive*

and Translation Studies of English and Chinese), vol. 2, Shanghai: Shanghai Foreign Language Education Press, 29–39.

Lü, Shuxiang (1942/1982) *Zhongguo Wenfa Yaolüe* (*Essentials of Chinese Grammar*), Shanghai and Beijing: The Commercial Press.

Lü, Shuxiang (1979) *Hanyu Yufa Fenxi Wenti* (*Problems in Chinese Grammatical Analysis*), Beijing: The Commercial Press.

Lü, Shuxiang (2002) 'Yufa yanjiu zhong de po yu li' ('Arguments and Refutations in Grammatical Studies'), in *Lü Shuxiang Quanji* (*The Complete Works of Lü Shuxiang*), vol. 13, Beijing: The Commercial Press, 402–404.

Lyons, J. (1968) *Introduction to Theoretical Linguistics*, Cambridge: Cambridge University Press.

Ma, Jianzhong (1898/1983) *Mashi Wentong* (*Ma's Grammar*), Beijing: The Commercial Press.

Piao, Chongkui (2003) 'Dange dongci zuo zhuyu de yuyi yufa kaocha' ('A Semantic and Grammatical Investigation of Single Verbs as Subjects'), *Chinese Language Learning* 6: 25–31.

Quirk, R., S. Greenbaum, G. Leech and J. Svartvik (1985) *A Comprehensive Grammar of the English Language*, London and New York: Longman.

Shen, Jiaxuan (1999) *Buduicheng he Biaojilun* (*Asymmetry and Markedness Theory*), Nanchang: Jiangxi Education Publishing House, Reprinted in Beijing: The Commercial Press, 2015.

Shen, Jiaxuan (2015) 'Xingshilei de fenyuhe' ('On Division of Form Classes'), *Modern Foreign Languages* 1: 1–14.

Shi, Dingxu (2011) *Mingci he Mingcixing Chengfen* (*Nouns and Nominal Phrases*), Beijing: Beijing University Press.

Shi, Youwei (2014) 'Diyi shezhi yu hanyu de shici' ('First Establishment and Full Words in Chinese', in *Yinghan Duibi yu Fanyi* (*Contrastive and Translation Studies of English and Chinese*), vol. 2, Shanghai: Shanghai Foreign Language Education Press, 40–70.

Wang, Dongmei (2001) 'Xiandai hanyu dongming huzhuan de renzhi yanjiu' ('A Cognitive Study of the Categorial Shift Between Nouns and Verbs in Contemporary Chinese'), Doctoral Dissertation, Department of Linguistics, Graduate School of Chinese Academy of Social Sciences. Revised version, 2010, Beijing: China Social Sciences Press.

Wang, Li (1954) *Zhongguo Yufa Lilun* (*A Theory of Chinese Grammar*), Beijing: Zhonghua Book Company.

Wu, Chang'an (2012) 'Hanyu mingci dongci jiaorong moshi de lishi xingcheng' ('The History of the Fusion of Nouns and Verbs in Chinese'), *Studies of the Chinese Language* 1: 17–28.

Xu, Guozhang (1991) *Xu Guozhang Lun Yuyan* (*Xu Guozhang on Language*), Beijing: Foreign Language Teaching and Research Press.

Xu, Shu and Jingchun Tan (2006) 'Guanyu Xiandai Hanyu Cidian (di wu ban) cilei biaozhu de shuoming' ('An Explanation of the Word Class Labels in *The Contemporary Chinese Dictionary* (Fifth Edition)'), *Studies of the Chinese Language* 1: 74–86.

Yuan, Yulin (1995) 'Cilei fanchou de jiazu xiangsixing' ('Family Resemblance of Lexical Categories'), *Social Sciences in China* 1: 154–170.

Yuan, Yulin (2010a) Hanyu he yingyu zai yufa fanchou de shixian guanxi shang de pingxingxing: ye tan hanyu li mingci/dongci yu zhicheng/chenshu, zhuyu yu huati, juzi yu huaduan' ('Parallels in the Realization of Grammatical Categories between Chinese and English: On Noun/Verb and Reference/Predication, Subject and Topic, Sentence and Utterance in Chinese'), *Journal of Sino-Tibetan Linguistics* 4: 139–168.

50 Breaking with earlier assumptions

Yuan, Yulin (2010b) 'Hanyu buneng chengshou de fanyi zhiqing: cong qu fanchouhua jiaodu kan hanyu dongci he mingci de guanxi' ('The Unbearable Lightness of the Translation of Deverbal Nouns from Indo-European Languages into Chinese: Rethinking the Relation between Verbs and Nouns in Mandarin Chinese from a Perspective of the Decategorization of Verbs'), *Essays on Linguistics* 41: 15–61.

Zhan, Weidong (1998) 'Guanyu NP de VP pianzheng jiegou' ('On the Modifier-Head Structure of NP *de* VP'), *Chinese Language Learning* 4: 24–28.

Zhan, Weidong (2012) 'Cong yuyan gongcheng kan zhongxin kuozhan guiyue he binglie tiaojian' ('A Language Engineering Perspective on Violation of Head Extension Principle and Coordination Condition'), *Linguistic Sciences* 5: 449–462.

Zhu, Dexi (1982) *Yufa Jiangyi* (*Lectures on Chinese Grammar*), Beijing: The Commercial Press.

Zhu, Dexi (1983) 'Zizhi he zhuanzhi: hanyu mingcihua biaoji *de zhe zhi* de yufa gongneng he yuyi gongneng' ('Self-designation and Transferred Designation: The Grammatical and Semantic Functions of Chinese Nominalizers *De, Zhe, Zhi*'), *Dialect* 1: 16–31.

Zhu, Dexi (1985) *Yufa Dawen* (*Answering Questions about Chinese Grammar*), Beijing: The Commercial Press.

Zhu, Dexi (1987) 'Juzi he zhuyu: yin'ouyu yingxiang xiandai shumian hanyu he hanyu jufa fenxi de yige shili' ('Sentences and Subjects: An Example of How Indo-European Languages Influence Modern Written Chinese and Syntactic Analysis of Chinese'), *Chinese Teaching in the World* 1: 31–34.

2 The problems

2.1 The problem of defining nouns

A grammatical system needs to take consistency and simplicity as the highest standards (see Section 2 of Introduction). A system that is not consistent or simple is certainly problematic, which does not need to be proved by more linguistic facts. This chapter presents the problems with the current Chinese word class system based on the traditional noun-verb distinction. These problems are big because they are closely related to the grammatical system as a whole. The previous chapter criticizes the practice of being entangled in side issues, which is as much a symptom of the same fault as ignoring and avoiding issues of global importance.

The first problem is how to define Chinese nouns in the traditional framework that distinguishes nouns from verbs. This is not a problem in Indo-European languages, because there are such morphological markers denoting gender, number, and case for defining nouns. Although the morphology of English has declined, it still exists: Nouns have their own special suffixes such as *-ness*, *-ation*, *-ment*, and *-ity*; most nouns can be singular or plural; nouns can be preceded by the article *a/an* or *the*. Even if a word or form is both nominal and verbal, it can be judged as a noun and distinguished from a verb as long as the plural marker *-s* or an article is added. But Chinese nouns cannot be defined in such a positive way. On this, Zhu Dexi argues in *Answering Questions about Chinese Grammar* (1985a) as follows:

> Some grammar books enumerate the "grammatical features" of nouns as (1) can be used as subjects and objects, (2) can be modified by attributes, (3) can be modified by quantifiers, and so on. The above three features are indeed grammatical functions of nouns, that is, they are the universals of nouns (all nouns have these functions). However, none of these three features can be called the exclusive grammatical features (individuality) of nouns, because verbs and adjectives also have these grammatical functions. . . . If these three features are used as the criteria for defining nouns, then almost all words that are normally considered verbs and adjectives would have to be grouped under the noun category.
>
> (p. 16)

DOI: 10.4324/9781003385899-3

52 *The problems*

With a clear difference between "grammatical features" and "grammatical properties" in mind, Zhu defines the grammatical features of a word class as the grammatical properties that are only possessed by the word class but not by other word classes, that is, the individuality that distinguishes this word class from other word classes. The three features mentioned earlier are not exclusive to nouns. So Chinese nouns can only be defined negatively, that is, they cannot generally be predicates.

Many people ignore this paragraph from Zhu or have doubts about it, yet this is a fact of the Chinese language. Verbs and adjectives can also be modified by quantifiers, whether monosyllabic or disyllabic, and they can take objects after taking quantifiers. There are numerous examples:

yǒu   yī diǎn   màn
have   a little   slow
'a little slow'

yǒu   xiēr   kuài
have   a little   fast
'a little fast'

sānfēn   zànchéng
three out of ten   favor
'three out of ten in favor'

qīfēn   fǎnduì
seven out of ten   against
'seven out of ten against'

yīfēn   tóngqíng
one out of ten   sympathize
'a little sympathy'

jiǔfēn   dānxīn
nine out of ten   worry
'very worried'

sān   dǎ   Zhùjiāzhuāng
three   assault   Zhu Family Village
'three assaults on the Zhu Family Village'

jiǔ   píng   sūlián xīuzhèngzhǔyì
nine   comment   Soviet revisionism
'nine comments on Soviet revisionism'

zhè   yī   cì   qù   xīzàng   duōkuī   le   nǐ
this   one   time   go   Tibet   thanks to   PSP   you
'this trip to Tibet is thanks to you'

zhè   zhǒng   kāi wánxiào   kě yàobudé
this   kind   joke   is not acceptable
'this kind of joke is not acceptable'

dǎoyǎn   Féng Xiǎogāng   zhè   sān gè   zhuǎnshēn   dōu   hěn   huálì
director   Feng Xiaogang   this   3 CL   turn   all   very   gorgeous
'the 3 turns of director Feng Xiaogang are all very gorgeous'

liǎng duì qíngrén de   zhè liǎng gè gàobié   dōu chéng   le   juébié[1]
two CL lovers   MM this two   CL goodbye   both become PSP eternal farewells
'these two goodbyes of the two pairs of lovers have both become eternal farewells'

An article by Lü Shuxiang (1944/1984) gives numerous examples of verbs modified by the classifier (*yī*) *gè* in early modern Chinese:

zuò   gè   zhǔnbèi
make   CL   preparation
'make a preparation'

yǒu   gè   xiàluò
have   CL   whereabouts
'have somebody's whereabouts'

tǎo   gè   fēnxiǎo
find out   CL   outcome
'find out the outcome'

zuò   gè   jìrèn
make   CL   mark
'leave a mark'

zhuāng   gè   lǎoshí
pretend   CL   honest
'pretend to be an honest man'

méi   gè   chénggōng
no   CL   succeed
'No success'./'None of them succeeded'.

mì   gè   zìwěn
seek   CL   suicide
'seek to commit suicide'

dé   gè   yīkào
get   CL   rely
'have someone to rely on'

54   *The problems*

yǒu   gè   fānshēn
have   CL   turnaround
'bring about an upswing'

zhàng   gè   gāncùi
pursue   CL   straightforward
'To do things in a straightforward manner'

mǎi   yī   gè   bù yányǔ
buy   one   CL   no words/silent/silence
'to bribe someone for the purpose of shutting him up'

chīkūi   zài   yī   gè   cōngmíng   hàoshèng
suffer loses   in   one   CL   clever   competitive
'to suffer losses because of someone's cleverness and competitiveness'

suànde   gè   tèděng   mǎhu
consider   CL   special grade   sloppy
'considered to be very sloppy'

yíng   gè   tājiāpiānyǒu
win   CL   make something exclusive to his family
'win something in order to make it exclusive to his family'

luò   gè   réncáiliǎngkōng
fall   CL   lose both people and money
'fall into a situation of losing both people and money'

dǎ   gè   xiōngsīzhuàng
beat   CL   bump into chest
'bump into each other's chests'

There are many more examples of verbs modified by *yī jiàn* 'a piece of', *yī duàn* 'a time of', *yī fān* 'a series of', and so on: (Cui 2013: 225–229)

yī jiàn   xūjīng
a thing of   to fear something unnecessarily
'a false alarm'

yī jiàn   guàài
a thing of   concern
'a thing of concern'

yī jiàn   qíyì
a thing of   strange
'a thing of strange'

yī jiàn   jīqiǎo
a thing of   ingenious
'a thing of ingenuity'

yī jiàn   jí tōngqíng
a thing of   very reasonable
'a thing of reasonability'

yī jiàn   bù shǒu nǚ'ér guīju
a thing of   to go against the rules of being a daughter
'a thing that goes against the rules of being a daughter'

yī duàn   xiāngsī
a time of   miss
'a time of lovesick'

yī duàn   jiāoxiū
a time of   shy
'a time of shyness'

yī fān   jiàoyù
a series of   lecturing
'a series of lecturing'

yī fān   qīhēi
a patch of   dark
'a patch of darkness'

yī chóng   nù
a burst of   anger
'a burst of anger'

yī tào   jiǎ yīnqíng
a set of   fake attention
'a set of fake attention'

Verbs and adjectives are also frequently found in the following sentence patterns:

wèn   gè   míngbai
ask   CL   clear
'to ask for a clear answer'

chī   gè   méigòu
eat   CL   not enough
'haven't had enough of something'

56 *The problems*

lái   yī   gè   bù   kēngshēng
come one CL   not   utter a word
'reply by not uttering a word'

hǎo   yī   gè   jiāoshūyùrén
good   one   CL   educate students
'What a good teacher!'

zhè   jiào   yī   gè   shuǎng
this   call   one   CL   wonderful
'What a wonderful feeling it is!'

nà   jiào   yī   gè   bàng
that   call   one   CL   awesome
'That's awesome!'

gǎo   tā   gè   shuǐluòshíchū
make   it   CL   come out in the wash
'Get to the bottom of it.'

dǎ   de   gè   luòhuāliúshuǐ
beat   CSC   CL   be badly beaten by someone
'clean someone's clock'

běifēng   nàgè   chūi
the north wind   that   blow
'How strongly the north wind blows!'

chǒu   tā   nàgè   pàng
look   he   that   fat
'Look at him, he is so fat!'

wǎng   chuángshàng   yī   tǎng
towards   on the bed   one   lie
'lie down on the bed'

chī   wán   le   yī   sàn
eat   over   PSP   one   leave
'finish eating and leave'

dòng   tā   gè   yī   dòng
move   he   CL   one   move
'Give him a move.'

shì   shàng   tā   yī   shì
try   on   he   one   try
'Give him a try.'

The problems 57

Although verbs are only quantified by a few classifiers such as *zhǒng* 'kind', *cì* 'time' and *gè* 'a', abstract nouns such as "*shìwù* 'thing', *guòchéng* 'process', *liángxīn* 'conscience', *zhànzhēng* 'war', *shǒushù* 'operation'" can also only be quantified by these classifiers. Just as nouns have temporary nominal quantifiers, verbs have temporary verbal quantifiers (Li 2011), as in:

chōu   yī   biānzi
whip   one   whip
'give a whip'

qiāo   yī   gùnzi
knock   one   stick
'knock a stick'

zhā   yī   zhēn
prick   one   needle
'prick a needle'

kǎn   sān   dāo
cut   three   knife
'cut three times'

fàng   liǎng   qiāng
fire   two   gun
'fire two shots'

shè   yī   jiàn
shoot   one   arrow
'shoot an arrow'

dǐng   yī   nǎodai
hit   one   head
'throw a headbutt'

chōu   yī   bāzhang
whip   one   slap
'take a slap'

chuō   yī   zhǐtou
poke   one   finger
'poke a finger.'

hēng   yī   bízi
hum   one   nose
'hum a nose'

58   *The problems*

tī   yī   jiǎo
kick   one   foot
'give a kick'

dǎ   yī   quán
beat   one   punch
'give a punch'

kàn   liǎng   yǎn
look   two   eye
'look twice'

jiào   yī   shēng
shout   one   sound
'give a shout'

mài   yī   bù
step   one   step
'take a step'

pǎo   liǎng   quān
run   two   lap
'run two laps'

sòng   yī   chéng
give   one   ride
'give a ride'

Temporary verbal quantifiers can also appear before verbs, such as *yī zhēn zhā xiàqù* 'a needle was pricked into', *yī bāzhang chōu guòqù* 'a slap was taken', *liǎng quān pǎo xiàlái* 'two laps down'.

However, what contradicts himself is that Zhu lists "can be modified by quantifiers" as a grammatical feature of nouns in his *Lectures on Chinese Grammar*, and takes it as a criterion for distinguishing nouns together with the feature of "cannot be modified by adverbs". Although it is stated in *Answering Questions about Chinese Grammar* that it is not a grammatical feature of nouns to be modified by quantifiers, this criterion is often applied in specific grammatical analyses. For example, when distinguishing attributes and adverbials, it is determined that *huáng* 'yellow' in *zhè gè rén huáng tóufa* 'the man has yellow hair' is an attribute, and *yě* 'also' in *tā dìdi yě huáng tóufa* 'his brother also has yellow hair' is an adverbial. The reasoning is that *huáng tóufa* can be modified by quantifiers and is therefore substantive, whereas *yě huáng tóufa* cannot be modified by a quantifier and is therefore predicative (Zhu 1982: 46–47). It is not difficult to understand Zhu's ambivalence: from the standpoint of Chinese facts, nouns cannot be defined positively, and the feature "can be modified by quantifiers" is not

The problems 59

exclusive to nouns; from the standpoint of the traditional conceptual framework that distinguishes nouns from verbs, it is not allowed that nouns lack a positive definition, so the feature "can be modified by quantifiers" becomes the most likely criterion for defining nouns.

Some argue that universal reference through reduplication can be taken as the grammatical feature of nouns, yet what is actually reduplicated is not nouns but quantifiers (including verbal quantifiers such as *cìcì* 'every time' and *biànbiàn* 'every time'). Consider the following examples:

kēkē 'CL-CL'   —   * shùshù 'tree-tree'
duǒduǒ 'CL-CL'   —   * yúnyún 'cloud-cloud'
dīdī 'CL-CL'   —   * shuǐshuǐ 'water-water'
pǐpǐ 'CL-CL'   —   * mǎmǎ 'horse-horse'

Tā mǎi le jǐ píng suānnǎi, píngpíng dōu yǒu guàiwèi.
he buy PSP several CL-bottle yogurt bottle-bottle all have strange taste
'He bought several bottles of yogurt, and every bottle had a strange taste.'

Tā mǎi le jǐ cì suānnǎi, cìcì dōu yǒu guàiwèi.
he buy PSP several CL-times yogurt times-times all have strange taste
'He bought yogurt several times, and every time it had a strange taste.'

* Tā mǎi le jǐ píng/cì suānnǎi, nǎinǎi dōu yǒu guàiwèi.
he buy PSP several CL-bottle/times yogurt yogurt-yogurt all have strange taste
'He bought several bottles of yogurt/yogurt several times, and every yogurt had a strange taste.'

If nouns and verbs are distinct from each other and are both subsumed by the super-category *shící* 'full words', then both of them should be defined positively. Some argue that by giving a positive definition of the verb as a way to determine its grammatical features, the scope of the noun would be delimited at the same time. But the premise of this is that full words have a positive definition, and obviously they cannot be defined as "nouns and verbs are collectively called notional words". In *Lectures on Chinese Grammar*, Zhu (1982: 39) explains full words as follows: "functionally, full words can act as subjects, objects or predicates". If the word *or* in this explanation is understood as conjunctive, then only verbs conform to this explanation while nouns do not, because nouns cannot generally be used as predicates. If the word *or* is understood as disjunctive, it is the same as saying that "nouns and verbs are collectively called full words", thus rendering the connotations of full words empty. Seeing these shortcomings, Lü Shuxiang (1979: 35) claims, "It seems that no definite conclusion can be reached just by pondering over 'full words' and 'empty words'; the difference between them is not of great practical significance either". Only in the verbs-as-nouns framework can traditional nouns be negatively defined.[2] The grammatical features of the super-nouns (including verbs) are "can be modified by quantifiers" and "can function as subjects and objects". Once both super-nouns and verbs have been clearly defined, the part of super-nouns that remains after the removal of verbs (i.e. traditional nouns, also known as "small nouns") does not need to be defined positively. Instead, they can only be negatively defined, that is, they cannot generally be used as predicates. (See Chapter 3, Section 3 for details.)

When Zhu says that Chinese nouns are negatively defined, he is only a step away from the verbs-as-nouns framework, which was already truly remarkable at that time. His definition of nouns in *Lectures on Chinese Grammar*—that they can be modified by quantifiers but not by adverbs—is essentially a negative definition, which exactly applies to small nouns in the verbs-as-nouns framework. As long as we break free from the traditional idea that nouns and verbs are distinct from each other, we will immediately step into the verbs-as-nouns framework. It is those who still insist on the noun-verb distinction that have the obligation to clarify positively what grammatical features the nouns in their framework have that are possessed only by nouns but not by verbs.

2.2 The problem of nouny verbs

2.2.1 The difficulty of delimiting the scope

According to Zhu Dexi (1982, 1985a, 1985c), "nouny verbs" are verbs with nominal characteristics, which can also be considered words classed as nouns and verbs, such as *yánjiū* 'research', *diàochá* 'survey', *zhǔnbèi* 'prepare'. They are only found in written Chinese and are all disyllabic verbs. Although the grammatical features of nouny verbs or the criteria for distinguishing them are not quite consistent in Zhu's discussions, they can be summed up as follows: 1) Can be the object of the verb *yǒu* 'have/there be'; 2) can be the object of dummy verbs such as *jìnxíng*, *jiāyǐ*, *jǐyǔ*, *yǔyǐ*, *zuò*, without the modification of adverbs and taking no objects, but some can be modified by quantifiers; 3) can modify nouns directly without adding *de*; 4) can be directly modified by nouns; 5) can only be juxtaposed by *hé* 'and' instead of *bìng* 'also'.

Nouny verbs are identified on the basis of the idea that nouns and verbs are distinct from each other but with a little overlap. As shown in the following figure, the overlapping part, where nouny verbs belong, can only take up a small portion, otherwise it should not be counted as class overlap.

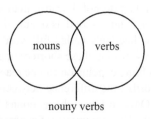

Figure 2.1 Nouny verbs

The problems   61

There are two problems with this understanding of nouny verbs. First, it is difficult to delimit the scope of the category with certainty using the proposed criteria. Second, the definition of the category leads to contradictions inside the theory and to the inconsistency of the whole grammatical system. As to the first problem, Qiu Rongtang (1994) explains in detail that the results of the previous five criteria are difficult to make consistent with each other. For example, some of disyllabic verbs that cannot be the objects of dummy verbs can be the object of *yǒu* 'have/ there be'; and some of them can be directly modified by nouns, such as *míxìn* 'be superstitious', *fāxiàn* 'discover', *gùlü* 'scruple', *shīwù* 'mistake', *zhòngtián* 'farm', *liúxíng* 'be popular', *jiàngjiū* 'be meticulous', *zhǐwàng* 'hope'. The disyllabic verbs that can be the object of dummy verbs cannot necessarily be directly modified by nouns, especially the disyllabic verbs consisting of a monosyllabic verb and a monosyllabic complement, such as "*tígāo* 'improve', *chéngqīng* 'clarify', *chámíng* 'ascertain', *pīzhǔn* 'approve', *sùqīng* 'purge', *jiūzhèng* 'rectify', *cūihǔi* 'destroy', *gǎizhèng* 'correct', and also disyllabic verbs that express mental states, such as *zūnzhòng* 'respect', *zhòngshì* 'value', *zhùyì* 'notice', *kěndìng* 'affirm', *xìnrèn* 'trust', *zànshǎng* 'appreciate'. What can be directly modified by nouns are not limited to nouny verbs or even to disyllabic verbs. Instead, it can be monosyllabic verbs as in "*wōlǐ fǎn* 'internal strife', *jiědì liàn* 'sibling love', *gūsǎo zhēng* 'a dispute between a man's sister and his wife', *húmǎ huì* 'Hu Jintao-Ma Ying-jeou dialogue', *ōuzhōu yóu* 'a trip to Europe', *shírì tán* 'Decameron (10 days' talk)', *bǎirì ké* 'pertussis (100 days of coughing)', *běnzì kǎo* 'textual research on the original character', *shuāngrì xiū* '2 days' off'. Taking the feature "can be directly modified by nouns" as a criterion results from the belief that nouns can be used as attributes but not as adverbials. However, there are many cases of nouns being used as adverbials. The recently published *A Descriptive Grammar of Modern Chinese* (Zhang 2010: 4) even argues that "nouns can directly modify verbs" is a feature of Chinese grammar that is different from English grammar. The following pairs of examples show that disyllabic nouns and verbs often alternate when used as adverbials:

xiàoliǎn xiāngyíng 'welcome somebody with a smiling face'	*wēixiào xiāngyíng* 'offer a welcoming smile'
xiànchǎng cǎifǎng 'live interview'	*zàichǎng cǎifǎng* 'interview on the spot'
gōngfèi dúbó 'publicly funded doctoral studies'	*fùfèi dúbó* 'pay tuition to pursue one's PhD'
dījià chūshòu 'sell at a low price'	*jiǎnjià chūshòu* 'lower price to sell'
zhǎngshēng huānyíng 'welcome with applause'	*gǔzhǎng huānyíng* 'applause to welcome'
gāoxīn yánpìn 'extend the employment period with a high salary'	*tíxīn yánpìn* 'pay a higher salary to extend the employment period'

62 *The problems*

wǎngluò liánxì
'contact via the Internet'

diǎnqiú huòshèng
'win via penalty kicks'

tuántǐ cǎigòu
'group purchasing'

shíwù zhòngdú
'food poisoning'

shàngwǎng liánxì
'go online to contact'

fáqiú huòshèng
'kick a penalty kick to win'

zǔtuán cǎigòu
'form a group to purchase something'

guòshí zhòngdú
'be poisoned from eating too much'

Most of the disyllabic verbs that directly modify nouns are not nouny verbs, as in *chūfā dìdiǎn* 'place of departure', *dǎjià yuányīn* 'reason for the fight', *tiàowǔ zīshì* 'dance postures', *jiéhūn fèiyòng* 'cost of marriage', *táopǎo lùxiàn* 'an escape route', *chūxí dàibiǎo* 'delegates in attendance', *tǎoyàn chéngdù* 'level of annoyance', *fàngjià rìqī* 'date of vacation', *xiàtái gànbù* 'a fallen cadre', *shuōhuà kǒuqì* 'tone of voice', *jīngguò dìdiǎn* 'place to pass', *xǐhuān duìxiàng* 'favorite people', *shuìmián fāngshì* 'sleeping style', *shànggǎng tiáolì* 'onboarding requirements', *tiàodòng fànwéi* 'jump range'. Most of the nouns directly modified by typical verbs are abstract nouns, and most of the nouns directly modified by nouny verbs listed by Zhu are also abstract nouns. Consider the following two columns for comparisons:

Phrases with disyllabic verbs that can be preceded by dummy verbs such as *jinxing, jiāyǐ, yǔyǐ, jǐyǔ*	Phrases with disyllabic verbs that cannot be preceded by dummy verbs such as *jinxing, jiāyǐ, yǔyǐ, jǐyǔ*
jiàoyù fāngzhēn 'education policies' (*jìnxíng jiàoyù*)	*yùrén fāngzhēn* 'policies of educating people' (*jìnxíng yùrén)
dòuzhēng zhéxué 'philosophy of struggle' (*jìnxíng dòuzhēng*)	*táopǎo zhéxué* 'philosophy of escape' (*jìnxíng táopǎo)
zhāopìn tiáolì 'recruitment requirements' (*jìnxíng zhāopìn*)	*zhāorǎn tiáolì* 'requirements for recruiting employees' (*jìnxíng zhāorén)
biǎodá kǒuqì 'tone of expressions' (*jìnxíng biǎoshù*)	*shuōhuà kǒuqì* 'tone of speaking' (*jìnxíng shuōhuà)
xiěshēng gōngjù 'sketching tools' (*jìnxíng xiěshēng*)	*huàhuà gōngjù* 'drawing tools' (*jìnxíng huàhuà)
chōngxǐ fāngshì 'way of flushing' (*jiāyǐ chōngxǐ*)	*xǐzǎo fāngshì* 'way of bathing' (*jiāyǐ xǐzǎo)
xiūxì shíjiān 'rest time' (*yǔyǐ xiūxī*)	*shuìmián shíjiān* 'sleep time' (*yǔyǐ shuìmián)
pángtīng míngdān 'list of spectators' (*jǐyǔ pángtīng*)	*chūxí míngdān* 'list of attendance' (*jǐyǔ chūxí)

The problems 63

Disyllabic verbs, including nouny verbs, can also take an object when modifying a noun, as in:

dàodá shíjiān 'time of arrival' | *dàodá Běijīng shíjiān* 'time of arrival in Beijing'

shìyìng nénglì 'ability to adapt' | *shìyìng huánjìng nénglì* 'ability to adapt to the environment'

jiějué bànfǎ 'solution' | *jiějué wèntí bànfǎ* 'solution to the problem'

fùxí qíngkuàng 'review' | *fùxí gōngkè qíngkuàng* 'review of lessons'

qiángjiān zùi 'crime of rape' | *qiángjiān nánrén zùi 'crime of raping a man'*

zìzhì jī 'homemade machine' | *zìzhì suānnǎi jī* 'homemade yogurt machine'

qīnfàn àn 'infringement cases' | *qīnfàn yǐnsī àn* 'cases of infringement of privacy'

guǎimài zùi 'crime of abduction and trafficking' | *guǎimài értóng zùi* 'crime of child abduction and trafficking'

Generally speaking, monosyllabic verbs can directly modify nouns only if they are followed by an object, such as *kuà shìjì réncái* 'trans-century talent', *yìn jiǎchāo jīqì* 'counterfeit money printing machine', *liúměi bóshì* 'a person who earns a PhD degree in the United States', *dǎguǎi mínjǐng* 'anti-trafficking police'. However, the ability of taking an object is an important criterion for Zhu to distinguish verbs from nouns. Some nouny verbs can be modified by quantifiers when they function as the objects of dummy verbs. This hardly shows that they have nominal characteristics, because verbs can also be modified by quantifiers (see the previous section). Again, there are exceptions to the adverbial modification of nouny verbs when they function as the objects of dummy verbs, as in *jìnxíng xiānghù píngjià* 'evaluate each other', *jìnxíng dàsì chūhuò* 'ship aggressively', *jìnxíng sìyì sōubǔ* 'raid indiscriminately', *yǔyǐ jíshí bàodào* 'report in real time', *jiāyǐ shāoxǔ gǎibiàn* 'change a little'.[3]

In short, if all the criteria are satisfied, the scope of the nouny verbs would be very narrow, whereas if only one criterion is satisfied, the scope of the nouny verbs would be very broad. The collocational differences between various dummy verbs (for example, *fàngxíng* 'let go' can be preceded by *jǐyǔ* and not by *jìnxíng*; *zhīchí* 'support' can be preceded by *jiāyǐ* and not by *zuò*) and the difficulty of distinguishing between homophone dummy verbs *zuò* make the criteria for distinguishing nouny verbs even more difficult to apply, and their scope even more difficult to delimit.[4] The scope of dummy verbs varies according to the number, strictness, and priority of different criteria, so it is no wonder that some people advocate expanding the scope while others suggest narrowing it. Nowadays some people criticize that the word class labels of the same nouny verb are often inconsistent in language engineering labels. This is because the scope of nouny verbs is difficult to delimit, and the reason behind this is that, as explained in section 3 of the previous chapter, verbs that are also nouny are indistinguishable in terms of their nouniness.

64   *The problems*

2.2.2   *The inconsistency of the system*

The main problem with nouny verbs is not that the scope is difficult to delimit but that the theory and the grammatical system are inconsistent. Otto Jespersen likens the V-ing form of English verbs to a hybrid of verbs and nouns, which has a mixture of verbal and nominal characteristics. Consider the following pair of sentences:

Brown deftly painting his daughter is a delight to watch.
Brown's deft painting of his daughter is a delight to watch.
Brown deftly painting his daughter is a delight to watch.
Brown's deft painting of his daughter is a delight to watch.

The V-ing form *painting* in the first sentence is modified by the adverb *deftly* and followed by the object *his daughter* and thus behaves like a verb. However, in the second sentence it exhibits nominal characteristics as it is qualified by the 3 attributes *Brown's*, *deft*, and *of his daughter*. Zhu argues that Chinese nouny verbs 'are a similar phenomenon', and he considers such structures as *méiyǒu yánjīu* and *diàochá hěn zhòngyào* to be ambiguous:

méiyǒu yánjīu 'no research$_N$'	*méiyǒu lìshǐ yánjiū* 'no historical research'; *méiyǒu yīxiē yánjiū* 'no adequate research'
méiyǒu yánjīu 'no research$_V$'	*méiyǒu mǎshàng yánjiū* 'not to research immediately'; *méiyǒu yánjiū wénxué* 'not to research literature'
diàochá hěn zhòngyào 'survey$_N$ is important'	*Chèdǐ de fāngyán diàochá hěn zhòngyào* 'A thorough survey of dialects is important'.
diàochá hěn zhòngyào 'survey$_V$ is important'	*Chèdǐ de diàochá fāngyán hěn zhòngyào* 'It is important to survey dialects thoroughly'.

What makes the problem even more serious is that this analysis renders constructions such as *qù hěn zhòngyào* 'visit is very important' and *méi fāxiàn tiào* 'jump has not been found' also ambiguous:

qù hěn zhòngyào 'visit$_N$ is very important'	(*Liú Xuándé de dìsān cì qù hěn zhòngyào* 'Liu Xuande's third visit is very important'.)
qù hěn zhòngyào 'visit$_V$ is very important'	(*jiēèrliánsān dì qù máolú hěn zhòngyào* 'It is important for Liu Xuande to visit the thatched cottage one after another'.)
méi fā xiàn qù 'visit $_n$ has not been found'	'Liu Xuande's third visit has not been found'.
méi fā xiàn qù 'visit $_v$ has not been found'	'It has not been found that Liu Xuande visited the thatched cottage one after another'.

tiào hěn zhòng yào 'jump $_n$ is very serious'

'Foxconn's eleventh jump is very serious'.

tiào hěn zhòng yào 'jump $_v$ is very serious'

'It is very serious to continuously jump from a tall building'.

méi fāxiàn tiào 'no jump$_N$ has not been found'

(*méi fāxiàn Fùshìkāng de dìshíyī tiào* 'Foxconn's eleventh jump has not been found'.)

méi fāxiàn tiào 'no jump$_V$ has not been found'

(*méi fāxiàn liánxùbúduàn dì tiào gāolóu* 'Jumping from a tall building has not been repeatedly found'.)

However, monosyllabic verbs such as *qù* and *tiào* are only verbs rather than nouns in the framework that distinguishes nouns from verbs. Thus, they do not belong to nouny verbs. Meanwhile, Zhu strongly opposes that they have been nominalized, because he thought it was against the principle of simplicity.

This problem can be summarized as follows: The related tenets of Zhu's grammatical system are two assertions, A and B. Assertion A is that when verbs function as subjects and objects, they are still verbs without undergoing nominalization, while assertion B is that nouny verbs have a mixture of nominal and verbal characteristics and are functionally similar to the V-ing form of English verbs. The source of the problem is that we could not affirm A if we affirm B, and we could not affirm B if we affirm A, and A and B would contradict each other if we affirmed both of them. Many people are more or less aware of this internal contradiction. In order to resolve this contradiction, there are two coping strategies; one is to adhere to B and amend A, the other is to adhere to A and amend B. Many people take the first strategy by retreating from the position of A and thinking that verbs are nominalized to some extent or in some way when they are used as subjects and objects. It has been shown in Chapter 1 that to adopt this strategy is to take a regressive step. It not only fails to distinguish between primary and secondary problems but also focuses on the minor and peripheral parts of them. As a result, it becomes a thankless job and a huge price to pay because the strategy will lead us not only to abandon the principle of simplicity in constructing a grammatical system but also to amend the head feature extension of grammatical structures (see the next section), which is quite thankless and costly. The delay in solving the old problem of *zhè běn shū de chūbǎn* 'the publication of this book' is not due to the irrelevance of Occam's razor or the restrictions of head feature extension but to the mispositioning of nouny verbs and the misunderstanding that only some verbs in Chinese have the nominal characteristics. This is to address the secondary problem of the strength of nouniness within verbs when the general pattern of the noun-verb relationship in Chinese has not been properly identified. To use an analogy, discussing the ownership of Kinmen or the Penghu Islands without understanding the relationship between Taiwan and China is a way of failing to distinguish between priorities and of putting the cart before the horse.

66 The problems

Instead, we adopt the second strategy to take a step further from assertion A and believe that the words in Chinese that have a mixture of nominal and verbal characteristics and are similar to the V-ing forms in English are not nouny verbs but the whole class of verbs, because Chinese in fact embodies the verbs-as-nouns framework. To establish the category of nouny verbs is nothing more than to pick within the class of verbs a part of words that are highly nouny and slightly verbal. Establishing the verbs-as-nouns framework is not equivalent to denying that verbs differ in terms of their nouniness. Instead it leads us to highlight this difference from the perspective of form (see Chapter 4 in Volume II for details).

2.3 Head feature convention and coordination condition

2.3.1 Violation of head feature convention

Following the principle of simplicity, it cannot be said that the word *chūbǎn* 'publish' in the phrase *zhè běn shū de chūbǎn* 'the publication of this book' has changed from a verb to a noun. However, asserting that it is still a verb would violate head feature extension or head feature convention of a grammatical structure. It states that if a head is extended, the resulting grammatical structure shares the same head features. *Chūbǎn* is a verb, but the extended phrase *zhè běn shū de chūbǎn* with *chūbǎn* being its head is nominal. This is the problem that *zhè běn shū de chūbǎn* violates the theory of endocentric constructions (Shi 1981).

Treating *chūbǎn* as a nouny verb does not solve the problem, because *chūbǎn* in *zhè běn shū de bù chūbǎn* 'the non-publication of this book' and *qù* in *tā de qù* 'his going' must be verbal in the framework that distinguishes nouns from verbs. Some people say that this is head-feature convention at work and that Bloomfield's view of endocentric constructions is problematic (Si 2006; Chen 2009). However, Huang Hebin (2014) points out that their doubts are actually a misreading of Bloomfield's view of endocentric constructions. Some people also say that the theory of endocentric constructions is not fully applicable to Chinese and "can't be copied blindly" (Fang 1997: 261). Zhu Dexi (1985b) and others scholars (e.g. Lu 1985; Jin 1987; Xiang 1991) try to revise the definition of endocentric construction to make it applicable to Chinese, but these revisions are still unsatisfactory (see Shi 1988; Wu 2006). And the attempt to amend it shows that the violation of head-feature convention is not a trivial matter, because it is closely related to hierarchical analysis and X-bar theory in generative grammar, and they are based on each other.

Now someone asks, "What if you follow the head-feature convention, and what if you violate it?" The implication is that it makes little difference whether you violate the convention or not. In our opinion, the consequences of this violation are serious: it would undermine the recursion of language. In addition to being a feature that distinguishes human language from animal communication systems, recursion also signifies the creative capacity of human language. One of the most important insights of the generative grammar theory is that human language "makes infinite use of finite means" (Chomsky 1965: 8, quoting von Humboldt 1836: 91). According to *Encyclopedia of Language and Linguistics* (Brown 2006:

The problems 67

414), a simple set of recursive rules can be represented as follows (the arrow →
stands for 'can consist of'):

i. X → Y
ii. X → X Z

The rules state that an X can consist of a Y or an X followed by a Z. What makes
these rules recursive is that X is the output of Rule b and also the input to Rule a
and Rule b. These two rules characterize any of the following sequences:

i. Y
ii. Y Z
iii. Y Z Z
iv. Y Z Z Z

In fact, they account for any sequence that contains a Y followed by any number of
Zs, that is, an infinite set of sequences. Rule b is the head-feature convention. The
essence of the head-feature convention is that a thing is defined by itself, or more
precisely, by itself as a constituent. The combination of *bàba de shū* 'dad's book'
is defined by *shū* 'book' used as a constituent. As *shū* is a noun, *bàba de shū* is
nominal, and the further expanded *bàba de bàba de shū* 'dad's dad's book' (which
can be expanded recursively) is also nominal. When a language abandons its head
feature convention, it loses its recursiveness and also ceases to be creative.

Lyons (1968: 331) also points out,

> [T]here is an essential, language-independent, relationship between N and
> NP and between V and VP. . . . NP and VP are not merely mnemonically-
> convenient symbols, but stand for sentence-constituents which are neces-
> sarily nominal and verbal, respectively, because they have N and V as an
> obligatory major constituent.

He continues to argue that it would not only be perverse, but it should be theoretically impossible for any linguist to propose such rules as 'NP→V + VP, NP→V,
VP→T (article) + N'. There are languages around the world that are able to express
complex meanings in other ways than recursion (see Evans & Levinson 2009),[5]
but they cannot violate the head feature convention or destroy the recursiveness.
As a computational linguist, Bai Shuo (2014) argues that, aside from Chomsky's
personal cult, Chinese should also be a language that X-bar theory is compatible
with and that the performance of a Context-Free Grammar parser can be well guar-
anteed if it is compatible with X-bar. Compatibility is definitely great news for
computational linguistics.

In the previous discussion, we assume that *chūbǎn* is the head of *zhè běn shū de
chūbǎn*, so is there any problem with the confirmation of the head? A generative
grammar solution (Cheng 1999; Si 2002, 2004; Xiong 2005) analyzes *zhè běn shū
de chūbǎn* as a determiner phrase (DP), *de* being the head D of the phrase. Due

to its [+ N] feature, D determines the nominal nature of the whole DP. This DP analysis differs from the traditional one in that it focuses mainly on generalization, namely identifying structural parallelisms between determiner phrases (DPs) and inflectional phrases (IPs; Abney 1987).

Consider the following Chinese examples with structural parallelisms:

i. *Shāngwù zhè běn shū de chūbǎn Shāngwù de chūbǎn (zhè běn shū) zhè běn shū (yóu Shāngwù) de chūbǎn*
ii. *Shāngwù chūbǎn le zhè běn shū Shāngwù chūbǎn le (zhè běn shū) zhè běn shū (yóu Shāngwù) chūbǎn le*

IP is the extension of functional category I (tense) to verb phrase VP, and DP is the extension of functional category D (determiner) to noun phrase NP. If the Spec position is vacant, *zhè běn shū* can shift to it, which results in *zhè běn shū de chūbǎn* and *zhè běn shū chūbǎn le*.

As shown from the tree diagram in Figure 2.2, it is a good idea to generalize the two structures, but it is extremely against the language intuition of native speakers of Chinese to treat both *de chūbǎn* and *chūbǎn le* as immediate constituents. From any point of view, prosody, semantics, or structure, *de* together with its preceding component counts as an immediate constituent. The analysis of *de chūbǎn* relies on examples that are extremely special, and obviously special cases cannot prove structural parallelisms (see Chapter 6, Section 2.1). Based on their linguistic intuitions for Chinese, even other scholars who work in generative grammar (e.g. Li 2008; Shi 2008; Tang 2006) do not accept it. Various problems with this analysis have been thoroughly reviewed by Zhou Guoguang (2005, 2006), Wu Chang'an (2006), and Pan Haihua and Lu Shuo (2013). As Zhou Ren (2012) points out, the major difficulty with *de* being the head is that the remainder should

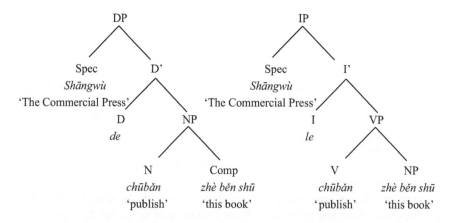

Figure 2.2 DP analysis of *Shāngwù zhè běn shū de chūbǎn* and IP analysis of *Shāngwù chūbǎn le zhè běn shū*

The problems 69

be syntactically and semantically different from the original whole structure once the head is removed, but the two most common types of noun phrases, as in *mùtou de fángzi* 'wooden house' and *hóng de huā* 'red flower', do not follow this pattern.

In our opinion, this analysis disregards the principle of simplicity. The previous parallel analysis assumes that the node of *chūbǎn* in DP is a noun, otherwise there is no parallelism between DP and IP. In the absence of such parallelism, there is no basis for a DP analysis of *zhè běn shū de chūbǎn*. Realizing this, Xiong Zhongru (2005) proposes a new functional category n with the feature [+ N] to assign the category feature of [+ N] to *chūbǎn*. First, n expands the verb phrase *chūbǎn zhè běn shū* into the noun phrase nP, and then D expands nP into DP. The purpose of setting up the functional category n is to explain how *chūbǎn* is nominalized,[6] not to mention that it is specifically designed for the previous DP analysis. The problem here is that proposing to nominalize *chūbǎn* in Chinese is superfluous and violates the principle of simplicity.

A slightly different analysis holds that *zhè běn shū de chūbǎn* is formed with the insertion of *de* in the subject-predicate structure *zhè běn shū chūbǎn* 'this book is published'. According to this analysis, some affirm that *de* is the head with the feature [+ N] (Lu 2003), and others assert it to be a self-referential nominalization marker (Yuan 2010b). Such analysis stays away from the nominalization of *chūbǎn*, but it needs to divide a unified *de* into two, one as in *zhè běn shū de fēngmiàn* 'the cover of this book' (the *de₃* defined by Zhu Dexi) and the other as in *zhè běn shū de chūbǎn* 'the publication of this book'. Can Occam's razor be used to solve these theoretical problems without adding new entities? There are also more new and challenging problems that result from this approach.

First, *zhè běn shū chūbǎn* without the insertion of *de* can also be used as the subject or object. The same subject-predicate phrases with or without *de* can be frequently found in a paragraph:

Měiguó de jièrù shì kěndìng de. Wúfēi shì yìng jièrù háishì ruǎn jièrù, yǐjí jièrù lìdù dàxiǎo de wèntí. . . . . . . Suǒyǐ měiguó jièrù shì yǒu tiáojiàn de, zhèxiē tiáojiàn yě shì wǒmén kěyǐ lìyòng de, yào ràng měiguó gǎnjué dào tā de jièrù jiāng fùchū tā suǒ bùnéng chéngshòu de dàijià, zhèyàng tā jiù huì xuǎnzé bú jièrù huò shǎo jièrù. (quoted from Wan 2010)

'US involvement is certain. It is nothing more than hard intervention or soft intervention, as well as the level of the intervention. . . . So there are conditions for the US to intervene, and they are also available to us to make the US feel that its intervention will pay a price that it cannot bear, so that it will choose not to intervene or to intervene less'.

If *de* is identified as the head of *Měiguó de jièrù* 'the involvement of USA', then what is the head of *Měiguó jièrù* 'the involvement of USA'? Does separating the heads of the two phrases help us better understand the phrases or hinder us from doing so? If *Měiguó jièrù* contains an implied head *de*, the phrases such as *túshū chūbǎn* 'publication of books', *wèntí yánjiū* 'study of problems', and *zhéxué sīkǎo* 'philosophical thinking' can all be said to imply a *de*. What sets it apart from the

70   *The problems*

assertion that a verb implies a nominalization marker when it appears in the subject or object position?

Second, Shi Dingxu (2008) points out that the structure with an insertion of *de* followed by a verb is not limited to the subject-predicate structure, and there are many other structures such as:

Miànxiàng   *jīcéng*   *de*   *fúpínbāngkùn*   *yīnggāi*   *chíxù*   *xiàqù.*
towards   grassroots   MM   poverty   should   continue   down
                                  alleviation and
                                  assistance

'*The grassroots-oriented poverty alleviation and assistance* should continue'.

Dàjiā   *duìyú*   *míngwùhuà*   *lǐlùn*   *de*   *pīpíng*   *dōu* *hěn* *zhōngkěn.*
everyone   towards   nominalization theory   MM   criticism   all very pertinent

'*Everyone's criticism of the nominalization theory* is very pertinent.'

Bàozhǐ   *shàng* *shuō* *de*   *zuò* *hángtiānfēijī* *lǚxíng* *mùqián* *hái* *wúfǎ*   *shíxiàn.*
newspaper on   report MM   sit space shuttle travel now   yet unable realize

'*The space shuttle travel that is reported in the newspaper* cannot be realized yet now.'

It is difficult or impossible to restore these underlined structures to subject-predicate structures by removing *de*. Therefore, it is infeasible to account for all possible cases through the insertion of *de* into the subject-predicate structure.[7]

Third, the subject-predicate structure of *zhè běn shū chūbǎn le* 'this book has been published' cannot take the insertion of *de* as *zhè běn shū de chūbǎn le*. If *zhè běn shū chūbǎn* is regarded as a phrase and *zhè běn shū chūbǎn le* as a sentence, then this contradicts the important point that Chinese sentences and phrases follow a single set of construction principles.

Fourth, is the insertion of *de* creates a semantic difference as in:

a. *Nǐ*   *méiyǒu*   *tā*   *de*   *qínfèn.*
    you   don't have   him   MM   diligence
    'You don't have his diligence.'

b. *Nǐ*   *méiyǒu*   *tā*   *qínfèn.*
    you   don't have   him   diligent
    'You are not as diligent as him.'

Sentence *a* can mean that you are not diligent, while sentence *b* only means you are not as diligent as he is. This shows that *tā de qínfèn* 'his diligence' is not simply the insertion of *de* between the subject *tā* and the predicate *qínfèn*. In short, by pressing down the gourd and floating the scoop, this problem seems to have been solved, but the other end becomes problematic.

In response to many criticisms about the analysis treating *de* as the head, those who insist on it claim that such criticisms are unfounded since the head of generative grammar is the head of the deep structure and the head of structural grammar is the head of the surface structure (Si 2006). Nevertheless, the comment 'this head is not that head' also applies to them. Following the logic of the debate, we acknowledge that it is not impossible to analyze *de* as the head and intend to remind that such analysis poses more problems than it solves and that to prove that there is no violation of the head feature convention entails proving that *chūbăn* is not the head in the structuralist analysis. As Li Yafei (2015) argues in the framework of generative grammar, although the word order does not necessarily reflect the structural arrangement at the deep level, the word order exhibits its essential characteristics. To judge the pros and cons of the two analyses, it remains crucial to take the facts of the Chinese language into account rather than the dominant school of linguistics and to utilize consistency and simplicity as evaluative criteria to overcome the differences between the various schools of linguistics.

2.3.2 *Dissatisfaction with the coordination condition*

The coordination condition of a grammatical structure states that the two conjoined components should belong to the same word class or category except for ad hoc uses. Consider the examples in English: (Radford 1988: 76)

John wrote [to Mary] and [to Fred]. (= PP and PP)
John wrote [a letter] and [a postcard]. (= NP and NP)
*John wrote [a letter] and [to Fred]. (= NP and PP)
*John wrote [to Fred] and [a letter]. (= PP and NP)

Generative grammarians use coordination conditions to test whether two components belong to the same syntactic category, which is known as the coordination test. This test proves, for example, that determiners and adjectives do not belong to the same category because they cannot be conjoined:

*[$_D$my] and [$_A$lazy] son
*[$_A$silly] and [$_D$these] ideasg

It can also be used to show that complements and adjuncts are two distinct categories, the former being the sister node of N and the latter being the sister node of the N-bar:

a student [of Physics] and [of Chemistry] (complement and complement)
a student [with long hair] and [with short arms] (adjunct and adjunct)
*a student [of Physics] and [with long hair] (complement and adjunct)
*a student [with long hair] and [of Physics] (adjunct and complement)

72 The problems

In Chinese, it obviously dissatisfies the coordination condition of grammatical structures to treat *chūbǎn* in the subject or object position as a verb. It is very common for coordinate structures such as *túshū hé chūbǎn* 'books and publication' or *zhè běn shū hé tāde chūbǎn* 'this book and its publication' to function as the subject or object. When a noun and a verb do not belong to the same category, how can they form a coordinate structure? It is perverse and theoretically untenable to propose that there is such a coordinate structure as "NP and VP". Could it be that there is a problem with the coordination condition or with the definitions of nouns and verbs in Chinese?

Yuan Yulin (2010a) argues that *túshū hé chūbǎn* does not dissatisfy the coordination condition, because *chūbǎn* is what Zhu calls the "nouny verb". It exhibits the verbal characteristics in *chūbǎn zhèxiē túshū* 'to publish these books' and the nominal characteristics in *túshū hé chūbǎn* 'books and publication'. To prove this, he provides the following examples:

túshū hé chūbǎn 'books and publishing'	**shū he chū* ***'books and publish'
zìkǎo shūjí hé diànzǐ chūbǎn 'self-study books and e-publishing'	**zìkǎo shūjí hé mǎshàng chūbǎn* ***'self-study books and immediately publish'
jíbìng hé zhìliáo 'diseases and treatment'	**bìng hé zhì* ***'diseases and to treat'
chángweì jíbìng hé shíwù zhìliáo 'gastrointestinal diseases and food treatment'	**chángweì jíbìng hé jíshí zhìliáo* ***'gastrointestinal diseases and promptly treat'
shāngpǐn hé xiāoshòu 'goods and sales'	**huò hé maì* ***'goods and sell'
bǎojiàn shāngpǐn hé jìjié xiāoshòu 'health commodities and seasonal sales'	**bǎojiàn shāngpǐn hé jìjiàng xiāoshòu* ***'health commodities and forthcoming sell'

According to him, the examples in the right column are not acceptable, because the monosyllabic *chū*, *zhì*, and *maì* are not nouny verbs, and *chūbǎn*, *zhìliáo*, and *xiāoshòu* modified by adverbs only exhibit verbal characteristics. However, a quick search on the Internet reveals a large number of coordinate structures, in which what can be conjoined with nouns is by no means limited to nouny verbs, and even if they are nouny verbs, they can be modified by adverbs (including bù 'not'):

> *zuì yǔ fá* 'crime and punish', *leì yǔ xiào* 'tears and laugh', *xìng yǔ sǐ* 'sex and die', *xìng yǔ shuì* 'sex and sleep', *mèng yǔ xiǎng* 'dreams and think', *rén yǔ dòu* 'people and fight', *qíng yǔ biàn* 'love and change', *shíjiān yǔ máng* 'time and busy', *yìshù yǔ pěng* 'art and support', *chī yǔ yíngyǎng* 'eat and nutrition', *Shànghǎirén yǔ chī* 'Shanghai people and eat', *chángshòu yǔ chīyán* 'longevity and eat salt', *luǒtǐ yǔ chūshū* 'nudity and publish', *shènbìng yǔ chūzhěnzi* 'kidney disease and break out in a rash', *záwén yǔ màrén*

The problems 73

'essays and scold', *nǚrén yǔ huāqián* 'women and spend money', *mǎifáng yǔ fēngshuǐ* 'buy a house and fengshui', *mángwén yǔ yùrén* 'braille and educate people', *qióngrén hé mǎifáng* 'the poor and buy a house', *shuìmián yǔ zuòmèng* 'sleep and dream', *nián yǔ áonián* 'year and survive a year', *fójiào yǔ jiāofó* 'Buddhism and teach Buddhism', *àiqíng yǔ áozhōu* 'love and make porridge', *dúshūrén hé dúshū* 'intellectuals and read', *bǐjià hé biǎnzhí* 'compare prices and depreciation', *chēhuò hé dǔlù* 'car accidents and block a road', *guàhào gōngsī yǔ kànbìng* 'registered companies and see a doctor', *chūntiān hé fángbìng* 'spring and prevent diseases', *gǔ yǔ zuòrén* 'stocks and behave as a human being', *lājī guǎnggào yǔ áimà* 'spam ads and get scolded', *yǎnqián déshī yǔ shòuqióng* 'immediate gains and losses and suffer poverty', *yīyèqíng yǔ zuò gōngchéng* 'one-night stands and do a project', *zǎoqī jiàoyù yǔ kàndiànshì* 'early education and watch TV', *Sūnzǐ Bīngfǎ yǔ qiǎng fǎntán* 'Sun Tzu's Art of War and grab the bounce', *qǔcáizhīdào yǔ qiǎng yínháng* 'the way to get money and rob a bank', *mèngjìng hé xīntiào* 'dreams and heartbeats', *mèng yǔ kūqì* 'dreams and cry', *zuì yǔ jùpà* 'sins and fear', *shōugòu jí qítā* 'acquire and others', *gǔjià yǔ zhǎngdiē* 'stock prices and rise and fall', *tuìchū hé tuìchū zhuàngtai* 'exit and exit status', *yújiā hé mànpǎo* 'yoga and jog', *yāndǒu yǔ dàozǒu* 'pipes and walk backward', *rìjì yǔ tōukuī* 'diary and peep', *jìyìfǎ hé kuàidú* 'mnemonics and skim', *jīngshén de dǐsè yǔ jiànbiàn* 'spiritual background and gradually change', *shēngsǐ yǔ pěngshā* 'life and death and praise and kill', *zhīqíngquán yǔ bùzhīqíng* 'right to know and don't know', *zérèn yǔ búzuòwéi* 'responsibility and take no actions', *qióngrén de zūnyán yǔ bù xiūrǔ* 'dignity of the poor and be not humiliated', *fángchǎnshāng hé sǐ kángjià* 'real estate agents and firmly raise the prices', *chéngxìn hé bù zhēteng* 'honesty and don't flip-flop', *tóngshòushǒu yǔ xiā zhēteng* 'the bronze animal head and flip-flop blindly', *sùshí wénhuà hé xìjiáomànyàn* 'fast food culture and chew slowly', *wǔqī gànxiào hé shàngshānxiàxiāng* 'May 7 cadre school and go and work in the mountains and the countryside', *lìrùn hé chíxù fāzhǎn* 'profit and develop sustainably', *zǎoqī zhěnduàn yǔ jíshí zhìliáo* 'early diagnosis and treat timely', *cāozuò cèlüè yǔ jíshí jiěpán* 'operation strategies and analyze the stocks market promptly', *àiguózhīxīn hé nǔlì gōngzuò* 'patriotism and work hard', *shèqū wèishēng fúwù yǔ kànbìng guì* 'community health services and medical treatment is expensive', *nǚrén áimà yǔ làng nǚrén* 'women get scolded and promiscuous women'

Likewise, the coordination of adjectives with nouns is not limited to nouny adjectives which can be identified by yǒu 'have/there be', and they can also be modified by the adverb bù 'not':

cái yǔ kuáng 'talent and arrogant', *rén yǔ tān* 'man and greedy', *lì yǔ měi* 'strength and beautiful', *wǒ yǔ shuài* 'me and handsome', *kù yǔ kù* 'trousers and cool', *hé yǔ hé* 'nuclear war and peaceful', *nèihuánjìng hé wěn* 'inner environment and stable', *hūnyīn yǔ gūdú* 'marriage and lonely', *àomàn yǔ*

74 *The problems*

piānjiàn 'proud and prejudice', *yǔjì hé lǎnsǎn* 'rainy seasons and lazy', *xiǎowù hé cōngmíng* 'small things and smart', *guānggǎn yǔ piāoyì* 'sense of light and graceful', *tiāncaí yǔ qínfèn* 'genius and diligent', *liúmáng hé bú zhàngyì* 'hooliganism and unrighteous', *cǎomín hé bù shíxiàng* 'grassroots people and insensible', *nǔrén de dàdù hé bùānquángǎn* 'women's generous and sense of insecurity'

It is not difficult for these coordinate structures to be the subject and object of a sentence:

Jí   lì   yǔ   meǐ   yú   yì   shēn.
combine strength and beautiful to   one   body
'Strength and beauty are combined into one.'

Shíjiān hé   máng búshì tuīcí   de   lǐyóu.
time   and   busy not   refusal MM   reason
'Time and being busy are not reasons for refusal.'

Miáoxiě dǐcéng   baìxìng de   leì yǔ   xiào.
portrait underclass people   MM   tear and   laugh
'The tears and laughter of the underclass are portraited.'

Wǒ   tǎoyàn tā   de   àomàn   yǔ   piānjiàn.
I   hate   him   MM   proud   and   prejudice
'I hate his pride and prejudice.'

Bìngfeī weìle lìyì   hé   chūmíng.
not   for   profit and   famous
'It is not for profit and fame.'

Chēhuò   hé   dǔlù   hùweí   yīnguǒ.
car accident and   road blockage be mutually   cause and effect
'Car accidents and road blockages are mutual causes and effects.'

Mèngjiàn   shé   hé   beìzhuā.
dream   snake and   be caught
'(I) dreamed of a snake and being caught.'

Wǒ   aì   nǐ   de   tiáojiàn   yǔ   bùzhēng.
I   love you   MM   condition and   don't contend
'I love your financial stability and non-contending attitude.'

Some are strongly written, some are heavily colloquial, most of them are disyllabic, and monosyllabic and polysyllabic words are also allowed. Chinese do not consider these expressions to be special, but when they are translated into English, all the verbs therein would have to be converted into nouns. The problems of analysis in the previous section persists in coordinate structures. For example,

The problems 75

some people consider *chūbǎn* 'publication' in *zhè běn shū hé tā de chūbǎn* 'this book and its publication' to be a verb (*de* is inserted between the subject *tā* and the predicate *chūbǎn*), *chūbǎn* in *túshū hé chūbǎn* 'books and publication' to be a nouny verb, and the two *bǎohù* 'protection' in *bǎnquán bǎohù yǔ tèbié bǎohù* 'copyright protection and special protection' to be a noun and a verb, respectively. These considerations obviously exaggerate the difference between the two components of the coordination and complicate a problem that is originally simple. The dissatisfaction with coordination condition and the violation of the head feature convention are two symptoms of the same disease, and the results are naturally not ideal to treat the headache with the head and the foot pain with the foot. Many of the "N *hé* V" examples listed earlier can be converted to "N *de* V" structures:

rén de tān 'the greed of man', *lì de měi* 'the beauty of force', *rén de dòu (bǐ gǒu de dòu lìhai)* 'the fights of man (are fiercer than the fights of dogs)', *wǒ de gūdú* 'my loneliness', *Shànghǎirén de chī* 'the eating of Shanghainese', *qíng de biàn yǔ búbiàn* 'the changing and unchanging of love', *nǚrén de huāqián* 'the spending of women', *qióngrén de mǎifáng* 'the purchase of houses by the poor', *gǔjià de zhǎngdiē* 'the fall and rise of stock prices', *xiǎowù de cōngmíng* 'the cleverness over small things', *fángchǎnshāng de sǐ kángjià* 'the firm raising of prices by real estate agents', *tóngshòushǒu de xiā zhēteng* 'the blind flip-flop about the bronze animal head', *yǔjì de lǎnsǎn* 'the laziness during rainy seasons', *cǎomín de bù shíxiàng* 'the insensibility of grassroots people'

In fact, the simplest solution is to admit that the verbs in Chinese are both verbs and nouns and to adopt the verbs-as-nouns theory. If so, the violation of the head feature convention and dissatisfaction with the coordination condition no longer exist. In the words of Lu Bingfu (2014), the violation of the head feature convention becomes a "false problem". By way of analogy, the newly established Shanghai Pilot Free-Trade Zone is negatively defined. As long as industries are not on the "negative list" such as gambling and sex trade, they are allowed to enter. Similarly, neither *qù* nor *chūbǎn* is on the negative list, and they certainly can enter this position.

2.4 The indeterminate syntactic functions of word classes

Earlier works on Chinese grammar once held the view that words belong to no definite classes, and their classes can only be identified within their sentential context (Li 1924: 6), but later, this view was largely abandoned in favor of the notion that words belong to definite classes, but these classes serve no fixed syntactic functions. As Zhu Dexi (1985a: 4–5) argues, Chinese differs from Indo-European languages in that word classes do not serve fixed syntactic functions, that is, they have multiple functions. Verbs serve not only as the predicate but also as the subject and object; adjectives can also be the subject, object, predicate, and adverbial in addition to being attributive; nouns can be attributive in addition to being the subject

76 *The problems*

and object, and they can also serve as the predicate under certain circumstances; adverbs serve only as the adverbial. In fact, under certain circumstances, verbs can also be used as attributes (as in *diàochá gōngzuò* 'investigation work', *hézuò xiàngmù* 'cooperation project') and adverbials (as in *pīnmìng pǎo* 'desperately run', *qūbié duìdài* 'discriminately treat'), and nouns can also be used as adverbials (as in *jítǐ cānjiā* 'attend as a group', *zhòngdiǎn zhǎngwò* 'master with a focus'); these are not necessarily less common than nouns functioning as predicates. Taken together, no one-to-one correspondence can be found between the three major word classes of nouns, verbs, adjectives and the syntactic functions.

However, as Hu Mingyang (1995) points out, word classes are identified to facilitate syntactic analysis, and they should be linked more closely to syntactic constituents. According to some, word class properties cannot capture the complete distribution of words, and in order for word class properties to fully reflect the distribution of words, it would have to be one category per word (Zhan 2013). Certainly, we agree with this statement, and we object to constant subcategorization. Nevertheless, this statement is not fully true, as word class properties should also reflect the main distribution of words. Then what is the main distribution of words to reflect when explaining grammar? The most important thing is how a word functions as the subject, object, predicate, attribute, or adverbial in a sentence. For nouns and verbs, it is important to know how they function as the subject, object, or predicate. If the identified word classes do not help distinguish whether there is a subject-predicate, predicate-object, or attribute-head relationship between words, then the main point of identifying word classes will be lost. When linguistic typologists compare word class systems across languages, they also first compare these main distributions of words (see Croft 1991; Hengeveld 1992). The belief that words belong to no definite classes eliminates the need for identifying word classes. The identification of word classes also becomes pointless if they are believed to serve no definite syntactic functions.

Since word classes serve no fixed syntactic functions, verbs can function as subjects and objects. They are still verbs when they are used as subjects and objects. This statement means that Chinese verbs can be directly used as subjects and objects without any morphological changes. In contrast, verbs in English need to undergo morphological changes to serve as subjects and objects. We have adopted two different methods and standards for the identification and conversion of word classes in Chinese. In identifying word classes, we rely on the so-called generalized morphology, that is, the combining ability and status of words with other words and components, in view of the lack of morphological markers in Chinese. In deciding whether word-class conversion has occurred, we still insist on the narrow morphological standard, treating verbs in the subject and object positions as verbs as long as they do not take nominalization markers and ignoring the generalized morphology of the verbs altogether. This treatment at least provides a rebuttal for those who insist that words belong to no definite classes: Since word-class conversion can use the narrow morphological standard, why is the identification of word classes not allowed to do the same? If the narrow morphological standard is adopted, Chinese content words cannot be classified. (Gao 1953) This leads to

The problems 77

a paradox: in order to oppose the notion that words belong to no definite word classes, we propose that word classes serve no definite syntactic functions, but our proposal in turn leads to the word-class indeterminacy of a word.

In order to resolve this paradox, Shen Jiaxuan (1999: Chapter 10), inspired by Croft (1991), proposes a correlated markedness pattern between word classes and syntactic constituents. In this pattern, {noun, subject-object}, {adjective, attribute}, {verb, predicate} constitute three unmarked combinations, while all the other combinations such as {noun, predicate}, {verb, subject-object), {adjective, predicate} are marked combinations to different degrees. The determination of "marked" and "unmarked" depends not only on morphological markers, but also on the generalized morphology, including the distribution and frequency of words. As this pattern indicates, there are correspondences and non-correspondences between word classes and syntactic constituents. As for the correspondences, nouns are typically used as subjects and objects, verbs as predicates, and adjectives as attributes. As for the non-correspondence, nouns have the atypical functions of being the predicate or the attribute; verbs have the atypical functions of being the subject, object, or attribute; and adjectives have the atypical functions of being the predicate, subject, or object. Therefore, this pattern is neither a one-to-one correspondence nor a complete separation between word classes and syntactic constituents but something in between. In Indo-European languages, there is not exactly a pattern of complete correspondence, and in Chinese, there is not exactly a pattern of complete separation. Instead, they exhibit the same pattern of correlated markedness.

However, the problem of word classes in Chinese is still not entirely resolved. The correlated markedness pattern seems to reveal a language universal, that is, there are both correspondences and non-correspondences between word classes and syntactic constituents in all languages. But it does not explain the characteristics of the Chinese word-class system as opposed to Indo-European languages or why Chinese has a higher level of non-correspondence than Indo-European languages. More importantly, as stated in Section 2.3 of the previous chapter, word classes have both properties of continuity and discreteness, and continuity cannot be used to negate discreteness. The correlated markedness pattern does not have a definite answer to whether *chūbǎn* 'publication' in *zhè běn shū de chūbǎn* 'the publication of this book' is a verb or a noun. In terms of discreteness, the question still remains of how to link word classes and syntactic constituents. Sentence-building rules are combinations of discrete word classes. Using nouns and verbs, Chinese sentences can have:

S→NP + VP

Wǒ   bú   qù.
I   won't go
'I won't go.'

Màicài de   lái   le.
the vegetable seller   come   PSP
'The vegetable seller comes here.'

78   *The problems*

Sùliào de   bù   jiéshi.
plastic   not   strong
'Plastic things are not strong.'

S→NP + NP

Xiǎo Wáng   Shànghǎi rén.
Xiao Wang   Shanghai people
'Xiao Wang is from Shanghai.'

Jīntiān   zhōngqiūjié.
today   Mid-Autumn Festival
'Today is Mid-Autumn Festival.'

Zhè běn shū   tā de.
This book   his
'This book is his.'

S→VP + VP

Guāng   kū   méi yòng.
only   cry   useless
'Crying only is useless.'

Bú   zhuàngqiáng   bú   bàxiū.
not   hit-wall   don't   give up
'Don't give up until you hit the wall.'

Tǎnbái   cái   yǒu   chūlù.
confession   only   have   way out
'Confession is the only way out.'

S→VP + NP

Táo   chántou.
escape   coward.
'To escape is a coward'. (Escape? You coward!)

Bù   sǐ   (jīnnián)   zhěng   yībǎi suì.
not   die   (this year)   full   100 years old
'He will be 100 years old (this year) if he hasn't died.'

Kàn   shàngqù   yīgeyàng.
look   DIR   the same
'It looks the same.'

The problems   79

These exhaust all the possibilities of combining NP and VP into a full sentence. Similarly, all nine possible pairings of nouns, verbs, and adjectives can be used to form attribute-head phrases in Chinese:

A + N   *wěidà guójiā* 'great country'
xiānhóng méigui 'bright red rose'
gāoyǎ yìshù 'elegant art'
měilì gūniang 'beautiful girl'

N + N   *shíyóu guójiā* 'oil country'
xuèhàn gōngchǎng 'sweatshop'
duǎnyǔ jiégòu 'phrase structure'
rénwù xíngxiàng 'character image'

V + N   *chūzū qìchē* 'taxis'
yǎngzhí duìxiā 'farmed prawns'
kàngrì qīngnián 'the youth in the War of Resistance against Japan'
biǎoxiàn fāngshì 'mode of expression'

N + A   *shìjué píláo* 'visual fatigue'
hǎipài jīmǐn 'Shanghai-style agility'
shēnghuó biànlì 'everyday conveniences'
zhèngzhì mǐngǎn 'political sensitivity'

N + V   *qìchē chūzū* 'car rental'
fángwū bǔtiē 'housing subsidies'
jīngjì zhīyuán 'financial support'
xìjié miáoshù 'detailed description'

A + V   *yánlì pīpíng* 'severe criticism'
yěmán bānjiā 'a savage move'
píngděng jiāoshè 'equal bargaining'
kuāzhāng miáoxiě 'exaggerated description'[8]

V + A   *shěnshì píláo* 'examining fatigue'
xiāngqīn kǒngjù 'dating fear'
gǎngǎo jiāolǜ 'anxiety arising from catching up on manuscript'
miànshì jǐnzhāng 'interviewing anxiety'

A + A   *xūjiǎ jiànkāng* 'false health'
píngjūn fùyù 'average affluence'
pǔtōng féidà 'common obesity'
nándé hútu 'a muddled state that is hard to get'

V + V   *bānjiā bǔzhù* 'moving allowance'
zūshòu guǎnlǐ 'sales and rental management'
zhuìjī diàochá 'aircraft crash investigation'
dàilǐ jìzhàng 'agency bookkeeping'

The rule S→NP + VP, as Zhu Dexi (1985a: 64) argues, "is not applicable in Chinese", but there is no way to dissociate this basic rule from the current

80 *The problems*

dominant generative grammar. Then, is this rule universal? Sapir (1921: 126) argues that the distinction between nouns and verbs is "imperatively required for the life of the language". What is the point of distinguishing between nouns and verbs in Chinese? Some computational linguists want to mark V in the attribute-head A + V phrase as N (Huang et al. 2009). The intention to solve some problems in this manner is understandable, but not caring about existing problems is abnormal. It is not just that we would not object to studying Chinese through generative grammar, but that this type of study has important value on its own. To do so, however, it is necessary to resolve the issue of the inapplicability of the S→NP + VP rule in Chinese, which is raised by Zhu (1985a: 64). At the very least, it cannot be ignored, and a reasonable explanation must be provided. The next chapter will demonstrate in detail that Chinese nouns and verbs are in an inclusion pattern containing both distinction and unification, and the relationships between nouns and verbs, between subjects-objects and predicates are skewed containing both correspondences and non-correspondences. Only by accepting the verbs-as-nouns framework can the S→NP + VP rule mentioned earlier be maintained to a *limited* extent in Chinese, and only in this framework can the significance of distinguishing between nouns and verbs in Chinese be partially preserved.

2.5 Multi-class words

Nouny verbs are defined as words classed as nouns and verbs, which is based on the distinction between nouns and verbs. It has been shown in Section 2.2 that there are no such nouny verbs in Chinese, since the so-called verbs are actually nouns or, more specifically, dynamic nouns. It is inevitable that some problems will arise when the description of Chinese is based on the idea that A and B are distinct with only a small overlap. Besides nouny verbs, the words classed as verbs and adjectives also cause problems. Zhu Dexi (1982: 55–56) defines verbs and adjectives as follows:

Any word in the predicate that cannot be modified by *hěn* 'very' or can take an object is a verb.
Any word in the predicate that can be modified by *hěn* 'very' but cannot take an object is an adjective.

Words like *wěiqu* 'aggrieved', *duānzhèng* 'correct', and *kuāndà* 'lenient' belong to class overlap between verbs and adjectives: "Such words are verbs *when* they take an object, and they are adjectives *when* they do not take an object"(emphasis mine). These multi-class words are actually identified based on their sentence context rather than on their definitions. The word *wěiqu* 'aggrieved' should fit the definition of adjectives if it is a word of class overlap between verbs and adjectives, but it does not, since it can take an object under certain conditions. Furthermore, it does not meet the definition of verbs because it can be modified by *hěn* 'very' depending on its context. In this regard, Zhou Ren (2014, 2015) asserts that to identify words classed as verbs and adjectives is to destroy the positive definitions of both verbs and adjectives. In practice, it is also difficult to implement; the most challenging

The problems   81

aspect of marking word classes in *The Contemporary Chinese Dictionary* is how to divide these words into classes.

There is also a problem with the class overlap between distinguishing words (also known as non-predicative adjectives) and adverbs. For example, there is a lot of debate about the word *bìrán* 'inevitable'. Zhu Dexi (1985a: 21) claims that the word only appears in three positions: Adverbial (as in *bìrán shībài* 'inevitable failure'), attributive (as in *bìrán qūshì* 'inevitable trend') and before the particle *de* (as in *bìrán de qūshì* 'inevitable trend'), and this distribution is exactly the sum of distinguishing words and adverbs, and thus *bìrán* is a word of class overlap between distinguishing words and adverbs. However, both Chen Xiaohe (1999) and Song Rou (2009) call attention to their definitions: Distinguishing words are defined as bound words that can only appear before nouns or the particle *de*, and adverbs are defined as those function words that can only serve as adverbials. According to them, both definitions contain the same word *only*, their connotations are totally exclusive, their denotations do not intersect, and therefore a logical fallacy occurs. In our opinion, this logical fallacy is directly related to the improper definitions of attributes and adverbials, and ultimately it is closely related to the traditional distinction between nouns and verbs. (See Sections 3 and 4 of Chapter 1 in Volume II.)

It is impossible for distinguishing words to share class overlap with adverbs and other word classes of multiple functions. Some grammar books describe the distinguishing words as sharing class overlap with nouns, verbs, and adjectives,[9] such as *yìwài* 'accidental', *zhuānyè* 'professional', *gāodù* 'high-level' with nouns, and *guóyíng* 'state-run', *zǔchuán* 'ancestral', and *jūnyòng* 'military' with verbs, but this is also logically fallacious upon closer consideration. To identify a word of class overlap between distinguishing words and nouns is to assert that it is both a distinguishing word and a noun, but according to the definition of distinguishing words, it is impossible for that word to be both a distinguishing word and a noun. In the same way, it is impossible for adverbs to share class overlap with other word classes of multiple functions. Zhou Ren (2014, 2015) states that since we insist that there is no one-to-one correspondence between word classes and sentence constituents, it is practically impossible to allow multi-class words in the identification of Chinese word classes. He contends that class overlap is essentially a process of categorizing individual words, which artificially undermines the overall nature of a word class. This statement makes much sense. In fact, as pointed out by Li Yuming (1996), there is not much difference between such words as *yìwài* 'accidental', *zhuānyè* 'professional', *gāodù* 'high-level', and such nouns as *suānxìng* 'acid', *chuántǒng* 'tradition'. Their differences are consistent in the following left and right columns:

i. *yìwài (de) shōuhuò* 'an accidental gain'
    fāshēng yìwài 'have an accident'
    zhuānyè jùtuán 'professional troupe'
    yǔyánxué zhuānyè 'linguistics major'
    gāodù de zérèngǎn 'strong sense of responsibility'
    fēixíng (de) gāodù 'height of flight'

82 The problems

ii. *suānxìng tǔrǎng* 'acidic soil'
   tǔrǎng chéng suānxìng 'the soil is acidic'
   chuántǒng sīxiǎng 'traditional thought'
   wǒmen de chuántǒng 'our tradition'

Examples of distinguishing words serving as subjects or objects are common and natural,[10] as in:

pǎo chángtú 'run long distance'
(*chángtú zhèngqián* 'Long-distance transport can earn money'.)

cún huóqī 'open a demand deposit account'
(*huóqī lìlǜ dī* 'Demand deposit rates are low'.)

chuàng chū gèngduō de míngpái 'create more famous brands'
(*míngpái bù hǎo chuàng* 'Famous brands are hard to create'.)

biǎoxiàn chū wēiruò de yángxìng 'show faint positivity'
(*yángxìng bù kěpà* 'Being positive is not terrible'.)

duó gāochǎn 'strive for high yields'
zuò kōngtóu 'make short trades'
chéng zhōngxìng 'be neutral'
fùyú chuàngzàoxìng 'be rich in creativity'
lùchū yīshù cǎisè 'reveal a bunch of colors'

In Li's interpretation (1996: 3), these distinguishing words "are merely manifestations and solidifications of nominal properties, and are specializations of grammatical functions of nominal properties as attributes". When the so-called distinguishing words *xīnshì* 'new-type', *zhòngxíng* 'heavy-lift', *gāojí* 'high-ranking', *yōuděng* 'superior-class', *dàhào* 'large-size' are used as attributes, they fulfil in part the grammatical functions of nouns and are thus only a little less abstract and more concrete than the corresponding adjectives *xīn* 'new', *zhòng* 'heavy', *gāo* 'high', *yōu* 'superior', *dà* 'large'. Consider the following paired examples:

xuéyuàn fēnggé 'academic style'	*xuéyuàn shì fēnggé* 'the style of academy'
tuǒyuán jiégòu 'elliptical structure'	*tuǒyuán shì jiégòu* 'the structure of ellipse'
jīngdiǎn zhùzuò 'classic works'	*jīngdiǎn xìng zhùzuò* 'the works of classic'

Distinguishing words such as *shèbàn* 'community-run', *guóyíng* 'state-run', *zǔchuán* 'ancestral', and *jūnyòng* 'military' are condensed forms of verb phrases, and therefore it is also common and natural for them to be subjects and objects:

gōngshè kāibàn 'community-run'	*shèbàn* 'community-run'
guójiā jīngyíng 'state-run'	*guóyíng* 'state-run'
zǔzōng chuánliú xiàlái 'inherited from ancestors'	*zǔchuán* 'ancestral'
jūnshì shàng shǐyòng 'for military use'	*jūnyòng* 'military'

Li (1996: 7) concludes that, in terms of substantives and predicatives, distinguishing words belong to substantives and that the functional mobility of distinguishing words indicates "a trend of substantives developing towards predicatives in Chinese". According to Zhou Ren (2014, 2015), class overlap is impossible between nouns and distinguishing words, and nouns can be attributive by their very nature since they are multifunctional. According to the verbs-as-nouns theory, the distinguishing words are a type of nouns that have not fully developed (grammaticalized) into predicative words. (See Section 2 of Chapter 4 in Volume II.)

In short, the premise of A and B with class overlap is that A and B are distinct with a small overlap. If it is an inclusion pattern of A and B, then there is no such thing as class overlap. What we can discuss in the inclusive patter is which words in A are developing towards B and how the level of development is. Section 3 of the Concluding Remarks in Volume II will explain that most of the pairs of grammatical categories in Chinese belong to the inclusion pattern. Considering this, it is easier to see why Chinese needs to adopt the continuous view of word classes (Yuan 1995, 2005; Shen 1999). It is even possible to say that the extensiveness of the inclusion pattern in Chinese provides a theoretical foundation for adopting a continuous view of word classes in Chinese.

The reason why multi-class words becomes problematic is that we lack a theoretical explanation for the multifunctionality of Chinese word classes. In the past, only the phenomenon that adjectives can serve as predicates was explained. The explanation is that, in Chinese, verbs include adjectives, which could be regarded as a kind of intransitive verbs (Chao 1968: 292). As for the other multi-functional phenomena, no explanation has been provided and there are only ad hoc discussions. In order to go deeper in research, we must ask not only how but also why. Why in Chinese can verbs function as subjects and objects, adjectives as adverbials, nouns often as attributes and sometimes as predicates and adverbials under certain conditions? The verbs-as-nouns framework will provide a unified explanation for these questions. (See Section 5 of Chapter 1 in Volume II.)

2.6 Other problems

The multifunctionality of Chinese word classes involves the type and definition of syntactic constituents, which are also problematic. The first problem concerns the type of predicates. In Chinese, compared with verbs or verb phrases functioning as subjects and objects, nouns or noun phrases functioning as predicates, as in *Xiǎo Wáng huáng tóufa* 'Xiao Wang, yellow hair', *Lǎo Wáng Shànghǎi rén* 'Lao Wang, person from Shanghai', are indeed special (so nouns cannot be typically used as predicates), but they are even more special compared with Indo-European nouns that *cannot* be directly used as predicates. If we admit that there are no restrictions on the types of predicates in Chinese and both verbs and nouns can serve as predicates, the assertion of nouns' predicativity may directly lead to the consequences of noun-verb confusion and words belonging to no definite classes. Thus it is not difficult to understand that in discussing the word class systems current Chinese grammar books present the fact that nouns can be directly used as predicates but

84 The problems

avoid or understate the question of how to explain it, not to mention the inadequacy of describing the fact (see Chen 2008).

It is also problematic to define attributes and adverbials in Chinese grammar, and their definitions are related to the types of predicates. The current definition of adverbials (the modifiers in the modifier-head predicative phrases) cannot be self-justified when encountering noun-predicate sentences such as *jīntiān gāng xīngqī èr* 'Today is just Tuesday' and *Xiǎo Wáng yě huáng tóufa* 'Xiao Wang also has yellow hair'. Moreover, no matter what changes are made to the definition of adverbials within the current framework of word classes, they are ineffective. In addition, the division of complements and objects is also theoretically inconsistent. On the one hand, the object can be a verbal constituent, and its semantical roles can be the patient or the result. On the other hand, the subsequent verbal constituent of the verb that represents the result is treated as a complement, and the object and the complement are regarded as two equal syntactic constituents. This is logically confusing. All these problems arise from the traditional distinction between nouns and verbs and can be properly solved by adopting the verbs-as-nouns theory. To avoid redundancy, details will not be supplied here. For more information, see Chapters 5 and 6 in this volume (predicate issues) and Chapter 1 in Volume II (complement and adverbial issues).

In the history of Chinese, disyllabification is a major event where monosyllabic words changed into disyllabic words. What exactly is its grammatical function? This is also a problem. Why do mono- vs. disyllabic word pairings ({monosyllabic + disyllabic} and {disyllabic + monosyllabic}) distinguish between two types of grammatical structures (attribute-head and predicate-object)? For example, *chūzū chē* 'taxi' is usually understood as an attribute-head nominal structure, while *zū qìchē* 'rent a car' must be taken as a predicate-object structure. Currently, there are two conflicting interpretations. One is that disyllabification makes monosyllabic verbs change from simple verbs to words classed as nouns and verbs, as in *gōng* 'attack' → *gōngjī* 'attack' and *chóu* 'prepare' → *chóubèi* 'prepare'. This statement is derived from the definition of nouny verbs in Section 2. The other is that the disyllabic verbs in modern Chinese are drifting towards nouns (Chen 1987). The contradiction is: Since *gōngjī* 'attack' and *chóubèi* 'prepare' have become nominalized after disyllabification, how can they drift towards nouns? These two interpretations are not only theoretically inconsistent but also fail to explain the important fact that many monosyllabic nouns can no longer be used as verbs after disyllabification, as in *chē* 'vehicle; transport' → *chēliàng* 'vehicle', *jiào* 'cellar v. & n.' → *dìjiào* 'cellar n.'. The root of the problem is still the traditional word-class notion of distinguishing between nouns and verbs. Chapters 4 and 5 in Volume II provide detailed analysis and solutions.

Identifying problems is often even more important in scientific research than solving them. This is because advances in research occur only when problems are faced rather than avoided. Further, existing problems cannot be treated one at a time in isolation when they are in fact linked together. Any solution to such problems must address their shared root cause. In the current discussion this root cause is nothing other than a lack of clarity in how the two most basic categories—nouns and verbs—relate to each other. After identifying the source of the problems, the

The problems 85

next step is to treat it comprehensively. To do this, the problem of word classes must be considered together with the problems related to "subjects", "sentences", the functions of "disyllabification", the status of word classes in the study of typology, and even the very notion of what a category is.

Notes

1 The last two examples are adapted from those provided by Zhang Bojiang.
2 Zhou Ren (2014) argues that Chinese word classes should be negatively defined.
3 The facts are pointed out by Zeng Qian and the examples are provided by him.
4 See Section 4 of Chapter 6 for the grammatical function of dummy verbs.
5 They refer to juxtaposition. For example, the use of *túshū hé chūbǎn* 'books and publication' to express the meaning of *túshū de chūbǎn* 'the publication of books', and the use of *nǐ qù, wǒ bú qù* 'you go, I won't' to express the meaning of *rúguǒ nǐ qù, wǒ bú qù* 'if you go, I won't go'. Juxtaposition does not violate the head feature convention, and it simply does not make use of it.
6 C.-T. James Huang (2010) proposes the functional category G, first changing *chūbǎn* into a gerund, then generating a gerund phrase, and then generating a DP.
7 Yuan Yulin (2010b) explained it by introducing 'potential subject' and 'potential object', which is arbitrary and extremely complicated.
8 The adverbial-head phrase is actually a kind of dynamic attributive-head phrase in Chinese (see Section 4 of Chapter 1 in Volume II).
9 For example, *A Descriptive Grammar of Modern Chinese* edited by Zhang Bin (2010) contains chapters on the words of class overlap between distinguishing words and nouns/verbs/adjectives, though it tries to limit the scope of multi-class words.
10 Zhu Dexi (1985a: 20) think that only juxtaposition allows this kind of use as in *jíxìng hǎo zhì, mànxìng nán zhì* 'Acute diseases are easy to treat, whereas chronic ones are difficult to treat'. This is not true: a counterexample without juxtaposition might be *wǒ dé de shì jíxìng* 'I have got an acute disease'.

References

Abney, S. (1987) 'The English Noun Phrase in Its Sentential Aspect', Doctoral Dissertation, Cambridge, MA: MIT Press.

Bai, Shuo (2014) 'Lun *zhe ben shu de chuban* yu X-bar lilun de jianrongxing' ('On the Compatibility of *Zhe Ben Shu de Chuban* with X-bar Theory'), http://blog.sina.com.cn/s/blog-729574a00102uzf6.html.

Brown, K. (ed) (2006) *Encyclopedia of Language and Linguistics*, 2nd ed., Amsterdam: Elsevier Ltd.

Chao, Yuen Ren (1968) *A Grammar of Spoken Chinese*, Berkeley and Los Angeles: University of California Press. Translated as *Hanyu Kouyu Yufa* by Lü Shuxiang in 1979, Beijing: The Commercial Press, and as *Zhongguohua de Wenfa* (Revised edition) by Pang-hsin Ting in 2002, Hong Kong: The Chinese University of Hong Kong Press.

Chen, Guohua (2009) 'Cong *de* kan zhongxinyu gouzao yu zhongxinyu de cilei' ('Centre Construction and the Word Class of Its Centre'), *Foreign Language Teaching and Research* 2: 92–98.

Chen, Manhua (2008) *Tici Weiyu Ju Yanjiu* (*A Study of Sentences with Substantive Predicate*), Beijing: China Federation of Literary and Art Circles Publishing House.

Chen, Ningping (1987) 'Xiandai hanyu mingcilei de kuoda' ('The Expansion of Noun Classes in Modern Chinese'), *Studies of the Chinese Language* 5: 379–389.

86   The problems

Chen, Xiaohe (1999) 'Cong zidong jufa fenxi jiaodu kan hanyu cilei wenti' ('The Issues of Chinese Word Classes from the Perspective of Automatic Syntactic Parsing'), *Language Teaching and Linguistic Studies* 3: 63–72.

Cheng, Gong (1999) *Yuyan Gongxing Lun* (*Linguistic Universalism*), Shanghai: Shanghai Foreign Language Education Press.

Chomsky, N. (1965) *Aspects of the Theory of Syntax*, Cambridge, MA: MIT Press.

Croft, W. (1991) *Syntactic Categories and Grammatical Relations*, Chicago: University of Chicago Press.

Cui, Shanjia (2013) *Hanyu Ouhua Yufa Xianxiang Zhuanti Yanjiu* (*Thematic Studies on the Phenomena of Chinese Europeanized Grammar*), Chengdu: Bashu Press.

Evans, N. and S. C. Levinson (2009) 'The Myth of Language Universals: Language Diversity and Its Importance for Cognitive Science', *Behavioral and Brain Sciences* 32: 429–492.

Fang, Guangtao (1997) *Fang Guangtao Yuyanxue Lunwen Ji* (*Essays in Linguistics by Fang Guangtao*), Beijing: The Commercial Press.

Gao, Mingkai (1953, October) 'Guanyu hanyu de cilei fenbie' ('On the Differences Between Word Classes in Chinese'), *Studies of the Chinese Language*: 13–16.

Hengeveld, K. (1992) 'Parts of Speech', in M. Fortescue, P. Harder and L. Kristoffersen (eds) *Layered Structure and Reference in a Functional Perspective*, Amsterdam: John Benjamins, 29–55.

Hu, Mingyang (1995) 'Xiandai hanyu cilei wenti kaocha' ('An Investigation of the Word Classes in Modern Chinese'), *Studies of the Chinese Language* 5: 381–389.

Huang, C. T. James (2010) 'Cong *ta de laoshi dang de hao* tan qi' ('On *Ta de Laoshi Dang de Hao* and Related Problems'), in *Lü Shuxiang Xiansheng Bainian Danchen Jinian Wenji* (*Essays in Commemorating the Centenary of the Birth of Lü Shuxiang*), Beijing: The Commercial Press, 126–143.

Huang, Changning, Zixia Jiang and Yumei Li (2009) 'Xingrongci zhijie xiushi dongci de a+v jiegou qiyi' ('Verb Modified by Adjective Directly: An Ambiguous Construction of a+v'), *Studies of the Chinese Language* 1: 54–63.

Huang, Hebin (2014) 'Zhiyi liangge wenti yu yige nanti: dui bushi xiangxin jiegouguan de renshi' ('Questions about Two Problems and One Puzzle: An Understanding of Bloomfield's View on Endocentric Construction'), *Journal of Foreign Languages* 4: 41–48.

Jin, Lixin (1987) 'Guanyu xiangxin jiegou dingyi de taolun' ('A Discussion on the Definition of Endocentric Construction'), *Chinese Language Guide* 7: 30–32.

Li, Jinxi (1924) *Xinzhu Guoyu Wenfa* (*The New Chinese Grammar*), Beijing: The Commercial Press.

Li, Xiang (2011) 'Cong shixian jizhi he jiwu leixing kan hanyu de jieyong dongliangci' ('Can Verb Classifiers Be Borrowed from Nouns?'), *Studies of the Chinese Language* 4: 313–325.

Li, Yafei (2015) 'Yetan hanyu mingci duanyu de neibu jiegou' ('Revisiting the Internal Structure of Chinese Noun Phrases'), *Studies of the Chinese Language* 2: 99–104.

Li, Yen-hui Audrey (2008) 'Duanyu jiegou yu yulei biaoji: *de shi zhongxinci*?' ('Phrase Structures and Categorical Labeling: *De* as a Head?'), *Contemporary Linguistics* 2: 97–108.

Li, Yuming (1996) 'Feiwei xingrongci de cilei diwei' ('The Word-Class Status of Non-Predicative Adjectives'), *Studies of the Chinese Language* 1: 1–9.

Lu, Bingfu (1985) 'Guanyu yuyan jiegou de neixiang waixiang fenlei he hexin de dingyi' ('On Classes of Endocentricicity and Exocentricity and a Definition of Nucleus in Linguistic Construction'), *Yufa Yanjiu he Tansuo* (*Studies and Explorations on Grammar*) 3: 338–351.

Lu, Bingfu (2014) 'Shen Jiaxuan mingdong baohan lilun zhengfan shuo' ('Pros and Cons of Shen Jiaxuan's Verbs-as-Nouns Theory'), in *Yinghan Duibi yu Fanyi* (*Contrastive and Translation Studies of English and Chinese*), vol. 2, Shanghai: Shanghai Foreign Language Education Press, 71–83.

Lu, Jianming (2003) 'Dui NP+de+VP jiegou de chongxin renshi' ('A New Understanding of the NP+de+VP Structure'), *Studies of the Chinese Language* 5: 387–391.

Lü, Shuxiang (1944/1984) 'Ge zi de yingyong fanwei: fulun danweici qian yizi de tuoluo' ('The Uses of *ge* as a Classifier, with Remarks Concerning the Dropping of *yi* before *ge* and Other Classifiers'), in *Hanyu Yufa Lunwen Ji* (*Studies in Chinese Grammar*), Beijing: The Commercial Press, 145–177.

Lü, Shuxiang (1979) *Hanyu Yufa Fenxi Wenti* (*Problems in Chinese Grammatical Analysis*), Beijing: The Commercial Press.

Lyons, J. (1968) *Introduction to Theoretical Linguistics*, Cambridge: Cambridge University Press.

Pan, Haihua and Shuo Lu (2013) 'DeP fenxi suo dailai de wenti jiqi keneng de jiejue fang'an' ('The Problems of the DeP Analysis and Its Possible Solution'), *Studies in Language and Linguistics* 4: 53–61.

Qiu, Rongtang (1994) 'Mingdongci zhiyi: ping Zhu Dexi xiansheng guanyu mingdongci de shuofa' ('Some Doubts about Nouny Verbs: Review of Zhu Dexi's Statement on Nouny Verbs'), *Chinese Language Learning* 6: 15–20.

Radford, A. (1988) *Transformational Grammar: A First Course*, Cambridge: Cambridge University Press.

Sapir, E. (1921) *Language*, New York: Harcourt, Brace & World.

Shen, Jiaxuan (1999) *Buduicheng he Biaojilun* (*Asymmetry and Markedness Theory*), Nanchang: Jiangxi Education Publishing House, Reprinted in Beijing: The Commercial Press, 2015.

Shi, Dingxu (2008) '*De* he *de* zi jiegou' ('*De* and *De*-Construction'), *Contemporary Linguistics* 4: 298–307.

Shi, Guangan (1981) '*Zhe ben shu de chuban* zhong *chuban* de cixing: cong xiangxin jiegou lilun shuoqi' ('The Word Class of *Chuban* in the Phrase *Zhe Ben Shu de Chuban* in Terms of Endocentric Construction'), *Current Research in Chinese Linguistics* 4: 8–12.

Shi, Guangan (1988) 'Xiandai hanyu de xiangxin jiegou he lixin jiegou' ('Endocentric Construction and Exocentric Construction in Modern Chinese'), *Studies of the Chinese Language* 4: 265–273.

Si, Fuzhen (2002) 'Hanyu de biaojuci *de* ji xiangguan de jufa wenti' ('The Chinese Complementizer *De* and the Related Syntactic Problems'), *Language Teaching and Linguistic Studies* 2: 36–42.

Si, Fuzhen (2004) 'Zhongxinyu lilun he hanyu de DeP' ('The Head Theory and DeP in Chinese'), *Contemporary Linguistics* 1: 26–34.

Si, Fuzhen (2006) 'Zhongxinyu lilun he Bulongfei'erde nanti' ('The Head Theory and the Bloomfieldian Puzzle'), *Contemporary Linguistics* 1: 60–70.

Song, Rou (2009) 'Cong yuyan gongcheng kan hanyu cilei' ('A Study on the Chinese Word Classes from the Perspective of Language Engineering'), *Essays on Linguistics* 40: 23–38.

Tang, Sze-Wing (2006) 'Yi *de* wei zhongxinyu de yixie wenti' ('On *De* as a Head in Chinese'), *Contemporary Linguistics* 3: 205–212.

von Humboldt, W. (1836) *On Language: The Diversity of Human Language-Structure and Its Influence on the Mental Development of Mankind*, P. Heath (trans.), Cambridge: Cambridge University Press.

88 *The problems*

Wan, Quan (2010) 'Yupian zhong de canzhaoti-mubiao goushi' ('The Reference-Point Construction in Discourse'), *Language Teaching and Linguistic Studies* 6: 38–45.

Wu, Chang'an (2006) '*Zhe ben shu de chuban* yu xiangxin jiegou lilun nanti' ('*Zhe Ben Shu de Chuban*: A Challenge to Bloomfield's Theory of Endocentric Construction'), *Contemporary Linguistics* 3: 193–204.

Xiang, Mengbing (1991) 'Lun *zhe ben shu de chuban* zhong *chuban* de cixing: dui hanyu dongci xingrongci mingwuhua wenti de zairenshi' ('On the Word Class of *Chuban* in the Phrase *Zhe Ben Shu de Chuban*: Revisiting the Nominalization of Chinese Verbs and Adjectives'), *Journal of Tianjin Normal University* 4: 75–80.

Xiong, Zhongru (2005) 'Yi *de* wei hexin de DP jiegou' ('A DP Structure Headed by *De*'), *Contemporary Linguistics* 2: 148–165.

Yuan, Yulin (1995) 'Cilei fanchou de jiazu xiangsixing' ('Family Resemblance of Lexical Categories'), *Social Sciences in China* 1: 154–170.

Yuan, Yulin (2005) 'Jiyu lishudu de hanyu cilei de mohu huafen' ('The Fuzzy Partition of Chinese Word Classes Based on Degree of Membership'), *Social Sciences in China* 1: 164–177.

Yuan, Yulin (2010a) 'Hanyu he yingyu zai yufa fanchou de shixian guanxi shang de pingxingxing: ye tan hanyu li mingci/dongci yu zhicheng/chenshu, zhuyu yu huati, juzi yu huaduan' ('Parallels in the Realization of Grammatical Categories between Chinese and English: On Noun/Verb and Reference/Predication, Subject and Topic, Sentence and Utterance in Chinese'), *Journal of Sino-Tibetan Linguistics* 4: 139–168.

Yuan, Yulin (2010b) 'Hanyu buneng chengshou de fanyi zhiqing: cong qu fanchouhua jiaodu kan hanyu dongci he mingci de guanxi' ('The Unbearable Lightness of the Translation of Deverbal Nouns from Indo-European Languages into Chinese: Rethinking the Relation between Verbs and Nouns in Mandarin Chinese from a Perspective of the Decategorization of Verbs'), *Essays on Linguistics* 41: 15–61.

Zhan, Weidong (2013) 'Jisuanji jufa jiegou fenxi xuyao shenmeyang de cilei zhishi: jianping jinnian lai hanyu cilei yanjiu de xin jinzhan' ('What Kind of Word Class Knowledge Is Required for Computer Analysis of Syntactic Structure: A Review of Recent Advances in Chinese Word Class Research'), *Studies of the Chinese Language* 2: 178–190.

Zhang, Bin (ed) (2010) *Xiandai Hanyu Miaoxie Yufa* (*A Descriptive Grammar of Modern Chinese*), Beijing: The Commercial Press.

Zhou, Guoguang (2005) 'Dui *zhongxinyu lilun he hanyu de DeP* yiwen de zhiyi' ('*Head Theory and DeP in Chinese* Revisited'), *Contemporary Linguistics* 2: 139–47.

Zhou, Guoguang (2006) 'Kuohao beilun he de-X de yugan: yi *de* wei hexin de DP jiegou yinan qiujie' ('Revisiting the De-X Structure: The Bracketing Paradox and Linguistic Intuition'), *Contemporary Linguistics* 1: 71–75.

Zhou, Ren (2012) 'N *de* V jiegou jiushi N *de* N jiegou' ('N *de* V Construction is N *de* N Construction'), *Studies of the Chinese Language* 5: 447–457.

Zhou, Ren (2014) 'Hanyu cilei huafen ying zhongshi paitafa' ('On the Importance of Exclusion Method in Dividing Chinese Word Classes'), *Chinese Language Learning* 1: 9–19.

Zhou, Ren (2015) 'Jianleishuo fansi' ('Reflections on Multi-Class Words in Chinese'), *Linguistic Sciences* 5: 504–516.

Zhu, Dexi (1982) *Yufa Jiangyi* (*Lectures on Chinese Grammar*), Beijing: The Commercial Press.

Zhu, Dexi (1985a) *Yufa Dawen* (*Answering Questions about Chinese Grammar*), Beijing: The Commercial Press.

The problems 89

Zhu, Dexi (1985b) 'Guanyu xiangxin jiegou de dingyi' ('On the Definition of Endocentric Constructions'), *Yufa Yanjiu he Tansuo (Studies and Explorations on Grammar)* 3: 19–23.

Zhu, Dexi (1985c) 'Xiandai shumian hanyu li de xuhua dongci he mingdongci' ('Delexicalized Verbs and Nouny Verbs in Modern Written Chinese'), *Journal of Peking University (Philosophy and Social Sciences)* 5: 1–6.

3 The verbs-as-nouns framework in Chinese

3.1 The ABCs of how Chinese and Indo-European languages differ

Chapter 1 discusses how Zhu Dexi has taken an important step towards breaking free from the shackles of traditional concepts derived from Indo-European languages. He maintains that Chinese does not have "nominalization", as is apparent from the ability of verbs to serve as predicates and as subjects and objects without underdoing any changes in form. This demonstrates that they remain verbs when filling subject and object roles.

This chapter will show that a further step forward on the foundation laid by Zhu is all that is needed to solve the problems delineated in Chapter 2. Specifically, it proposes that the reason why verbs do not undergo "nominalization" is that they are essentially a type of nouns. To be precise, they are dynamic nouns. From this, it follows that Chinese nouns and verbs are structurally related in the verbs-as-nouns framework.

This can be demonstrated from many different angles. We begin our discussion with the ABCs of how Chinese grammar differs from Indo-European grammars, with the ABCs here meaning the "common sense" approach. To attain this knowledge we have had to travel a long road under the domination of traditional concepts whose prominence comes from their having been proposed first.

A. *Tā kāi fēijī.*
he fly plane
*He fly a plane.
'He flies a plane'.

B. *Tā kāi fēijī.*
he fly plane
*He flies plane.
'He flies a plane'.

C. *Kāi fēijī róngyì.*
fly plane easy
*Fly a plane is easy.
'Flying a plane is easy'.

DOI: 10.4324/9781003385899-4

The verbs-as-nouns framework in Chinese   91

A shows that unlike verbs in Indo-European languages the Chinese verb *kāi* does not undergo inflection to function as a sentence's predicate. English verbs inflect. Its verb *fly* must be changed into *flies* in A. In this sense, Chinese verbs are intrinsically predicative expressions, and there is no distinction in Chinese between a verb's base form and the form it has when functioning as a predicate.

B shows that the Chinese noun *fēijī* undergoes no "referentialization" process like nouns in Indo-European languages to serve as a referring expression in a sentence. In contrast, the basic lexical item *plane* in English has to be realized as *a plane, the plane(s)*, or *planes* to function as a grammatical referring expression. It is in this sense that Chinese nouns are basic referring expressions.

C shows that Chinese verbs, unlike their Indo-European counterparts, do not undergo the process of nominalization or "noun-object assignment" or referentialization to be used as nouns in sentences (functioning as referring expressions in the subject and object positions). English has this kind of process. *Fly* has to be changed into *flying* or *to fly* to function as a noun.

Taken together, A, B, and C support the following conclusions: Chinese verbs (predicative expressions) are nouns (referring expressions); verbs are a subclass of nouns, dynamic nouns, or simply gerunds. Zhu Dexi has already argued for and emphasized two of the three points given earlier, A and C. The only addition being proposed here is B.[1]

Some have raised doubts about the two points A and C. Although Chapter 1 has already addressed these doubts, a few additional comments are made here about point A. Some people concede that *kāi* does not undergo morphological changes in *tā kāi fēijī* 'he flies planes', before offering as a counterexample to the claim in A the occurrence of *kāi* with the aspect markers *le, zhe*, and *guo* in the sentences *tā kāi le fēijī le* 'he flew a plane', *tā kāi zhe fēijī ne* 'he is flying a plane', and *tā kāi guò fēijī* 'he has flown a plane'.

The response to the previous argument is as follows: First, comparisons should be made on the same level. The addition of *le, zhe*, and *guò* does not involve an inflectional change to the base form of the verb *kāi*. Chinese aspect markers are introduced at a different linguistic level from the one for the inflectional changes (*flies, flew, flying*, and *flown*) to the English verb *fly*. If the past tense and past participle forms of an English verb are irregular, they must be listed in the lexicon, as is the case for "*fly, flew, flown*". Second, morphological markers must be divided into those which are obligatory and those which are optional. In Chinese, the inclusion of *le, zhe*, and *guò* is optional (Lü 1979: 92). Consider the following sentences:

Tā   kāi   huílái   (le)   Yī   jià   fēijī.[2]
he   fly   back   PSP   one   CL   plane
'He flew a plane back.'

Tā   yībiān   kāi   (zhe)   fēijī   yībiān   pāizhào.
he   while   fly   DUR   plane   while   take-pictures
'He took pictures while flying a plane.'

92　*The verbs-as-nouns framework in Chinese*

Tā	*céngjīng*	*kāi*	*(guò)*	*fēijī*	*chūhǎi.*
he	used-to	fly	EXP	plane	out-sea

'He used to fly out to the sea.'

In contrast, *He fly a plane* in English is absolutely ungrammatical and cannot function as a sentence. Cross-linguistic comparisons should first compare items in terms of whether both languages' examples are grammatical.

Beginning here, the focus of the discussion will now turn to point B of ABC. Consider the following example:

Lǎohǔ	*shì*	*wēixiǎn*	*dòngwù.*
tiger	be	dangerous	animal

'*Tigers* are dangerous animals./*The tiger* is a dangerous animal.'

Lǎohǔ	*lóngzi*	*lǐ*	*shuìjiào*	*ne.*
tiger	cage	in	sleep	MP

'*The tiger* is sleeping in the cage./*The tigers* are sleeping in the cage.'

Tā	*zuótiān*	*zhōngyú*	*kànjiàn*	*lǎohǔ*	*le.*
he	yesterday	at last	see	tiger	PSP

'He saw *the tiger(s)/a tiger/tigers* at last yesterday.'

Lǎohǔ 'tiger' in the first sentence is generic, referring to a kind of animal. Chinese just uses *Lǎohǔ*. English, in contrast, cannot use *tiger* alone in a sentence.

Lǎohǔ in the second sentence is definite, referring to a certain tiger or certain tigers. The Chinese is still just *lǎohǔ*, whereas English can use neither *tiger* nor *tigers* alone to express definiteness.

Lǎohǔ in the third sentence can be definite, indefinite, specific, or generic depending on the context. In Chinese, *lǎohǔ*, unchanged and free standing, expresses all these meanings. To do the same, English needs to use different forms and phrases like *the tigers*, *a tiger*, or *tigers*.

In Chinese, definiteness and indefiniteness can be distinguished by word order, without morphological changes. A common example is *kèrén lái le* 'the guest(s) came' (definite) as opposed to *lái kèrén le* 'a guest/some guests came' (indefinite). The previously cited three example sentences with *lǎohǔ* also show that the bare noun *lǎohǔ* can serve as different types of referring expressions, and that bare verbs like *shì* 'to be', *shuìjiào* 'to sleep', and *kànjiàn* 'to see' are capable of functioning as predicates without any morphological changes. In contrast, English verbs must undergo formal changes. For example, *be* is inflected as *is* or *are* and *see* as *saw*, with *sleep* undergoing a change in *is sleeping*, and so on. In short, for words extracted from the lexicon in Chinese, those marked as "nouns" can be directly realized as "referring expressions", and those marked as "verbs" can be directly realized as "predicates".

In some Chinese dialects, mainly in the subject position, classifiers have a usage that seems similar to the definite article, as for example in the Yantai dialect sentence *Jiān wūr zhēn dà hang* (*Zhè jiān wūzi zhēn dà a*) 'This room is really big'. However, Liu Tanzhou and Shi Dingxu (2012) point out that apart from marking definiteness, classifiers can mark nominal expressions as specific, generic, and indefinite (e.g. *Nǐ suíbiàn bāng wǒ zhǎo ge xiǎohái ba, gè sìwǔsuì de jiù xíng* 'Find any child for me as you like, as long as he or she is four or five years old'). They even mark referentless nominal, as in *Jù huà dōu shuō bù qīng* (*Lián jù huà dōu shuō bù qīng*) 'Not even a single utterance can be made clear'. Since the same form can be used to mark various kinds of reference, it is problematic to say it is an article. To claim that a language has articles as a lexical category, it should at least be similar to English in having an opposition like the one between *the* and *a*. Liu and Shi (2012) characterize this usage of Chinese classifiers as marking a "subjective comment", expressing the emotions and attitudes of the speaker. The subjective comment function is even more evident in the following "classifier + verb" structures:

Gè	*tiāo*	*shìr*	*hang,*	*qiānwàn*	*bùnéng*	*tiāo*
CL	pick	persimmon	MP	on-no-account	cannot	pick

dàijiār	*de.*
with-sharp-point	MM

'When picking persimmons, on no account pick the ones with sharp points or big spikes.'

Xiǎo Zhāng	*kěnéng*	*shuì*	*le,*	*tā*	*gè*	*shuì*	*yībān*
Xiao Zhang	may	sleep	PSP	he	CL	sleep	average

rénr	*bǐbuliǎo.*
people	not-compare

'Xiao Zhang may have gone to sleep. Most people can't compare with him in sleeping.'

Tā	*gè*	*zuòfàn*	*miē*	*jiào*	*zuòfàn?*
He	CL	cook	MP	call	cook

'Can his cooking be called cooking?'

Āiyā,	*kē*	*shù*	*gè*	*gāo*	*a.*
INT	CL	tree	CL	tall	MP

'Oh, this tree is so big!'

Gè	*háizi*	*gè*	*fánqì*	*rén*	*nè!*
This	child	CL	annoy	people	MP

'This child really gets on people's nerves.'

94 *The verbs-as-nouns framework in Chinese*

In view of these examples, it is better to say that the classifier *gè* is a subjectivity marker than to hold that it has uses like an article.[3]

It is not the case that we were unaware of point B before now. Rather, it is simply that it was not considered important. Most Chinese students of English can easily describe the differences captured in the two points A and C. In contrast, they would find it relatively difficult to do the same for the differences in B, even though it is important for them to know that the sentences *he flies plane* and *he fly a plane* are equally ungrammatical in English. It is because we are in the habit of looking at Chinese from a Chinese perspective that we fail to consciously note that Chinese bare nouns can directly function as referring expressions or as subjects and objects. This is actually an important characteristic that differentiates Chinese from Indo-European languages. This is exactly the kind of habit we want to break. For Chinese learning English, even if people achieve a high level of proficiency, they still often make one mistake, leaving off an article before a noun where one is required.[4] We simply cannot imagine that it is absolutely necessary to add the article *le* in front of the telephone number 3777 to express "in case of danger immediately dial 3777" in French. Only by so doing is the sentence in accord with French grammar. Conversely, Westerners learning Chinese do not dare say directly *wǒ bèiqǐ shūbāo huíjiā* 'I am carrying bookbag and returning home'. Instead, they say *wǒ bèiqǐ wǒde shūbāo huí wǒde jiā* 'I am carrying my bookbag and returning to my home'. They are not accustomed to bare nouns used as referring expressions in Chinese.

Point B has long been ignored by us. However, there are a number of Western formal semanticists who consider it very important. For example, Chierchia (1985, 1998) proposes that bare nouns extracted from lexicons in different languages fall into three types, each represented by French, English, and Chinese.

French: [– arg]   [+ pred]
English: [+ arg]   [+ pred]
Chinese: [+ arg]   [– pred]

[± arg] denotes whether a bare noun can serve as an argument of a sentence. This mainly concerns whether or not the bare noun can be a subject or object. [± pred] denotes whether they can fill the predicate function. Words that function as arguments directly belong to the semantic type entity, *e* (entity). Otherwise, they are only predicates. Bare nouns in Chinese can directly function as subjects or objects, and their semantic type is *e*. Bare nouns in French cannot act as subjects or objects directly; their semantic type is predicate $<e, t>$. The semantic type of bare nouns in English is a mixture of the Chinese and French types. Bare nouns in English generally function as predicates $<e, t>$. However, their plural forms can directly serve as subjects and objects and so are entities $<e>$. French and English bare nouns need to undergo semantic type shift before filling the slots of subjects or objects. It is a shift from predicate function to entity. Chinese bare nouns enter subject and object roles with no need for such a shift, because they are lexically entities. It is from the perspective of "semantic type" that formal semanticists examine the differences among Chinese, French, and English. The linguistic phenomena the formal

The verbs-as-nouns framework in Chinese   95

semanticists focus on are the same as the ones we do. The differences they explicate are identical to those we emphasize.[5] Huang Shizhe (2008) sees the importance of this feature of Chinese and uses it to explain the collocational characteristics of adjectives and nouns in Chinese.

Some have expressed doubts about point B. For example, Yuan Yulin (2010) argues that data from actual Chinse texts show that in many cases Chinese makes extensive use of quantifiers, demonstrative pronouns, and restrictive phrases to express referential and quantified situations of the concepts nouns refer to. In addition, there are cases in English where bare nouns are used as subjects and objects. This obliterates the differences between Chinese and Indo-European languages, and this confuses the general with the particular. There are cases where bare nouns serve as subjects and objects in English. This is a fact. But these are special cases. In contrast, it is quite common for Chinese bare nouns to be used as subjects or objects. Another way to describe the differences between English and Chinese is as follows: English bare nouns are non-referential and so do not denote individuals, whereas Chinese bare nouns are referentially unspecified. See Section 1 of Chapter 4 for discussion.

3.2 The "skewed distribution" of nouns and verbs

The determination of nouns and verbs in Chinese is traditionally based on "the noun-verb distinction", even though their actual distribution does not support this distinction and does support the verbs-as-nouns framework. The term and linguistic phenomenon "skewed relation"[6] was discussed by Yuen Ren Chao (1959a, 1968) on numerous occasions. It refers to a relationship of partial correspondence. For example, the Heavenly Stems *Jia* and *Yi* as used in the Chinese ordinal system correspond to A and B, respectively, when the Roman letters are used to mark an ordered sequence. There is a one-to-one correspondence between the Heavenly Stems and the Roman letters in this case. In contrast, in a skewed relationship, *Jia* corresponds to A at the same time that *Yi* corresponds to both A and B. The 5 main types of patterns where the distribution of nouns and verbs display a skewed distribution are as follows:

Type I

Nouns typically function as subjects and objects but not as predicates; verbs, on the other hand, function as predicates and as subjects and objects. As has already been explained earlier in detail, Zhu Dexi treats this skewed distribution as highly significant. Here is a new fact to supplement the discussion. *Zhe* 'this' can occur with verbs in the same way it does with nouns, to strengthen their referential force when they occur as subjects and objects (Fang 2011):

Wǒ	*zhè*	*tóutòng*	*yě*	*yǒu*	*hǎo*	*duō*	*nián*	*le.*
I	this	headache	also	have	good	many	year	PSP

'I have had headaches for many years.'

96 *The verbs-as-nouns framework in Chinese*

Cf.

Wǒ   zhè   <u>tóutòngbìng</u>   yě   yǒu   hǎo   duō   nián   le.
I   this   headache-disease   also   have   good   many   year   PSP
'I have had the headache disease for many years.'

Wǒ   jiù   pèifú   tā   zhè   <u>chī</u>,   tā   kěshì   tài   néng   chī   le.
I   INT   admire   he   this   eat   ta   really   too   can   eat   PSP
'I admire him for this eating of his. He really can eat.'
(I admire this eating of his—his capacity for food is great beyond all measure.)

Cf.

Wǒ   jiùshì   pèifú   tā   zhè   <u>fànliàng</u>,   tā   kěshì   tài   néng   chī   le.
I   INT   admire   he   this   appetite   he   really   too   can   eat   PSP
'I admire him for this appetite of his. He really can eat.'

Type II

Adjectives rather than adverbs typically modify nouns. Both modify verbs. Zhu Dexi also treats this skewed distribution as highly significant. It establishes that Chinese adjectives can function as attributes and as adverbs. For example, *kuài* 'fast' occurs as the modifier in both *kuài chē* 'express bus' and *kuài zǒu* 'walk fast'. This is different from adjectives in Indo-European languages, which generally serve only as attributes.

In writing, attributive-*de* and adverbial-*de* also show a skewed distribution. The adverbial-*de* is only an adverbial marker; the *de* in *piāoliàng de yīfú* 'beautiful clothes' can only be written in attributive-*de* instead of adverbial-*de*. In contrast, *de* marks both attributes and adverbials, as in *wǒ zhēnde hěn ài nǐ* 'I really love you', *zhè jiàn shì shífēn de róngyì* 'This is very easy'. Similar examples are found in Lü Shuxiang and Zhu Dexi (1979):

Zhōngguó   rénmín   jiěfàngjūn   de   xùnsù   de
Chinese   people   liberation-army   MM   quickly   ATT-de/ADV-de

zhuǎnrù   fǎngōng,   shǐ   fǎndòngpài   jīnghuángshīcuò.
change-into   counterattack   make   reactionary   out-of-minds
'The Chinese People's Liberation Army quickly mounted a counterattack, scaring the reactionaries out of their minds.'

Gèbié   xìtǒng   hé   dānwèi zhǐ   zhùyì   gūlì   de
individual   system   and   unit   only   pay-attention-to   isolate   ATT-de/ADV-de

zhuā   shēngchǎn   ér   hūshì   le   zhígōng   shēnghuó.
grasp   production   whereas   neglect   PSP   employee   life
'Individual systems and units gave production their undivided attention and thus neglected their employees' lives.'

The verbs-as-nouns framework in Chinese   97

Lü Shuxiang and Zhu Dexi (1979) observe that "some people only uses the attributive-*de*". Zhu Dexi (1985: 45–46) offers the following examples:

zhōumì   de   xiǎngfǎ
thorough   ATT-de   idea
'thoughtful ideas'

zhōumì   de   diàochá   yīxià
thoroughly   ADV-de   investigate   one-time
'Investigate it carefully.'

zhōumì   de   diàochá   zhèlǐ   de   qíngkuàng
thoroughly   ADV-de   investigate   here   ATT-de   situation
'Investigate the situation here carefully.'

yǐjīng   zhōumì   de   diàochá   guò   le
already   thoroughly   ADV-de   investigate   EXP   PSP
'It has been investigated thoroughly.'

jìnxíng   zhōumì   de   diàochá
conduct   thorough   ATT-de   investigation
'Conduct a thorough investigation.'

zhōumì   de   diàochá   hěn   zhòngyào
thorough   ATT-de/ADV-de   investigation   very   important
'A thorough investigation is very important.'

Zhu points out that native speakers who have not been influenced by the current conventions in grammar textbooks use attributive-*de* in this way. Lü Shuxiang (1981) observes that the meticulous differentiation of attributive-*de* from adverbial-*de* in writing is originally something that came out of translation needs after the May 4th movement and that it arose under the influence of Western languages. An examination of early vernacular literature shows that *Outlaws of the Marsh* for the most part only uses attributive-*de*, with adverbial-*de* occurring in a few places. *Dream of Red Mansions* (a.k.a. *Dream of the Red Chamber/The Story of the Stone*) and *The Scholars* only use attributive-*de*.

Up until now, there are still differences in how everyone uses these two forms of *de* in writing. This is especially the case for noun-classifier reduplication. Here it is even rarer to make a strict distinction between the two *de* forms. Examples of this include *mǎduì yīgèquān yīgèquān de pǎo* 'The horse team ran in a circle', *yīlièchē yīlièchē de bèi sòngdào gè dìfāng qù* 'they are sent to various places by train', and *jìnxíng le zhútiáo zhúxiàng de xuéxí, yǐjiàn shì yīgè wèntí de tǎolùn* 'Learning was itemized, and discussion was conducted in a case-by-case manner'. Attributive-*de* and adverbial-*de* can be used interchangeably in all of the previous examples. In view of examples like these, Lü Shuxiang (1984) observes that it is best to leave

98 *The verbs-as-nouns framework in Chinese*

it to grammarians to argue over the times when using only attributive-*de* leads to difficulties in distinguishing attributes from adverbials, since it is not going to be an issue for the average person in writing.[7]

Sections 3 and 4 of Chapter 1 in Volume II will start with this skewed distribution in their discussion of the relation between attributes and adverbials.

Type III

The negation of nouns uses *méi*; usually, *bù* is not used with nouns. The negation of verbs uses *bù* and *méi*. In classical Chinese, *wú* is used to negate nouns, while *wèi* is usually not used with them. Verb negation uses both *wèi* and *wú*.

*bùchē	*méichē*	**wèichē*	*wúchē*
*bù-car	*méi*-car	**wèi*-car	*wú*-car
	'no car'		'no car'

búqù	*méiqù*	*wèihuí*	*(yǒu qù) wúhuí*
bú-go	*méi*-go	*méi*-return	(have-go) *wú*-return
'not going'	'did not go'	'still not returned'	'(have gone) no return'

In other words, *méi* and *wú* are capable of negating both verbs and nouns. This is quite different from the one-to-one correspondence in English *not* negating verbs and *no* negating nouns. Shi Yuzhi (1992: 36) uses *bù* and *méi* to differentiate quantities involving discreteness from those involving continuity, reaching the conclusion that nouns only have discreteness, whereas verbs have both continuity and discreteness. Chapter 3 in Volume II will further explain this skewed distribution and its connection to the verbs-as-nouns framework in Chinese.

Type IV

Noun conjunction uses *hé* and usually does not use *bìng*, and verb conjunction uses either *bìng* or *hé*. In fact, *hé* is used to conjoin not only two nominal constituents but also two verbal constituents, regardless of whether they are disyllabic or monosyllabic. Examples are as follows:

Wǒmen	*yào*	*jìchéng*	*hé*	*fāyáng*	*gémìng*
we	must	inherit	and	carry-forward	revolution

de	*yōuliáng*	*chuántǒng.*
MM	honorable	tradition

'We must inherit and carry forward the honorable traditions of the revolution.'

Zhōngyāng	*de*	*yǒuguān*	*wénjiàn,*	*wǒmen*	*zhèngzài*
Central-government	MM	relevant	document	we	are-doing

The verbs-as-nouns framework in Chinese 99

| *rènzhēn* | *de* | <u>*xuéxí*</u> | *hé* | <u>*tǎolùn.*</u> |
| conscientiously | ADV-de | study | and | discuss |

'We are studying and discussing conscientiously the central government's relevant documents.'

| *Duōyú* | *de* | *fángzi* | *zhǐ* | *néng* | <u>*mài*</u> | *hé* | <u>*chūzū.*</u> |
| surplus | MM | house | only | can | sell | and | rent |

'The surplus houses can only be sold and rented.'

| *Lǎoshī* | *jiǎng* | *de* | *nǐ* | *yào* | *rènzhēn* | *de* | <u>*tīng*</u> | *hé* | <u>*jì.*</u> |
| teacher | say | MM | you | must | carefully | ADV-*de* | listen | and | take-notes |

'You must carefully listen to and take notes on what your teacher says.'

There are those who assert that *yǔ* in the classical Chinese conjoins nominal constituents and *ér* verbal constituents. For them, this is evidence for the distinction between nouns and verbs. This is incorrect; the fact is that *ér* generally conjoins verbal constituents,[8] while *yǔ* conjoins both nominal and verbal constituents. *Yǔ* as a conjunction for verbal constituents is a common usage as shown in the following examples:

| *Zhī* | *kěyǐ* | *zhàn* | <u>*yǔ*</u> | *bùkěyǐ* | *zhàn* | *zhě,* | *shēng.* |
| know | can | fight | and | cannot | fight | people | win |

'He who knows when he can fight and when he cannot will be victorious' (Chapter 3 Offensive strategy, in *The Art of War*).

| *Sānshí* | *nián* | *chūn,* | *Jìn* | *rén* | *qīn* | *Zhèng,* | *yǐ* |
| 30th | year | spring | Jin | people | invade | Zheng | to |

| *guān* | *qí* | *kě* | *gōng* | <u>*yǔ*</u> | *fǒu.* |
| see | it | can | attack | and | not |

'In the spring of the 30th year, an officer from Jin made an incursion into Zheng, to see whether it could be attacked or not' (The 30th year of Duke Xi, in *Zuo Tradition*).

| *Xià* | *dì* | *bǔ* | *shā* | *zhī* | <u>*yǔ*</u> | *qù* | *zhī* |
| Xia | emperor | cast-oracles | kill | them | and | expel | them |

| <u>*yǔ*</u> | *zhì* | *zhī,* | *mò* | *jí.* |
| and | keep | them | none | auspicious |

'The Emperor of Xia cast oracles on whether to kill them, to expel them, or to keep them. None of the results were auspicious' (The Basic Annals of Zhou, in *Historical Records*).

The same is true of *hé* in modern Chinese. (Cited in Cui Shanjia 2013: 346–369)

| *Yě* | *cǎo* | *fán* | *bùfán,* | *yì* | *yīng* | *shēng* | <u>*hé*</u> | *chū.* |
| wild | grass | ordinary | extraordinary | also | should | sprout | and | grow |

'No matter whether wild grasses are ordinary or extraordinary, they should also sprout and grow' (From *Ode to Wide Grasses*, written by Su Zheng in Tang Dynasty).

100   *The verbs-as-nouns framework in Chinese*

Jiāo	*shēng*	*chóng*	*wèn,*	*wǒ*	*ér*	*bié*
soothing	voice	repeatedly	ask	my	son	separation

hòu	*cún*	*hé*	*wáng.*
since	alive	and	dead

'She repeatedly asked in a soothing voice, "Is my son alive or dead since our last separation?"' (From No. 11, *All Keys and Modes by Liu Zhiyuan*)

Yī	*zhī*	*shǒu*	*jiūzhù*	*zhè*	*sīpō*	*máoyī,*
one	CL	hand	grab	this	guy	furry-clothes

shǐ	*quánchuí*	*hé*	*jiǎotī.*
use	punch	and	kick

'One hand grabbed this guy by the furry clothes as he was punched and kicked' (From *Pottery Ghost*, author unknown, written in Yuan Dynasty).

Jiālǐ	*zhuāngtián*	*suī*	*bù*	*duō,*	*jiǎnshěng*	*zhe*	*chī*	*hé*
home	farmland	though	not	much	frugally	DUR	eat	and

chuān,	*kě*	*dào*	*yě*	*gòu*	*ǎn*	*guò.*
dress	but	come	also	enough	I	live

'Though my family does not have much farmland, by eating and dressing frugally, it comes to enough for me to live on' (From Chapter 9 of *The Rich and Noble Immortals*).

Hún	*hé*	*mèng,*	*sī*	*hé*	*xiǎng,*	*dōu*	*zuò*	*le*
soul	and	dream	think	and	imagine	all	make	PSP

qì	*fēng*	*āi*	*yuán.*
weep	phoenix	mourn	ape

'The soul and the dream, the thinking and the imagining, all made a weeping phoenix and a mourning ape' (From *The Jade Hairpin* by Gao Lian, Ming Dynasty). (This example of juxtaposing noun conjunction with verb conjunction further clarifies the question at hand.)

Some argue that English's juxtaposing of nouns using *and* along with its juxtaposing of verbs with *and* shows that it is not sensitive to the distinction between nouns and verbs, whereas Chinese, to the contrary, is.

This is not correct. The primary difference between English and Chinese is that English nouns and verbs cannot be coordinated in one and the same phrase while Chinese grammar permits this. For example, *zuì yǔ fá* (a noun and a verb) [the Chinese translation of *Crime and Punishment*] cannot be rendered into English literally as "crime and punish" but rather must be given as "crime and punishment". The phrase *àomàn yǔ piānjiàn* (an adjective and a verb) [the Chinese translation of *Pride and Prejudice*] cannot be expressed in English literally as "proud and prejudice" but must be translated as 'pride and prejudice'. (See Chapter 2, Section 3.2.)

Type V

In questions, the substitution for nominal constituents is *shénme* 'what' and usually not *zěnmeyàng* 'how about'. The substitution for predicative constituents is either *zěnmeyàng* 'how about' or *shénme* 'what'. *Zěnmeyàng* 'how about' can only substitute for predicative constituents. *Shénme* 'what' can substitute for nominal constituents as well as predicative constituents. The following examples are from Zhu Dexi (1961, 2010: 97):

Substituting nominal components	*Substituting predicative components*
Kàn shénme? watch what *Kàn diànyǐng.* watch movie '—What are you watching? —A movie'.	*Kàn shénme?* watch what *Kàn xiàqí.* watch play-chess '—What are you watching? —A chess game'.
Pà shénme? afraid what *Pà shāyú.* afraid shark '—What are you afraid of? —Sharks'.	*Pà shénme?* afraid what *Pà lěng.* afraid cold '—What are you afraid of? —The cold'.
Kǎolǜ shénme? think-about what *Kǎolǜ wèntí.* think-about problem '—What are you thinking about? —A problem'.	*Kǎolǜ shénme?* think-about what *Kǎolǜ zěnmeyàng bǎ gōngzuò zuòhǎo.* think-about how get job done '—What are you thinking about? —How to get the job done'.
Pútáo, píngguǒ, lí, grape apple pear *shénme dōu yǒu.* what all have 'Grapes, apples, pears, everything is there'.	*Chànggē, tiàowǔ, yǎnxì* sing dance play-act *shénme dōu huì.* what all capable 'Singing, dancing, acting, s/he can do everything'.

The five types of skewed distribution mentioned above can be summarized as follows:

Figure 3.1 The skewed distribution between nouns and verbs

102 *The verbs-as-nouns framework in Chinese*

Nouns correspond to slot A, but verbs correspond to slot B and slot A. The verb forms are the same whether they occur in slot A or slot B. There is no need for the nominalization of verbs, because they possess the same grammatical properties that nouns have. The reverse is not the case. This is the defining feature of the verbs-as-nouns framework in Chinese.

This series of skewed distributions tells us that for Chinese when we test a lexical item to determine whether it is a noun or a verb using methods concerning whether it can function as a subject or an object, or as an attribute or an adverbial, or be negated by *bù* or *méi*, or enter into coordinate structures marked by *hé* or *bìng*, or replace *shénme* 'what' or *zěnmeyàng* 'how about' in answer to a question, we are only able to confirm that that lexical item does not possess verbal properties. However, we cannot confirm that it does not possess nominal properties.

Content words in Chinese naturally possess nominal properties. Thus, it is not difficult to understand why Lü Shuxiang (1942/1982: 234) said that Chinese nouns cannot be negated, that is to say that there are no negative words in Chinese that exclusively negate nouns.[9] Nor is it difficult to understand the statement by Zhu Dexi et al. (1961) and Zhu Dexi (1985: 16). There is no way for us to identify a grammatical feature that only nouns have. This is because the so-called grammatical features of nouns are all shared by verbs. In fact, the grammatical features of nouns are discussed apophatically: Unlike verbs, nouns do not in general function as predicates. (See Chapter 2, Section 1.)

3.3 Two types of markedness: "unmarked" and "still-not-marked"

If categories A and B are not in an equivalency relationship, there are only two kinds of relationships possible between them. One is an exclusionary relationship expressible as if not this then that. This can be called an A-B opposition or an A-B separation. The other kind is an inclusive non-exclusionary relationship. This is called an A-B interdependent relationship or A-B in an inclusion relation. The former exclusionary relationship is like the one between the two categories *male* and *female*. If one is *male* one is not *female*; if one is *female* one is not *male*. The latter relationship is like the one between the categories *man* and *woman*. Members of the category *man* do not all belong to the category *woman*. But all members of the category *woman* belong to *man*. *Man* as a category includes *woman*. It is necessary to get rid of the prejudice discussed earlier. It is important not to think that there is only one kind of situation, one in which A and B are distinct. Note that A-B in an interdependent relationship and A-B in an inclusion relationship are two ways of referring to the same relation. "Interdependency" emphasizes not all members of A belong to B. "Inclusion" emphasizes that all members of B belong to A. Because the intent here is to emphasize the latter, this book will usually refer to the relation as the inclusion of B in A.

Because the idea of nouns and verbs as distinct is deeply rooted, many people want to restore the inclusion of verbs in nouns to an original separation of nouns from verbs. They propose within the verbs-as-nouns framework that the class of

The verbs-as-nouns framework in Chinese   103

nouns can be divided into two. One is "noun₁", a class in opposition to verbs. The other is "noun₂", a class equivalent to "content words". Thus, the relations between noun₁ and verbs are still those of separation. The implied meaning is that it is unnecessary to propose the inclusion of verbs in the noun category because it can be ultimately reduced to the noun-verb distinction.

From the perspective of markedness theory, the restoration discussed earlier is unreasonable and unworkable. Jakobson (1932, 1939) extended the theory of markedness, which originated in phonology (Trubetzkoy 1939), to morphology. In phonology, marked item and unmarked item constitute a relation of opposition, i.e. the marked item has a plus value for a feature F, whereas the unmarked item lacks the feature F. For example, /b/ has the feature [voiced] whereas /p/ lacks it. The two phonemes mutually exclude each other.

However, Jakobson found that there are two types of relations between marked items and unmarked items in morphology. One is the type of relation seen with the *male-female* opposition. Like that for /b/ and /p/, *male* lacks the feature F [feminine], whereas *female* has the feature F [feminine]. The other type is seen in the type of inclusion relation between *man* and *woman*, where the marked item *woman* has a plus value for the feature F [feminine], whereas the unmarked item *man* has been assigned neither the plus value nor the minus value for that feature.[10]

"A and B as separate" and "the inclusion of B in A" are two different markedness types that need to be distinguished from each other. A lot of people confuse the two types. For example, in discussing the pair of categories *male* and *female*, they say that *male* is unmarked and *female* is marked. Then, regarding the pair *man* and *woman*, they hold that *man* is unmarked while *woman* is marked. Apart from that, they adopt the same notation for the feature, using [– F] for unmarked items and [+ F] for marked items. This results in both *male* and *man* being marked as [– feminine]. As a result, they exacerbate the blurring together of two types of markedness.

In fact, the [– feminine] in the oppositional pattern for the unmarked term *male* expresses that that term definitely does not have the feature [feminine]. In contrast, the [– feminine] in the inclusion pattern involving the unmarked term *man* expresses that it is still uncertain whether the term is marked for the feature [feminine]. The word "unmarked" in English fails to capture this kind of difference. This often leads to a sense of helplessness when describing linguistic facts, because they do have this kind of difference.

Chinese makes a distinction between the negative adverbs *wèi* 'still-not' and *wú* 'have-not'. The unmarked (*wú*) item in the inclusion pattern should be re-analyzed as a still-not-marked (*wèi*) item using the notation [~ F] to differentiate it from [– F]. In this approach, *man* is marked [~ feminine]. Correspondingly, for marked items two kinds of situations need to be distinguished. Although both use the term "marked", for the "marked" of the oppositional pattern, it is the marking for what exists or is already realized. In contrast, for the "marked" of the inclusion pattern, marked is for a feature that comes out of nothing or one that arises out of nothing. Granted, by distinguishing "unmarked" from "still-not-marked", the two situations concerning "marked" are also distinguished, making it unnecessary to introduce names to differentiate them.

If corresponding relations between categories and features are used to express the differences between the "oppositional pattern" and the "inclusion pattern", the oppositional pattern corresponds to the one-to-one correspondence and the inclusion pattern to the skewed correspondence. The differences can be diagrammed as follows:

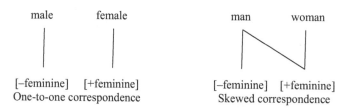

Figure 3.2 One-to-one correspondence vs. skewed correspondence

The "A-B opposition" is a type of marking involving a one-to-one correspondence. *Male* corresponds to the feature [– feminine] and *female* to [+ feminine] in the figure on the left. The "inclusion of B in A" is a type of marking involving a skewed correspondence. *Woman* corresponds to the feature [+ feminine] and *man* to both [– feminine] and [+ feminine] in the figure to the right.

If the relation in the pattern of "the inclusion of B in A" is explained by using the "A-B opposition", the explanation will be long-winded and still remains unclear. For example, if the oppositional pattern were adopted, it would be necessary to say that *man* represented two categories and could be divided into two homonyms, man_1 and man_2. Man_1 would represent male, and man_2, human beings. The one that would form the oppositional relation with *woman* would be man_1 and not man_2.

However, Kempson (1980) has long argued that the practice of splitting *man* into two homonyms is not workable. Using the word pair *dog-bitch* as an example, she argues that if *dog* is divided like *man* into dog_1 (male dog as opposed to female dog) and dog_2 (dog in its general sense), there should only be two readings for each sentence containing the homonym *dog*. The sentence "*He saw a dog*" can be read as "He saw one dog" or as "He saw one male dog". But in fact the sentence could be read in a third way: "He saw one dog and the dog is a male one". The following two sentences can illustrate the difference between the third and second readings:

He saw a dog, not a bitch.
He saw a dog, not a cat and not a bitch.

Moreover, regardless of what kind of method is adopted for dividing a sentence type, there is no way to eliminate the third reading. Following from this, Kempson

The verbs-as-nouns framework in Chinese   105

argues that it is only possible to regard *dog* as a single word (a polysemous word) and that it is not possible to divide it into two words (homonyms).

With the third reading, the utterance "*he saw a bitch*" can be used to answer the question "*did he see a dog or a cat?*", since a *bitch* must be a *dog*. She treats the phenomenon of polysemy as semantic indeterminacy, which is different from ambiguity, generality, or vagueness. Zhu Dexi (1980) discovered long ago that this kind of semantic indeterminacy cannot be distinguished using methods concerned with differentiating sentence types. Shen Jiaxuan (1991) further explored this issue and demonstrated that the linguistic phenomenon of indeterminacy is universal in human languages.

To summarize, the use of the inclusion pattern can already handle the relationship between the paired categories *man-woman* or *dog-bitch*. Moreover, an approach that strives to return the inclusion pattern to an oppositional one would double the effort for half the result. It would involve splitting off a category while still not being able to clarify anything.

This principle is extremely important when extended to the relationship between nouns and verbs. It would be difficult to interpret [verbless] sentences like *jīntiān yǐjīng xīngqīwǔ* 'today is already Friday' (literally, 'today already Friday') and *zhè gè rén jiǎnzhí piànzi ma* 'this person is simply a liar' (literally, 'this person simply a liar'), if nouns in the inclusion pattern were divided into two categories, noun$_1$ and noun$_2$. This is because *xīngqīwǔ* 'Friday' and *piànzi* 'liar' would be examples of both noun$_1$ and noun$_2$. As examples of noun$_2$, the possibility cannot be excluded that they function as predicates and are modified by adverbs. As examples of noun$_1$, they are not verbs, which is the word class that usually functions as predicates. This kind of an oppositional division has difficulty explaining the fact that verbs can be modified by adverbs while serving as the heads of noun phrases as in the following:

Tā	*de*	*bú*	*qù*
He	MM	not	go
'His not going'			

Zhè	*běn*	*shū*	*de*	*yǐjīng*	*chūbǎn*
This	CL	book	*de*	already	publish
'The fact of this book's already having been published'					

A move like revising the "Head Extension Principle" or one that posits another *de* would have problems that would be hard to resolve. (This is already discussed in Section 3 of the previous chapter.)

In contrast, the verbs-as-nouns framework can already explain the relation in Chinese between nouns and verbs as well. Moreover, to reduce this relation to an opposition between nouns and verbs would be redundant and would lose more than what is gained.[11]

Looked at from the perspective of the evolution of word classes, verbs split from nouns. If one is to talk "restoring" or "returning", the oppositional pattern should

106 *The verbs-as-nouns framework in Chinese*

be restored to the inclusion pattern and not the opposite. See Section 5 of Chapter 2 in Volume II for details.

We will now define the features for nouns and verbs in the verbs-as-nouns framework as follows:

Nouns: [+ referential], [~ predicative]
Verbs: [+ referential], [+ predicative]

Those words included as nouns other than verbs: [+ referential], [– predicative]

With respect to nouns, that is "all nouns", their feature is [+ referential], the possession of referentiality. What has not been determined from them is whether they have a predicative function, hence [~ predicative]. Typical of their distribution is that they can serve as subjects and objects, can at least be modified by *yīgè* 'one-entity' or *yīzhǒng* 'one-kind',[12] can be negated using *méi* 'not' or *méiyǒu* 'not-have', can be replaced by *shénme* 'what', can undergo modification with adjectives and nouns, and can be conjoined using *hé* 'and'. These are the defining features of nouns.

With respect to "verbs" (which are "dynamic nouns"), their features not only include [+ referential] for referentiality but also [+ predicative] for predicativity. Apart from the distribution properties of nouns, they can freely serve as predicates, can be negated using *bù* 'not', can be replaced using *zěnmeyàng* 'how about', can be modified by adverbs, and can be coordinated using *bìng* 'and'.[13]

Among nouns, those words other than verbs, that is to say "static nouns" (traditionally referred to as nouns) cannot be defined positively. They can only be defined negatively based on "all nouns" and "verbs" as not possessing predicativity [– predicative]. They cannot freely function as predicates.

It should be noted that the definition of "dynamic nouns" and "static nouns" and the relations between them in the inclusion framework is different from the definition of verbs and nouns and their relations to each other in the oppositional framework. In the inclusion framework, "dynamic nouns" are defined as [+ referential] [+ predicative], and "static nouns" are defined as [+ referential] [– predicative]. Although they are in opposition with respect to the feature [predicative], they are the same in terms of [referential]. In the oppositional framework, verbs are defined as [– referential], [+ predicative] and nouns are defined as [+ referential], [– predicative]. They are in opposition to each other with respect to the features [predicative] and [referential].

Some think that all that is necessary is for the words among nouns other than verbs (dynamic nouns) to be called "left-over nouns" in the inclusion framework for the relationship between "left-over nouns" and "verbs" to be the same as the relationship between "nouns" and "verbs" in the traditional oppositional framework. Such thinking betrays a misunderstanding. The difference between the two frameworks is not a question of names or terminology but rather one involving substance.

The definitions of "referentiality" and "predication" will be discussed in Section 1 of Chapter 4. A word class for "content words" that encompasses nouns and verbs is devoid of content in a framework that distinguishes nouns from verbs. In contrast, in the verbs-as-nouns framework, content words are nouns and they are words which refer to things, actions, and attributes. Only by having the feature [+ referentiality] does the "content word" have real properties. If content words are empty, the distinction between function words and content words will be practically pointless (Lü 1979: 35). However, Chinese language traditions have put an enormous amount of emphasis on this distinction (notwithstanding that there were different ways to differentiate them). This shows that "content words" cannot be empty, that they must be "full". The content is the content in their referentiality.

Having established the verbs-as-nouns framework, we will nevertheless use the pair "noun" and "verb" in writing to avoid prolixity and new terminology that adds to the readers' burden (Lü 1979: 10). For example, in saying that the "verbs" *zhà* 'explode' and *sǐ* 'die' have predicative functions that "nouns" lack, it is not implied that they are only verbs ('explode' and 'die', respectively) and not also nouns ('explosion' and 'death', respectively). For the most part, misunderstandings will not arise in context.[14]

There is a new development in "markedness theory", the "theory of markedness reversal". This and the verbs-as-nouns theory mutually support each other. This will be discussed in Chapter 5 of Volume II.

3.4 From the minor sentence theory to the verbs-as-nouns theory

The verbs-as-nouns framework can be derived from Yuen Ren Chao's "minor sentence" theory. The minor sentence theory (Chao 1968: 57–83) is captured in three sentences: 1) Full sentences can be composed of minor sentences; 2) minor sentences can be the basis for a sentence; 3) minor sentences can be free standing. Before moving on to the verbs-as-nouns framework, this theory will be introduced in the following paragraph.

The definition of a Chinese sentence is "a segment of speech bounded at both ends by pauses" (Chao 1968: 57). Chinese sentences thus defined may be structurally classified into *full* and *minor* sentences. A full sentence consists of two parts, a subject and a predicate, whereas a minor sentence does not have the subject-predicate form. The subject and predicate of a full sentence are "separated from each other by a pause, a potential pause, or one of the four pause particles: *A (~ia)*, *ne*, *me*, and *ba*". These are the "formal features" of a full sentence (1968: 67). In light of the formal features of a full sentence, we arrive at "the surprising, and yet obvious, conclusion that a full sentence is a complex sentence consisting of two minor ones" (1968: 83). This is because *a, ne, me,* and *ba* occur both as interrogative particles at the end of questions and as pause particles after a subject. Consider the following examples:

Zhè	*gè*	*rén*	<u>*a,*</u>	*yīdìng*	*shì*	*gè*	*hǎo*	*rén.*
this	CL	person	MP	must	be	CL	good	person

'This man (as for), must be a good man.'

108 *The verbs-as-nouns framework in Chinese*

Cf.:

Tā	*shì*	*năr*	*de*	*rén*	*a?*
he	Be	where	ATT-de	person	MP

'Where is he from?'

Tā	*zìjǐ*	*de*	*xiǎoháir*	*na,*	*yě*	*bú*	*dà*	*tīng*	*tāde*	*huà.*
he	self	MM	child	MP	also	not	much	listen	his	words

'His own children (if it is a question of), do not listen to him much, either.'

Cf.:

Xiǎoháir	*dōu*	*shàng*	*năr*	*qù*	*le*	*na?*
child	all	go	where	DIR	PSP	MP

'Where have all the children gone?'

Tā	*cízhí*	*de*	*yìsi*	*me [mə],*	*yǐjīng*	*dǎxiāo*	*le.*
he	resign	MM	idea	MP	already	cancel	PSP

'His idea of resigning (as for), has already been canceled.'

Cf.:

Nǐ	*zhīdào*	*tā*	*yào*	*cízhí*	*le*	*ma?*
you	know	he	is going to	resign	PSP	MP

'Do you know that he is going to resign?'

Zhàngfū	*ba,*	*zhǎo*	*bù*	*zhǎo*	*shìr;*	*háizimen*
husband	MP	find	not	DUR	job	children

ba,	*yòu*	*bùkěn*	*niànshū.*
MP	either	won't	study

'The husband (if you consider him), can't find a job; the children (if you consider them), won't study, either.'

Cf.:

Wǒmen	*wènwèn*	*tāde*	*zhàngfū*	*ba?*
we	ask	her	husband	MP

'Shall we ask her husband?'

"The close parallel between the pause particles and the interrogative particles is no mere accident, but derives from the nature of the subject as a question and the predicate as an answer" (1968: 82). We have the following degrees of integration between questions and answers: 1) 2-person conversation, 2) posing and then answering one's own question, and 3) combining a question and answer into a full sentence with no intervening pause between the two. The following are examples of these phenomena:

i. *Fàn a? Hái méi dé nà.* —Rice?—It's not ready yet.
    Fàn nà? Dōu chī wánle. —Rice?—It's all eaten up.

ii. *Fàn a, hái méi dé nà.* Rice, it's not ready yet.
   Fàn nà, dōu chī wánle. Rice, it's all eaten up.

iii. *Fàn hái méi dé nà.* Rice it's not ready yet.
    Fàn dōu chī wánle. Rice it's all eaten up.

With respect to full sentences, a predicate can do without a subject in forming a stand-alone sentence, and a subject can form a stand-alone sentence without a predicate. Notwithstanding that this is not acceptable from the perspective of Indo-European languages that take the verb as the nucleus of a sentence, it is a fact that Chinese is this way. That the language has this formal feature is obvious, neat, and irrefutable, and its importance is self-evident.[15]

Conversations are not limited to "questions and answers". They can include a variety of "initiations and responses". For example, your saying *wǒ bù lái* 'I won't come' can trigger my response *wǒ bú qù* 'I won't go'. From this it follows that the complex conditional sentence *nǐ bù lái, wǒ bú qù* 'if you won't come, I won't go' is a full sentence made up of two minor sentences. In addition to the possibility of following a conditional clause with the same sort of pause or pause particle discussed earlier, a *de huà* can always be added after one as in *Yàoshi bù kěn de huà, nà jiù suàn le* 'if s/he is unwilling, just forget it'.[16] This is not restricted to just conditional clauses. Concessive, cause or reason, temporal, and locative clauses can also occur as subjects as in the following examples:

Suīrán   wǒ   xiǎng   fācái ...   *Wǒ   suīrán   xiǎng   fācái ...*
although   I   want   get rich   I   though   want   get rich
'Although I wish to get rich . . .'   'Although I wish to get rich . . .'

Yīnwèi   tā   tàitài   bìng   le ...   *Tā   yīnwèi   tàitài   bìng   le ...*
because   his   wife   sick   PSP   he   because   wife   sick   PSP
'Because his wife is sick . . .'   'Because his wife is sick . . .'

In these adverbial clauses of concession and cause or reason, "the so-called subordinate conjunctions can always follow the subject and modify the verb in the clause".[17]

Consider the following examples:

Wǒ   zuór   wǎnshàng   shàngchuáng   (de shíhòu),
I   yesterday   evening   go to bed   (when)

kèrén   hái   méi   quán   zǒu.
guest   yet   not   all   leave
'(When) I went to bed last night, not all the guests had left, yet'.

Dàjiā   yònggōng   (de dìfāng),   nǐ   bùnéng   dàshēngr   shuōhuà.
everybody   work hard   (where)   you   cannot   loud   talk
'You can't talk loudly, (where) everybody is studying.'

110 *The verbs-as-nouns framework in Chinese*

Wǒ   chī   wán   le   (yǐhòu)   nǐ   chī.
I   eat   TAM   PSP   (after)   you   eat
'You'll eat, (after) I'm done eating.'

Piào   hái   méi   mǎi   (yǐqián)   nǐ   bùnéng   shàng   chuán.
ticket   yet   not   buy   (before)   you   cannot   get on   boat
'You can't go on the boat before buying a ticket.'

The *de shíhòu* 'during the period of' and *de dìfāng* 'in the place of' in the neutral tone function like conjunctions. Although clauses containing these words can be translated as adverbial clauses in a foreign language, it is best to analyze such constructions as "an ordinary substantive subject" (Chao 1968: 119).

Although subordinate clauses use utterance final *le* 'perfective marker' along with its corresponding negative words *méi* 'not-have' and *méiyǒu* 'not have' to express time, they are still nevertheless similar to conditional clauses (cf. German *wenn*). Indeed, *le* 'perfective marker' can be used in conditional clauses:

Wǒ   sǐ   le   sāngshì   cóngjiǎn.   (Time)
I   die   PSP   funeral   simple
'When I die, the funeral should be simple.'

Wǒ   sǐ   le   nǐ   dǐnghǎo   zài   jià.   (Condition)
I   die   PSP   you   had better   again   marry
'If I die, you'd better marry again.'

In summary, questions can act as subjects, and "all the concessive, causal, conditional, temporal, and spatial clauses are in the last resort subjects" (Chao 1968: 120).

Full sentences occur "only in deliberate connected discourse" (Chao 1968: 83), whereas in daily conversation minor sentences are "normal and adequate" (Chao 1968: 83). Although minor sentences are often used in two-way dialogues in other languages, in Chinese minor sentences are "more primary and relatively even still more frequent" (Chao 1959b: 2). This has resulted in the "almost unlimited variety" (Chao 1968: 83) of structural types of subjects and predicates: Apart from nominal expressions, subjects can be words or expressions about time, place, and condition, verbal expressions, prepositional phrases, and subject-predicate clauses; apart from verbal expressions (including adjectival expressions), predicates can be nominal expressions and subject-predicate clauses. It is even possible for a Chinese sentence to be made up of a verbal subject and a nominal predicate, as in:

Táo,   chántou.
escape   coward
'To escape is a coward'. (Escape? You coward!)

(Tā)   bù   sǐ   yībǎi   suì   le.
(he)   not   die   one hundred   year old   PSP
'If he had not died, he would have been one hundred years old.'

Bù   xiàyǔ   yǐjīng   sān   gè   yuè   le.[18]
not   rain   already   three   CL   month   PSP
'It has been three months since it rained.'

Zhu Dexi (1985: 64) contends that the rewrite rule S→NP + VP in generative grammar "does not work for Chinese". Yuen Ren Chao has already given the reason for why it "does not work"—minor sentences are primary and their possible forms are unlimited.

Subject-predicate structures may serve as predicates, a phenomenon Chao (1955: 39) calls the "Chinese puzzle". The solution to this puzzle is that minor sentences are primary, and hence the terms "main subject" and "the clause subject". Chao (1968: 95) states that "the main subject of a sentence may be closely or loosely related to the S in the S-P clause predicate". Following are actual examples of this loose relationship:

Diànyǐngr   wǒ   kàn   bào   le,   méi   shénme   hǎo   de.
movie   I   read   newspaper   PSP   no   what   good   MM
'(As for) movies, I have looked over the papers, there aren't any good ones.'

Wǒ   jiéhūn   de   zǒng   sòng   zhège.   (Duìyú jiéhūn de rén, wǒ zǒng
I   marry   MM   always   send   this   *sòng zhège.)*
'(As for) me, (to) those getting married (I) always give this.'

Liúxué   de   shìqíng   zhèngfǔ   zǎo   guiding   le
study abroad   MM   thing   government   long ago   set   PSP

bànfǎ   le.
procedure   PSP
'(With regard to) the matter of studying abroad, the government set the procedures long ago.'

Zhōngguóhuà   "cigarette"   zěnme   shuō?
Chinese   "cigarette"   how   say
'How do you say "cigarette" in Chinese?' [when the questioner knows how to say "cigar"]

"Cigarette"   zhōngguóhuà   zěnme   shuō?
"cigarette"   Chinese   how   say
'How do you say "cigarette" in Chinese?' [when the questioner knows how to say it in French.]

Nǐ   fúshuǐ   xuéhuì   le   méiyǒu?
you   swim   learn   PSP   not
'Have you learned how to swim (among other things)?'

Many people now accept that the subject-predicate structure can be used as a predicate in Chinese. However, these same people do not accept that "minor

112 *The verbs-as-nouns framework in Chinese*

sentences are primary", even though these two phenomena are not theoretically autonomous, because the former is derived from the latter.

Minor sentences can be used alone. "A succession of two minor sentences does not necessarily make a full sentence. They may be two separate sentences if each has a conclusive sentence intonation" (Chao 1968: 105). Consider the following examples:

Zhè	*ge*	*rén!*	*Yě*	*bù*	*gēn*	*péngyǒu*	*dǎzhāohū!*
this	CL	guy	even	not	to	friends	say hello

'What's up with this guy! Doesn't even say hello to his friends!'

Tiānqì	*hěn*	*hǎo.*	*Dànshì*	*wǒ*	*bùnéng*	*chūqù.*
weather	very	beautiful	but	I	cannot	go out

'The weather is just beautiful. But I cannot go out.'

In the second example, the *hǎo* 'good' has a full third tone and is followed by a complete stop, and there are two sentences. If the full third tone or half third tone of *hǎo* 'good' is held until the onset of the next clause, the two of them form a compound sentence. It is because Chinese primarily depends on intonation and pauses to define sentences that commas or the equivalent punctuation marks are typically used throughout a paragraph. In contrast, English uses a large number of full stops.

In summary, in determining what is a Chinese sentence, it is not important if the subject and predicate are completely expressed. Instead, the factors of prosodic elements such as pause and intonation are "the most important" (Chao 1968: 107). See also Wang Hongjun (2011).

The proposition "Minor sentences are primary in Chinese" naturally entails the proposition "Subjects are topics in Chinese". Because minor sentences are primary, the subject-predicate structures perform the same grammatical functions with other structures. They can also occur as predicates (as in *Tā ěrduǒ ruǎn* 'His ears are soft— He is gullible'). It follows that the subjects in front of this type of predicate are still subjects and there is no point in treating them as topics that are other than subjects.

According to the previous explanation, we can infer the verbs-as-nouns framework from the "minor sentence" view as follows:

- All minor sentences can be subjects or topics of full sentences;
- Both subjects and topics are referential;
- All minor sentences (including predicative ones) can be referential.

This can be illustrated by the following example:

Zhì	*de*	*hǎo*	*ma.*	*Hái*	*huózhe*	*ne.*
cure	CSC	well	MP	still	alive	MP

Jīnnián	*yībǎi*	*suì*	*le.*
this year	one hundred	year old	PSP

'Cured. Still alive. One hundred years old this year.'

The verbs-as-nouns framework in Chinese   113

This example consists of three juxtaposed sentences. Each ends with sentence-final intonation. Pauses occur before and after each of them. The first two are subjectless minor sentences. The last one is a subject-predicate sentence.

If the sentence-final intonation and utterance-final pause are removed from *Zhì dé hǎo ma* 'cured', it can be combined with *Hái huózhe ne* 'still alive' to form the full sentence *Zhì dé hǎo ma hái huózhe ne* 'cured, still alive'. In this sentence, *Zhì dé hǎo* is the topic, *ma* is a topic marker, *hái huózhe* is the predicate, and *ne* draws the listener's attention to the fact "still alive'.

If the sentence-final intonation and utterance-final pause are removed from *Hái huózhe ne* 'still alive', it can be combined with *Jīnnián yībǎi suì le* 'this year one-hundred years old' to form the full sentence *Hái huózhe ne jīnnián yībǎi suì le* 'still alive, this year one-hundred years old'. In this sentence, *Hái huózhe* is a referential topic and *ne* a topic marker.

From this it follows that the predicate *hái huózhe* 'still alive' in the first full sentence is also referential.[19] The predicate in the first full sentence is the subject in the second full sentence, without any changes in form. In the traditional framework that distinguishes nouns from verbs, full sentences are primary and subjects are distinct from predicates. In the verbs-as-nouns framework, minor sentences are primary and subjects are not distinguished from predicates.

Note that the statement "predicates are referential" does not mean that only some predicates are referential. Rather, it affirms that all predicates are referential. This is the original meaning of the verbs-as-nouns theory. The referring expressions in the predicate position are typically predicative, but the predicate position does not exclude referring expressions that lack predicative functions. For this reason, nominal expressions can also function as predicates (See Chapter 6, Section 1.)[20] The verbs-as-nouns theory also helps to explain why flowing sentences abound in Chinese. Flowing sentences are in fact a series of juxtaposed referential minor sentences linked one after the other in spite of appearing to be separate from each other. See Section 3.3 of Chapter 6 for details.

3.5   Reduplication and the "super-noun"

The current system of word classes for Chinese first distinguishes nouns, verbs, and adjectives. Then it divides adjectives into two smaller classes, qualitative adjectives and stative adjectives, with most of the latter being reduplications of the former (Zhu 1956). However, an important fact of Chinese is that nouns, verbs, and adjectives, regardless of whether they are monosyllabic or disyllabic, can be changed into depictive expressions after undergoing reduplication. This kind of reduplication breaks down the boundaries between words and phrases. It also shows that the boundaries between words and phrases and between morphology and syntax are not that important in Chinese (Shi 2011). The following Putonghua examples are mainly quoted from Hua Yuming (2008):

114   *The verbs-as-nouns framework in Chinese*

The reduplication of nouns and noun phrases:

céng	Céngcéng	de	yèzi	zhōngjiān	diǎnzhuì	zhe
layer	Layers	and	leaf	middle	adorn	DUR

	xiē	bái	huā.
	Some	white	flower

'White flowers adorn the layers of leaves'.

sī	Hé	miàn	shàng	piāofú	zhe	sīsī	xiá	guāng.
ray	river	surface	upon	float	DUR	rays	sunset-glow	light

'Rays of light from the setting sun float upon the surface of the river.'

hǔ	Yǎnjīng	dèng	de	hǔhǔ	de.
tiger	eyes	bulge	CSC	tiger-like	MNN

'(His/Her) eyes bulged tiger-like.'

nián	Niánnián	jiǎng,	yuèyuè	jiǎng,	rìrì	jiǎng.
year	every-year	state	every-month	state	every-day	state

'It should be stated every year, every month, and every day.'

shānshuǐ	Shānshān	shuǐshuǐ	de	huà	gè	bùtíng.
mountain-river	mountains	rivers	MNN	paint	CL	non-stop

'(S/he) keeps on painting mountains and rivers.'

xìngtóu	Xìngxìngtóutóu	gǎn	huí	jiā	lái.
high spirits	high spirits	hurry	return	home	DIR

'(S/he) hurried home in high spirits.'

yāojing	Dǎbàn	de	yāoyāojingjīng	de.
goblin	dress up	CSC	goblin	MNN

'(She) dressed up like a goblin.'

wǔmiǎo	Miǎo	zhēn	tiào	zhe	wǔmiǎo	wǔmiǎo	de	zǒu.
five-second	second	hand	skip	DUR	five-second	five-second	MNN	walk

'The second hand skips forward five seconds at a time.'

dàbǎ	Chāopiào	dàbǎ	dàbǎ	de	wǎng	dài	lǐ	rēng.
good-handful	cash	good-handful	good-handful	MNN	to	bag	in	throw

'Heaping handfuls of cash were thrown into the bag.'

yībǎnshū	yībǎnshū	yībǎnshū	de	dú	xiàqù.
one-CL-book	one-CL-book	one-CL-book	MNN	read	DIR

'Keep reading one book after another.'

The reduplication of verbs and verbal phrases:

piāo	Piāopiāo	bái	xuě	fēiyáng	zài	kōng	zhōng.
flutter	fluttering	white	snow	fly	be-in	sky	middle

'Fluttering white snow fills the air.'

The verbs-as-nouns framework in Chinese 115

fēi	*Tā zài*	*huìchǎng*		*zhōng jìnjìnchūchū,*	*máng*	*de*	*fēifēi.*	
fly	he be-in	conference-hall		middle go-in-go-out	busily	CSC	fly	

'He kept going in and out of the conference hall, busily bouncing from one place to another.'

tiào	*Diànhuà*	*língshēng*	*jiānruì*	*de*		*jiào*	*le*	*qǐlái,*
jump	phone	ring	piercing	MNN		ring	PSP	DIR

	tóu	*yòu*	*kāishǐ*	*tiàotiào*	*de*	*tòng.*
	head	again	start	throbbing	MNN	ache

'The phone let out a piercing ring and s/he started to have a throbbing headache'.

dǒu	*Mǔqīn*	*chīlì*	*de*	*táiqǐ*	*shǒubì*	*dǒudǒu*	*de*	*zhǐ*
tremble	mother	struggle	MNN	raise	arm	tremble	MNN	point

	zhe	*qiáng*	*shàng*	*guà*	*de*	*gān*	*liáng*	*kuāng.*
	DUR	wall	on	hang	MM	dry	grain	basket

'After struggling to raise her arm, the mother's hand trembled as it pointed to the dry grain basket hanging on the wall'.

yáobǎi	*Huār*	*zài*	*fēng*	*zhōng*	*xiào*	*de*	*yáoyáobǎibǎi.*
sway	flower	be-in	wind	middle	laugh	CSC	sway

'The flowers swayed laughingly in the wind'.

zhǐdiǎn	*Tāmen*	*zhǐzhǐdiǎndiǎn*	*de*	*yìlùn*	*qǐlái.*
point-finger	they	point-finger	MNN	comment	DIR

'They began commenting, as they pointed the finger at someone.'

kūzhe	*Kū*	*zhe*	*kū*	*zhe*	*jiù*	*kēshuì*	*le.*
cry-DUR	cry	DUR	cry	DUR	then	fall-asleep	PSP

'(S/he) cried and cried and then fell asleep.'

yīchàn	*Chē*	*shēn*	*diān*	*de*	*yīchàn*	*yīchàn*	*de.*
shake	car	body	jolt	CSC	shake	shake	MNN

'The car shook as it jolted forward.'

The reduplication of adjectives and adjectival phrases:

bái	*Bǎ*	*liǎn*	*mǒ*	*de*	*báibái*	*de.*
white	get	face	paint	CSC	white	MNN

'Paint your face fairly white.'

màn	*Mànman*	*de*	*zǒu.*
slow	slow	MNN	walk

'Walk slowly.'

116 The verbs-as-nouns framework in Chinese

suíbiàn	*Suísuíbiànbiàn*	*shuō*	*le*	*jǐ*	*jù.*
casual	casually	say	PSP	several	sentence

'(S/he) made a few casual remarks.'

dàfāng	*Yīfú*	*yào*	*chuān*	*de*	*dàdàfāngfāng*	*de.*
generous	clothes	should	wear	CSC	tasteful	MNN

'Clothes should be worn tastefully.'

hěntàng	*Hěntàng*	*hěntàng*	*de*	*zuò*	*le*	*wǎn*	*jiāng*	*tāng.*
very-hot	very-hot	very-hot	MNN	make	PSP	CL	ginger	soup

'The freshly made ginger soup was piping hot.'

hěnxiǎoxīn	*Hěnxiǎoxīn*	*hěnxiǎoxīn*	*dì*	*jǐ*	*chū*	*yīdiǎn*	*jiāoshuǐ.*
very-careful	very-careful	very-careful	MNN	squeeze	out	a bit	glue

'A little bit of glue was squeezed out very carefully.'

Adding an XX reduplication to monosyllabic nouns, verbs, or adjectives forms stative adjectives.

Monosyllabic nouns + XX

yè chénchén	'deep in the night'
yǎn sōngsōng	'drowsy-eyed'
qíng qièqiè	'full of affection'
yuè méngméng	'as dim as moonlight'
xuè bānbān	'bloodstained'
xīn dàngdàng	'(state of mind) feel distracted'
lù tiáotiáo	'faraway'

Monosyllabic verbs + XX

tàn liánlián	'to sigh over and over again'
sòu shēngshēng	'persistent coughs'
dī liūliū	'rolling round and round'
hū xiàoxiào	'with a whistling sound'
sǐ hǔhǔ	'grim, ferocious, and in a tigerish mood'
xiào mīmī	'smiling'
mà bu liēliē	'foul-mouthed'

Monosyllabic adjectives + XX

báo xiāoxiāo	'as flimsy as raw silk'
lěng bīngbīng	'ice-cold'
qīng yōuyōu	'leisurely'
jìng qiāoqiāo	'very quiet'
ruǎn miánmián	'very soft'
hóng tōngtōng	'bright red'
chòu hōnghōng	'stinking'

The verbs-as-nouns framework in Chinese   117

Even the reduplicated X can be a noun, verb, or adjective:

X as nouns

lěng bīngbīng	'ice-cold'
tián mìmì	'sweet like honey'
hēi qīqī	'black like lacquer; pitch-black'
bái xuěxuě	'snow-white'

X as verbs

yuán gǔngǔn	'very round (to the extent that it rolls)'
xiāng pēnpēn	'aromatic (to the extent that the fragrance fills nostrils)'
dòng piāopiāo	'fluttering (moving as if it is floating)'
zhí tǐngtǐng	'bolt upright (when straightening one's back)'

X as adjectives

hóng tōngtōng	'bright red'
bái mángmáng	'(of mist, snow, floodwater, etc.) a vast expanse of white'
xiào yíngyíng	'smilingly (the whole face brimming with smiles)'
bìng yānyān	'look listless and sick'

The reduplicated XX can also be placed before the head. This is quite common in Chinese dialects. For example, in the Shanghai dialect, we may find:

qīqī hēi	'black like lacquer; pitch-black'
xuěxuě bái	'snow-white'
bīngbīng lěng	'ice-cold'
bǐbǐ zhí	'straight as a ramrod'
pēnpēn xiāng	'aromatic (to the extent that the fragrance fills nostrils)'
gǔngǔn yuán	'very round (to the extent that it rolls)'
tōngtōng hóng	'bright red'

Cai Shumei and Shi Chunhong (2007) studied various forms of reduplication found in the works of Yan Lianke. They discovered that the three word classes, nouns, verbs, and adjectives, have AABB and AXX reduplicative forms that function depictively.

Reduplicative forms of nouns

lànglàngtāotāo	'great waves'
bōbōlànglàng	'waves'
shānshānhǎihǎi	'mountains and seas'
shānshānlǐnglǐng	'mountain ridges'
tìtìlèilèi	'tears and snivel'
qiāngqiāngpàopào	'guns and cannons'
chóuchóuhènhèn	'enmity and hatred'

118 *The verbs-as-nouns framework in Chinese*

wùwùshénshén	'various things'
wùwùjiànjiàn	'various things'
yuányuányóuyóu	'causes and reasons'
jiāngjiānghúhú	'rivers and lakes'
gǔgǔkāngkāng	'rice chaff'
dìngdīngshéngshéng	'nails and ropes'
wāngwāngyángyáng	'boundless seas'
xiělínlín	'dripping with blood'
shuǐzhāzhā	'watery'
yāntuántuán	'smoky'
wùnóngnóng	'densely foggy'
hànzìzì	'sweaty'

Reduplicative forms of verbs

bābāwàngwàng	'look forward to'
kūkūhuànhuàn	'cry and call'
xǐxǐzhěngzhěng	'wash and tidy up'
téngténgwùwù	'fog drifting and swirling'
jiǎnjiǎncáicái	'cut and prune'
shǎnshǎnmièmiè	'flash on and off'
chànwēiwēi	'totter'
xiàoyínyín	'smile'
dàngjījī	'stimulate'
qìfènfèn	'indignant'
chánhuāhuā	'gurgle'

Reduplicative forms of adjectives

lièlièyányán	'intense and scorching'
hónghóngpàngpàng	'reddish and plump'
mùmùránrán	'dazed'
báibáiliàngliàng	'bright white'
róuróuhéhé	'soft and gentle'
báibáimángmáng	'(of mist, snow, floodwater, etc.) a vast expanse of white'
měiměilìlì	'wonderfully beautiful'
xiānmíngmíng	'highly distinctive'
qīngchīchī	'youthful and foolish'
jǐnpiāopiāo	'tightly fluttering'
báimángmáng	'(of mist, snow, floodwater, etc.) a vast expanse of white'
hóngyànyàn	'brilliant red'

Some AB forms that participate in reduplication are words. Others seem to be temporary combinations like *shānhǎi* 'mountains and seas', *xǐzhěng* 'wash and tidy up', and *lièyán* 'intense and scorching'. There is an especially large number of nominal AB reduplicative forms.

There are also quasi-reduplicated patterns which can be structurally represented as "*yī* X *yī* Y" (one X, one Y) or "*bàn* X *bàn* Y" (half X, half Y). Nouns, verbs, and adjectives all have depictive properties when they occur in these patterns (Shao 2013: 130–552):

X and Y as nouns

yīqiányīhòu	'one after the other'
yīzǎoyīwǎn	'every morning and evening'
yīfēnyīmiǎo	'every minute and every second'
bànrénbànguǐ	'half human and half ghost'
bànzǐbànxù	'half son and half son-in-law'

X and Y as verbs

yībèngyītiào	'skip along'
yīlāyīdǎ	'pull and hit'
yīpāoyījiǎn	'toss and pick up'
bànxìnbànyí	'half believe, half doubt'
bàntuībànjiù	'yield with a show of reluctance'

X and Y as adjectives

yīlěngyīrè	'one being cold, the other being hot'
yīchángyīduǎn	'one being long, the other being short'
yīkuàiyīmàn	'one being fast, the other being slow'
bànduìbàncuò	'half right and half wrong'
bànxīnbànjiù	'half new and half old'

It is quite common in Chinese dialects for there to be conditions where a reduplicated noun, verb, or adjective describes a state. Both Shi Qisheng (1997, 2011) and Lin Huayong (2011) provide a large number of examples of reduplicated nouns (and noun phrases) and verbs (and verb phrases) from Min and Yue dialects. Moreover, both consider reduplication to be an important morphological device in Chinese, as in the following examples:

Quanzhou

Qì	*gè*	*xiǎozǐ*	*(shēnggòu)*	<u>*hóuhóu,*</u>	*mùzhū*	<u>*shǔshǔ,*</u>
that	CL	guy	(grow like)	monkey-monkey	eyeball	mouse-mouse

shǔ	*dànzǎi*	*kuǎn*	*yě*	*wú.*
be	a bit	manner	also	absent

'That guy looks like a monkey. His eyes are mousy. He has got no appropriate manners'.

Qì	*gè*	<u>*chàngxiān*</u>	<u>*chàngxiān*</u>	*gè,*	*shǔxià*	*kàn*
that	CL	cosy-immortal	cosy-immortal	MP	once	look

jiù	*wú*	*shùnyǎn.*
then	not	pleasant-to-eyes

'He acts like some rich guy's spoiled brat. It's a pain to look at him'.

120 *The verbs-as-nouns framework in Chinese*

Fā	*le*	*jǐ*	*rì*	*shāo,*	*xínglù*	*qiāo*	*fú*	*fú.*
run	PSP	several	days	fever	walk	calf	float	float

'After running a fever for a couple of days, s/he walks like s/he's floating.'

Xiamen

Jí	*gǔ*	*nóng*	*zhúgāo*	*zhúgāo.*
this	CL	person	bamboo-pole (for punting)	bamboo-pole (for punting)

'She's tall and skinny like a bamboo pole.'

Wǒ	*xīn*	*lǐ*	*shā*	*hòuhuǐ*	*hòuhuǐ.*
my	heart	in	somewhat	regret	regret

'I feel a little regret in my heart.'

Shantou

Gè	*wù*	*dì*	*zhe*	*tóujiānǎi*	*tóujiānǎi*	*lìng,*
that	person	look	DUR	shopkeeper's wife	shopkeeper's wife	MP

wèidé	*jiùshì*	*yī*	*a?*
afraid	be	her	MP

'That person acts like a shopkeeper's wife. I am afraid she is the person.'

Liǎng	*rén*	*xínggòu*	*mó*	*mó*	*lìng.*
two	person	walk	adjoin	adjoin	MP

'The two walked next to each other.'

Gǎn	*gǎn*	*xíng!*
dare	dare	walk

'Walk boldly!'

Zhangzhou

Tiān	*bǔ*	*luòyǔ*	*bǔ*	*luòyǔ.*
sky	predict	rain	predict	rain

'It's going to rain.'

Lianjiang

Mǎo	*shīkuáng!*	*Yì*	*zhī*	*yì*	*zhī*	*lái.*
don't	worry	one	CL	one	CL	come

'Don't worry. Come one by one.'

Píngguǒ	*fàng*	*zài*	*xiāngdǐ*	*xiāngdǐ*	*ne.*
apple	place	be-in	box-bottom	box-bottom	MP

'The apples are at the bottom of the box.'

Wǒ	*rújīn*	*xiǎng*	*ǒu*	*xiǎng*	*ǒu*	*dànzuòdào.*
I	now	want	vomit	want	vomit	like that

'I'm feeling a bit nauseous right now.'

Jīnǎ <u>*ài*</u>   <u>*sǐ*</u>   <u>*ài*</u>   <u>*sǐ*</u>   *dàndào*   □*[tɛ²¹]*   *wa.*
hen   is going to   die   is going to   die   like that   □[tɛ²¹]   MP
'The hen is dying.'

<u>*Dǐngshàng*</u>   <u>*dǐngshàng*</u>   *jǐ*   *rì*   *kōngqì*   *chà*   *dào*   *sǐ.*
the last   the last   several   day   air   bad   to   death
'The air quality has been very bad over the last few days.'

Tiān   *hǎosì*   <u>*xiǎng*</u>   <u>*chū*</u>   <u>*rètóu*</u>   <u>*xiǎng*</u>   <u>*chū*</u>   <u>*rètóu*</u>   *dànzuòdào.*
sky   seem   want   out   the sun   want   out   the sun   like that
'It seems that the sun is coming out of the clouds.'

Wǒ   *dàbó*   *zài*   *[nei55]*   <u>*shǐniú*</u>   <u>*shǐniú*</u>   *zài.*
my   uncle   be-in   MP[nei⁵⁵]   use-ox   use-ox   MP
'My uncle is plowing the fields there.'

In particular, Shi Qisheng (1997) offers a large number of nominal reduplication examples in Shantou dialect:

bùbù	(reduplication of cloth)	'tough, chewy, and tasteless'
zhīzhī	(reduplication of juice)	'wet'
yóuyóu	(reduplication of oil)	'oily'
shāshā	(reduplication of yarn)	'the fabric is broken into messy yarns and is not strong'
shuǐshuǐ	(reduplication of water)	'watery'
bíbí	(reduplication of nose)	'shaped like liquid from one's nose'
mǎomǎo	(reduplication of mortise)	'round and bare'
yúnyún	(reduplication of cloud)	'the eyes can't see clearly as if in the fog'
cháichái	(reduplication of firewood)	'as thick-fibered and tasteless as firewood'
tiětiě	(reduplication of iron)	'as hard as iron'
xiānxiān	(reduplication of an immortal)	'lazy and indifferent'
shūshū	(reduplication of book)	'talk and behave in a bookish manner'

The local Daye dialect in Hubei province (a Gan dialect) has a type of stative adjectives with monosyllabic suffixes, the roots of which are also nominal, verbal, and adjectival (Wang 1994).

N + X   *fēngliū* 'the way a breeze blows', *rénliú* 'the appearance of being full of vigor), *rùlǐ* 'soft and elastic'

V + X   *xǐmǐ* 'happy', *kūbiǎn* 'cry bitterly', *chǎohǒu* 'noisy everywhere'

A + X   *tiánmǐn* 'very sweet', *xiāngpēn* 'fragrant', *hēiyǒu* 'dark'

122 The verbs-as-nouns framework in Chinese

The Northern Jin dialect even has reduplication examples of genitive pronouns (Fan 2012):

Wǒ wǒ yéye kě kànhǎo wǒ li!
I I grandfather actually think highly of I MP
'My grandfather actually thinks highly of me!'

Tā tā bàba kě yǒu běnshì li!
she she father actually have ability MP
'Her father is actually very capable!'

Nǐ nǐ dàye rénjia hái shí liǎ gè zì li!
you you grandfather sb. else even know two CL character MP
'Your grandfather even knows a few Chinese characters!'

Such reduplications have an obvious emotional component, such as *wǒwǒ yéye* being equivalent to 'my (lovely) grandfather' and *wǒwǒ* being depictive.

The Fuling dialect also frequently reduplicates monosyllabic verbs into stative adjectives. According to Li (2011), there are two forms:

i.

xiēxiē de zǒu	'walk with breaks'
mǐnmǐn de chī	'eat in sips'
shuǎshuǎ de zuò	'do playfully'
xiǎngxiǎng de kū	'cry and think alternately'
āiāi de jìng (jiǔ)	'propose a toast in turn'
suànsuàn de dǎ (pái)	'play cards with mental calculations'

ii.

Dēng yīzhí shǎn le shǎn de.	'The light keeps flickering'.
Huǒ yào xī bu xī de.	'The fire is going out'.
Nà jǐ kuài zhuān yào luò bu luò de	'Those few bricks seem to fall'.

In Putonghua, the expressions *chīfàn biéqiǎngqiǎng de* 'don't fight for getting food' and *tā tiāntiān zài wǒ miànqián huànghuàng de* 'he hangs about in front of me every day' are unacceptable, whereas the expressions *qiǎng lái qiǎng qù* 'snatch and grab' and *huàng lái huàng qù* 'keep wobbling' are permitted. This shows that dialects differ simply in the way they duplicate. Furthermore, Ye Zugui (2014) provides examples supporting the stative function of reduplications of verbs in various dialects (no matter whether they are northern or southern dialects) and of duplications of nouns, verbs, and adjectives in Jia Pingwa's novels.

Considering the previous facts, we can arrive at a conclusion as follows: If such words as *sī* 'silk' and *shānshuǐ* 'mountains and rivers', *dǒu* 'shake' and *yáobǎi* 'sway', *bái* 'white', and *dàfāng* 'generous' are classed into nouns, verbs, and adjectives, respectively, then it would not make sense to treat the resulting stative adjectives through reduplication and words like *bái* 'white' and *dàfāng* 'generous' as two subclasses of the same class in a grammatical system. Conversely, if they are treated as two subclasses of the same class, then it would be unreasonable to classify the words not yet reduplicated into three separate categories. The more sensible solution in Chinese would be to rename stative adjectives to depictive words or simply to depictives[21] and to group nouns, verbs, and adjectives as super-nouns. On the first level, super-nouns must be distinguished from depictive words, and then on the second level, super-nouns can be divided into nouns, verbs, and adjectives (more precisely, qualitative adjectives). In distinguishing among nouns, verbs, and adjectives, adjectives are first distinguished from nouns and verbs in terms of depictiveness (see Section 5 of Chapter 4 in Volume II), before making a limited distinction among nouns and verbs as they are in an inclusion pattern. It is less important to distinguish among nouns, verbs, and adjectives, as well as between words and phrases, as compared to the distinction between super-nouns and depictive words. Due to this, we find no concept of 'verbs' as opposed to 'nouns' but the concepts of 'nouns' and 'reduplication' in the traditional studies of Chinese writings.[22] (See also Chapter 4, Section 3.1.) Chinese is often said to lack morphology, but in fact reduplication is its most important morphology, which is different from those of Indo-European languages.[23]

As a result of the subjectivity of depictive words or depictives, Chinese values the distinction between nouns and depictives. This is closely related to the distinction between indicative and non-indicative negation in Chinese (see Section 1.2 of Chapter 3 in Volume II).

3.6 *De₃* and EZ in Iranian languages

Not all linguists who work in generative grammar analyze the *de* in *zhè běn shū de chūbǎn* 'the publication of this book' as the head of a noun phrase or as an element inserted in the subject-predicate structure. Such an analysis requires the creation of another *de* of a different nature besides the *de₃* defined by Zhu (1961). Whenever possible, we should avoid adding entities according to the principle of simplicity, and this principle transcends different schools of linguistics. The majority of scholars working in generative grammar hold the belief that nouns, verbs, and adjectives are distinct. However, Richard Larson, the author of the Larson's Shell Hypothesis, suggests that Chinese may be similar to some Iranian languages in that nouns are essentially a super-noun category that include verbs as well as adjectives. This speculation is made by comparing Chinese *de* with its counterpart auxiliary in Iranian languages on the basis of the Case theory of generative grammar.

Larson's (2009) article is titled "Chinese as a Reverse Ezafe Language". What is Ezafe? A particle similar to Chinese *de* is known as Ezafe (EZ) in some Iranian

124   *The verbs-as-nouns framework in Chinese*

languages. EZ comes in two varieties, default and reverse, and Farsi uses the default EZ:

del-**é**	sang	
heart-**EZ**	stone	'stone heart'
otâq-**é**	besyar kucik	
room-**EZ**	very small	'very small room'

Attributes are placed after their heads in Farsi, and EZs are attached to the heads. In the two previous examples, the heads are nouns, and the attributes are a noun and an adjective respectively.

hordan-**é**	âb	
drinking-**EZ**	water	'the drinking of water'

In this example, the head *hordan* is glossed as 'drinking', and it seems impossible to tell whether it is a verbal root or a nominal one (but see the following example). The head can also be an adjective or a preposition.

negæran-**é**	bæche	
worried-**EZ**	child-PL	'worried about the children'
beyn-**é**	mæn-o to	
between-**EZ**	you and me	'between you and me'

A reverse Ezafe (REZ) behaves like Chinese *de* in that the attribute precedes its head and the EZ is attached to the attribute, as in Gilaki:

John-**é**	xowne	
John-**REZ**	house	'John's house'
zak-**ə**	negarown	
child-**REZ**	worried	'worried about the child'
istaxr-**e**	dowri	
pool-**REZ**	around	'around the pool'

The heads in these three examples are a noun, an adjective, and a preposition, respectively.

âb-**e**	xurdan	
water-**REZ**	eat	'the drinking of water'

The head in this example is *xurdan* glossed as 'eat', which is probably a verbal root (see later examples for more discussion).

surx-**ə**	gul		
red-**REZ**	flower		'red flower'
daryaa(-**e**)	kinaar-**e**	xowne	
sea(-**REZ**)	next-**REZ**	house	'house beside the sea'

The verbs-as-nouns framework in Chinese   125

These two examples use an adjective and a prepositional phrase as attributes, respectively.

What Larson adopts is still the traditional analysis of the attribute-head structure, in which EZ or REZ is analyzed as a particle between the attribute and the head. Since neither the head nor the attribute is restricted to nouns in the traditional sense, which instead include adjectives, prepositions, and even verbs, Larson categorizes the words that serve as heads and attributes as 'super-nouns' and EZ as super-'s or super-*of*. Following Li (1985), he argues that the grammatical function of super-'s or super-*of* is to help case concord by coordinating the cases of neighboring constituents, where 'case' is the special property of nominal constituents. According to Larson, existing studies show that such an analysis and characterization of EZ in Iranian languages is plausible and concise within the theoretical framework of generative grammar.

The generalizability of super-'s or super-*of* in Iranian languages is consistent with that of *de*$_3$ in Chinese. Consider the examples:

bàba de shū	'Dad's books'	*shū de fēngmiàn*	'cover of the book'
chénzhòng de shū	'heavy books'	*shū de chénzhòng*	'the heaviness of books'
diàoyè de shū	'books with dropped pages'	*shū de diàoyè*	'the page-dropping of books'
zàiguǎn de shū	'the books available in the library'	*shū de zàiguǎn*	'the book's availability in the library'

According to Zhu (1961), regardless of whether the attributes preceding *de* are nouns, adjectives, or verbs, *de* is a postpositional enclitic of a nominal grammatical unit.[24] Larson (2009) further argues that regardless of whether the attributes preceding *de* or the heads following *de* are nouns, adjectives, or verbs, *de* is the particle that makes the neighboring nominal grammatical constituents exhibit case concord. He believes that this is the true nature of the Chinese word *de* that can only be seen clearly by comparing Chinese with the Iranian languages.

In the theoretical framework of orthodox generative grammar, in order to analyze the attribute constituents as nominal ones, it is necessary to assume that the predicative *chénzhòng* 'heaviness', *diàoyè* 'page-dropping', and *zàiguǎn* 'availability in the library' have undergone relativization or that they have been changed from finite to non-finite forms; in order to analyze the heads as nominal constituents, it is necessary to assume that these same predicative constituents have undergone nominalization, because the head of a noun phrase should be nominal, which requires no argumentation, otherwise it would violate the theory of "X-bar" (i.e., the head-feature convention). In Chinese, nominalization and relativization violate the principle of simplicity, so both are unnecessary. It is now possible to eliminate both nominalization and relativization with Larson's hypothetical super-nominality.

According to Larson, the role of *de* is to be a checker or concordializer of the cases of the nominal constituents, whereas in functional linguistics, the role of *de*

126 *The verbs-as-nouns framework in Chinese*

is to use the object of reference (attribute) to increase the identifiability of a noun phrase. These two arguments differ only in terms of observation angle and theoretical starting point: The first considers the abstract function of *de*, while the second considers its specific function, leading to the same conclusion but from a different perspective. See also Wan (2015).

Larson (2009: 31) emphasizes that "we cannot figure out Chinese using only Chinese". This is a good point. It is after comparing the Chinese word *de* to the Iranian EZ that the super-nominality of Chinese is identified. We believe that the converse statement also applies to Iranian or other languages and that Iranian cannot be figured out using only Iranian, and likewise, English cannot be figured out using only English. In Iranian languages, the super-nominality identified in generative grammar explicitly includes adjectives and prepositional phrases, but not verbs, which are generally considered to lack the [+ N] feature. However, the examples mentioned earlier of Farsi and Gilaki include the verbal roots *xurdan* 'eat' and *hordan* 'drinking'. If we look at these two languages with reference to Chinese, the verbs or verbal roots therein can also be considered to be super-nominal and the so-called prepositions *beyn* 'between' and *dowri* 'around' are originally location nouns. It would be worth the time of experts in Iranian languages to study this topic in more depth. Section 4 of Chapter 6 will explain how a deeper insight into the referentiality of English predicates can be gained by examining them in light of Chinese predicates. The following section will explain how Tagalog's so-called verbs and verbal roots can actually be analyzed as nouns and nominal roots.

3.7 The Tagalog verbs

The Tagalog language of the Philippines (an Austronesian language) provides circumstantial evidence that the Chinese nouns are super-nominal that include both verbs and adjectives. Based on historical linguistics, linguistic typology, and generative grammar, Kaufman (2009) argues that Tagalog's so-called verbal predicates are actually nominal and that its subject-predicate structure consists of two noun phrases linked by an implicit copula.

In line with Indo-European verb-centered grammatical views, Tagalog grammarians believe that verbs have four types of voice morphology—namely, actor voice (AV), patient voice (PV), locative voice (LV), and conveyance voice (CV)—and that each voice selects its corresponding argument—namely, agent, patient, locative, and conveyance—to act as the subject of a clause (with the case marker *ang*). For example, all the following four sentences express the same meaning of 'The cat (agent) ate a rat (patient) on the plate (locative) for the dog (conveyance)', but the verb *k-áin* 'eat' selects different subjects with different voice morphology.

i. a. k⟨um⟩áin   nang=dagà   sa=pinggan   pára sa=áso   **ang=púsa**
⟨AV:BEG⟩eat   GEN=rat   OBL=plate   for OBL=dog   NOM=cat

  b. k⟨in⟩áin-ø   nang=púsa   **ang=dagà**   sa=pinggan   pára sa=áso
⟨BEG⟩eat-PV   GEN=cat   NOM=rat   OBL=plate   for OBL=dog

c. k⟨in⟩áin-an nang=púsa nang=dagà **ang=pinggan** pára sa=áso
   ⟨BEG⟩eat-LV GEN=cat GEN=rat NOM=plate for OBL=dog

d. i-k⟨in⟩áin nang=púsa nang=dagà sa=pinggan **ang=áso**
   CV-⟨BEG⟩eat GEN=cat GEN=rat OBL=plate NOM=dog

This voice system is characterized by the "subjects-only" restriction on the extraction of nominal constituents during question formation, topicalization, and relativization. This restriction is common to Austronesian languages that preserve this voice system, which has caused widespread concern. Consider the following examples.

ii. a. Sino ang=b⟨um⟩ili nang=téla?
       who NOM=⟨AV:BEG⟩buy GEN=cloth
       'Who bought the cloth?'
   b. *Sino ang=b⟨in⟩ili-ø ang=téla?
       who NOM=⟨BEG⟩buy-PV GEN=cloth

iii. a. Ano ang=b⟨in⟩ili-ø nang=babái?
        what NOM=⟨BEG⟩buy-PV GEN=woman
        'What did the woman buy?'
    b. *Ano ang=b⟨um⟩ili ang=babái?
        what NOM=⟨AV:BEG⟩buy NOM=woman

In ii. a., the subject selected by the actor voice is the agent and hence it can be extracted to be the sentence-initial interrogative, whereas extracting the agent from a patient voice clause, as in ii. b., is ungrammatical. Likewise in iii. a., it is legitimate to extract the patient from a patient voice clause to be the sentence-initial interrogative, but extraction of the same patient from an actor voice clause is ungrammatical, as shown in iii.b. Topicalization and relativization are also subject to the same restriction, so no further examples will be provided. The more complicated sentences in i. also fall under this restriction.

Kaufman (2009) states that to explain this phenomenon, it is only necessary to adopt a universal restriction proposed earlier by generative grammar, namely the prohibition against extracting nominal constituents from noun phrases (or determiner phrases), thus eliminating the need for other more complex explanations. This simple explanation assumes a return to the traditional analysis of Tagalog: All predications are inherently copular, all predicates are inherently nominal, and all verbal voice morphology should actually be analyzed as nominal. This type of analysis is concise and can explain both synchronic and diachronic linguistic phenomena. For example, the following four translated sentences in English (all are copular clauses with a copula connecting two NPs) are a more literal rendering of what they mean in Tagalog (*ang* is the nominative case marker and *nang* is the genitive case marker):

128   *The verbs-as-nouns framework in Chinese*

iv. a. k⟨um⟩áin   nang=dagà   **ang=púsa**
        ⟨AV:BEG⟩eat   GEN=rat   NOM=cat
        'The cat was the eater of a rat.'

   b. k⟨in⟩áin-ø   nang=púsa   **ang=dagà**
        ⟨BEG⟩eat-PV   GEN=cat   NOM=rat
        'The rat was the eaten one of the cat.'

   c. k⟨in⟩áin-an   nang=púsa   nang=dagà   **ang=pinggan**
        ⟨BEG⟩eat-LV   GEN=cat   GEN=rat   NOM=plate
        'The plate was the cat's eating place of the rat.'

   d. i-k⟨in⟩áin   nang=púsa   nang=dagà   **ang=áso**
        CV-⟨BEG⟩eat   GEN=cat   GEN=rat   NOM=dog
        'The dog was the cat's "eating benefactor" of the rat.'

Kaufman (2009) emphasizes that Tagalog sentences like these are basic rather than derived. In comparison with English, AV and PV have morphologies that are equivalent to actor-oriented -*er* and patient-oriented -*ee*, although English nouns lack corresponding morphologies for LV and CV.[25] This is precisely the nature of the voice morphology in Austronesian languages such as Tagalog.

As can easily be seen, the previous four translated sentences in English are increasingly unnatural, but they become more natural when translated into Chinese topic-comment sentences:

v. a. *Māo,   chī   hàozi   de.*   (AV)
        cat   eat   rat   MM
        'Cats eat rats'.
   b. *Hàozi,   māo   chī   de.*   (PV)
        rat   cat   eat   MM
        'Rats are for cats to eat'.
   c. *Pánzi,   māo   zài   nàr   chī   hàozi   de.*   (LV)
        plate   cat   over   there   eat   rat   MM
        'Plates are the places for cats to eat rats'.
   d. *Gǒu,   māo   tì   tā   chī   hàozi   de.*   (CV)
        dog   cat   for   it   eat   rat   MM
        'Cats eat rats for dogs'.

These four Chinese sentences all use nominal phrases ending in *de* as predicates, and the copulas are hidden, so each sentence relies on a referential predicate to comment on its topic. Interestingly, the *de* in Chinese is equivalent to the Tagalog genitive marker *nang*, whereas the noun phrase marker *de* encompasses the Tagalog voice morphology, AV, PV, LV, and CV. This is an example of how simplicity works in Chinese.

The verbs-as-nouns framework in Chinese   129

In the previous translations, the constituents introduced by *ang* are actually treated as topics. Consequently, the word order in these Tagalog sentences disrupts the common information structure of "topic first, comment second". As Lu (2014) proposes, in order to reflect the fact that the sentence-initial verbs in Tagalog are actually nominal and to maintain the topic-comment structure, these four sentences can be interpreted as follows (bracketed translations are mine):

vi. a.   In the event of eating the rat, the cat is the agent.   (The one that ate the rat is the cat.)

b.   In the event of being eaten by the cat, the rat is the patient.   (The one that was eaten by the cat is the rat.)

c.   In the event that the cat eats the rat, the place is in the plate.   (The place where the cat ate the rat is the plate.)

d.   In the event that the cat eats the rat, the dog is the benefactor.   (The one for whom the cat ate the rat is the dog.)

"The cat", "the rat", "the plate", and "the dog" are all salient information introduced by *ang*. This salient information is indicated by morphological markers in the event nouns preceding them.

Back to the two questions in ii. and iii., the English translations do not exactly match the meaning of the original. More accurate Chinese translations would be *shéi mǎi de nà kuài bù* for ii. instead of *shéi mǎi le nà kuài bù* 'Who bought the cloth?', *nà nǚrén mǎi de shénme* or *shénme shì nà gè nǚrén mǎi de* for iii. instead of *nà nǚrén mǎi le shénme* 'What did the woman buy?' It is not a strange phenomenon for both subjects and predicates to be nominal; at least it is the case with Tongan (see Chapter 2 in Volume II for details). Chapter 6 will explore extensively the referentiality of Chinese predicates and the potential referentiality of English predicates.

As Kaufman (2009) points out, all the verb phrases that act as predicates in Tagalog are in fact noun phrases, and the underlying reason for this is that the roots of words in this language are all nominal, including those that denote typical actions. Consider the following examples:

vii.   dalawa=ng   **kuha**=ngà=lang   nang=i_isang   ibon
two=LNKw   take=EMPH=only   GEN=LIM_one   bird
'two takes (photos) of only one bird'

viii.   saan   ang=**lákad**=mo   ngayong   gabi
where   NOM=walk=2S.GEN   now:LNK   night
'Where is your walk tonight?'

The verbal root *kuha* in vii is preceded by a numeral, and *nang* is the genitive marker. Like *yī yā de liǎng chī* 'two meals out of one duck' in Chinese, what is glossed as 'two takes (photos) of only one bird' in vii. means that a bird was photographed twice. The verbal root *lákad* in viii. has the number-case marker that common nouns bear. What is glossed as 'Where is your walk tonight?' in viii. is

130   *The verbs-as-nouns framework in Chinese*

structurally similar to *Nǐ jīnwǎn nǎr de yī zǒu* 'Where are you going tonight?' Such roots denoting actions cannot be used as predicates without voice morphology, which indicates that the nouniness of these roots is not derived from their syntactic positions but rather is intrinsic. This can also be seen in utterances mixed with borrowed words and in Pidgin English mixed with Tagalog words. Consider the following examples:

ix. a.   mag-*ice-cream*   b.   mag-*basketbol*
         AV-ice-cream   AV-basketball
         'eat ice cream'   'play basketball'
x. a.   mag-*trabaho*   b.   p⟨um⟩*arada*
         AV-work   ⟨AV⟩stop
         'to work'   'to park'

In ix., the predicates are *ice-cream* from English and *basketbol* from Spanish, along with voice morphology. Both nouns have no corresponding verbs. Predicates in x. consist of borrowed Spanish nouns *trabaho* and *para*, both with corresponding verbs, and voice morphology. Similar examples are also found in Chinese:

xi.   *Nǐ   iPhone   le   ma*?
      you   iPhone   PSP   MP
      'Have you used iPhone?'

      Nǐ   5G   le   ma?
      you   5G   PSP   MP
      'Have you used 5G?'

xii. *Nǐ   parking   hǎo   le   ma*?
      you   parking   finished PSP   MP
      'Have you finished parking?'
      Nǐ   jīntiān   swimming   le   ma?
      you   today   swimming   PSP   MP
      'Have you swum today?'

The predicates in xi. are borrowed English nouns *iPhone* and *5G*, along with *le*. It may not be so much a rhetorical use of nouns as verbs temporarily but rather a recognition that predicates filled by verbs in Chinese are inherently nominal (see Chapter 6), since most people who say so are unaware whether these borrowed English words are nouns or verbs. As an additional justification, both sentences in xii. use noun forms of the verbs *park* and *swim*, even though these verbs do exist in English.

xiii. Let's make *pasok* ('enter') *na* to our class!
       Wait *lang*! I'm making *kain* ('eat') *pa*!
       Come on *na*, we can't make *hintay* ('wait') anymore!

The verbs-as-nouns framework in Chinese 131

The examples in xiii. are Pidgin English mixed with borrowed Tagalog words, which is exactly the reverse of what is described earlier. Because the roots *pasok* 'enter', *kain* 'eat', and *hintay* 'wait' denoting actions are nominal, they have to be preceded by the verb 'make' when inserted into English sentences. In Pidgin English mixed with borrowed Chinese words, the situation is similar, especially with Chinese verbs (which are actually gerunds) that are difficult to translate, as in xiv:

xiv. We can't make *zheteng* (flip-flop) anymore!
Let's do some *zouxue* (make itinerant performances), too!
He is doing *huyou* (deceive) again!

It is typical to begin with the use of words such as *zhēteng, zǒuxué, hūyōu* and then try to explain what these words mean. Without assuming these words are nominal, it is difficult to explain why they are preceded by *make* or *do*.

There is a similar situation with Chinese words that enter Japanese. Among those Chinese words denoting actions, even monosyllabic words (with strong verbiness), not to mention disyllabic words, become ようげん 'yōgen' only when す る (ずる, じる) is added, otherwise remain たいげん 'taigen', as in 検閲する 'review (troops, etc.)', 解放する 'liberate', 愛する 'love', 念ずる 'pray', and 任 じる 'appoint'.[26] The same is true for Chinese words that enter Korean, as in:

xv. Jeongbu-ga   dari-reul   geonseol-ha-oet-da.
government-NOM   bridge-ACC   build-do-past tense-statement
'The government built the bridges.'

The predicate in xv. consists of *geonseol* 'build' and *-hada* 'do'. The word *geonseol* is borrowed from Chinese *jiànshè* 'build' and these borrowed Chinese words can also take nominative and accusative case markers (Cui Jian, personal communication).

Simply put, what was once considered verbal roots are actually nominal roots. This insight is so important that *Theoretical Linguistics* dedicated a special issue (Vol. 35, No.1) to Kaufman's paper.[27] According to Baker (2009: 63), Kaufman's proposal is potentially elegant even though it is somewhat radical, and one source of the differences among languages is differences in their stocks of word classes. Following Kaufman (2009), Baker (2009: 63–64) also states that in linguistic typology if the noun-verb distinction is neutralized, it is neutralized in favor of nouns rather than verbs. He argues that Kaufman's analysis is correct, but it should be demonstrated with explicit or implicit evidence internal to Tagalog. Chapter 5 will demonstrate this cognitively mainly through English and Chinese examples.

Larson and Kaufman discuss their problems within the framework of generative grammar, but they are not bound by the traditional noun-verb distinction. In their minds, the principle of simplicity overrides differences between schools of linguistics. This deserves our serious attention.

132 *The verbs-as-nouns framework in Chinese*

Notes

1 Starting from the belief that nouns and verbs are distinct and neglecting morphological facts, Si Fuzhen (2014) oddly misinterpreted assertions in this paragraph. For example, "nouns are referring expressions" is misinterpreted as "referring expressions equal nouns".

2 Zhang Zhongxing strongly opposes adding *le* when it is optional. He considers its addition to be "redundant" and "useless". Wu Chang'an (2013: 463) contends that *le* can be added when special emphasis is needed.

3 It may be the case for some Chinese dialects that classifiers are obligatory when expressing definite reference. Even if this is confirmed, the phenomenon can be regarded as evidence that Chinese is undergoing the process of developing a formal grammatical distinction between definite and indefinite reference. However, this phenomenon would still not be like the fully grammaticalized distinction in Indo-European languages (see Section 5 of Chapter 2 in Volume II). Judging from the overall situation, the phenomenon does not affect the tenability of B.

4 For example, Chen Xinren (2010) offered the following data:

> I input the data into □ computer and ran the SPSS to analyze it.
> Chapter 4 will answer □ research questions raised in □ methodology chapter.
> Lu Bingfu (private conversation) believes when teaching Chinese to write English that learners would be correct at least 70% of the time if they first added an article before each and every noun and then removed the ones they felt were really not needed. If, in contrast, they first added no articles and then added a few based on context, they would probably be correct only 30% of the time. This is indeed speaking from experience.

5 Cheng and Sybesma (1999) argues that bare nouns in Chinese are not really bare, and that they are predicates and not entities. This obliterates the differences between Chinese and Indo-European languages. Their reasons are that 1) syntactically "only DPs (Determiner Phrases) can function as arguments" and 2) that an element like D (determiner) is implicitly present before a Chinese bare noun when it serves as an argument. But judging from the Principle of Simplicity, it is indeed unnecessary to posit an implied D for Chinese. Following this kind of "implicit" logic, English "a book" should implicitly contain a classifier like *běn* as in its Chinese counterpart *yī běn shū* 'one classifier book'.

6 Previously, I used the translated term *niǔqū guānxì* 'distorted relation' from Lü Shuxiang's translation (1979). However, Yuen Ren Chao (1970) translated it himself as *piāncè guānxì* 'skewed relation'. Yuen Ren Chao (1980: 52–53) also called this relation a *cēncī guānxì* 'unbalanced relation'. [Skewed relation or relationship works well here.]

7 The 1956 *Preliminary Grammatical System for Teaching Chinese* advocated that the uses for attributive-*de* and adverbial-*de* be kept separate. Later, this distinction was gradually popularized. However, the 1984 replacement for the preliminary system *Summary of the Grammatical System for Middle School Education* advocated that attributive-*de* and adverbial-*de* be used interchangeably.

8 Sometimes *ér* connects nominal components as in *shì hēiniú yě ér báití* 'It is a black cow with white hooves' or *cǐ yàn zhī chánglì ér jūn zhī dàmíng yě* 'This is a long-term benefit for Yan, and through this you can also achieve great fame'. These examples will be dealt with in Section 3.4 of Chapter 6.

9 *Méi chē* 'no car' is actually a contraction for *méi yǒu chē* 'there aren't any cars'. What *méi* negates is the verb *yǒu* 'have/there be'.

10 The original text reads as follows: The plus value of a feature is always marked (thus woman in English are 'marked for' + female) and its opposite is either a minus value (thus male is − female) or a zero value (thus man is). A difference should be made between unmarkedness and nonparticipation in an opposition.

The verbs-as-nouns framework in Chinese 133

11 There are those who start from mathematical logic and argue that the verbs-as-nouns theory is unclear and imprecise because it has not completely separated nouns from verbs (Si 2013). This is a strange statement. Regardless of which logic is adopted, it is always necessary to recognize that for the relationship between two categories (sets) A and B, besides the two being distinct from each other, there is the relationship of inclusion. If A and B are distinct, the intersection of A and B can be formed. If A includes B, then B is a subset of A. It is being unclear and imprecise not to distinguish between these two types of relations. Si (2013) also gives, as a reason to reject that verbs are included in the noun category in Chinese, the following distinct category assignments of *to* in English as a preposition (followed by a noun) and as a marker of infinitives (followed by a verb). However, *to* is separately assigned to two categories precisely because nouns and verbs are in opposition in English. The logic of this kind of argument is equivalent to saying that there must be an opposition between nouns and verbs in Chinese because there is one in English.

12 In so doing, it is unnecessary to isolate from nouns the place words *xīnjiàn yīgè běijīng* 'to build a new Beijing', time words *yòu shì yīgè zhōngqiū* 'another mid-autumn festival', and location words *zhēng jiù zhēng yīgè qiántou* 'to fight for a forefront'.

13 Guo Rui (2011) criticizes the verbs-as-nouns theory, saying that it should not deny that verbs functioning as subjects and objects still have predicativity. It should be noted that the verbs-as-nouns theory has never denied this.

14 That year, when Li Shutong was going to be a monk, a friend wrote a letter reproaching him saying, "I've heard that you don't want to be human, but instead want to be a monk". This is simply not treating monks as human. In fact monks are humans. That friend was just speaking casually. It is not possible for him to have believed that monks were not humans. This was only a convenient way of talking. It would have been really ridiculous if there really were people who thought monks were not human.

15 Some, while disregarding such an important formal feature like the one previously mentioned, do all they can to find hidden, fragmentary, and far-fetched evidence with the intent of proving that Chinese predicates the same finite-infinitive distinctions found in Indo-European languages. This penny-wise-pound-foolish approach is highly undesirable.

16 An inverted word order is used in old-style conditional clauses in English. This is circumstantial evidence that conditional clauses are close to questions. Consider the example: Should it rain tomorrow (/,/~/?/) that would be too bad. Yuen Ren Chao remarks that "/,/ and /?/ are usually phonetically indistinguishable" and that the intonation is "ambivalent" (1968: 119). Ten years later, John Haiman (1978) published a highly cited article in *Language* titled "Conditionals Are Topics". In fact, all he did was repeat Chao's position.

17 For this reason, Chinese words like *suīrán* 'although' and *yīnwéi* 'because' are better treated as adverbials that function like conjunctions (i.e. conjuncts) rather than as subordinate conjunctions.

18 There are even more examples of this in classical Chinese, e.g. *Xiāngzhòng rú qí nà bì, lǐ yě* 'Xiangzhong went to Qi with the marriage offerings of silk, and this visit was according to propriety' (*Zuo Tradition*, Second year of Duke Wen) and *Fá lǔ, qí zhī dàguò yě* 'To attack Lu is a great mistake for Qi' (*The Mozi*, Lu's Questions).

19 There are those who assert that *hái huózhe* 'still alive' can serve as an attribute only if *de* is appended after it as in *hái huózhe de rén* 'a person who is still alive'. For them this shows that *hái huózhe* is predicative and that it becomes a referential attribute only after a *de* is added after it. This assertion is incorrect. The function of *de* is not to cause a predicate to undergo "referentialization" or "nominalization". It is just like the *de* of *bàba de shū* 'father's book' (literally, "father de book"). Both function to increase the degree of identifiability of referring expressions. (See Section 6 of this chapter.)

134 *The verbs-as-nouns framework in Chinese*

20 To use an analogy, if a bar is usually a place for gays and lesbians to congregate, it is a bit out of the ordinary for an average person to visit the bar. However, such a patron is definitely not excluded.
21 Ding Shengshu (1940) uses 'depictive' as a generic term for adjectives and adverbs. According to him, *The Book of Poetry* contains numerous reduplicated words, most of which are depictive words, and verbs and nouns can also be reduplicated as in *căi căi fú yĭ* 'gather plantains' and *yàn yàn yú fēi* 'swallows fly'.
22 In *Ma's Grammar,* though *míngzì* 'noun', *dòngzì* 'verb', and *jìngzì* 'stative' (aka adjective) are equally distinguished, *dòngzì* is opposed to *jìngzì* in naming.
23 What ranks first in the top 10 words of Pidgin English is *hăohăo xuéxí, tiāntiān xiàng-shàng* 'Good good study, day day up'. It is because it highlights a very important difference between Chinese and English: the adjective *hăo* 'good' and the noun *tiān* 'day' are both reduplicated to become depictive.
24 There are some people who wrongly think that *de* is a nominalization marker; in fact, it's not, since the *de* in *mùtou de fángzi* 'a wooden house' plays hardly any role in that regard.
25 In English, the verb *amputate* requires two arguments: a subject and a direct object, which refer to the agent and the body part removed, respectively. It does not involves the argument of the person whose limb is amputated and therefore render the sentence **The doctor amputated John* unacceptable. This restricted argument structure, however, does not affect the formation of *amputee*, which refers precisely to the individual in question. Even though there is no syntactic argument corresponding to the participant in the amputation, it is possible to form the word *amputee* in that way as long as the conceptual meaning of the verb *amputate* is sufficient to guarantee the existence of a person undergoing amputation. This illustrates how Tagalog sentences are constructed.
26 As some scholars in Japanese linguistics argue, many Japanese words that denote actions are nouns by themselves and become verbs by adding a light verb する (in the terminology of generative grammar). Some even claim that certain derivative nouns like 食べ 'eating' and 飲み 'drinking' are not necessarily derived from verbs since the so-called verbal roots are probably nominal in nature. It is a question that deserves further investigation.
27 On the word class features of Tagalog, see also Himmelmann (2007) and LaPolla (2010).

References

Baker, M. C. (2009) 'On Some Ways to Test Tagalog Nominalism from a Crosslinguistic Perspective', *Theoretical Linguistics* 35(1): 63–71.
Cai, Shumei and Chunhong Shi (2007) 'Yan Lianke zuopin zhong de chongdie xingshi tanxi' ('An Analysis of the Reduplicative Forms in the Works of Yan Lianke'), *Language Teaching and Linguistic Studies* 4: 1–9.
Chao, Yuen Ren (1955) 'Notes on Chinese Grammar and Logic', *Philosophy East and West* V(1): 31–41, also in A. S. Dil (ed) *Aspects of Chinese Sociolinguistics: Essays by Yuen Ren Chao*, Stanford: Stanford University Press, 237–249. Translated as 'Hanyu Yufa yu Luoji Zatan' by Bai Shuo, in *Essays in Linguistics by Yuen Ren Chao*, 2002, Beijing: The Commercial Press, 796–808.
Chao, Yuen Ren (1959a) 'Ambiguity in Chinese', in S. Egerod and E. Glahn (eds) *Studia Serica Bernhard Karlgren Dedicata*, Copenhagen: Ejnar Munksgaard, 1–13, also in A. S. Dil (ed) *Aspects of Chinese Sociolinguistics: Essays by Yuen Ren Chao*, Stanford: Stanford University Press, 293–308. Translated as 'Hanyu Zhong de Qiyi Xianxiang' by Yuan Yulin, in *Essays in Linguistics by Yuen Ren Chao*, 2002, Beijing: The Commercial Press, 820–835.

Chao, Yuen Ren (1959b) 'How Chinese Logic Operates', *Anthropological Linguistics* 1(1): 1–8, also in A. S. Dil (ed) *Aspects of Chinese Sociolinguistics: Essays by Yuen Ren Chao*, Stanford: Stanford University Press, 250–259.

Chao, Yuen Ren (1968) *A Grammar of Spoken Chinese*, Berkeley and Los Angeles: University of California Press. Translated as *Hanyu Kouyu Yufa* by Lü Shuxiang in 1979, Beijing: The Commercial Press, and as *Zhongguohua de Wenfa* (Revised edition) by Pang-hsin Ting in 2002, Hong Kong: The Chinese University of Hong Kong Press.

Chao, Yuen Ren (1970) 'Guoyu tongyi zhong fangyan duibi de ge fangmian' ('Aspects of Contrasting Dialects in the National Language Unity'), *Bulletin of the Institute of Ethnology, Academia Sinica* 29: 37–42.

Chao, Yuen Ren (1980) *Yuyan Wenti* (*Language Issues*), Beijing: The Commercial Press.

Chen, Xinren (2010) 'Zhongguo xuesheng eryu chanchu zhong de guangtu keshu mingci duanyu: gainian renzhi yu yuyan biaozheng' ('Bare Count Noun Phrases in Chinese Students' Second Language Output: Conceptual Cognition and Linguistic Representation'), *Foreign Languages Research* 1: 15–20.

Cheng, Lisa and R. Sybesma (1999) 'Bare and Not-So-Bare Nouns and the Structure of NP', *Linguistic Inquiry* 30(4): 509–542.

Chierchia, G. (1985) 'Formal Semantics and the Grammar of Predication', *Linguistic Inquiry* 16(3): 417–443.

Chierchia, G. (1998) 'Plurality of Mass Nouns and the Notion of "Semantic Parameter"', in S. Rothstein (ed) *Events and Grammar*, Dordrecht: Kluwer Academic Publishers, 53–103.

Cui, Shanjia (2013) *Hanyu Ouhua Yufa Xianxiang Zhuanti Yanjiu* (*Thematic Studies on the Phenomena of Chinese Europeanized Grammar*), Chengdu: Bashu Press.

Ding, Shengshu (1940) 'Shi juan'er fuyi "caicai" shuo' ('"Caicai" in Poems *Mouse-ear* and *Plantain*'), *(Guoli) Beijing Daxue Sishi Zhounian Jinian Lunwen Ji (yi bian shang) (An Anthology of Essays Commemorating (National) Peking University's 40th Anniversary (Part II, Section A))*, Beijing: The Publishing Team of National Peking University, 1–15.

Fan, Xiaolin (2012) 'Jinbei fangyan lingshu daici de chongdie' ('The Reduplication of Possessive Pronouns in Northern Shanxi Dialect'), *Studies of the Chinese Language* 1: 56–57.

Fang, Mei (2011) 'Beijinghua de liangzhong xingwei zhicheng xingshi' ('Two Patterns of Action Reference in Colloquial Beijing Mandarin'), *Dialect* 4: 368–377.

Guo, Rui (2011) 'Zhu Dexi xiansheng de hanyu cilei yanjiu' ('Zhu Dexi's Study on Parts of Speech in Chinese'), *Chinese Language Learning* 5: 14–26.

Haiman, J. (1978) 'Conditionals Are Topics', *Language* 54: 564–569.

Himmelmann, N. (2007) 'Lexical Categories and Voice in Tagalog', in P. K. Austin and S. Musgrave (eds) *Voice and Grammatical Functions in Austronesian Languages*, Stanford: CSLI.

Hua, Yuming (2008) 'Hanyu chongdie gongneng de duoshijiao yanjiu' ('A Multi-Dimensional Study on the Functions of Reduplication in Chinese'), Doctoral Dissertation, School of Literature, Nankai University.

Huang, Shizhe (2008) 'Yuyi leixing xiangpei lun yu duozhong yuyan xingming jiegou zhi yanjiu' ('A Study of the Configuration of Semantic Types and AN Construction'), *Chinese Linguistics* 2: 53–61.

Jakobson, R. (1932) 'Structure of the Russian Verb', in L. R. Waugh and M. Halle (eds) 1984, *Russian and Slavic Grammar: Studies, 1931–1981*, The Hague: Mouton, 1–14.

Jakobson, R. (1939) 'Zero Sign', in L. R. Waugh and M. Halle (eds) 1984, *Russian and Slavic Grammar: Studies, 1931–1981*, The Hague: Mouton, 151–160.

Kaufman, Daniel (2009) 'Austronesian Nominalism and Its Consequences: A Tagalog Case Study', *Theoretical Linguistics* 35(1): 1–49.

136 *The verbs-as-nouns framework in Chinese*

Kempson, R. M. (1980) 'Ambiguity and Word Meaning', in S. Greenbaum, G. Leech and J. Svartvik (eds) *Studies in English Linguistics for Randolph Quirk*, London: Longman, 7–16.

LaPolla, Randy J. (2010) 'Feilübin tajialuoyu de cilei fanchou' ('The Word Classes of Tagalog'), *Essays on Linguistics* 41: 1–14.

Larson, R. K. (2009) 'Chinese as a Reverse *Ezafe* Language', *Essays on Linguistics* 39: 30–85.

Li, Wenli (2011) 'Cong xiuci jiaodu kan fuling fangyan danyinjie dongci chongdie' ('The Reduplication of Monosyllabic Verbs in Fuling Dialect from a Rhetorical Perspective'), *Contemporary Rhetoric* 5: 2–13.

Li, Yen-hui Audrey (1985) 'Abstract Case in Chinese', Unpublished PhD Thesis, University of Southern California.

Lin, Huayong (2011) 'Lianjiang yueyu de liangzhong duanyu chongdieshi' ('Two Types of Reduplicated Phrases in the Yue Dialect of Lianjiang'), *Studies of the Chinese Language* 4: 364–371.

Liu, Tanzhou and Dingxu Shi (2012) 'Yantaihua zhong budai zhishici huo shuci de liangci jiegou' ('Bare Classifier Phrases in the Yantai Dialect'), *Studies of the Chinese Language* 1: 38–49.

Lu, Bingfu (2014) 'Shen Jiaxuan mingdong baohan lilun zhengfan shuo' ('Pros and Cons of Shen Jiaxuan's Verbs-as-Nouns Theory'), in *Yinghan Duibi yu Fanyi* (*Contrastive and Translation Studies of English and Chinese*), vol. 2, Shanghai: Shanghai Foreign Language Education Press, 71–83.

Lü, Shuxiang (1942/1982) *Zhongguo Wenfa Yaolüe* (*Essentials of Chinese Grammar*), Shanghai and Beijing: The Commercial Press.

Lü, Shuxiang (1979) *Hanyu Yufa Fenxi Wenti* (*Problems in Chinese Grammatical Analysis*), Beijing: The Commercial Press.

Lü, Shuxiang (1981) 'Guanyu *de di de* he *zuo zuo*' ('On *de/di/de*, and *zuo/zuo*'), *Chinese Learning* 3: 52–53.

Lü, Shuxiang (1984) 'Guanyu *de di de* de Fenbie' ('The Difference between *de, di* and *de*'), in *Yuwen Zaji* (*A Miscellany of Linguistic Essays*), Shanghai: Shanghai Educational Publishing House, 50–51.

Lü, Shuxiang and Dexi Zhu (1979) *Yufa Xiuci Jianghua* (*Talks on Grammar and Rhetoric*), 2nd ed., Beijing: China Youth Publishing Group.

Shao, Jingmin (2013) *Hanyu Yufa de Dongtai Yanjiu* (*Dynamic Studies of Chinese Grammar*), Beijing: The Commercial Press.

Shen, Jiaxuan (1991) 'Yuyi de buquedingxing" he wufa fenhua de duoyiju' ('Semantic Indeterminacy and Indistinguishable Ambiguous Sentences'), *Studies of the Chinese Language* 4: 241–250.

Shi, Qisheng (1997) 'Lun shantou fangyan zhong de chongdie' ('On Reduplications in Shantou Dialect'), *Studies in Language and Linguistics* 1: 72–85.

Shi, Qisheng (2011) 'Hanyu fangyan zhong cizu de xingtai' ('The Morphology of Phrases in Chinese Dialects'), *Studies in Language and Linguistics* 1: 43–52.

Shi, Yuzhi (1992) *Kending yu Fouding de Duicheng yu Buduicheng* (*The Symmetry and Asymmetry of Affirmation and Negation*), Taipei: Taiwan Student Book Company Limited.

Si, Fuzhen (2013) 'Jianyue zhiwen' ('Simplicity of Linguistic Theory Formulation and Evaluation'), *Linguistic Sciences* 5: 497–504.

Si, Fuzhen (2014) 'Yeshuo hanyu he yin'ouyu chayi de ABC' ('On the ABCs of the Differences between Chinese and Indo-European Languages', in *Yinghan Duibi yu Fanyi* (*Contrastive and Translation Studies of English and Chinese*), vol. 2, Shanghai: Shanghai Foreign Language Education Press, 156–164.

The verbs-as-nouns framework in Chinese 137

Trubetzkoy, N. S. (1939) *Principles of Phonology*, C. A. M. Baltaxe (trans.), Berkeley: California University Press, 1969.

Wan, Quan (2015) 'Zuowei houzhi jieci de *de*' ('Postposition *De*'), *Contemporary Linguistics* 1: 85–97.

Wang, Guosheng (1994) 'Dayehua li de zhuangtai xingrongci' ('Stative Adjectives in Daye Dialect'), *Journal of Hubei Normal University* 2: 81–89+93.

Wang, Hongjun (2011) 'Hanyu yufa de jiben danwei yu yanjiu celüe (zuozhe buji)' ('The Eseential Units of Chinese Grammar and Research Strategies (Author's Addendum)'), in *Jiben Danwei de Xiandai Hanyu Cifa Yanjiu* (*A Study of Morphology of Basic Units in Modern Chinese*), Beijing: The Commercial Press, 414–420.

Wu, Chang'an (2013) *Yuyan Wengao* (*Studies of Language*), Changchun: Northeast Normal University Press.

Ye, Zugui (2014) 'Hanyu fangyan zhong miaomoxing dongci chongdie de xiucixue kaocha' ('A Rhetorical Study of the Reduplication of Depictive Verbs in Chinese Dialects'), *Contemporary Rhetoric* 5: 76–83.

Yuan, Yulin (2010) 'Hanyu buneng chengshou de fanyi zhiqing: cong qu fanchouhua jiaodu kan hanyu dongci he mingci de guanxi' ('The Unbearable Lightness of the Translation of Deverbal Nouns from Indo-European Languages into Chinese: Rethinking the Relation between Verbs and Nouns in Mandarin Chinese from a Perspective of the Decategorization of Verbs'), *Essays on Linguistics* 41: 15–61.

Zhu, Dexi (1956) 'Xiandai hanyu xingrongci yanjiu' ('A Study of Adjectives in Modern Chinese'), *Linguistic Research*: 83–111.

Zhu, Dexi (1961) 'Shuo *de*' ('On *De*'), *Studies of the Chinese Language* 12: 1–15.

Zhu, Dexi (1980) 'Hanyu jufa zhong de qiyi xianxiang' ('Ambiguity in Chinese Syntax'), *Studies of the Chinese Language* 2: 81–92.

Zhu, Dexi (1985) *Yufa Dawen* (*Answering Questions about Chinese Grammar*), Beijing: The Commercial Press.

Zhu, Dexi (2010) *Yufa Fenxi Jianggao* (*Lecture Notes on Grammatical Analysis*), Beijing: The Commercial Press.

Zhu, Dexi, Jiawen Lu and Zhen Ma (1961) 'Guanyu dongci xingrongci mingwuhua de wenti' ('On the Nominalization of Verbs and Adjectives'), *Journal of Peking University* (*Humanities and Social Sciences*) 4: 51–64, also in Dexi Zhu (1980) *Xiandai Hanyu Yufa Yanjiu* (*Studies in Modern Chinese Grammar*), Beijing: The Commercial Press, 193–224.

4 Realizational relations and constitutive relations

4.1 "Reference" and "predication" as primary concepts

For the verbs-as-nouns framework to be established in Chinese, it must first be clarified that Chinese nouns and verbs are respectively referring and predicative expressions (see Chapter 3, Section 1). Some scholars define nouns and verbs as two primary concepts that are universal in human languages, with nouns having the feature [+ N] and verbs having the feature [+ V]. However, their definitions are of no real value, since each human language actually distinguishes between nouns and verbs according to their syntactic distribution. The problem is how to determine that one category of words distinguished according to their distribution in one language is the same as a distributionally defined category of words in another language and that they both belong to the same class of nouns or verbs.

The only approach other than one that defines categories according to lexical meaning is one that uses the primary concepts "reference" and "predication" to define lexical categories. In this approach, all words used referentially are nouns, and those used as predicates are verbs. Zhang Bin (2014) argues at the very beginning of his paper that "Language is a tool for expressing meaning, and its original functions are reference and predication". Scholars who take nouns and verbs as primary concepts develop analyses that depend on referential concepts like "generic reference, definite reference, and indefinite reference". Linguistic typologists usually use "reference" and "predication" as the cross-linguistic basis for their comparative studies of different languages' lexical categories. Of the two, reference is more basic than predication. This is because the predication of an activity or event necessarily includes reference to that activity or event.

"Reference" is by no means the same as "denotation". Denotation concerns the possible relationship between words and the non-linguistic objects they may name. Reference, on the other hand, concerns the specific relationship between a word and a particular object established through the actual use of that word at a certain time and in a certain place. (Jiang 2013) Pierce divides signs into three categories: Icon, symbol, and index. A referring expression in linguistics is not only an icon and a symbol but also an index. The term "index" originally meant "pointing with an index finger". Recently, some scholars working on the origins and evolution of language have proposed that "pointing" was the initial or preliminary phase in the

DOI: 10.4324/9781003385899-5

Figure 4.1 Realizational metaphors and constitutive metaphors

development of human language (Kita 2003; Bejarano 2011; Arbib 2012; Diessel 2013). With our fingers, we are able to point at events and things both within and outside of our field of vision. In addition, we can point to the past and the future as well as to what exists only in our imaginations. Animals lack these abilities. For example, when a woman says, "My husband is doing an experiment in the lab now", while raising her hand and pointing backwards over her head towards the right, she is referring to her husband (a person), the lab (an object), and the experiment (an event). That is to say, it is possible to point to actions, activities, and events. Another example would be my use of my index finger to point to a fashionably dressed young woman who is smoking. My objective is to draw your attention to the woman and to convey to you my feelings about the situation. This is done to enable you to understand the meaning behind my pointing. From this it follows that the linguistic term "reference" is essentially a pragmatic concept, closely related to language use and the speaker's intention. According to Hopper and Thompson (1984), referring expressions in language refer to "discourse-manipulable participants". These are either topics to be commented on or objects to be manipulated or affected by an action.

With respect to the concept of reference, there is the distinction between what is referential and what is nonreferential. Referential can be further divided into definite, indefinite, generic, and specific reference. Each of these distinctions is defined according to the particular cognitive state of a discourse participant. (See Chen 1987). In predicate logic, there is a distinction between referentially saturated and referentially unsaturated expressions. Chierchia (1985) holds that only words which can directly serve as an argument refer to "entities" and takes this as a criterion for identifying a significant difference between nouns in French and English and nouns in Chinese. French and English nouns cannot directly serve as a sentence's arguments. From this it follows that they refer to "properties" rather than "entities". In contrast, nouns in Chinese can directly serve as an argument and thus refer to "entities". Arguments for the most part are the subjects and objects of sentences. Referentially, they belong to one of the four categories, generic, specific, definite, and indefinite. Chinese nouns are referentially saturated; English nouns are not. Section 1 of Chapter 3 already explained this difference by contrasting the Chinese bare noun *lǎohǔ* 'tiger' and the English bare noun 'tiger'.

Some people cast doubts on the claim that both the subject and object of a sentence are referential. They contend that Zhu Dexi classifies subjects and objects into two types—referential and predicative—and state that a way to distinguish

140 *Realizational relations and constitutive relations*

the two types of expressions is through substitution. "What" can replace referential subjects and objects; "how" can replace those that are predicative. Those who raise such questions do not actually understand Zhu's original intention. He always opposes using meaning to assert that verbs that function as subjects and objects undergo either nominalization or transformation into the name of an object. In the past, there were people who used referentialization to justify positing nominalization or transformation into the name of an object. Zhu proposed that subjects and objects can be either referential or predicative as a way to criticize the positing of referentialization. He dismissed this approach asking, "What is the point of positing referentialization since both subjects and objects can be predicative?" (Zhu et al. 1961).

The verbs-as-nouns theory supports Zhu's viewpoint and moreover provides it with an explanation: Since predication is also referential, there is no need for the referentialization of verbs. However, those who believe in the noun-verb distinction insist that nominalization should at least be recognized, to some extent. They even go so far as to propose that nominalization occurs at different levels. Their point of view is totally at odds with what Zhu genuinely intended.

Further, notwithstanding that Zhu used "what" and "how" to differentiate referential subjects and objects from predicative ones, he observed that "how" can only substitute for a predicative constituent. "What", on the other hand, can replace either a nominal constituent or a predicative one. This kind of skewed distribution with respect to substitution is precisely the kind of evidence that supports the proposed inclusion of verbs in nouns (the inclusion of predicative expressions in referring ones), which is explained in Section 2 of Chapter 3.

4.2 "Realizational relations" and "constitutive relations"

4.2.1 "Realizational metaphors" and "constitutive metaphors"

Grammatical categories are abstract; pragmatic categories are concrete. According to the theory of metaphor in cognitive linguistics, metaphor uses a concrete concept to explain a similar abstract one. There are two types of metaphor, "realizational" and "constitutive" (Ungerer & Schmid 1996: 147–149). For example, when someone says, "Your computer has been infected by a virus. Kill it as soon as possible", the "virus" mentioned is an example of a metaphor, which, with the aid of the familiar concrete concept of a physical virus, refers to a similar but abstract concept of something hidden in the computer program. Moreover, with the popularization of computers, such terms as "virus", "firewall", "desk", and "menu" have become familiar to people and entered into everyday use. However, many computer scientists disapprove of using these metaphors. They believe that the metaphorical use of these words should be avoided because they do not sound like scientific terms and may obscure the real situation. Even though many scientific notions, like the Big Bang theory in astronomy, are themselves metaphors, and many scientists believe that the use of metaphors cannot be avoided (Boyd 1993; Kuhn 1993; Feng 2006), the skeptical attitude towards metaphors

Realizational relations and constitutive relations 141

and attempts to purify scientific language by scientists have never been given up (Radman 1997: 44).

This shows that for at least some experts, the metaphorical use of words like "virus" and "firewall" only serves explanatory functions. Their use is to explain abstract and unfamiliar concepts with concrete and familiar ones.

These metaphors, however, are not only explanatory but also constitutive for ordinary users of computers, especially for novices. For them, the metaphors themselves constitute the abstract concepts related to computers. It would be impossible for these users to understand the abstract concepts without the help of the metaphors. When someone new to computers gradually becomes an expert through learning, constitutive metaphors become purely explanatory. This process of transition may be quite long. The point of transition in the continuum at which a constitutive metaphor becomes an explanatory one may not be clear. However, the two ends of the continuum are distinct.

Compare the definitions of "virus" given in two different dictionaries (since the first definitions for *virus*$_1$ in both dictionaries are concerned with a physical virus in a human body, they are not discussed here):

The Contemporary Chinese Standard Dictionary: *virus*$_2$ is an unauthorized self-replicating program designed and spread to destroy other programs. It can destroy documents saved in the computer and even the hardware so as to prevent the computer and its network from functioning properly.

The Contemporary Chinese Dictionary: *virus*$_2$ refers to a computer virus.

Though *The Contemporary Chinese Dictionary* has another entry for "computer virus" and gives a similar definition to that for *virus*$_2$ in *The Contemporary Chinese Standard Dictionary*, its approach is different from the other dictionary's. As a medium-sized Chinese dictionary, *The Contemporary Chinese Dictionary* treats "computer virus" as an adequate definition for *virus*$_2$ for common readers, who may have no need for the detailed entry for "computer virus". But if it were a small-sized dictionary, it would even be unnecessary to have a separate entry for "computer virus". Actually, no matter how detailed a definition might be, it would still be hard to tell whether it is all-inclusive and accurate. Take a newly emerged virus named "Trojan virus" (a metaphor too) for example. To highlight its imperceptibility, some people have differentiated the "Trojan virus" from "virus (with an emphasis on its spreadability)". Thus it can be seen that in a dictionary without a separate entry for "Trojan virus", even though the definition of "virus" is given in as much details as the one in *The Contemporary Chinese Standard Dictionary*, it is still lacking (in that it fails to include the imperceptibility of the virus). Moreover, even with a more detailed definition of computer virus, it would still be difficult for readers other than experts to understand what exactly is being defined because other terms used in the definition like "software", "hardware", "save", and "network" are all metaphors. In a word, the dictionaries' entries not only reflect differences in approach to dictionary compilation but also show that the distinction between explanatory and constitutive metaphors is present in how a metaphor like "virus" is defined.

142   *Realizational relations and constitutive relations*

When a speaker takes a concrete concept to explain an abstract one, he intends to help the listener to realize and understand the abstract concept through the concrete one. Thus, the "explanatory" relation between two concepts can also be taken as a "realizational" relation, in which the concrete concept is the realization of the abstract one. From this it follows that the distinction between "explanatory" metaphors and "constitutive" metaphors is the distinction between "realizational" metaphors and "constitutive" metaphors. The following figure illustrates this:

In the figure to the left, the dotted circle above stands for an abstract concept and the solid circle for a concrete one. As is illustrated previously, a realizational metaphor is formed through a process of realization of an abstract concept by a concrete one. In contrast, a constitutive metaphor does not go through such a process of realization. The abstract concept is constituted by the concrete one. Some people cast doubt on this by arguing that the boundary between the realizational relation and the constitutive relation is vague. The fact is, however, that this distinction is clearly made in both Indo-European languages and Chinese. The former marks the distinction formally; the latter does not. The distinction between the realizational relation and the constitutive relation is not only relevant for analyzing metaphors but also for studying other aspects of language and for other aspects of human activities as well.

4.2.2   *Universality of the realizational-constitutive distinction*

Metaphor is more than a rhetorical device or a characteristic of language. It is an aspect of human cognition. Our concepts and conceptual systems are, to a high degree, metaphorical in nature. They are governed by metaphor (Lakoff & Johnson 1980: 3). Politicians often put forward realizational metaphors and, intentionally or not, cause people to understand them as constitutive metaphors to promote their political agenda. Lakoff (1992) gives as an example what the US authorities did before launching the Gulf War. The authorities used metaphors like "WAR IS POLITICS PURSUED BY OTHER MEANS" and "POLITICS IS BUSINESS" to create in people's minds the idea that war was just like negotiating prices in a business deal. What was hidden was war's brutality, death, and bloodshed. In saying this, Lakoff shows that there are at least some American intellectuals who are against the use of this kind of political metaphor. For them, these metaphors are only realizational rather than constitutive.

Rawls (1955) was the first to propose that the rules governing human social activities can be divided into "regulative rules" and "constitutive rules":

Regulative rules (RR): regulating an already existing activity, for example, transportation rules.
Constitutive rules (CR): making up a practice of which the rule is a part, for example, rules for ball games.

RR can be summarized as follows: If Y, then X should be done. For example, when driving, one should follow the traffic rules of stopping for a red light and

Realizational relations and constitutive relations 143

going on green; or if someone is a military officer, that person should follow the rule of wearing a tie when dining. Such practices as driving and eating happen whether or not there are RRs covering them. RRs are formulated in the form of an order. For example, the transportation rule "Do not cross the street when the light is red" is set down as an order, regulating the interests of and social relations between parties who are not related to the rule itself and manifesting people's expectation towards normal social practices as well. Whoever does not observe RRs may still be able to drive or eat, but they will be fined or otherwise punished.

CR can be summarized as follows: If X takes an action in the setting of E, then X is regarded as Y. For example, a goal is scored in a football game when a player kicks or heads the ball past the goal line between the goalposts and under the cross-bar, or a person who goes through certain procedures in a wedding ceremony is regarded as the one presiding over the ceremony. A CR is a part of a practice which does not exist independently of the rule system itself. It is not an order for people to do or not do something. Rather, it is something that makes up or defines the manner of a new practice, embodying people's beliefs about the social practice. A breach of a CR will not incur penalties but will bring about a failure to achieve the expected results. For example, a football player cannot score a goal by pushing the ball into the goal by the hand, nor can a player in Chinese chess checkmate the general if the person does not move the knight diagonally.

Regulative rules are, by their nature, realizational rules, realizing through regulation the social practices that people expect. For example, normal traffic is realized through the regulations found in traffic rules. Thus, regulative rules are different from constitutive rules in the same way that realizational rules are different from those rules.

Nevertheless, either a realizational rule or a constitutive rule can change into the other. As mentioned earlier, when a person becomes an expert with computers, such metaphors as "virus" will be converted from constitutive to realizational ones. In contrast, rules for human social practices often change from realizational into constitutive ones. For example, the family institution was originally built to accommodate raising children, whose chances for survival were better by living with their parents. Hence, a rule system for the family institution was set up to regulate family life, forbidding incest on the one hand and fostering within-family altruism on the other. These realizational rules regulated the relations among the members of a family and defined what was allowed or demanded from each of its members. However, over time, these rules have become a part of our concept of family. They define and govern family internal relations even in families where its original regulative use no longer exists. These include, for example, adopted children, stepparents, and foster families. For such cases, these rules can only be regarded as constitutive. They have become a part of the cultural system. Another example is the collection of procedures for the changing of the guard ceremony at Buckingham Palace in London. At first, they were realizational rules. They were set up to regulate the guards' work and for the purpose of security and protection. As the ritual turned into a ceremony, the rules came to define the ceremony

144   *Realizational relations and constitutive relations*

internally, with no external end served, and hence they became a constitutive system (Kasher & Sadka 2001).

This pair of concepts, realizational relation and constitutive relation, is also used in political science. Tong (2008) provides the follow example of this. The police are responsible for law enforcement in Western countries. If they are called to deal with a fight a husband and wife are having in their home, they handcuff the husband and leave without saying much of anything. The question of who is in the right and who is at fault is left to be decided in court. In contrast, the police in China would first try to mediate between the two parties, even if that meant suffering a few blows. In China, the police are responsible for maintaining not only the legal order but also the moral order of the society. While the political order in the West is realized through the moral order, it is, in China, constituted by it.[1]

Before the 2008 Olympic Games, Beijing's municipal government adopted some regulative measures, for example, limiting the driving of a car to alternative days based on whether its license plate number was even or odd and requiring the sweeping and repair of streets and buildings. These measures caused a lot of inconveniences for the city's residents. The Director of Public Security offered an explanation for these measures by saying that people clean up their homes and put on new clothes to welcome guests when somebody in their family gets married. Hosting the Olympic Games in China is analogous to the nation holding a wedding ceremony. These measures by the Chinese government, however, were regarded in the West as self-propaganda and coercing public opinion. But what they did not understand is that it was not only the Chinese government but also ordinary people that wanted to leave the guests with a favorable impression.

This case shows that when discussing the relationship between "nation (*guó*)" and "family (*jiā*)", in the West the "family" is simply the means through which the "nation" is realized. The nation is the nation. The family is the family. The nation's affairs are its affairs. Family matters are its own matters. On the other hand, in China, the "nation" is not only realized through "family" but also constituted by it; it is an extended family, whose business is the business of all people. This way of conceptualizing "nation" and "family" is reflected succinctly in the Chinese words *guójiā* 'nation-family' and *jiā* 'family' respectively, just like the word *shìwù* 'matter-thing'. As *shì* 'matter' can be considered *wù* 'thing', *shì* being an abstract *wù*, *guó* 'nation' is equivalent to *jiā* 'family', being an extended *jiā*.

4.2.3   Yǒu *'have/there be' and* shì *'be'*

The difference between what is realizational and what is constitutive can be seen, from a different angle, as the difference between *yǒu* 'have/there be' and *shì* 'be'. For example, 'there is' (*yǒu*) traffic only when people observe traffic rules (realizational rules). People 'are' (*shì*) playing chess only when they follow the rules of chess (constitutive rules). With respect to the "virus" example, it is only by having the realizational metaphor that 'there is' (*yǒu*) the concept of a computer virus. It is only through the constitutive metaphor that the abstract concept can 'be' (*shì*) a

Realizational relations and constitutive relations   145

computer virus. In fact, as we understand and think, we constantly encounter the difference between *yǒu* and *shì*. For example, a well-known quotation on the relation between Chinese paintings and poems from the famous poet Su Dongpo of the Song Dynasty goes, "In poems there are paintings; in paintings there are poems". On a passage of description in *A Dream of Red Mansions*, a famed literary critic known for his critical studies of the Chinese classic novel, Zhou Ruchang commented in his article "The Essentials of Poeticization" that the famous quotation might as well be rephrased as "Poetry is painting, and painting poetry". It can be seen that there is a difference between Su Dongpo's and Zhou Ruchang's understanding of the relationship between poetry and painting. Su thinks that it is a realizational relation, a *yǒu* 'have/there be' relation. Zhou believes it is a constitutive relation, a *shì* (be) relation.

As another example, there are four sentences in *The Heart of Prajna Paramita Sutra*, 'Form does not differ from emptiness; emptiness does not differ from form. Form itself is emptiness; emptiness itself is form'. The first two sentences relate to the realizational relation between form and emptiness, a *yǒu* 'have/there be' relation. Form cannot be separated from emptiness, and emptiness cannot be separated from form. Only if there is emptiness is there form; only where there is form is there emptiness. The other two sentences concern the constitutive relationship between form and emptiness, a *shì* 'be' relation. Form is emptiness, and emptiness form.

There have been many philosophical discussions concerning the differences between the two concepts *yǒu* 'have/there be' and *shì* 'be'. Taking language as his starting point, Chao (1955; also in Dil 1976) observes that the English concept of being (*shì*) must be linked with the concept of 'there be' (*yǒu*). In contrast, the Chinese concept of *shì* 'be' need not to be linked with the concept of *yǒu* 'have/there be'. The former is independent of the latter.

Although Ancient Chinese did not have a copular such as *shì* 'be', the absence of a word for *shì* 'be' is not the same as lacking the concept 'being'. The concept *shì* 'be' is a never-questioned and self-evident default concept for the Chinese. Thus, the significant philosophical question in the West, 'being and nonbeing', can never be a question in Chinese philosophy. It is not necessary for Chinese people to find a single word to express this concept. The word *shì* 'be' in modern Chinese is used only for emphasizing affirmatives. Accordingly, it can be said that the realizational relation and the constitutive relation in English are not independent of each other, but they are in Chinese. This issue will be further investigated in Chapter 3 of Volume II when the division between *shì* and *yǒu* and its philosophical background is discussed.

4.3 Comparisons between Chinese and Indo-European Languages

4.3.1 *Nouns in English and Chinese*

Grammatical concepts or categories are largely metaphorical in nature (Shen 2006a), hence either realizational or constitutive. This pair of relations can be

146 *Realizational relations and constitutive relations*

used to illustrate a significant difference between Chinese and Indo-European languages: The abstract grammatical categories and the concrete pragmatic categories in Indo-European languages are in a realizational relation while those in Chinese are constitutive.

English has realization processes and methods that apply to abstract nouns/ verbs to enable their "realization" as referring/predicative expressions in discourse. In Chinese, on the other hand, nouns/verbs are constituted out of referring/predicative expressions without the application of realization processes or methods. See Figure 4.1 for realizational metaphors and constitutive metaphors.

In the *Zhōngyī Yàoxué Míngcí 'Terms/Nouns of Traditional Chinese Medicine'* issued by China National Committee for Terminology in Science and Technology (CNCTST), the so-called terms (nouns) of traditional Chinese medicine (TCM) include such disyllabic words as *zīyīn* 'nourish Yin', *bǔxuè* 'enrich blood', *míngmù* 'improve eyesight', and *tōngbí* 'relieve stuffy nose' and monosyllabic words like *qiē* 'cut', *chǎo* 'stir-fry', *tàng* 'heat', and *zhēng* 'steam', all of which are grammatically verbs. How can they be included as "nouns" in TCM? Obviously, the "nouns" specified in that book are actually names (referred to as 'terms' in specialist terminology). However, they are not the nouns grammarians put in opposition to verbs. To put it succinctly, the words *qiē* 'cut', *chǎo* 'stir-fry', *zīyīn* 'nourish *yin*', and *bǔxuè* 'enrich blood' are all "names". They are the names for actions. This is all totally correct.

Shi Ming 'Interpreting Names' by Liu Xi of the Eastern Han includes the names for objects like *tiān* 'heaven', *dì* 'earth', *shān* 'mountain', and *shuǐ* 'water'; *fù* 'father', *mǔ* 'mother', and *xiōngdì* 'brother'; *rì* 'sun', *yuè* 'moon', and *xīngxiù* 'star constellation'; *méi* 'brow', *yǎn* 'eye', *shé* 'tongue', and *chǐ* 'tooth'; *bǐ* 'writing brush', *mò* 'ink stick', *zhǐ* 'paper', and *yàn* 'ink stone'; *gǔ* 'drum', *sè* '25-stringed plucked instrument', *shēng* 'reed pipe wind instrument', and *xiāo* 'vertical bamboo flute'. It also includes the names for actions like *qū* 'hurry', *xíng* 'walk', *bēn* 'run fast', and *zǒu* 'run'; *shì* 'look', *tīng* 'listen', *guān* 'watch', and *wàng* 'look far into the distance'; *zuò* 'sit', *wò* 'lie', *guì* 'kneel', and *bài* 'bow'; *jǔ* 'savor', *jué* 'chew', *tǔ* 'spit', and *chuǎn* 'pant'; *chuò* 'sob', *jiē* 'sigh', *yī* 'astonish', *wū* 'lament'; *hǎo* 'love', *è* 'dislike', *shùn* 'follow', and *nì* 'violate'.

In *The Contemporary Chinese Dictionary*, the word *míngcí* 'noun' is defined as follows:

> *Míngcí* 'noun': ① a word that is used to name a person or a thing, such as *rén* 'person', *niú* 'cow', *shuǐ* 'water', *yǒuyì* 'friendship', *tuántǐ* 'group', *jīntiān* 'today', *zhōngjiān* 'middle', *Běijīng* 'Beijing', and *Kǒngzǐ* 'Confucius'. ② (used with a suffix "-r") a term or a word similar to a term (not limited to grammatical nouns), such as *huàxué míngcí* 'chemistry terms', or *xīn míngcír* 'new terms'.

Definition ① quoted earlier refers to 'grammatical nouns', examples of which exclude words representing actions. Definition ② contains a small inaccuracy. It includes a note on the use of a suffix "-r", suggesting that nouns in this sense usually have the form of names (*míngcír*). However, neither *huàxué míngcí* 'chemistry terms' nor *zhōngyī yàoxué míngcí* 'terms of Traditional Chinese Medicine' can be suffixed with "-r". It would be good to modify Definition ② into "names (used with a suffix "-r") or terms" and place it before Definition ①, for "nouns" are "names" in the eyes of general readers but not grammarians.[2]

Chinese have no problem with verbs being treated as nouns. Westerners, on the other hand, have their doubts about this. To accommodate Westerners, the book *Terms of Traditional Chinese Medicine* translates the names as English nouns rather than using the verbs' original forms. The book nominalizes the verbs by adding suffixes such as *-ness, -ation, -ment*, and *-ity* or with *-ing*. The same approach is adopted by CNCTST for terms in other branches of science because, for the British in general (including grammarians), a noun is a noun, and a noun refers to a person or thing. For them, a verb is a verb, and a verb describes an action or activity. A verb can be used to refer to an action or activity only after undergoing a process of nominalization. In contrast, verbs in Chinese like *qiē* 'cut', *chǎo* 'stir-fry', *zīyīn* 'nourish Yin', and *bǔxuè* 'enrich blood' can be used directly to name actions or activities without undergoing the process of nominalization.

The use of a verb to "refer" to an action or activity is what is called an "ontological metaphor". Such metaphors treat an abstract event or activity as a concrete entity. Ontological metaphors can also be either realizational or constitutive; they are realizational in English but constitutive in Chinese. For the British people, a change in lexical form is the process and method by which an abstract concept of an event or activity is realized as a concrete concept of an entity as in the following examples:

explode   → explosion
excite   → excitement
propose   → proposal
sell   → selling

For the Chinese, however, an event or activity is an entity. Or to put it differently, it is constituted by an entity. There is no process of "realization". Thus, no change in lexical form is needed. According to Lakoff and Johnson (1980: 30), ontological metaphors in English can be expressed as follows:

EXPLOSION IS AN ENTITY
THINKING IS AN ENTITY
HOSTILITY IS AN ENTITY
HAPPINESS IS AN ENTITY

However, a Chinese would ask a question like the following about this form of expression (not the ontological metaphor per se): Given that the lexical forms of EXPLOSION and THINKING already mark them as entities, which is the same as saying "an entity is an entity", can they still be regarded as metaphors? It does not

148 *Realizational relations and constitutive relations*

make any sense. They can only count as metaphors and be meaningful if they are expressed as follows:

EXPLODE IS AN ENTITY
THINK IS AN ENTITY
HOSTILE IS AN ENTITY
HAPPY IS AN ENTITY

For Chinese-speaking Chinese, Western talk about ontological metaphors seems unimportant and superfluous. After all, actions or activities are themselves entities.

In short, the Chinese word *míngcí* 'noun' is a dual metaphor: On the one hand, it is used as the concrete pragmatic concept *míngcír* (a referring expression) to refer to or understand the abstract grammatical concept *míngcí* 'noun'. On the other hand, it is used as a concrete *míngcí* 'noun' that refers to people or things to refer to abstract events and activities. Hence, it is an ontological metaphor. Chinese and English treat the two metaphors differently. In English, both of them are realizational; in Chinese, they are both constitutive.

The following correspondences exist between the "noun" metaphor and the "virus" metaphor: The relation between a "computer virus" (abstract) and a "physical virus" (concrete) is constitutive for a computer novice but realizational for a computer expert. Similarly, the relation between the grammatical "noun" (abstract) and the pragmatic *míngcír* (concrete) is constitutive for the Chinese but realizational for the British; hence the relation between an activity (abstract) represented by a verb and an entity (concrete) represented by a noun is also constitutive for the Chinese but realizational for the British.

When we imitate Western grammar to construct Chinese grammar, it is not unacceptable to render the English word "noun" into Chinese as *míngcí* 'noun', *míng* 'name', or *míngzì* 'name'. Nevertheless, the translations may not capture the essence of the original word. That is why we must understand a significant difference between Chinese *míngcí* and English nouns. We often say, "I'm looking for a word". We also say, "I'm looking for a *míngcír* (terms not limited to grammatical nouns)". Their meanings are completely the same. From this it can be seen that Chinese "content words" are naturally "nouns" and referring expressions. They refer to things and to actions. For the Chinese, once a name (*míng*) is given, it is "used" to refer to an entity (otherwise it would not be a "name") and can directly function as various referring expressions in language use, hence referentially saturated (see Section 3.1).

4.3.2 Sentences and utterances

"Sentence" is generally regarded as a grammatical unit while "utterance" is taken to be a pragmatic one. With respect to the pair of concepts "type" and "token", "sentence" is an abstract "type", and "utterance" a concrete "token". Though a Chinese "sentence" is regarded by most people as equivalent to an English "sentence", they are not equivalent. Rather, a Chinese sentence corresponds more closely to an

Realizational relations and constitutive relations   149

"utterance" in English, as stated by Jiang Wangqi (2006). According to Yuen Ren Chao's minor sentence theory introduced in Section 3.4 of Chapter 3, a sentence in Chinese is often defined as a segment of speech bounded at both ends by pauses. A minor sentence that does not express a complete subject-predicate relation only needs to end with utterance-final intonation to count as an independent sentence. Following his view, Zhu (1987) argues that though an English sentence consists of a subject and a predicate, subjectless Chinese sentences have freely occurred in all varieties of Chinese since the ancient language of the Pre-Qin period up until and including the modern spoken language. Subjectless sentences have always been as independent and complete as sentences with subjects. Therefore, in his opinion, the traditional hypothesis of subject ellipsis is not an adequate explanation for the existence of subjectless sentences. Zhu classifies subjectless sentences into the following five categories:

i. No subject could be placed in any position:

Dǎshǎn   le.
hit-lightening   PSP
'There is lightening.'

Lúndào   nǐ   qǐngkè   le.
turn   you   treat-guests PSP
'It's your turn to treat.'

ii. The constituent about which something is predicated is not in the position of a subject:

Rè   de   wǒ   mǎntóudàhàn.
hot   CSC   me   drenched-with-sweat
'It's so hot that my face is drenched with sweat.'

Yǒu   gè   guówáng   yǒu   sān   gè   érzi.
have   CL   king   have   three   CL   sons
'There is a king who has three sons.'

iii. The subject about which something is predicated is of general reference:

Xué   ér   shí   xí   zhī,   bú   yì   yuè   hū?
learn   and   often   review   it   not   also   happy   MP
'Isn't it a pleasure to review and reflect frequently while learning?'

iv. The subject of predication is the speaker or the listener:

Dǎsuàn   xiě   běn   shū.
plan   write   a   book
'I plan to write a book.'

Nǎtiān   huílái   de?
which-day   come-back   MP
'When did you come back?'

150 *Realizational relations and constitutive relations*

v. The subject of predication can be inferred from the context:

Wǔyáng hóu   Fán Kuài   zhě,   pèirén   yě.
Wuyang-Marquis Fan Kuai   MP   Pei-county-person   MP

. . . Yǐ   túgǒu   wéishì,   yǔ   gāozǔ   jù   yǐn.
. . . on   kill-dog live-on   with   Gaozu   both seclusion
'Fan Kuai, Marquis of Wuyang, was born in Pei county. . . . He was once a dog
butcher, and lived in seclusion with Gao Zu (Liu Bang) of the Han Dynasty.'

Zěnmeyàng?   — Hái   búcuò.
how   — still not-bad
'How was it?   — It was not bad'.
(A conversation between two people after watching a movie)

Translations of these sentences into English need to include subjects. That is why
Zhu concludes that what counts as a sentence in Chinese can only be determined
based on pauses and intonation. This definition of "sentence" for Chinese is exactly
the same as the one for "utterance" in English (Lyons 1968: 172; Crystal 1997).

As a matter of analytical methodology, Chao (1968: 42–56) adheres to the
principle of talking about ellipsis as little as possible. In his opinion, one-verb
declarative sentences such as *Duì* 'Correct!', *Xíng* 'Okay', *Yǒu* 'There is' *Shuāi*
'Fall—Mind you, you will fall down', and *Tàng* 'Hot—It's hot' should be considered self-sufficient, because they can be supplied with more than one kind of
subject in some cases, and in others, no form can serve as their subject. Take the
sentence *Duì* 'Correct!' for example. It is possible sometimes to treat it as reduced
from the sentence *Nǐ shuōde duì* 'What you say is correct', but there is no reason to
deny that it could also be a reduced form of *Nǐ shuōde huà duì* 'The words you said
were right', or *Nǐ shuōde nèigè duì* 'The one you mentioned was right', or even a
teacher's comment on students having correctly done what the teacher taught them
to do. Phrases like . . . *de shíhòu* (the time), . . . *de dìfāng* (the place), or . . . *de rén*
(the person) can probably be added after the subjects in sentences like *chīfàn děi
shǐ kuàizi* (eat-rice have-to use chopsticks, 'when you eat, you need to use chopsticks'), and *mǎipiào qǐng páiduì* (buy-ticket please wait-in-line, 'if you want to
buy a ticket, please queue up') where the connection between the subject and the
predicate are fairly loose, but it is difficult to decide which specific one applies to it.
However, given that it is unclear which of these possible phrases should be added,
it is best to treat *chīfàn* 'have meal' and *mǎipiào* 'buy a ticket' as the verbal subjects
of their sentences. As for sentences with the copula *shì* 'be' as the predicate, like
rénjia shì fēngnián 'They are a bumper year' (They have a bumper year), there is
no specific word or words that can be considered omitted or understood. Elaborations that fill in assumed omitted material like *rénjia de nián shì fēngnián* 'The year
they had was a bumper year' or *rénjia shì gè fēngnián de rénjia* 'That family is
one which had a bumper year' all sound awkward. Sentences like *jīnr xiàwǔ tǐcāo*
'This afternoon physical exercise' should be regarded as having nominal predicates
because it cannot be determined whether the omitted verb is *yǒu* 'have/there be',
shàng 'take up as a class hour', or *jiāo* 'teach'.

Realizational relations and constitutive relations 151

Lü (1979: 67–68) also adheres to this principle of analysis. He argues that "there were grammarians in the past who took logical propositions as the starting point for their approach to ellipsis. In so doing, it was inevitable that they would misuse the theory of 'ellipsis'". Important here is that "there are conditions placed on ellipsis in this theory". One of these conditions is that "there is only one expression that can be used to fill in deleted material".[3]

Jiang (2006) takes a step further and argues that the concept of "sentence" in Western research on language as represented by English studies has gradually become detached from that of "utterance" and evolved into an abstract unit, the "sentence". In Chinese, on the other hand, the sentence has remained a concrete unit of use.

This evolution is the process of grammaticalization (Shen 1994, 1998), through which usage hardens into grammar or the organization of composition hardens into syntax. The pragmatic unit "utterance" in English has gone through the process of grammaticalization and evolved into a syntactic unit "sentence". In contrast, the "sentence" in Chinese has not been totally grammaticalized into a syntactic unit. In terms of realizational and constitutive relations, the abstract "sentence" in English is realized in discourse as the concrete "utterance". In Chinese, what a sentence constitutes is a unit of discourse. Following is an illustration of this difference:

English sentence and utterance realizational relation
Chinese "sentence" and "discourse unit" constitutive relation

4.3.3 Subjects and topics

It is generally accepted that "subject" and "predicate" belong to grammatical categories, whereas "topic" and "comment" fall into pragmatic ones. The former pair is abstract; the latter pair, concrete. In Indo-European languages, subjects are subjects and topics are topics. The two are distinct constructs with different properties. But Chinese is different from them in that, as observed by Yuen Ren Chao, the subject in Chinese sentences is literally the subject matter to talk about, and the predicate is the comment on that matter. He elaborates on his ideas regarding the grammatical meaning of subject and predicate, writing that it is more appropriate to take subject and predicate in Chinese as topic and comment (Chao 1948: 35, 1968: 45). The subject-predicate relation in Western languages is mostly an actor-action relation. However, in Chinese, the proportion of the sentences with this kind of subject-predicate relation is very low, perhaps not much higher than 50%. Even in copular sentences, it is not definite that the subject will be equal to what occurs after the verb *shì* 'be'. Nor does the subject before an adjectival predicate have to possess the properties denoted by the adjective. The following are examples to illustrate this:

zhè jiàn shì zǎo fābiǎo le (This matter has long been published.)
zhè guā chīzhe hěn tián (Literally, 'this melon eat-DUR very sweet'. This melon tastes very sweet.)

152 *Realizational relations and constitutive relations*

tā shì gè Rìběn nǚrén (Literally, it means 'he is a Japanese woman'. But in context it means *tāde yòngrén shì gè Rìběn nǚrén* 'his servant is a Japanese woman'.)

The subjects of the two sentences *tāde yòngrén shì gè Rìběn nǚrén* and *tā shì gè Rìběn nǚrén* have the same grammatical form.

Subjects referring to a time, place or condition present an important contrast when compared to English as in the following pairs of examples:

ia. *Jīnr lěng* 'Today is cold'.
ib. *Jīnr bú qù le* '(We are, one is, etc.) today not going anymore'.
iia. *Zhèr shì nǎr* 'Where is here? [Where are we?]'
iib. *Zhèr bùnéng shuōhuà* 'Here (one) can't talk'.
iiia. *Tā sǐ le de huà jiǎnzhí bùkān shèxiǎng* 'It is simply unthinkable that he would die'.
iiib. *Tā sǐ le de huà, jiù bù róngyì jiějué le* '(In the) event of his death, (things) will be difficult to settle'.

For the b sentences in each of the aforementioned pairs, the English translation has to be supplied with a subject as the actor while the expression referring to a time, place, or condition becomes an adverb. However, the Chinese subject only serves to introduce the topic of discourse, and there is no difference between the subjects of the sentences in each pair in terms of their grammatical form (Chao 1968: 52).

Chao (1968: 70–71) further argues that sometimes the looseness of subject-predicate relations in Chinese

> would be ungrammatical in another language. . . . A purist, especially one who knows some Occidental language, is likely to correct his children or students when he hears such sentences, but goes on using them when not listening to himself—as who does?

He goes on to cite a frequently encountered situation in poems and couplets to prove that the grammatical meaning of subject in Chinese is topic. For example, consider a poem by Li Bai. *Yún xiǎng yīshang huā xiǎng róng* (Clouds think garments;/flowers think face. [less literally, 'Clouds remind one of her garments;/ flowers remind one of her face'.]), and the lines *qín lín qiūshuǐ tán míngyuè, jiǔ jìn dōngshān zhuó báiyún* (A lute near autumn waters play to the bright moon;/wine near the eastern mountain sip the white clouds [and less literally, 'With a lute near autumn waters, one plays under the bright moon;/with wine near the eastern mountains, one sips under the white clouds'.]).

In a paper on Chinese logic, Chao (1955) points out one of the divergences between Chinese and English. Those who have followed recent developments in formal logic are familiar with the paradoxes of material implication: Any given proposition implies a true proposition and a false proposition implies any proposition. But, in his opinion, the apparently paradoxical forms of material implication

Realizational relations and constitutive relations   153

are not without their popular expression in Chinese, and the paradoxes are, sometimes, not so paradoxical in Chinese logic. For example, people often say in Chinese: "If *p* is true, my name is not Wang". That is to say that for a speaker, a false proposition implies anything including even that his "name is not Wang". Another example is: "Only if the sun rises in the west, will such and such (impossible) things happen". Hence, the occurrence of the impossible implies anything including the sun's rising in the west. In our opinion, the reason why the paradoxes are not so paradoxical in Chinese is that the Chinese subject is a topic that is loosely related to the predicate. Both the conditional clause "If *p* is true" and the clause "Only if the sun rises in the west" are subjects and so are also topics. (See Chapter 3, Section 4.)

There are innumerable examples of subjects functioning as topics. According to Liu (2012), there are seemingly unusual comparative sentences in the Wu dialect. In these comparatives, the subject must be understood as a topic. Examples of this can be found in the Shaoxing dialect of Keqiao where there are sentences like *Xiǎo Wáng shì Xiǎo Lǐ cháng* (Xiao Wang is Xiao Li long), meaning 'Xiao Li is taller than Xiao Wang'. In this sentence, the subject "Xiao Wang" is in fact the base of comparison while "Xiao Li" is the comparative's subject. Actually, Chinese does not lack examples of taking the base of comparison rather than the subject of a comparative as the sentence topic, as in *Xiǎo Wáng ma, háishì Xiǎo Lǐ gāo* 'As for Xiao Wang, Xiao Li is taller than him'. Such comparative expressions with *háishì* 'still is' can often be heard in the Wu dialect in districts other than Shaoxing (Lin & Zheng 2014). This shows that the seemingly unusual comparative of the Shaoxing dialect is not so unusual after all. Zhang (2013) offers many interesting examples of this from Chinese idioms.

Since the Chinese subject is a topic, the Chinese concept of topic is different from the English one. Chafe (1976) is also aware of this kind of difference and claims that topics in different languages have different properties. While the English topic is a contrastive constituent in sentence-initial position, the Chinese topic sets a spatial, temporal, or personal framework or scope for the following predication. Consider the following examples:

The play, John saw yesterday. (The topic is a focus of contrast.)

Nàxiē   shùmù   shùshēn   dà.
those   trees   tree-trunk   big
'Those trees' trunks are big.'

Nà   gè   rén   yángmíng   qiáozhì   zhāng.
that   CL   person   foreign-name   George   Zhang
'That person has a foreign name, George Zhang.'

Xīngqītiān   dàjiā   bú   shàngbān.
Sunday   people   not   work
'On Sundays, people do not go to work'.
The English translation of the sentence adds a preposition before 'Sunday'.

154 *Realizational relations and constitutive relations*

Tiānkōng   wūyún   zhērì.
sky   dark-clouds block-the-sun
'In the sky, the dark clouds blocked out the sun'.
The English translation also adds a preposition before 'the sky'.

The subject-predicate structure in Chinese is free to serve as a predicate, commenting on the preceding topic, like in *shùshēn dà* and other examples mentioned earlier. Since a topic's properties in Chinese are different from those in English, the subject-topic relation in Chinese also differs from the one in English. This can be illustrated in terms of the realizational relation and the constitutive relation as shown here:

English: Subject—topic   realizational relation
Chinese: Subject—topic   constitutive relation

In the previous English example, the subject "John" is not realized as a topic. From the perspective of grammaticalization, the grammatical category "subject", which developed out of the pragmatic category "topic" through a process of emptying, has already become detached from topic. It has become a separate abstract category. In Chinese, on the other hand, "topic" has yet to become a syntactic category through a process of emptying. "Subject" has remained a concrete category, a category of use, up until now.

It has already been confirmed in many languages that the category "subject" evolved from the category "topic". For example, Givón (1979: 301) investigates the use of English among uneducated Americans. He found that the sentence type in i. was gradually developing into the sentence type in iii. with the rise of 'he-rides' as a new verb, and these changes may continue:

i. My ol'man, he rides with the Angels.
ii. My ol'man he-rides with the Angels.

"My ol'man" in i. is no other than a topic, and "he" is a subject referring back to the topic. "My ol'man" becomes a subject in ii. In some other languages, a pronoun like "he" can be attached to a verbal predicate and then abbreviated into a formal marker in agreement with the subject, thus giving rise to the grammatical category of subject. Simply put, a subject is a grammaticalized topic.[4] Therefore, though we may still use the commonly accepted term "subject" when discussing Chinese grammar, we should always bear in mind that the subject has not yet been highly grammaticalized in Chinese, and its grammatical meaning is still topic. Lapolla and Poa (2006) hold the same opinion and make ample arguments in support of it.

Two questions need to be addressed. Since some people, in spite of the principle of talking about ellipsis as little as possible (Chao 1968), still make efforts to supply a sentence with a so-called null subject and treat it as different from a topic, the first question to be addressed is whether it is possible to find such a subject. The following are idiosyncratic copular sentences with "recovered" subjects provided by Zhang and Tang (2010, 2011):

Nà chǎng dàhuǒ, (yuányīn) shì diànxiàn pǎo le diàn. 'That fire, [the cause] is the electricity leakage through the electric wires'.
Wǒ (diǎn de cān) shì zhájiàngmiàn. '[The food] I [ordered] is noodles with mixed sauce'.

In fact, given certain contexts, there are many other possible "null subjects" for the previous sentences, as in:

Nà chǎng dàhuǒ, (jiēguǒ) shì diànxiàn pǎo le diàn. 'That fire, [the consequence] is the electricity leakage through the electric wires'.
Wǒ (yòng de cáiliào) shì zhájiàngmiàn. '[The material] I [used] is noodles with mixed sauce'.

The speaker "I" of the last sentence may be an avant-garde artist who is talking about a special material used for a device. Theoretically speaking, as long as the variety of contexts is infinite, the possible choices for a null subject are limitless. Those who favor the hypothesis of null subjects take the topic-subject relation as a possessive relation in a broad sense and believe that a particle *de* 'a marker of modification' could be inserted to indicate the possessive relation, as in *Tā (de yòngrén) shì gè Rìběn nǚrén* 'He (his servant) is a Japanese woman'. Nevertheless, Chao (1968: 57–58) points out that the insertion of *de* will result in a change not only in the sentence structural but also in its meaning. Compare the following two pairs of sentences:

Tā	*dùzi*	*dà*	*le.*		*Tā*	*ěrduo*	*ruǎn.*
she	abdomen	big	PSP		he	ear	soft
'She is pregnant'.					'He is gullible'.		

Tā	*de*	*dùzi*	*dà*	*le.*	*Tā*	*de*	*ěrduo*	*ruǎn.*
she	MM	abdomen		PSP	he	MM	ear	soft
'Her abdomen has become big'.					'His ears are soft'.			

The primary meaning of *Tā dùzi dà le* is 'She is pregnant' while *Tā de dùzi dà le* means 'Her abdomen has become big (for some reason)'. *Tā ěrduo ruǎn* can be used to indicate that 'He is gullible' while *Tā de ěrduo ruǎn* simply means 'His ears are (physically) soft'. Generally speaking, the sentences with *de* are more likely to be taken literally, and those without *de* often have a specialized or a figurative meaning. (Chao 1968: 97) Moreover, the change with *de* is not available to all sentences without it. For example, *Jīnr tiān hǎo* 'Today, the weather is good' can be changed into *Jīnr de tiān hǎo* 'Today's weather is fine'. But *Jīnr Wáng xiānshēng lái* 'Today, Mr. Wang is coming' cannot be changed to **Jīnr de Wáng xiānshēng lái* 'Today's Mr. Wang is coming'. Therefore, it is not reasonable or feasible in Chinese to fill out null subjects.

4.3.4 So-called syntactic topics

The second question to be addressed is whether there is a so-called syntactic topic. As for the sentence *Zhèběn shū wǒ bù dǎsuàn xiě le* 'This book I am not going to write', both Yuen Ren Chao and Zhu Dexi treated *zhèběn shū* 'this book' as subject (a large subject) and *wǒ bù dǎsuàn xiě le* 'I am not going to write' as predicate, which is a subject-predicate structure on its own with *wǒ* 'I' as subject (a small subject). But later, some functional grammarians analyzed *zhèběn shū* as topic and *wǒ* as subject, treating grammatical and pragmatic categories on the same plane, which incurred criticisms from Zhu Dexi and many other scholars. After that, some scholars (i.e. Chen 1996; Xu & Liu 1998: 57) proposed the concept "syntactic topic" and treated *zhèběn shū* as an example of it, arguing that a syntactic topic is, like a subject, determined by its position in the sentence and placed before the subject. If they were right, the subject *wǒ* would not be a topic in the pragmatic sense, and the subject-topic relation in Chinese would not be a constitutive one. This proposal of "syntactic topic", however, is not reasonable, as it causes problems. Consider how an English subject is distinguished from a topic:

i. *The play* lasts two hours.
ii. The play, John saw yesterday.
iii. As for *the play*, the actress is beautiful.

"The play" in i. is a subject, which is not only an argument of the verbal predicate but also in agreement with it. "The play" in iii., in contrast, is a topic, which is neither an argument of the predicate nor in agreement with it, and, moreover, it has been preceded by a topic marker "as for". "The play" in ii. is something between subject and topic, for it is an argument of the predicate, but is not in agreement with it. As a result, of "agreement" and "argument", the two criteria for identifying subject or topic, the former is determining, as confirmation of an argument may be equivocal in some instances. Because of this, Western grammarians regard "the play" in ii. as a topic and believe argument structure is fundamental to syntactic structure. Thus they add a determiner to this topic, hence the concept of "syntactic topic", i.e. the topic of arguments. The "syntactic topic" is placed in the NP position ahead of the sentence S' as illustrated in the following tree diagram:

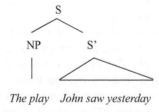

Figure 4.2 The tree diagram of *The play, John saw yesterday*

This is not a common sentence pattern in English. It is transformed from the common pattern *John saw the play yesterday* by moving *the play* from the object position to the beginning of the sentence and making it stressed, in order to give prominence to the contrastiveness of *the play* (What he saw is a play, not a film). This process is known as "topicalization". To put it in a nutshell, subject and topic in English belong to two separate and distinct categories, with the former being a syntactic category and the latter a pragmatic one. The "syntactic topic" is located on the interface between syntax and pragmatics and can be treated as a syntactic constituent, as illustrated in Figure 4.3:

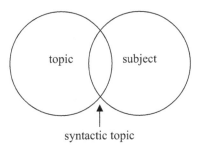

Figure 4.3 Syntactic topic

However, this type of topic-subject relation in English, separate but with a little overlap, does not apply to Chinese. First, there is no subject-predicate agreement in Chinese. Due to the lack of that important formal criterion for defining subject and topic in Indo-European languages, Chinese grammarians have to make judgments based on whether it is an argument or not. But when meaning is the only criterion for identifying an argument, it can be challenging. Take, for example, the sentence *Xiàng bízi cháng* 'The trunk of an elephant is long'. We can tell from the sentence that *bízi*, instead of *xiàng*, is the argument of the predicate *cháng*. Consequently, *bízi* can be identified as the subject and *xiàng* the topic. Yet, it is difficult to identify the arguments in the following sentences:

Xiàng   xìnggé   wēnshùn.
elephant disposition mild
'An elephant's disposition is mild.'

Zhè   bǎ   dāo   qiēròu   kuài
this CL   knife cut-meat fast
'This knife cuts meat easily.'

Zhè   dǐng màozi nǐ   héshì.
this CL   hat   you suit
'This hat suits you.'

If *xìnggé* were an argument of *wēnshùn*, then why not the *xiàng* a second argument? If *qiēròu* 'cut-meat' were an argument of *kuài*, then why not *zhè bǎ dāo* an argument too? And if *nǐ* were an argument of *héshì*, why not *zhè dǐng màozi*? What makes the situation even more complicated is that, besides the sentence *Xiàng bízi cháng* 'The trunk of an elephant is long', we may also say:

Bízi	xiàng	zuìcháng,	bózi	chángjǐnglù	zuìcháng.
nose	elephant	the-longest	neck	giraffe	the-longest

'As for noses, the elephant has the longest; as for necks, the giraffe has the longest.'

When illustrated with a tree diagram, the argument *bízi* would be placed before S' while the non-argument *xiàng* would be the subject of S'. In fact, a Chinese subject needs not serve as an argument of the predicate verb. What is more important is that Chinese sentences can go without subjects, which are still regarded as normal sentences in Chinese. For example, in the sentence *Zhè běn shū wǒ bù dǎsuàn xiě le* 'This book I am not going to write', *bù dǎsuàn xiě le* 'not going to write' is also a normal sentence by itself which can be labeled as S'' as illustrated in the following tree diagram. Thus, there is no reason to deny *wǒ* 'I' (before S'') as a topic.

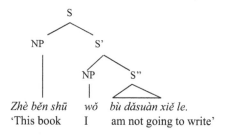

Figure 4.4 The tree diagram of *Zhè běn shū wǒ bù dǎsuàn xiě le*

That is why Shen (1999: 235) points out that the "syntactic topic" treatment simply replaces the labels of "large subject" and "small subject" with "syntactic topic" and "subject", respectively. Then it is not surprising that Yuan (1996) redefines *zhè běn shū* as "topical subject", which is in essence a "large subject". In fact, there are both similarities and differences between the "large subject" and the "small subject". If their similarities are to be highlighted, both can be referred to as "subject", with different adjectives, "large" or "small"; if their differences are to be emphasized, they can be labeled as "(syntactic) topic" and "subject" respectively. Whatever the case is, the Chinese "topic" has not been fully grammaticalized into a syntactic category. If the subject is analyzed as an argument, it is simply a special type of topic, i.e., the "syntactic topic", which still falls into the pragmatic category of topic. Therefore, the "subject" which is essentially a topic is, by its very nature, still a pragmatic category. The inclusion of subject in topic in Chinese can be illustrated with the following figure:

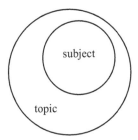

Figure 4.5 The inclusion of subject in topic in Chinese

Just as there is no nominalization of verbs in Chinese, there is no topicalization of subject either; both hypotheses violate the principle of simplicity. Some people may fear that the proposed inclusion framework would erase the distinction between the major components of a sentence that serve as an argument and those that do not. That fear is unnecessary, because the inclusion framework does not remove the distinction but simply reduces its distinctiveness, which draws it closer to the linguistic facts of Chinese and thus eliminates possible theoretical inconsistencies. In Chinese, those who insist on a topic-subject distinction need to give "topic" a positive definition, which is, however, a daunting task.

Many people have accepted Li and Thompson's (1976) view that English is a subject-prominent language while Chinese is a topic-prominent language. It, however, takes as its premise the dichotomy between subject and topic, and is also based on Indo-European languages. It does not conform to the facts of the Chinese language. In comparison with Yuen Ren Chao's assertion that subjects are essentially topics, this is more of a step back than a step forward in exploring the features of the Chinese language.

With the help of the concepts "realizational relation" and "constitutive relation", we can now explain the differences between English and Chinese in the three categories "sentence", "subject/predicate", and "noun/verb":

Table 4.1 English and Chinese "sentence", "subject/predicate", and "noun/verb" in terms of realizational and constitutive relations

	sentence/utterance	*subject/predicate— topic/comment*	*noun/verb—reference/ predication*
English	realizational	realizational	realizational
Chinese	constitutive	constitutive	constitutive

Concepts such as "sentence", "subject/predicate", and "noun/verb" are all among the most essential conceptual tools or theoretical constructs to study grammar. As all of them demonstrate the same difference between Chinese and English, the two languages cannot be considered to be different in random aspects but in fundamental grammatical systems. As we have mentioned earlier in this book,

160 *Realizational relations and constitutive relations*

Chinese linguists can continue to use traditional terms like "sentence", "subject/predicate", and "noun/verb" for convenience and for comparative studies between Chinese and other languages, but we must always keep in mind that their connotations and denotations are systematically different from their English counterparts.

Some people do not quite understand how my concepts of realizational/constitutive relations relate to and differ from Zhu Dexi's compositional/realizational relations (see Chapter 2, Section 2.2). Here is a brief explanation. We inherit most of Zhu Dexi's scholarly legacy and only suggest examining the relation between phrases and sentences in Indo-European languages along the abstract-concrete dimension, that is, studying Indo-European languages with reference to Chinese. Chinese has long been studied from the perspective of Indo-European languages, but why are people upset when we do the opposite? As seen from the perspective of Chinese, the compositional relations of Indo-European languages are actually indirect realizational relations, whereas their Chinese counterparts are direct realizational relations. To highlight the difference between direct and indirect realizational relations, we use the term "constitutive relation" for "direct realizational relation" and retain the term "realizational relation" for "indirect realizational relation". The second concern is that such terms make it easier for linguistics to communicate with other disciplines that have widely adopted this pair of terms "realizational/constitutive". (See suggestions offered by Wang Juquan 2014.)

4.3.5 Head feature convention revisited

The concepts of realizational/constitutive relations provide a new perspective on the phrase *zhè běn shū de chūbǎn* 'the publication of this book' that violates the head feature convention (see Chapter 2, Section 3). According to the conceptual integration theory of cognitive linguistics (Fauconnier & Turner 2003), Chinese words, phrases, and sentences are primarily formed through conceptual integration rather than grammatical derivation, as compared with the Indo-European languages. (See Shen 2006b, 2006c, 2007, 2008.)

The phrase *zhè běn shū de chūbǎn* 'the publication of this book' is a result of integrating the two concepts expressed by *zhè běn shū de N* 'this book's *N*' and *chūbǎn le zhè běn shū* 'published this book'. *N* refers to a thing such as the cover or content of the book, *chūbǎn* predicates an event, and the whole phrase *zhè běn shū de chūbǎn* refers to an event. Integration of concepts always involves compressing two concepts and leaving out parts of them. The conceptual integration of *zhè běn shū de chūbǎn* leaves out the tense feature of *chūbǎn le zhè běn shū* (we cannot add a tense particle *le* to *zhè běn shū de chūbǎn*) and part of the nominal features of *zhè běn shū de N* (we can say *zhè běn shū de chíchí bù chūbǎn* by adding adverbs *chíchí* 'very late' and *bù* 'not').

The head feature convention posits that the part determines the feature of the whole, and thus the feature of the whole must match the head feature. In contrast, the conceptual integration theory assumes that the property of the whole does not rely entirely on its components, so the integrated concept cannot always be disintegrated and restored as an extension of the head. For example, *dà shù* 'big tree' can be understood as an extension of the head *shù* 'tree', but *dàchē* 'livestock-drawn cart or wagon' cannot be taken as an extension of *chē*. Moreover, there is nothing wrong with saying *yī liàng xiǎo dàchē* 'a small cart or wagon', but one cannot say *yī kē xiǎo dà shù* 'a small big tree'. That is because *dàchē* as an integrated concept is not structurally or semantically the sum total of *dà* and *chē*.

Chinese and Indo-European languages have different levels of conceptual integration. There is a low level of integration in Indo-European languages like English where the phrase *the publication of this book* can easily be disintegrated and restored to become an extension of the head, whereas *zhè běn shū de chūbǎn* 'the publication of this book' in Chinese is integrated so highly that it cannot be disintegrated and restored as an extension of the head.

Why do Chinese and Indo-European languages have different levels of integration? The answer lies in the distinction between direct and indirect integration, the former being on a higher level of integration whereas the latter is on a lower level. The Chinese phrase *zhè běn shū de chūbǎn* is the result of direct integration, because *chūbǎn* as a predicative expression and *chūbǎn* as a referring expression are in a constitutive relation. In contrast, the English phrase *the publication of this book* is the result of indirect integration, because *publish* as a predicative expression and *publication* as a referring expression are in a realizational relation, requiring a process of realization. Thus, the so-called problem of *zhè běn shū de chūbǎn* violating the head feature convention can also be resolved from the perspective of integrating concepts in constitutive and realizational relations. This is logically consistent with the resolution proposed in Section 3 of Chapter 2.

4.4   Chinese grammar and usage

4.4.1   *Grammatical classes and usage classes*

Linguists agree that grammatical and pragmatic dimensions should be distinguished, but the verbs-as-nouns theory claims that Chinese nouns and verbs are referring and predicative expressions respectively. This leads to a confusion: Are these two dimensions lumped together in the theory? As a matter of fact, there is no clear distinction in Chinese between grammatical and pragmatic categories (because grammar is included in usage in Chinese), which is exactly a key feature of the Chinese language. Therefore, the verbs-as-nouns theory cannot by any means be viewed as lumping grammatical and pragmatic dimensions together. This can be further demonstrated from a variety of perspectives.

While Zhu Dexi suggests that the grammatical and expression (or pragmatic) dimensions must be distinguished, he has also realized that Chinese differs from Indo-European languages in the way they relate usage to grammar. In his view, phrases and sentences in Chinese are in a relation of "abstract grammatical structures" and "concrete utterances". This implies that Chinese sentences are actually utterances. He illustrates the differences between Chinese and Latin word order by

162   *Realizational relations and constitutive relations*

using the sentence *Bǎoluó kànjiàn le Mǎlì* 'Paul saw Mary', which may be written in six different ways in Latin (Zhu 1985: 3):

Paulus vidit Mariam.   *Mariam vidit Paulus.*
Paulus Mariam vidit.   *Mariam Paulus vidit.*
Vidit Paulus Mariam.   *Vidit Mariam Paulus.*

Unlike Latin, Chinese word order is less flexible. Besides this difference, Zhu adds, "While six variations of word order in Latin do not affect the syntactic structure, changing the word order in Chinese frequently results in various syntactic structures. This suggests that word order in Chinese is more significant than in Indo-European languages". With the help of context, this statement can be understood as follows. Although the subject-predicate-object structure does not change when the word order in Latin changes, pragmatic elements like topic, focus, and viewpoint do change. However, in Chinese, both usage and grammatical structure are impacted by the change in word order. As an example, consider the following:

Wǒ   bù   chī   yángròu.
I   not   eat   mutton
'I don't eat mutton.'

Yángròu   wǒ   (kě)   bù   chī.
mutton   I   actually   not   eat
'Mutton, I don't eat.'

While the sentence structure of *Wǒ bù chī yángròu* is subject-verb-object, *Yángròu wǒ (kě) bù chī*, like *Xiàng bízi cháng*, is in a subject-subject-predicate structure, with a subject-predicate phrase being its predicate.

A second example can be seen in the different grammatical structures formed with different types of verbs. According to Zhu (1980), in terms of syntactic distribution, transitive verbs can be divided into *dǎ* 'hit' type and *ái* 'suffer' type, and intransitive verbs into *diào* 'fall' type and *wán* 'play' type, and different word orders of different types of verbs may represent different grammatical structures. Therefore, changes in word order also affect the grammatical structure in Chinese:

Nǐ lín zháo yǔ méiyǒu? 'Did you get caught in the rain or not?' (Structurally the
   same as *Bùshí ái zháo quántóu méiyǒu?* 'Did Bush take any punches or not?')
Yǔ lín zháo nǐ méiyǒu? 'Did the rain catch you or not?' (Structurally the same as
   Quántóu dǎ zháo Bùshí méiyǒu? 'Did the fists hit Bush or not?')

Tā zhù zài chénglǐ 'He lives in the city'. (Structurally the same as *Háizi diào zài
   jǐnglǐ* 'The child fell into the well'.)
Tā zài chénglǐ zhù 'He is living in the city'. (Structurally the same as *Háizi zài wūlǐ
   wán* 'The child is playing in the room'.)

Realizational relations and constitutive relations 163

This can also be demonstrated from another perspective. Consider the following examples:

> i. *Zhè   běn   shū   chūbǎn   le.*
>   this   CL   book   publish   PSP
>   'This book has been published.'

> ii. *?Zhè   běn   shū   chūbǎn.*
>   this   CL   book   publish

Zhè   běn   shū   chūbǎn,   nà   běn   shū   bù   chūbǎn.
this   CL   book   publish   that   CL   book   not   publish
'This book will be published, but that one will not.'

Zhè   běn   shū   chūbǎn   bù   chūbǎn?   Zhè   běn   shū   chūbǎn.
this   CL   book   publish   not   publish   this   CL   book   publish
'(Will) this book be published or not? It will.'

In the i. group, the sentence marked with ? cannot occur by itself, but it can be said in a parallel structure or as a reply to a question. Then, to which dimension, grammatical or pragmatic, should we ascribe the distinction between i. and ii.? Since grammar rules are obligatory, *this book publish* in English is not acceptable in any case because it violates English grammar rules. But it can be accepted in Chinese in certain contexts as in i., which implies that i. and ii. only differ in the pragmatic dimension, and that the sentence marked with ? in ii. is simply unacceptable in usage but not in grammar.

This assertion, however, would set us up for a dilemma, since more similar problems remain unsolved, for example:

> i. *Jīnr   guài   lěng   de.*
>   today   quite   cold   MP
>   'It is quite cold today.'

> ii. *?Jīnr   lěng.*
>   today   cold

Jīnr   lěng,   zuór   nuǎnhuo.
today   cold   yesterday   warm
'Today it is cold; yesterday it is warm.'

Jīnr   lěng   bù   lěng?   Jīnr   lěng.
today   cold   or   not   today   cold
'Is it cold or not today? It is cold today.'

As is explained earlier, *Jīnr lěng* in ii. is acceptable only when it occurs in a parallel structure or as a reply to a question. Therefore, *Jīnr lěng* that stands alone should also be considered unacceptable in usage but not in grammar, and

164 *Realizational relations and constitutive relations*

the distinction between i. and ii. should also be taken as a difference in usage. If *lěng* 'cold' and *guài lěng de* 'quite cold' are grouped into two different categories based on the previous distinction, like Zhu Dexi who classifies *lěng* and *guài lěng de* as a qualitative and a stative adjective respectively, those two categories fall still into usage classes rather than grammatical classes. However, most people, including Zhu, treat the distinction between i. and ii. as a grammatical issue and regard qualitative and stative adjectives as two grammatical categories. What is left to discuss if we argue that the distinction between i. and ii. is a usage issue and exclude it from our discussion on grammatical issues given that this kind of distinction is highly prevalent in Chinese and is evident in a significant number of examples? It is ironically common for those who claim they avoid usage issues in their grammatical studies to use examples such as these. As a matter of fact, since the so-called grammatical categories and units in Chinese are constituted by pragmatic categories and units, it is virtually impossible to discuss grammatical issues without addressing usage, or there is not much left to discuss.[5]

There is still an aspect of demonstration that needs to be addressed. In generative grammar, intransitive verbs are syntactically classified into unergative verbs like *bìng* 'be sick' and *xiào* 'laugh' and unaccusative verbs like *sǐ* 'die' and *lái* 'come'. There is also evidence in Chinese that supports such a classification, for example:

Wáng	*Miǎn*	*de*	*fùqīn*	*bìng*	*le.*
Wang	Mian	MM	father	be sick	PSP

'Wang Mian's father was sick.'

*Wáng	*Miǎn*	*bìng*	*le*	*fùqīn.*
Wang	Mian	be sick	PSP	father

Wáng	*Miǎn*	*de*	*kèrén*	*xiào*	*le.*
Wang	Mian	MM	guest	laugh	PSP

'Wang Mian's guests laughed.'

*Wáng	*Miǎn*	*xiào*	*le*	*kèrén.*
Wang	Mian	laugh	PSP	guest

Wáng	*Miǎn*	*de*	*fùqīn*	*sǐ*	*le.*
Wang	Mian	MM	father	die	PSP

'Wang Mian's father died.'

Wáng	*Miǎn*	*sǐ*	*le*	*fùqīn.*
Wang	Mian	die	PSP	father

'Wang Mian suffered a loss from his father's death.'

Wáng	*Miǎn*	*de*	*kèrén*	*lái*	*le.*
Wang	Mian	MM	guest	come	PSP

'Wang Mian's guests came.'

Wáng	*Miǎn*	*lái*	*le*	*kèrén.*
Wang	Mian	come	PSP	guest

'Wang Mian encountered the visits of his guests.'

Shen (2006b, 2009) points out that these two classes of intransitive verbs differ in usage instead of grammar. While *Wáng Miǎn bìng le fùqīn* is not acceptable, both of the following sentences are acceptable:

Wáng	*Miǎn*	*jiā*	*bìng*	*le*	*yī*	*gè*	*rén.*
Wang	Mian	family	be sick	PSP	one	CL	person

'One of Wang Mian's family members was sick.'

Wáng Miǎn bìng le yī gè gōngrén
Wang Mian be sick PSP one CL worker
'One of Wang Mian's workers was sick'.
(Wang Mian understood as an employer)

Liu (2009) even provides a large number of Chinese sentences in which verbs like *bìng* 'be sick' or *xiào* 'laugh' are followed by an object:

(Fēidiǎn de shíhòu) Xiǎo Lǐ yě bìng le yī gè mèimèi.
SARS MM time Xiao Li also be sick PSP one CL younger sister
'(During the SARS period,) one of Xiao Li's younger sisters also fell sick.'

Guō Dégāng yīkāikǒu, wǒmen sā jiù xiào le liǎ.
Guo Degang start-to-speak we three then laugh PSP two
'The minute Guo Degang started to speak, two of us three broke into laughter at his performance.'

Zàichǎng de rén kū le yī dà piàn.
on the scene MM people cry PSP one big CL
'Most of the people cried on the scene.'

Búdào qīdiǎn, wǒmen sùshè jiù shuì le liǎng gè rén
not 7 o'clock our dormitory already sleep PSP two CL person
'It's not 7 p.m. yet. But two of our dormitory mates already fell asleep.'

Búdào liùdiǎn, nà qún háizi jiù qǐ le Tiāntiān hé Nàonào liǎng gè.
not 6 o'clock that CL child already get up PSP Tiantian and Naonao two CL
'It's not 6 a.m. yet. But two of the children, Tiantian and Naonao, already got up.'

Lìdìngtiàoyuǎn (quánbān) yǐjīng tiào le sānshí gè tóngxué le.
standing-long-jump whole-class already jump PSP thirty CL students PSP
'Thirty students of the class have already taken the standing long jump test.'

Wǒ dàxué tóngxué yǐjīng líhūn le hǎo jǐ gè le.
my college classmates already divorce PSP quite several CL PSP
'Quite a few of my college classmates have already divorced.'

Tāmen bàngōngshì jiēlián gǎnmào le sān sì gè rén.
their office in a row catch a cold PSP three four CL person
'Three or four colleagues in their office caught a cold in a row.'

Jīntiān shàngwǔ zhè tái pǎobùjī yīlián páo guò sān gè dàpàngzi.
today morning this CL treadmill succession run EXP three CL fatty
'A succession of three fatties were seen running on this treadmill this morning.'

166 *Realizational relations and constitutive relations*

In Chinese, depending on certain contexts, intransitive verbs may be followed by an object, and transitive verbs may take no objects. According to Lu Bingfu (in a personal correspondence), the English sentence *The window broke* is transformed from *I broke the window* with a different argument structure, and this transformation called "ambitransitive alternation" can only happen with certain transitive verbs. However, the Chinese sentence *Chuāngzi dǎpò le* 'The window broke' cannot be considered to represent a new argument structure as compared to the sentence *Wǒ dǎpò le chuāngzi* 'I broke the window'. It is simply a change in usage, for almost all sentences with transitive verbs can be changed in this way, as in:

Wǒ   chī   le   yángròu.
I   eat   PSP   mutton
'I ate mutton.'

Yángròu   chī   le.
Mutton   eat   PSP
'Mutton has been eaten.'

The coordination condition can be still another possible perspective. As discussed in Section 3.2 of Chapter 2, the juxtaposed nouns and verbs in Chinese violate the coordination condition. However, by applying common sense, we may realize that the coordination test only requires that the elements to be coordinated belong to the same class and doesn't specify which class. That is to say, the elements can be of the same class in terms of grammar, meaning, or usage. Even though English requires its elements to belong to the same grammatical class, it does not absolutely exclude those of the same semantic or pragmatic class. Consider the following examples:

Any change is bound to have numerous *academic and cost* implications.
John is *a banker and extremely rich.*

Both previous sentences contain a coordinated part consisting of a nominal constituent and an adjectival constituent. *Academic* and *cost* in the first sentence are both attributes that modify the noun that follows, and *a banker* and *extremely rich* are both predicative complements preceded by the copula *be*. Halliday (1994: 227) also uses a choice question *plain or with cream?* as an example to illustrate that any two functionally equivalent elements (serving as modifiers) can be coordinated.[6] The unacceptability of the following sentence is simply due to the fact that the two elements conjoined are not of the same semantic category (Fillmore 1968: 22):

?? *John* and *a hammer* broke the window.

The semantic role of *John* in the previous sentence is an agent while that of *a hammer* is an instrument, though both of them are nominal phrases. The two coordinated

Realizational relations and constitutive relations 167

elements in the following sentences are neither of the same grammatical category nor semantic category but of the same pragmatic category, both functioning as a comment of the same topic (Matthews 1981: 214):

The other notes [you do need] and [would be better in the text].
The cakes [you'll need on Wednesday] and [are better made fresh].

It can be seen from the previous examples that English and Chinese have different restrictions for the coordination condition. Coordinated elements in English must fall into the same grammatical category (those that fall into the same semantic or pragmatic category are considered exceptional), whereas in Chinese they need only be of the same semantic or pragmatic category. The coordinated elements in *túshū hé chūbǎn* 'books and publishing' and in *zhè běn shū hé tā de chūbǎn* 'this book and its publishing' are all referring expressions in usage, with the only difference being that one refers to a thing and the other to an action.

Since Chinese grammatical categories and units are constituted by pragmatic categories and units, Chinese grammatical studies should shift their focus from grammar to usage, from grammaticality to acceptability of usage.[7]

4.4.2 The grammar and usage of answering questions

Two articles by Yuen Ren Chao (1955, 1959) on Chinese logic discuss how Chinese and Indo-European languages differ in the way of answering questions. Indo-European languages follow the logic of being "affirmative" or "negative", whereas the Chinese language works on the logic of being "true" or "false" and uses statements of agreement or disagreement. For example, if a Chinese speaker agrees that *Zánmen méiyǒu xiāngjiāo* 'We have no bananas', s/he will say *Shìde, zánmen méiyǒu xiāngjiāo* 'Yes, we have no bananas'; if s/he does not agree with another's criticism *Nǐ yīdiǎn méi jiàoyǎng* 'You're not educated at all', s/he will reply *Búshì, wǒ yǒu jiàoyǎng* 'No, I am educated'. *Shìde* 'yes' in Chinese responses means "What you said is true. I agree", and *búshì* 'no' means "What you said is false. I don't agree". Conversely, in English, the reply to show agreement is *No, we don't have bananas*, and to show disagreement is *Yes, I am educated*, in which *yes* introduces an affirmative response and *no* introduces a negative response.

When typologists investigate languages, they usually first study different sentence types such as declarative, interrogative, and imperative sentences. Among interrogative sentences, yes-no questions are their primary concern. Responses to yes-no questions are of two types (Liu 2008: 26–27), i.e., the answer-positioning type and the Q&A-relationship type. The two types are distinguished depending on how they respond to negative yes-no questions. As an answer-positioning type, the English answer to the negative yes-no question *Didn't John go there?* would be "Yes" if John did go, as it would be followed by an affirmative response "he did". If John did not go, the answer would be "No", followed by a negative response "he didn't". In contrast, Chinese responses to negative yes-no questions belong to the Q&A-relationship type. If Lao Zhang actually went there, the Chinese answer to

168 *Realizational relations and constitutive relations*

the negative yes-no question *Lǎo Zhāng méiyǒu qù ma?* 'Didn't Lao Zhang go there?' would be *bù* 'no' (equivalent to *búshì* 'is not', or *búduì* 'not right'), because the following response *tā qù le* 'he did' is inconsistent with the propositional content of the question. If Lao Zhang did not go there, the response would be *shì* 'yes' (equivalent to *shìde* 'yes', *duì* 'right', or *duìde* 'right'), because the following response *tā méi qù* 'he didn't' is consistent with the propositional content of the question. In this regard, Japanese is of the same Q&A-relationship type as Chinese, and Russian adopts both types. Nevertheless, the answer-positioning type is the primary and unmarked type. This idea of the two types is fully consistent with Yuen Ren Chao's view introduced at the beginning of this section.

A lot of people know from experience that Chinese learners of English and foreign learners of Chinese often make mistakes in their responses to negative yes-no questions, causing misunderstandings in cross-linguistic communication. Then what is the root cause of this significant difference between Chinese and English? The answer lies in that English is a grammar-type language while Chinese is a usage-type language. A grammar-type language distinguishes among different grammatical categories such as sentences, subjects and predicates, nouns and verbs, while a usage-type language distinguishes between pragmatic categories such as utterances, topics and comments, referring and predicative expressions. Similarly, affirmation and negation are grammatical categories and means, while agreement and disagreement are pragmatic categories and means. The Chinese responses *shìde* 'yes' and *búshì* 'is not' are a judgment not only on the truth value of the propositional content but also on whether the speech act of the interlocutor is right or wrong. In fact, *shìde* is often replaced by (*nǐ*) *shuō de shì* 'what (you) said is right' and *búshì* by (*nǐ*) *shuō de búshì* 'what (you) said is not right', as in:

(*Nǐ*) *shuō de shì, zánmen méiyǒu xiāngjiāo.* 'What (you) said is right. We have no bananas'.
(*nǐ*) *shuō de búshì, wǒ yǒu jiàoyǎng.* 'What (you) said is not right. I am educated'.

The Q&A-relationship type is therefore not only related to the affirmative or negative responses but also to whether the propositional content of the question is agreed upon or not, as opposed to the answer-positioning type, which is grammar-type and only related to the affirmative or negative responses that follow. By applying the theory of grammaticalization, it can be interpreted that the means of expressing agreement or disagreement have been grammaticalized in English into the affirmative or negative forms of predicates. But such grammaticalization has not been fulfilled in Chinese, as a result of which pragmatic means remain in use.

The operation of Chinese logic on the truth values of propositions is also related to the referentiality of Chinese predicates (see Chapter 6). A truth-value judgment involves determining not only whether the *shì* 'matter' to be predicated is true or false but also whether the *wù* 'thing' to be referred to is true or false. Ultimately, it is a judgment on the truth value of the *wù* 'thing' to be referred to, for a *shì* 'matter' could also be regarded as an abstract *wù* 'thing'.[8] We may judge whether something is true or false, but we cannot determine whether anything is affirmative or negative, as affirmative or negative assertions typically apply to matters rather than things. To sum up, the English affirmative *yes* and the negative *no* are both responses to the predicative predicates in interrogative sentences, whereas the Chinese responses *shìde* 'yes' and *búshì* 'is not', which indicate the truth value of a proposition, are responses to the referential utterances, including the utterances referring to actions.

4.4.3 Usage includes grammar

Chinese and Indo-European languages differ in how usage is related to grammar, which can be illustrated with the following figure:

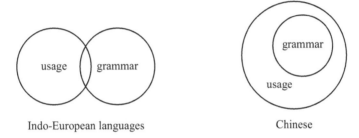

Figure 4.6 The relationship between usage and grammar in Indo-European languages and in Chinese

In Indo-European languages (especially Latin), changes in usage are generally different from those in grammar, and there is an interface between usage and grammar. Chinese, however, does not have an interface between usage and grammar, as changes in usage are also often changes in grammar, with the latter included in the former. That is, grammar has split off from usage in Indo-European languages but not yet in Chinese, where usage and grammar are still in an inclusion pattern. In Chinese, the grammar as the essence of language structure is included in its usage.[9] This inclusion pattern implies that, on the one hand, usage and grammar are not separated from each other because grammatical issues are also usage issues but, on the other, they are independent of each other, because not all usage issues are grammatical issues.[10]

Rules of Chinese word order are comparatively simple and can be summarized as follows: Subjects precede predicates, objects follow the verbs, and all modifiers appear before their heads. Are they only grammar rules and not usage rules? The answer is that they are usage rules as well. Subjects and predicates in Chinese are in fact topics and comments respectively, and the order in which topics precede comments is in accordance with the general principle of information structure. The order of objects after verbs in spoken language aligns with the spatial order of natural gestures in deaf individuals' natural sign language (Yau 2014: 78). In Ancient Chinese, objects typically come after verbs except for pronoun objects. This also conforms to the principle of information structure that more informative and less identifiable constituents tend to be placed towards the end of a sentence. In languages with a dominant order of objects preceding verbs, it is generally possible for an object of various types to be moved after the verb, but pronoun objects are excluded from this possibility. Lu (2005) argues from the perspective of word order typology that the word order of modifiers preceding their heads is stable and optimal since it conforms not only to the identifiability precedence principle but also to the semantic proximity principle. Zhang (2011) also holds that the word order of syntactic structure in Chinese substantially mirrors that of pragmatic structure. Chinese word order, to put it simply, is a kind of "natural order", whose rules are by no means in conflict with pragmatic principles.

To argue that Chinese usage includes grammar is not to deny the distinction between them but to emphasize the unified aspect of the two. Recent years have seen quite a number of Chinese grammarians suggest studying Chinese from three dimensions, namely grammar, semantics, and pragmatics. Historically, it was the semiotician Morris (1938) who first proposed separating these three dimensions as early as the 1930s. According to him, signs are formally related to each other in "syntactics" (equivalent to "grammar"), to objects in "semantics", and to interpreters in "pragmatics". Hence, there is nothing new about the three-dimensional approach. Moreover, generative grammar uses the three dimensions as the basis for its arguments (except that dimensions are called modules), and maintains their discreteness and autonomy while firmly opposing the idea of lumping them together. The advocates of a three-dimensional approach to Chinese grammar actually argue for integrating rather than segregating the three dimensions in exploring the linguistic facts of Chinese. Section 6 of Chapter 4 in Volume II will explain this further.

If the relationship between usage and grammar is viewed from the dynamic evolutionary perspective of "grammaticalization of usage", Figure 4.6 can be revised as follows:

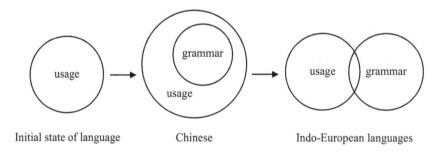

Initial state of language   Chinese   Indo-European languages

Figure 4.7 Grammaticalization of usage

Figure 4.7 illustrates how usage in the initial state of language evolved into grammar in Indo-European languages, which split off from usage and stood in opposition to it. Although grammar appears in the usage of Chinese, it has not yet split off. Usage and grammar are still in an inclusion pattern in Chinese. It follows that Indo-European languages are more grammaticalized than Chinese. The

Realizational relations and constitutive relations 171

inclusion of grammar in usage in Chinese provides a logical explanation for the statement that Chinese grammar is based on usage. Despite the separation of grammar from usage in Indo-European languages, it can still be said from an evolutionary perspective that English grammar is also based on usage, for this sequence of evolution depicted in Figure 4.7 is universal in human languages. Although a logical explanation is not necessarily consistent with a historical interpretation, it is certainly better for them to be consistent in explaining linguistic facts. Our explanation achieves such logical-historical consistency: Logically, there is a possible pattern in which usage includes grammar; historically, there is a phase in which usage includes grammar. It is in this logical-historical sense that we argue that Chinese is a usage-type language.

Notes

1 We have a compound term "moral court". This compound is also the name of a TV program with high ratings.
2 In the trial edition of *The Contemporary Chinese Dictionary* when first published, the note in parentheses in Definition ② only said, "not limited to nouns". Later editions added the word "grammatical" before nouns. This implies that the editors of the first test edition believed that "nouns" of course meant "grammatical nouns" in the note "not limited to nouns". Later, they realized that there was a problem and added "grammatical" because the word *míngcí* 'noun' is generally understood as *míngcír* 'name'. This modification shows a shift of the editors' perspective from grammarians to general readers. This was a laudable change.
3 Qi Gong (1997: 2) argues that to omit too much will leave the audience with a sense of it being evasive rhetoric. He offers a vivid analogy: Apes have tails, but humans do not; is this due to evolution, or is it that human beings have chosen to "omit" the tail?
4 There are occasionally sentences in colloquial English with loose subject-predicate relations, for example, (*Who's responsible for delivering which sandwiches?*) *I'm the sandwiches on the table. And you're those sandwiches that John put in the refrigerator, remember?* (Ward 2004: ex.18). Despite this, the morphological agreement between the predicate verb and the subject should still be maintained. From this, it can be seen that the subject in English is a grammaticalized topic.
5 Zhang Bojiang (2009) argues that the D category (determiners) in generative grammar is actually pragmatic in nature in Chinese.
6 My thanks go to Randy J. LaPolla who reminded me of Halliday's view and the example cited.
7 For example, the question of whether the sentence *Tāliǎ kāifáng shì wǒ zhàokāi de yántǎohuì* 'They stayed in a hotel is I organized the seminar' (That they stay in a hotel is to attend a seminar there organized by me) is grammatical or not is problematic by itself, because it may be the best way of expressing the idea and retaining its liveliness and humor under certain circumstances like the following:

> The job that wily boss gave me is to cover up whatever he and his mistress do. That they go sightseeing abroad is to be on a business trip abroad with me; that they dine together is to discuss business with me; that they stay in a hotel is to attend a seminar there organized by me.
>
> (Quoted from *Aimless Beautiful Life* by Hong Huang)

8 The philosopher Husserl holds that what can be judged as true or false includes not only propositions but also names, whose truth value is more fundamental than propositions'. This is Husserl and Frege's dispute about "truth". (See Gao 2013.) The view that names

172　*Realizational relations and constitutive relations*

can be true or false is consistent with the traditional Chinese philosophical tenet "names must reflect reality" (Wang Wenbin 2014).

9　In mainstream Chinese philosophy, ontology and methodology are inseparable, suggesting the abstract *Dao* is manifested in concrete *qi* (tangible objects). See Section 3 of the Concluding Remarks in Volume II.

10　It is exactly because usage and grammar are also independent of each other that we still need two sets of terms for them, such as "nouns/verbs" and "referring expressions/predicative expressions".

References

Arbib, M. A. (2012) *How the Brain Got Language: The Mirror System Hypothesis*, Oxford: Oxford University Press.

Bejarano, T. (2011) *Becoming Human: From Pointing Gestures to Syntax*, Amsterdam: John Benjamins.

Boyd, R. (1993) 'Metaphor and Theory Change: What Is "Metaphor" a Metaphor for?', in Andrew Ortony (ed) *Metaphor and Thought*, 2nd ed., Cambridge: Cambridge University Press, 481–532.

Chafe, W. L. (1976) 'Givenness, Contrastiveness, Definiteness, Subjects, Topics and Point of View', in C. N. Li (ed) *Subject and Topic*, New York: Academic Press, 25–55.

Chao, Yuen Ren (1948) *Mandarin Primer*, Cambridge, MA: Harvard University Press.

Chao, Yuen Ren (1955) 'Notes on Chinese Grammar and Logic', *Philosophy East and West* V(1): 31–41, also in Dil (ed) 1976, 237–249. Translated as 'Hanyu Yufa yu Luoji Zatan' by Bai Shuo, in *Essays in Linguistics by Yuen Ren Chao*, 2002, Beijing: The Commercial Press, 796–808.

Chao, Yuen Ren (1959) 'How Chinese Logic Operates', *Anthropological Linguistics* 1(1): 1–8, also in A. S. Dil (ed) 1976, 250–259.

Chao, Yuen Ren (1968) *A Grammar of Spoken Chinese*, Berkeley and Los Angeles: University of California Press. Translated as *Hanyu Kouyu Yufa* by Lü Shuxiang in 1979, Beijing: The Commercial Press, and as *Zhongguohua de Wenfa* (Revised edition) by Pang-hsin Ting in 2002, Hong Kong: The Chinese University of Hong Kong Press.

Chen, Ping (1987) 'Shi hanyu zhong yu mingcixing chengfen xiangguan de sizu gainian' ('Explanation of Four Pairs of Concepts Related to Nominal Expressions in Chinese'), *Studies of the Chinese Language* 2: 81–92.

Chen, Ping (1996) 'Pragmatic Interpretations of Structural Topics and Relativization in Chinese', *Journal of Pragmatics* 3: 1–17.

Chierchia, G. (1985) 'Formal Semantics and the Grammar of Predication', *Linguistic Inquiry* 16(3): 417–443.

China National Committee for Terminology in Science and Technology (2006) 'Zhongyi yaoxue mingci' ('Terms in Traditional Chinese Medicine'), serially published in *China Terminology*: 1–4.

Crystal, David (1997) *A Dictionary of Linguistics and Phonetics*, 4th ed., Oxford: Blackwell Publishers Ltd.

Diessel, H. (2013) 'Where Does Language Come From: Some Reflections on the Role of Deictic Gesture and Demonstratives in the Evolution of Language', *Language and Cognition* 5(2–3): 239–249.

Dil, A. S. (ed) (1976) *Aspects of Chinese Sociolinguistics: Essays by Yuen Ren Chao*, Stanford: Stanford University Press.

Fauconnier, G. and M. Turner (2003) *The Way We Think: Conceptual Blending and the Mind's Hidden Complexities*, New York: Basic Books.

Feng, Zhiwei (2006) 'Shuyu mingming zhong de yinyu' ('Metaphors in Term Naming'), *China Terminology* 3: 19–20.

Fillmore, C. J. (1968) 'The Case for Case', in E. Bach and R. T. Harms (eds) *Universals in Linguistic Theory*, New York: Holt, Rinehart and Winston, 1–88.

Gao, Song (2013) 'Zhenli zhi zheng: Husai'er yu Fuleige lun zhen' ('The Debate of the Theory of Truth between Husserl and Frege'), *Philosophical Research* 5: 73–81.

Givón, T. (1979) *On Understanding Grammar*, New York, San Francisco and London: Academic Press.

Halliday, M. A. K. (1994) *An Introduction to Functional Grammar*, 2nd ed., London: Edward Arnold Publishers Ltd.

Hopper, P. J. and S. A. Thompson (1984) 'A Discourse Basis for Lexical Categories in Universal Grammar', *Language* 60: 703–752.

Jiang, Wangqi (2006) 'Hanyu de *juzi* yu yingyu de *sentence*' ('The Chinese *Juzi* and the English *Sentence*'), in Zijian Yang (ed) *Yinghanyu Bijiao yu Fanyi (English-Chinese Comparative Study and Translation)*, vol. 6, Shanghai: Shanghai Foreign Language Education Press, 198–217.

Jiang, Yan (2013) '*Yuyixue* Daodu' ('Introduction to *Semantics*'), in Kate Kearns (ed) *Semantics*, 2nd ed., Beijing: World Publishing Corporation, 15–54.

Kasher, A. and R. Sadka (2001) 'Constitutive Rule Systems and Cultural Epidemiology', *Monist* 84: 438–449.

Kita, Sotaro (ed) (2003) *Pointing: Where Language, Culture, and Cognition Meet*, Mahwah, NJ: Lawrence Erlbaum Associates.

Kuhn, T. S. (1993) 'Metaphor in Science', in A. Ortony (ed) *Metaphor and Thought*, 2nd ed., Cambridge: Cambridge University Press, 533–542.

Lakoff, G. (1992) 'Metaphor and War: The Metaphor System Used to Justify War in the Gulf', in Martin Pütz (ed) *Thirty Years of Linguistic Evolution*, Amsterdam and Philadelphia: John Benjamins, 463–481.

Lakoff, G. and M. Johnson (1980) *Metaphors We Live By*, Chicago and London: University of Chicago Press.

LaPolla, R. and D. Poa (2006) 'On Describing Word Order', in F. Ameka, A. Dench and N. Evans (eds) *Catching Language: The Standing Challenge of Grammar Writing*, Berlin: Mouton de Gruyter, 269–295.

Li, C. N. and S. A. Thompson (1976) 'Subject and Topic: A New Typology of Language', in Charles N. Li (ed) *Subject and Topic*, New York: Academic Press, 457–490.

Lin, Su'e and Xing Zheng (2014) 'Ningbohua *haishi* chabiju' ('The Comparative Constructions with *Haishi* in Ningbo Dialect'), *Dialect* 1: 21–27.

Liu, Danqing (ed) (2008) *Yufa Diaocha Yanjiu Shouce (A Handbook for Grammatical Investigation and Research)*, Shanghai: Shanghai Educational Publishing House.

Liu, Tanzhou (2009) 'Yiyuan feizuoge dongci dai binyu xianxiang' ('The Phenomenon of Unergative Intransitive Verbs Taking Objects'), *Studies of the Chinese Language* 2: 110–119.

Liu, Danqing (2012) 'Hanyu chabiju he huati jiegou de tonggouxing: xianhe fanchou de kuozhangli yili' ('The Homogeneity of Comparison and Topic Structure in Chinese: An Illustration of the Expansive Power of Mighty Categories'), *Studies in Language and Linguistics* 4: 1–12.

Lu, Bingfu (2005) 'Yuxu youshi de renzhi jieshi: lun kebiedu dui yuxu de pubian yingxiang' ('Word Order Dominance and Its Cognitive Explanation: The Pervasive Influence of Identifiability on Word Order'), *Contemporary Linguistics* 1: 1–15, 2: 132–138.

174 *Realizational relations and constitutive relations*

Lü, Shuxiang (1979) *Hanyu Yufa Fenxi Wenti* (*Problems in Chinese Grammatical Analysis*), Beijing: The Commercial Press.

Lyons, J. (1968) *Introduction to Theoretical Linguistics*, Cambridge: Cambridge University Press.

Matthews, P. H. (1981) *Syntax*, Cambridge: Cambridge University Press.

Morris, C. W. (1938) 'Foundations of the Theory of Signs', in O. Neurath, R. Carnap and C. Morrris (eds) 1939, *International Encyclopaedia of Unified Science*, Chicago: Univrsity of Chicago Press.

Qi, Gong (1997) *Hanyu Xianxiang Luncong* (*Essays on Chinese Language Phenomena*), Beijing: Zhonghua Book Company.

Radman, Z. (1997) *Metaphors: Figures of the Mind*, Boston: Kluwer Academic Publisher.

Rawls, J. (1955) 'Two Concepts of Rules', *Philosophical Review* 64: 3–32.

Shen, Jiaxuan (1994) 'Yufahua yanjiu zongguan' ('A Survey of Studies on Grammaticalization'), *Foreign Language Teaching and Research* 4: 17–24.

Shen, Jiaxuan (1998) 'Yuyongfa de yufahua' ('Grammaticalization of Pragmatics'), *Foreign Languages in Fujian* 2: 1–8, 14.

Shen, Jiaxuan (1999) *Buduicheng he Biaojilun* (*Asymmetry and Markedness Theory*), Nanchang: Jiangxi Education Publishing House, Reprinted in Beijing: The Commercial Press, 2015.

Shen, Jiaxuan (2006a) 'Yufa yinyu he yinyu yufa' ('Grammatical Metaphor and Metaphorical Grammar'), *Yufa Yanjiu he Tansuo* (*Studies and Explorations on Grammar*) 13: 1–14.

Shen, Jiaxuan (2006b) '*Wang Mian si le fuqin* de shengcheng fangshi: jianshuo hanyu rouhe zaoju' ('The Generative Mechanism of Sentences Like *Wang Mian Si le Fuqin*: Sentence Generation by Blending in Chinese'), *Studies of the Chinese Language* 4: 291–300.

Shen, Jiaxuan (2006c) 'Rouhe he jieda' ('Blending and Haplology'), *Chinese Teaching in the World* 4: 5–12.

Shen, Jiaxuan (2007) 'Yetan *ta de laoshi dang de hao* ji xiangguan jushi' ('On *Ta de Laoshi Dang de Hao* and Related Constructions'), Paper presented at the 15th Annual Conference of the International Association of Chinese Linguistics, New York, also in *Contemporary Research in Modern Chinese* (Japan), 9: 1–12.

Shen, Jiaxuan (2008) 'Yiwei haishi yiqing: xi *ta shi qunian sheng de haizi*' ('Moving What? On Emotional Movement in *Ta Shi Qunian Sheng de Haizi*'), *Studies of the Chinese Language* 5: 387–395.

Shen, Jiaxuan (2009) 'Jiliang deshi he jijiao deshi: zailun *Wang Mian si le fuqin* de jushi yiyi he shengcheng fangshi' ('Gain and Loss: Do You Mind It or Not?: A Further Discussion of the Construction Meaning and the Generative Mechanism of *Wang Mian Si le Fuqin*'), *Language Teaching and Linguistic Studies* 5: 15–22.

Tong, Yanqi (2008) 'Zhongguo zhengfu yu baixing: zhengzhixue yanjiu zhaji' ('The Chinese Government and People: Notes on Political Science Research'), *Observation and Communication* 22, Center for Chinese & Global Affairs, Peking University.

Ungerer, F. and H.-J. Schmid (1996) *An Introduction to Cognitive Linguistics*, London and New York: Longman.

Wang, Juquan (2014) 'Shen Jiaxuan xiansheng hanyu cilei wenti xinguandian shuping' ('A Summary and Critique of Shen Jiaxuan's Viewpoints on Chinese Word Classes'), in *Yinghan Duibi yu Fanyi* (*Contrastive and Translation Studies of English and Chinese*), vol. 2, Shanghai: Shanghai Foreign Language Education Press, 117–133.

Wang, Wenbin (2014) 'Hanyu dui xingwei dongzuo de kongjianhua biaozheng: yi *da/xiao*+V geshi weili' ('A Probe into the Spatializing Representation of Actions in Chinese: Taking for Example the Pattern of *da/xiao*+V'), in *Yinghan Duibi yu Fanyi* (*Contrastive and*

Translation Studies of English and Chinese), vol. 2, Shanghai: Shanghai Foreign Language Education Press, 134–147.

Ward, Gregory (2004) 'Equatives and Deferred Reference', *Language* 80: 262–289.

Xu, Liejiong and Danqing Liu (1998) *Huati de Jiegou yu Gongneng* (*Topic: Structural and Functional Analysis*), Shanghai: Shanghai Educational Publishing House.

Yau, Shun-chiu (2014) *Shijue Yuyanxue Gaiyao* (*An Outline of Visual Linguistics*), Beijing: The Commercial Press.

Yuan, Yulin (1996) 'Huatihua jiqi xiangguan de yufa guocheng' ('Topicalization and Its Related Grammatical Process'), *Studies of the Chinese Language* 4: 241–254.

Zhang, Bin (2014) 'Zhicheng he chenshu' ('Reference and Predication'), *Research on Chinese as a Second Language* 11: 1–4.

Zhang, Bojiang (2009) 'Hanyu xianding chengfen de yuyong shuxing' ('The Pragmatic Status of Determiners in Chinese'), *Studies of the Chinese Language* 3: 195–207.

Zhang, Bojiang (2011) 'Hanyu de jufa jiegou he yuyong jiegou' ('Mapping from Pragmatic Structures to Syntactic Structures in Chinese'), *Chinese Language Learning* 2: 3–12.

Zhang, Bojiang (2013) 'Hanyu huati jiegou de genbenxing' ('The Fundamental Nature of Topic Structures in Chinese'), in *Mucunyingshu Jiaoshou Huanli Jinian Zhongguoyu Wenfa Luncong* (*Collection of Papers on Chinese Grammar in Honor of Professor Hideki Kimura on the Occasion of His 60th Birthday*), Tokyo: Hakuteisha, 130–141.

Zhang, Heyou and Sze-Wing Tang (2010) 'Yu kongyulei xiangguan de teyixing *shi* zi ju de jufa yuyi' ('On the Syntax and Semantics of the Idiosyncratic Copular Sentences and Empty Categories'), *Contemporary Linguistics* 1: 14–23.

Zhang, Heyou and Sze-Wing Tang (2011) 'Kongyulei de yunzhun ji putonghua yueyu huatilei xiciju de jufa chayi' ('Licensing of Empty Categories and the Syntactic Variation of Copular Topic Sentences in Mandarin and Cantonese'), *Linguistic Sciences* 1: 58–69.

Zhou, Ruchang (2005) 'Shihua de yaoyi' ('The Essence of Poetics'), in *Honglou Shi'er Ceng* (*Twelve Floors of the Red Mansion*), Taiyuan: Shuhai Press, 99–105.

Zhu, Dexi (1980) 'Hanyu jufa zhong de qiyi xianxiang' ('Ambiguity in Chinese Syntax'), *Studies of the Chinese Language* 2: 81–92.

Zhu, Dexi (1985) *Yufa Dawen* (*Answering Questions about Chinese Grammar*), Beijing: The Commercial Press.

Zhu, Dexi (1987) 'Juzi he zhuyu: yin'ouyu yingxiang xiandai shumian hanyu he hanyu jufa fenxi de yige shili' ('Sentences and Subjects: An Example of How Indo-European Languages Influence Modern Written Chinese and Syntactic Analysis of Chinese'), *Chinese Teaching in the World* 1: 31–34.

Zhu, Dexi, Jiawen Lu and Zhen Ma (1961) 'Guanyu dongci xingrongci mingwuhua de wenti' ('On the Nominalization of Verbs and Adjectives'), *Journal of Peking University* (Humanities and Social Sciences) 4: 51–64, also in Dexi Zhu (1980) *Xiandai Hanyu Yufa Yanjiu* (*Studies in Modern Chinese Grammar*), Beijing: The Commercial Press, 193–224.

5 The asymmetry between nouns and verbs

5.1 Nouns used as verbs and verbs used as nouns

In the verbs-as-nouns framework, the relationship between nouns and verbs is not one of opposition or equivalence, and verbs are only a subcategory of nouns. This chapter argues that if nouns and verbs are related such that one includes the other, it must be that the noun category includes verbs but not vice versa. In the words of Baker (2009), if there is a neutralization between nouns and verbs, they must be neutralized in favor of nouns rather than verbs (see Section 7, Chapter 3). Under verb-centered grammatical views, however, many people assume verbs to be the resulting neutralized words. The discussion of the skewed distribution of nouns and verbs in Chinese in Section 2 of Chapter 3 supports Baker's argument. For example, whether in the positions of subjects and objects or in the head positions after the modifiers, if neutralization occurs between nouns and verbs, the resulting neutralized words are always nouns, not verbs (see Section 4 of Chapter 1 in Volume II). It ultimately comes down to skewed distribution of cognitive asymmetry between the concepts of things and actions, which is not isolated to Chinese.

Zhang Hanyu, the protagonist of the movie *Assembly*, won the Hundred Flowers Award for Best Actor. When a reporter asked him about his future plans, he replied, "*Yǎnyuán shì gè dòngcí, béngguǎn shénme, zǒngzhī nǐ yào pāi (xì), bùnéng xiánzhe.* '*Actor* is a verb. Anyway, you have to shoot (movies). You can't just sit around'" (*Beijing Evening News*, Sept. 13, 2008). The utterance *Yǎnyuán shì gè dòngcí* 'Actor is a verb' is concise, vivid, and witty. It is a unique rhetorical use because *yǎnyuán* 'actor' is obviously a noun. Such expressions have recently caught on, for example:[1]

Mìngyùn *búshì míngcí érshì dòngcí, mìngyùn búshì fàngqì érshì zhǎngwò.*
destiny is not noun but verb destiny is not give up but master
'*Destiny* is not a noun but a verb; *destiny* is not to give up but to master.'

Wánměi shì gè dòngcí, dàn shì yī gè méiyǒu wánchéngshí de dòngcí.
perfect is CL verb, but is one CL not perfect tense MM verb
have
'*Perfect* is a verb, but it does not have a perfect tense.'

DOI: 10.4324/9781003385899-6

The asymmetry between nouns and verbs   177

Xuě,   bù   dāndan   shì   míngcí.
snow   not   merely   is   noun
'*Snow* is not merely a noun.'

However, most people do not say that *Pāixì shì gè míngcí* 'Shooting (movies or TV series) is a noun' unless they are grammar experts who study word classes. Instead, people say:

Zǒuxué	*shì*	*gè*	*xīn*	*míngcír.*
make itinerant performances	is	CL	new	noun

'*Zǒuxué* "make itinerant performances" is a new noun.'

Pāituō	*shì*	*gè*	*gǎngtái*	*míngcí.*
dating	is	CL	Hong Kong and Taiwan	noun

'*Pāituō* "dating" is a noun in Hong Kong and Taiwan.'

Qiēmài	*shì*	*gè*	*zhōngyīyào*	*míngcí.*
pulse-taking	is	CL	Chinese medicine	noun

'*Qiēmài* "pulse-taking" is a noun in Chinese medicine.'

No one would think there is anything special about such expressions, although in the eyes of some grammar experts, *zǒuxué, pāituō,* and *qiēmài* are all verbs. When you are asked to solve a riddle to guess at a new noun, you will not be surprised to find out that the answer is *zǒuxué.* Some people claim that the "nouns" in these sentences refer to "names", and they are not the "nouns" as opposed to "verbs" in grammar books. This makes sense. As noted in Section 3.1 of the previous chapter, the Chinese word *míngcí* differs from the English word "noun" in that its primary meaning is "name" and thus it is also known as *míngcír.* What it means as opposed to "verb" in grammar books is only its secondary meaning. In spite of this, it is still important to emphasize that even in a framework that distinguishes nouns from verbs, the use of nouns as verbs (for predication) is particular, and the use of verbs as nouns (for reference) is generally accepted. Here are some examples of nouns used as verbs in modern Chinese:[2]

Línzǒu	*hái*	*dài*	*le*	*yī*	*xiá*	*huǒchái.*
before leaving	also	bag	PSP	a	box	matches

'Before leaving, (he) also packaged a box of matches.'

Wǒ	*yě*	*lái*	*shūnǚ*	*yīxià.*
I	also	come	fair maiden	a while

'Let me also act like a fair maiden for a while.'

Wǒ	*yě*	*guānliáo*	*guānliáo.*
I	also	bureaucrat	bureaucrat

'Let me also behave like a bureaucrat.'

Tā	*kě*	*zhēn*	*néng*	*Ā Q*	*zìjǐ.*
he	actually	true	can	Ah Q	self

'He can always find ways to comfort himself like Ah Q.'

178 *The asymmetry between nouns and verbs*

Ràng	*tā*	*zìgě*	*zuǐ*	*shàng*	*kuàigǎn*	*qù.*
let	him	by oneself	mouth	on	pleasure	DIR

'Let him enjoy mouth pleasure on his own.'

Wǒ	*yě*	*dàkuǎn*	*guò*	*yīhuí.*
I	also	tycoon	EXP	once

'I also was once a tycoon.'

Tā	*jiù*	*nàme*	*hé*	*mǔqīn*	*jùlí*	*zhe.*
she	just	so	with	mother	distance	DUR

'She kept distancing from her mother in that way.'

When typing the previous sentences on the computer, wavy lines appeared on the words such as *hái dàile, guānliáo guānliáo, jùlí zhe*. The spelling and grammar checker was reminding us that we had made a mistake in the wording of the sentences. This demonstrates how special and rhetorical their usage is. It is also possible for some nouns used as verbs to become real verbs. For example, *dìng dīngzi* 'nail the nail', *xiù zhe shǒu* 'put hands in one's sleeves', *xù miánǎo* 'stuff a cotton coat with cotton', *duī chéng duī* 'pile up a pile', and *ràng chóng zhù le* 'eaten by insects' have ceased to be a special usage, and thus are no longer considered nouns used as verbs.

Now consider the following examples of verbs used as nouns:

Xiào	*bǐ*	*kū*	*hǎo.*
laugh	than	cry	better

'Laughing is better than crying.'

Wǒ	*pà*	*zhuā.*
I	be afraid of	scratch

'I am afraid of being scratched (by cats).'

Dǎ	*shì*	*téng,*	*mà*	*shì*	*ài.*
beat	is	love	scold	is	love

'Both beating and scolding are love.'

Tā	*zhǔguǎn*	*túshū*	*chūbǎn.*
he	be in charge of	book	publish

'He is in charge of book publishing.'

Lǎoshī	*de*	*chēngzàn*	*fǎnér*	*ràng*	*tā*	*bú*	*zìzài.*
teacher	MM	praise	instead	make	him	not	comfortable

'The teacher's praise made him uncomfortable instead.'

Wǒmen	*yào*	*wèi*	*pǔtōnghuà*	*de*	*tuīguǎng*	*jìnlì.*
we	have to	for	Putonghua	MM	promote	do our best

'We have to do our best for the promotion of Putonghua.'

Yǒu	*jìzhě*	*wèn*	*tā*	*jīnhòu*	*yǒu*	*shénme*	*dǎsuàn.*
there is	reporter	ask	him	future	have	what	plan

'A reporter asked him what is his future plan.'

In all of these sentences, verbs are used either as subjects or as objects. When they are typed into the computer, no wavy lines appear, and no one would find them strange. Some verbs used as nouns do not refer to the action itself but to the action-related agents, results, instruments, etc. For example, in *Tā shì biānjí* 'He is an editor', *zhēngqìjī zhè yī fāmíng* 'the invention of the steam engine', and *Bié bǎ bāozhuāng sīhuài* 'Don't damage the package when tearing it', the verbs have changed into real nouns. Examples like these are outside of the scope of our discussion.

Both verbs used as nouns and nouns used as verbs in Chinese show no morphological changes, but from our linguistic intuition we can infer that there is an asymmetrical relationship between them. Using verbs as nouns is common and conventional, whereas using nouns as verbs is special and rhetorical. The source of this intuition will be discussed in Section 4. According to Wang Dongmei (2001: 104), the number of instances of using verbs as nouns is 57 times greater than that of using nouns as verbs in modern Chinese, and using nouns as verbs is more common in ancient Chinese than it is in modern Chinese, but it remains a minority and a special phenomenon in comparison with verbs used as nouns. Wang Kezhong (1989) discusses the word class flexibility in classical Chinese, most of which are nouns used as verbs; the book rarely discusses the flexible use of verbs as nouns, and all of those mentioned are used to refer to their related entities (e.g., *sǐ* 'die' to *sǐzhě* 'the dead', *jū* 'dwell' to 'residence'). In *A Draft Grammar of Chinese* (1982: 66–69), Chen Chengze argues that verbs used as nouns such as *zú* 'death' in *Huìgōng zhī zú* 'Duke Hui's death' are a flexible use of its original usage without any functional shift in word classes, whereas nouns used as verbs such as *xuě* 'snow' in *Wǎn lái tiān yù xuě* 'It is getting dark and is likely to snow' are a flexible use of its non-original usage as its word class has changed. This is a very insightful point.[3]

5.2 The universality of the asymmetry between nouns and verbs

5.2.1 *The similarities between Chinese and other languages*

The asymmetry between nouns and verbs is common in other languages as well. In English, verbs used as nouns must be morphologically changed, as in:

Seeing is believing.
To see is to believe.

By adding *-ing* to the end, or inserting an infinitive marker *to*, they remain verbs, but are in nonfinite forms. Contrary to this, the words *proposal*, *creation*, and *excitement*, which are derived from *propose*, *create*, and *excite*, respectively, have become real nouns and they can no longer be considered verbs used as nouns.

180   *The asymmetry between nouns and verbs*

Can nouns be used as verbs in Chinese like they are in English? Of course. This was once thought by some to be a feature of classical Chinese, which not only had a wide range of uses but also many kinds. Here are some examples:

Ěr	*yù*	*Wúwáng*	*wǒ*	*hū?*
you	want	king of Wu	me	MM

'Are you making me the king of Wu?'

(The 10th year of the reign of Duke Ding, in *Zuo Tradition*)

Hòufēi	*shuài*	*jiǔ*	*pín*	*cán*	*yú*	*jiāo.*
queen	lead	nine	concubine	silkworm	in	countryside

'The queen led nine concubines to raise silkworms in the countryside.'

(Respecting Agriculture, in *Master Lü's Spring and Autumn Annals*)

Guāng	*xǐ,*	*nǎi*	*kè*	*Wǔ*	*Zixū.*
Guang	happy	then	guest	Wu	Zixu

'Guang was happy and treated Wu Zixu as a distinguished guest.'

(Hereditary Household of Wu Taibo, in *Historical Records*)

In fact, English nouns used as verbs are no less common than those in classical Chinese, both in terms of number and type and seem to be more common than those in modern Chinese. In Clark and Clark (1979), more than 1,300 examples of modern English are collected in nine categories and nearly fifty subcategories, some of which are listed as follows:

Mummy trousers me.
I am crackering my soup.
The boy porched the newspaper.
I guitared my way across the US.
She certainly had me fooled.
She mothered all her young lodgers.
They Christmas-gifted each other.
The farmer barned the cows.
The story has been scripted for movie.
Don't saint the reformer!
The car rear-ended the van.
The guard quickly armed him out of the way.
We were stoned and bottled as we marched down the street.
My sister Houdini'd her way out of the locked closet.
The mayor tried to Richard Nixon the tapes of the meeting.

Wavy lines appear when these sentences are typed into a computer, indicating that they are also very special rhetorical expressions in English. It is worth noting that Clark and Clark (1979) do not refer to the underlined words as "nouns used as verbs" but rather as "innovative denominal verbs", since they originate

The asymmetry between nouns and verbs 181

from nouns but have become real verbs. It echoes Jespersen's (1924: 62) statement. When some English grammarians consider the *tead* in *We tead at the vicarage* to be a noun used as a verb, Jespersen (1924: 62) argues,

> The truth is that we have a real verb, just as real as *dine* or *eat*, though derived from the substantive *tea*—and derived without any distinctive ending in the infinitive. To form a verb from another word is not the same thing as using a substantive as a verb, which is impossible.

When Jespersen asserts it is "impossible" to use a noun as a verb, he only uses this word for convenience.

In English, when a verb is used as a noun, it undergoes morphological changes by adding -*ing* to the end or inserting an infinitive *to*, but grammarians do not assert that the verb becomes a real noun. When a noun is used as a verb, its infinitive has no distinctive ending, but it is considered a real verb. Why is this? This is because when *tea* is used as a verb without a distinctive ending, it has the same morphological differences in "tense" and "number/person" as common verbs *dine* or *eat*, with -*ed* in the past tense and an -*s* in the third person singular. It is this structural parallelism (see Chapter 6, Section 2.1) that plays a decisive role.

In fact, both nouns used as verbs and verbs used as nouns are rather vague expressions. At least three levels of use should be distinguished: Common use, temporary use, and word-class conversion. By doing so, differences and similarities between English and Chinese can be more clearly observed.

In English, verbs used as nouns such as *seeing* and *believing* are temporary uses where the prototypical verb is temporarily changed into a nonfinite form, while nouns used as verbs such as *tead* are word-class conversion where the nouns have already become real verbs. In Chinese, verbs used as nouns such as *xiào* 'laughing' and *kū* 'crying' are common use without any morphological changes, while nouns used as verbs such as *shūnǚ* 'fair maiden' are temporary use, which can be temporarily followed by a verbal classifier complement *yīxià* 'in a short while' like a verb. Unlike English, there is no such morphological change like "tea→tead" with these nouns in Chinese, so they are not considered to have been converted into real verbs. It is important not to overlook the similarities between English and Chinese, where using verbs as nouns is much more common than using nouns as verb, and the asymmetry between nouns and verbs is found in both languages.

Table 5.1 Comparison between English and Chinese at three levels of using nouns as verbs and verbs as nouns

	Common use	*Temporary use*	*Word-class conversion*
English		*Seeing* is *believing*.	We *tead* at the vicarage.
Chinese	*Xiào* bǐ kū hǎo.	*Wǒ yě lái shūnǚ yīxià.*	
	'Laughing is better than crying'.	'Let me also act like a fair maiden for a while'.	

182   *The asymmetry between nouns and verbs*

There are cognitive reasons for this asymmetry (see Section 4), and it is common in other languages as well. For example, in Iroquoian of North America, nouns are used as subjects and objects but rarely as predicates (Mithun 2000); in Manipuri (a Tibetan-Burmese language), verbal roots can be nominalized with nominal suffixes, while nominal roots cannot be changed into verbs with verbal affixes; and in Maori (an Austronesian language of New Zealand), both nouns and verbs can serve as subjects, objects and predicates on the surface, but on closer examination, nouns are still restricted from being predicates in describing events (Anwood 2000). Likewise, the !Xun language of the Khoisan family of African languages allows the subject to be a verb like English *drink* but does not allow the predicate to be a noun like English *water*:[4]

mí   má   cŋ$ g‖ú.
I   TOP   drink   water
'I drink water.'

cŋ$ má   kàhin.
drink   TOP   is-good
'Drink (water) is good.'

*mí   má   g‖ú   dèbe.
I   TOP   water   kid
*'I water kid. (I feed the kid with water).'

Within the framework of generative grammar, Baker (2009: 64–65) illustrates the asymmetry between nouns and verbs as follows: "[V]erbs license specifiers within their maximal projections (the verb phrase), whereas nouns (and adjectives) do not. In other words, verbs are intrinsically predicates, whereas nouns can only become predicates by combining with a functional head (Pred)". One ground of argument is that there are some intransitive verbs that can act as unaccusative predicates whose only argument behaves like the object rather than the subject of a transitive verb, whereas nouns never function as unaccusative predicates because their subjects are never generated directly inside the noun phrase but only inside the predicate phrase (PredP). The other ground of argument is that, in many languages such as Italian, Russian, Hebrew, and Japanese, the subject argument of some verbs can be incorporated into the predicate verb in a way that the subject of a nominal predicate cannot. As an example, consider Mohawk (an Iroquoian language of North America):

i. *Wa'-ka-wír-ʌ'-ne'.*
    FACT-NsS-baby-fall-PUNC
    'The baby fell'.

ii. **Wa'-t-ka-wir-ahsʌ'tho-'.*
    FACT-DUP-NsS-baby-cry-PUNC
    'The baby cried'.

iii. *Ka-nerohkw-a-nuhs-a'.
Ns-box-Ø-house-NSF
'That box is a house'.

In i., the predicate is an unaccusative verb ʌ' 'fall', into which the subject argument *ka-wir* 'the baby' can be incorporated. In ii., the predicate is an unergative verb *ahsʌ'tho* 'cry', into which the subject argument cannot be incorporated. Nouns in this language can be used as predicates, but when it happens, the subject argument cannot be incorporated, as in iii. *ka-nerohkw* 'that box' cannot be incorporated into the nominal predicate *a-nuhs* 'house'. This fact reveals that verbs can take objects when they are used as predicates, among which transitive verbs certainly can and intransitive verbs at least partly (e.g. unaccusative verbs) can take objects at the bottom (surface as subjects) and that the subjects incorporated into unaccusative verbs are actually the objects at the bottom, but nouns cannot take objects at the bottom when they are used as predicates.[5]

As Zhu Dexi (1985: 5) argues, the relationship between word classes and syntactic constituents in Chinese is complex, but one of his observations holds true, namely, that nouns can serve as predicates only "under certain conditions". In his schema, there is a dotted line between nouns and predicates, unlike the solid line between verbs and subjects/objects.

As a matter of fact, this asymmetric relationship is not specific to Chinese but is universal to all languages.

5.2.2 From usage to grammar

What are the reasons for creating denominal verbs? Clark and Clark (1979) contend that this is largely due to the least effort and economy of expression. Using Grice's (1975) Cooperative Principle, particularly the maxim of quantity, conversational participants always seek to avoid redundancy. In the sentence *I guitared my way across the US*, the meaning that requires many words to convey is condensed into a single word *guitar*. A denominal verb is particularly useful in technical fields where actions occur frequently but no verbs are readily available to express them. In the computer industry, for example, denominal verbs as in "*key* in the data", "*flowchart* the program", "*program* the system", "*output* the results", and "*CRT* the trace" (display tracking records on a CRT video monitor) are invented, but laypeople are

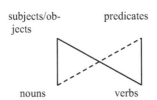

Figure 5.1 The relationship between nouns/verbs and syntactic constituents in Chinese

184   *The asymmetry between nouns and verbs*

unaware that they are derived from nouns. The use of new technologies has also led to some established denominal verbs, such as *xerox* (to make copies), *telephone* (to make phone calls), *wire* (to send telegrams), and *paperclip* (to pin something on with paper clips). As a result of the economy of expression, 3 benefits can be obtained. First, there is precision. It is more precise to say *autoclave the scalpels* to the hospital sterilization workers than to say *sterilize the scalpels*. Second, there is vividness. In a biography of a politician, the denominal verb *Richard Nixon* is obviously more vivid than the common verb *erase* in the sentence *The mayor tried to Richard Nixon the tapes of the meeting*. Third, there is humor. A newspaper columnist once joked that "The *SF Progress* is not a biweekly, as *erratum'd* here yesterday, but a semi-weekly", in which the denominal *erratum* makes the remark witty and humorous. There is no doubt that excessive pursuit of economy will lead to difficulties in understanding. For example, "Karen *weekended* in the country" sounds good, but "Karen *Saturdayed* in the country" sounds awkward because it is unintelligible, unless it is deliberately used for comic effects.

As previously mentioned, the nouns used as verbs in Chinese expressions such as *dìng dīngzi* 'nail the nail', *duī chéng duī* 'pile up a pile', and *ràng chóng zhù le* 'eaten by insects', have become real verbs, thus losing their rhetorical force. The same is true in English. According to Clark and Clark (1979), some innovative denominal verbs have become well established denominal verbs. Underlined words in *smoke a pipe*, *park the car*, *land the plane*, for example, are no longer perceived by most people as derived from nouns. A continuum exists between purely coined verbs and fully established verbs, making it difficult to draw a sharp line between them. According to Clark and Clark (1979), it generally consists of six stages:

i. Complete innovations: (Being used for the first time)

> *Let us cease to sugar-coat, let us cease to white-wash, let us cease to bargin-counter the Bible!*
> *When you're starting to Sunday School MPs, then I think you're going too far.*

ii. Near-innovations: (Having been used for more than once)

> *Let's chopstick for dinner again.*
> *Ruth Buzzi houseguested with Bill Dodge.*

iii. Half-assimilated transparent idioms: (Professionals is no longer aware that they are derived from nouns)

> *I'll key in the data at once.*
> *This time CBS satellited the broadcast.*

iv. Assimilated transparent idioms: (Easy to understand when first heard and know they are derived from nouns)

> *We bicycled to his house.*
> *The documents were paperclipped together.*

The asymmetry between nouns and verbs   185

v. Partly specialized idioms: (Most people become unaware of their origin from nouns)

He used to smoke a pipe.
The plane finally landed on a lake.

vi. Opaque idioms: (No one is aware of their origin from nouns)

They decided to boycott the conference.[6]
He is slated for ambassador to Australia.[7]

A similar division can be made in Chinese, which has six stages in the same order:

i. *Tā   jiù   nàme   hé   mǔqīn   jùlí   zhe.*
   She   just   so   with   mother   distance   DUR
   'She kept distancing from her mother in that way.'

ii. *Bié   Ā Q   le!*
    don't   Ah Q   PSP
    'Don't comfort yourself like Ah Q!'

iii. *Jiàn   huíchē   jiàn,   jìnrù   duìhuàkuāng.*
     key   Enter   key   enter   dialog box
     'Press the Enter key to enter the dialog box.'

iv. *Diàntī   huài   le,   yào   tuǐ   zhe   le.*
    elevator   stop working   PSP   have to   leg   DUR   PSP
    'The elevator stopped working, so I have to take the stairs on foot.'

v. *Gāng   jiào   le   yī   pī   báicài.*
   just   cellar   PSP   one   CL   cabbage
   '(I) just pickled a batch of cabbage in the cellar.'

vi. *Nóngfū   zài   lièrì   xià   chē   shuǐ.*
    farmer   exist   scorching sun   under   watermill   water
    'The farmer irrigates water with a watermill under the scorching sun.'

In general, language evolves from innovations to idioms, from usage to grammar. A process of grammaticalization takes place from nouns to innovative denominal verbs and further to idiomatic denominal verbs (see Section 2 of Chapter 4 in Volume II).

5.2.3   *The particularity of nominal predicates*

While verbs are commonly used as nouns, using nouns as verbs is uncommon and rhetorical. In this regard, Chinese and English are similar. What is different between them is that there are a lot of non-rhetorical uses of nouns as predicates in Chinese, such as *Lǎo Wáng Shànghǎi rén* 'Lao Wang is Shanghainese' and *Shù shàng sān zhī xǐquè* 'There are three magpies on the tree'. Even so, these nominal predicates are still relatively unique compared with verbal predicates.

186   *The asymmetry between nouns and verbs*

It has been pointed out that such nominal predicates are normally used in judgmental and existential sentences, which are limited to the affirmative form. The negative form requires the addition of the predicate word *shì* 'be'. For example, *Jīntiān bù xīngqīsān* 'Today not Wednesday'/*Jīntiān búshì xīngqīsān* 'Today is not Wednesday', *Wǒ bà bù gōngchéngshī* 'My father not an engineer'/*Wǒ bà búshì gōngchéngshī* 'My father is not an engineer', *Shù shàng bù sān zhī niǎo* 'three birds not in the tree'/*Shù shàng búshì (méiyǒu) sān zhī niǎo* 'There are no three birds in the tree'. There are also cases where *bù* 'not' directly modifies nouns, such as *Rén bù rén, guǐ bù guǐ* 'neither a human nor a ghost' and *bù sān bú sì* 'neither one thing nor the other'. These expressions are highly rhetorical, and their normal counterparts are *Tā búshì rén, yě búshì guǐ* 'He is neither a human nor a ghost' and *Zhège shùzì búshì sān yě búshì sì* 'The number is neither 3 nor 4'.

Almost all Chinese verbs can take objects when used as predicates, though the distinction between transitive and intransitive verbs is unclear. Generally speaking, *shā* 'kill' is a transitive verb and *sǐ* 'die' is an intransitive verb. However, in *sǐ le zhè tiáo xīn* 'give up the idea', *sǐ le xǔduō rén* 'many people died', *sǐ* can take agentive objects. Consider *sǐ* 'die' and *fēi* 'fly' taking instrument objects and cause objects as follows:

Guózú	*tīchéng*	*nàyàng*	*hái*	*guò*	*de*	*tǐng*	*hǎo*	*de,*	*nǐ*	*sǐ*	*shá?*
national football team	kick	like that	still	live	CSC	fairly	good	MM	you	die	what

'Even though the national football team stinks, they are still living well, so what do you die for?'
(Used to dissuade people from committing suicide)

Táotài	*Sūlián*	*fēijī*	*hòu,*	*Éluósī*	*fēi*	*shá?*
eliminate	Soviet	aircraft	after	Russia	fly	what

'After eliminating Soviet aircrafts, what does Russia fly?'
(In a title of a newspaper article)

In *chóurén yǐ shā* 'the enemy has been killed' and *fùrú bù shā* 'women and children will not be killed', *shā* 'kill' does not take an object; the patients function as the subjects. In *Zhè shì wǒ de bào, nǐ kàn ma?* 'This is my newspaper, do you want to read it?', *kàn* 'read' (transitive) doesn't take an object. If *ta* 'it' is inserted as the object of *kàn* 'read', the sentence takes on a completely new meaning. It will almost amount to saying that *Nǐ yào kàn zhè zhóng dōngxi ma?* 'Do you want to see this kind of stuff?' Transitive and intransitive verbs differ not in whether they take objects but in the kind of objects they take (Chao 1968: 61, 292; Zhu 1982: 58).

As mentioned earlier, intransitive verbs in Chinese can be divided into two groups. The first group includes verbs like *sǐ* 'die' and *lái* 'come' and the second group includes verbs like *bìng* 'sick' and *xiào* 'laugh'. The second group of verbs cannot take objects in Indo-European languages. As a matter of fact, there appears to be no obvious difference between these two groups of verbs in Chinese. The first group can certainly take objects, as in *sǐ le yī gè háizi* 'a child died'; the second group is also capable of taking objects, even at their surface structure, provided the

The asymmetry between nouns and verbs   187

context is appropriate, as in *Zàicháng de rén kū le yī dà piàn* 'Most of the people cried on the scene' and *Fēidiǎn de shíhòu Xiǎo Lǐ yě bìng le yī gè mèimei* 'One of Xiao Li's younger sisters also fell sick during the SARS period'. (See Chapter 4, Section 4.1 for more examples.)

Using structural parallelism, Zhu Dexi (1985: 51–53) demonstrates that the verbal and temporal classifiers after predicate verbs are also objects, e.g., *yī cì* 'once' in *xǐ yī cì* 'wash once' and *yī tiān* 'one day' in *zhù yī tiān* 'stay for one day'. Lü Shuxiang (1979: 74) proposes that nouns after predicate verbs should be regarded as one and the same constituent called "complements".[8] It is even more important to understand that nominal predicates rarely accept objects of any kind, unless they appear in extremely common colloquial expressions like *Nǐ duǎnxìn wǒ* 'You text-message me'. When nominal predicates take objects, they are often used rhetorically, e.g. *Kànlái yào tuǐ yīzhèn le* 'It looks like I have to go on foot for a while', *Wǒ yě dàkuǎn yī huí* 'Let me also act like a tycoon this time' (taking verbal and temporal classifiers as objects). Thus, to say that Chinese nouns cannot serve as predicates is roughly equivalent to saying that nouns used as predicates cannot take objects. This is consistent with the pattern illustrated with Mohawk in the previous section based on Baker (2009).

It is also likely that nominal predicates possess some subjective meaning; they are often more lyrical and expressive than their corresponding verbal predicates. Here are some examples from Chen Manhua (2008) and Xu Denan (1984) (with modifications):

Āqìng	*sǎo*		*shì*	*wǒ*	*de*		*bǎomǔ.*	—	*Dàyànhé,*	*wǒ*	*de*		*bǎomǔ.*
Aqing	sister-in-law		be	I	MM		nanny	—	Dayanhe	I	MM		nanny
'Sister Aqing is my nanny'.								—	'Dayanhe, my nanny'.				

Zhè	*shì*	*shénme*	*huà?*	—	*Zhè*	*shénme*	*huà?*
this	be	what	word	—	this	what	word
'What are these words?'				—	'What these words?'		

Tā	*shì*	*gè*	*báichī.*	—	*Nǐ*	*cái*	*báichī*	*ne!*
he	be	CL	idiot	—	you	actually	idiot	MP
'He is an idiot'.				—	'Actually, you idiot!'			

Tā	*shì*	*liúxuéshēng.*	—	*Hái*	*liúxuéshēng*	*ne,*	*gǒupì!*
he	be	international student	—	still	international student	MP	bullshit
'He is an international student'.			—	'An international student? bullshit!'			

Sentences with "yī 'one' + classifier" being predicates are also emotionally charged (Chu 2001: 414). Examples include *máo xiǎohái yī gè* 'only a kid', *guānggùn yī tiáo* 'only a bachelor', shénjīngbìng yī gè 'only a psychopath'. As Yuen Ren Chao (1968: 64) notes, nouns are often juxtaposed in poetry to present scenes without describing the specific activities of things, e.g. *tíyīng wǔyàn* 'crying warblers and dancing swallows' and *xiǎoqiáo liúshuǐ fēihóng* 'small bridges,

188 *The asymmetry between nouns and verbs*

flowing water, and flying rainbows'. Zhang Jiangzhi (2013) devotes Chapter 5 to discussing the particularity of nominal predicates. According to Zhou Ren (2012), nominal predicates are also particular in that they cannot be combined or changed.

5.3 Contextual expressions

When nouns are used as verbs, something new is always added to their original meaning, and the added content varies depending on the context. Most semantic theories distinguish between denotational expressions like *man, blue, walk, day,* and *bachelor* and deictic expressions like *he, over there, yesterday,* and *the bachelor*. For an expression to be denotational, it must have a fixed sense and denotation. For example, the fixed sense of *bachelor* is 'unmarried man', and its denotation is unmarried men in every real or imaginary world. Likewise, a deictic expression must have a fixed sense and denotation, but its reference shifts depending on the context. For example, the fixed sense of *he* is 'male person', and its denotation is a male person in every real or imaginary world, but its referent changes with the time, place, and circumstances of its utterance. Clark and Clark (1979) point out that innovative denominal verbs are neither denotational nor deictic but constitute a new category of contextual expressions (contextuals), whose senses and denotations change with the context. As an example, consider the innovative denominal English verb *siren*:

i.   *The fire stations siren<u>ed</u> throughout the raid.*
ii. *The factory siren<u>ed</u> midday and everyone stopped for lunch.*
iii. *The police siren<u>ed</u> the Porsche to a stop.*
iv. *The police car siren<u>ed</u> up to the accident.*
v.   *The police car siren<u>ed</u> the daylights out of me.*

The denominal verb *sirened* means 'turn on the alarm' in i., 'tell time with the siren' in ii., 'warn with the siren' in iii., 'drive fast with the siren wailing' in iv., and 'threaten with the siren' in v. There is no end to the number of contexts and meanings.

For another example, the denominal verb *bottle* have many other senses apart from 'put a liquid into a bottle' as in *bottle the beer* and 'attack by throwing bottles' as in *bottle the demonstrators*. Suppose both the speaker and the hearer know that Max has a hobby of sneaking up and stroking the back of people's legs with a bottle. In such a context, *bottle* would be probably understood as 'rub the back of the leg with a bottle', as in *Well, this time Max has gone too far. He tried to bottle a policeman*.

Using nouns as predicates was described by Yuan Renlin (1989) of Qing Dynasty as using "full words as empty words" or "dead words as living words" in his book *On Functional Words*. He claims that context determines whether full words are used as empty or living words, that all dead words can be brought to life but only in certain cases, and that even dictionaries cannot exhaust all the possible flexible uses. Clearly, Yuan Renlin had already sketched out what Clark &

The asymmetry between nouns and verbs 189

Clark intended to say. Most flexible uses of nouns as verbs in classical Chinese are also contextual expressions. As an example, consider the noun *shì* 'generation; life, lifetime; age, era, epoch; world'. As Chen Chengze (1982: 9) explains, *shì* means 'succeeding generations' in *Wúguó yóu shì* 'succeeding generations in ruling Wu', 'handing down' (with the connotation of 'death') in *Jĭnggōng zǎo shì* 'Duke Jing died young', 'lifetime' in *yù qiú chángshēng jiǔshì* 'seek longevity', and 'a hereditary title' in *xī wǒ xiānwáng shì hòu jì* 'my ancestors were officials in agriculture for several generations'.

Some scholars who study these phenomena under the theory of generative grammar contend that denominal verbs are not created but derived. McCawley (1971), for example, holds that the predicate verb *nailed* in the following example i. is derived from the deep structure ii.:

i. John *nailed* the note to the door.
ii. CAUSED a NAIL to HOLD x ON y

But deep structures like ii. are not capable of covering the various meanings of *sirened* and *shì* in different contexts. Green (1974: 221) argues that verbs originating from instrumental nouns, such as *hammer* in *hammer in a nail*, are derived based on the purpose for which the instrument is designed and the way NP rules are typically applied. However, the bottle example earlier indicates that the bottle was not designed to smash people, much less to stroke their legs.

In short, innovative denominal verbs cannot be derived and they emerge from pragmatic conditions. A speaker who observes the cooperative principle believes that, based on the speaker's shared knowledge (both general and specific) with the hearer, the hearer can easily arrive at an understanding that the source noun of the verb plays one role in the situation described by the denominal verb and other related nouns play other roles. Clark and Clark (1979: 809) conclude that it is regrettable that the mainstream grammar theories do not consider the ability to form and understand contextual expressions as "an intrinsic part of our capacity to use language".

Returning to the sentence *Yǎnyuán shì gè dòngcí* '*Actor* is a verb', it is also a contextual expression. In different contexts, it may mean keeping shooting movies or TV series, making itinerant performances all year round, or turning fake couples into real ones by way of shooting.

5.4 The cognitive reason for the asymmetry between nouns and verbs

Why is the asymmetry between nouns and verbs universal? Ultimately, it is because there is a difference in the way each individual perceives and acts on things. Specifically, an idea of a thing can be independently conceived, and it is perfectly possible to visualize it without associating it with any action. It is impossible, however, to imagine an action without associating it with something related to it at the same time, because the concept of action is always attached to related things. For example, the concept of "beating" cannot exist independently of the concept of

190   *The asymmetry between nouns and verbs*

"person", whereas the concept of "person" can be entirely separated from the concept of "beating" (cf. Langacker 1987: 299). Changing a verb to refer to something, such as changing *chī* 'eat' to *chī de* 'what to eat', does not add anything conceptually, since the concept of "eating" already entails the person who eats and the thing eaten. In contrast, if a noun refers to an action, such as *nǎi* 'milk' in *nǎi háizi* 'milk the baby', something must be added conceptually. It is no wonder that Pan et al. (1996) object that using *jūn* 'army' (noun) as a verb to represent the meaning of *zhùjūn* 'garrison' in classical Chinese is not a flexible use of word classes, since *zhùjūn*, which consists of a verb *zhù* and a noun *jūn*, contains an additional concept of action. Due to this cognitive asymmetry, in Chinese we can use "verb + *de*" to refer to related nouns, but we cannot use "noun + *de*" to refer to related verbs:

zàofǎn de (nóngmín)	**nóngmín de (zàofǎn)*
'the rebelling (peasant)'	**'peasants' (rebellion)'*
jiànzào de (qiáoliáng)	**qiáoliáng de (jiànzào)*
'the built (bridge)'	**'bridge's (building)'*
huàtú de (gōngjù)	**gōngjù de (huàtú)*
'painting (tool)'	**'tool's (painting)'*

The phrase *yǎnyuán hé zǒuxué* 'actor and making itinerant performances' is a juxtaposition of the noun *yǎnyuán* 'actor' and the verb *zǒuxué* 'make itinerant performances'. No one would object to saying that the juxtaposed *zǒuxué* is a noun referring to an action. However, if one were to posit that the juxtaposed *yǎnyuán* is a predicate verb, most people would disagree. As Hopper and Thompson (1984) point out, verbs used as nouns denote actions that are regarded as entities, whereas nouns used as verbs do not denote entities that are regarded as actions but actions that are associated with those entities. Verbs that are used as nouns still denote actions (though in discourse the actions are referred to rather than predicated), so they still retain the verbal feature and are not common nouns. For example, English V-ing verbs can still be modified by *not* and other adverbs, as in *We are talking about John not/soon having a sabbatical*. The same is true for verbs in Chinese that are used as subjects or objects, as in *Wǒmen zài tánlùn Lǎo Zhāng de chíchí bù xiūjià* 'We are talking about Lao Zhang's not taking a sabbatical soon'. Since the nouns used as verbs no longer indicate entities but related actions, they have lost their nominal features and have become verbs instead. Thus these verbs derived from nouns require the tense/number markers -ed or -s in English and can be followed by *le, zhe, guò*, and verbal classifier complements in Chinese:

We squirrel<u>ed</u> away $500 last year.
She breakfast<u>s</u> with the mayor on Tuesdays.
Wǒ yòu dàkuǎn <u>le</u> yī huí. 'I acted like a tycoon once again'.
Wǒ hái méiyǒu bókè <u>guò</u>. 'I haven't blogged yet'.

In several studies of aphasia, verbs have been reported to be more difficult to retrieve than nouns for people with aphasia. If people with aphasia are asked to

The asymmetry between nouns and verbs   191

describe a scene in the kitchen in which various actions took place: A sink over-flowing, a woman fumbling, a boy almost knocked over the stool when reaching for the cookie box, and a girl watching, they would utter something almost full of nouns: *Water . . . man, no woman . . . child . . . no, man . . . and girl . . . oh dear . . . cupboard . . . man, falling . . . jar . . . cakes . . . head . . . face . . . window . . . tap . . .*

As Aitchison (1994: 102) points out, this is not because nouns are more numer-ous than verbs but because nouns are conceptually independent and do not undergo syntactic relations. Also, children prefer nouns over verbs in acquiring new words.

Using verbs as nouns conforms to ontological metaphors (see Chapter 4, Section 2.1). According to Lakoff and Johnson (1980: 31), "[w]e use ontological metaphors to comprehend events, actions, activities, and states. Events and actions are concep-tualized metaphorically as objects, activities as substances". It is only when events, actions, and activities are viewed as objects and substances that they can be referred to and quantified. As human cognitive features make it easier to deal with concrete concepts than abstract ones, metaphorical processes are unidirectional by nature, using concrete concepts to explain abstract ones rather than vice versa. Using verbs as nouns is akin to treating abstract activities as concrete substances, whereas concrete substances would not be treated as abstract activities unless the reasons were specific.[9]

In a nutshell, the cognitive reason for the asymmetry between nouns and verbs is the asymmetry between the concepts of *wù* 'thing' and *shì* 'matter'. The asym-metry can be summarized in two clauses: "Matters *are also* things; things *are like* matters". The reason why things *are like* matters is that matters *are also* things. In Chinese, verbs *are also* nouns, and nouns are only used *like* verbs, and the reason why Chinese nouns can be used *like* predicate verbs is that Chinese verbs (predica-tive expressions) *are also* nouns (referring expressions).

5.5   Distinguishing between generality and particularity

5.5.1   Chinese is not a precategorial language

The use of verbs as nouns is relatively common, whereas the use of nouns as verbs is quite uncommon. To develop a Chinese grammatical system, it is essential to distinguish between general and particular phenomena.

The asymmetry between verbs used as nouns and nouns used as verbs is fre-quently ignored in favor of the idea that Chinese, particularly Late Archaic Chi-nese, allows for both verbs and nouns to be flexibly used in the same context. For example, Bisang (2008, 2013) contends that Late Archaic Chinese was a precat-egorial language, i.e., a language whose lexical items are not preclassified in the lexicon prior to their entry into the syntactic level. This claim is based on Evans and Osada's (2005: 366) criteria for establishing lack of word class distinctions. According to them, languages lacking a noun-verb distinction can be considered monocategorial if they satisfy the following three criteria:

i. Compositionality: The composition of word meaning and syntactic position (subjects, objects, and predicates) may fully predict the semantic differences of a word in different syntactic positions.

192 *The asymmetry between nouns and verbs*

ii. Bidirectionality: Words denoting actions can serve as subjects and objects, and words denoting things can serve as predicates.

iii. Exhaustiveness: Most words satisfy the previous two criteria.

All words in Late Archaic Chinese at the lexical level, according to Bisang (2008), satisfy these three criteria. In particular, he argues in detail that the first criterion is satisfied since words denoting persons serving as predicates appear in transitive and intransitive sentences to convey different meanings.

i. *Jūn*   *jūn,*   *chén*   *chén,*   *fù*   *fù,*   *zǐ*   *zǐ.*
    prince   prince   minister minister father father son   son
    'Let the prince behave like a prince, the minister like a minister, the father like a father and the son like a son.'

ii. *Wú*   *yú*   *Yán Bān*   *yě*   *zé*   *yǒu*   *zhī*   *yǐ.*
    I   to   Yan Ban   MP   thus   friend   him   MP
    'What I am to Yan Ban, I treat him as a friend.'

The intransitive clause's predicate in i., *jūn* 'king', means acting like a king or becoming a king, whereas the transitive clause's predicate in ii., *yǒu* 'friend' means making someone become a friend, making someone act like a friend, considering someone a friend, or thinking someone acts like a friend.

Words denoting tools serving as predicates also have different meanings when used in transitive and intransitive clauses.

iii. *Jūnzǐ*   *bú*   *qì.*
     gentlemen not   implement
     'The gentleman is not an implement.'

iv. *Jí*   *qí*   *shǐ*   *rén*   *yě*   *qì*   *zhī.*
    reach   his   employ   man   MP   instrument   them
    'As for his employment of people, he uses them as instruments.'

v. *Gōngzǐ*   *nù*   *yù*   *biān*   *zhī.*
    prince   get angry   want   whip   him
    'The prince got angry and wanted to whip him.'

In iii., *qì* 'implement' is used as the intransitive sentence's predicate, and its semantic meaning is to become or be used as an implement. In iv., *qì* 'instrument' is used as the transitive clause's predicate, and its semantic meaning is to make something become an instrument or be used as an instrument. In v., *biān* 'whip' is also used as the transitive clause's predicate, and its semantic meaning is to apply the whip on someone or something.

These illustrations lead him to the conclusion that the composition of lexical meaning and syntactic position can be used to infer and predict the semantic change that takes place when a noun is used as a predicate in different sentential contexts, thereby satisfying the criterion of compositionality. Such inferences and predictions are, in fact, very limited in scope since, as stated in Section 3, nouns

The asymmetry between nouns and verbs   193

become contextuals when used as predicates, and their meanings change in different contexts, therefore defying predictions.

As further evidence of unpredictability, the action denoted by a noun differs and is unique to different languages. According to Zhu Dexi (1988), the English word *water* has only the sense of watering and irrigation and does not refer to swimming, whereas the Chinese counterpart *shuǐ* 'water' can refer to swimming in classical Chinese as in *Jiǎ zhōují zhě, fēi néng shuǐ yě, ér jué jiānghé* 'Those who make use of boats may not know how to swim, and yet they manage to get across rivers' (selected from *Encouraging Learning* in *Xunzi*).

The bidirectionality criterion is also invalid. The use of words denoting things as predicates is not symmetrical with the use of words denoting actions as subjects and objects. Unlike the latter, which is a common phenomenon with predictable meaning, the former is a particular phenomenon with unpredictable meaning. As in modern Chinese, there are two types of words denoting actions or properties used as subjects and objects in Late Archaic Chinese: One is transferred designation, and the other is self-designation. Following are some examples:

vi. *Rén*   *zhě*   *lè*   *shān.*
humane   marker   enjoy   mountain
'Those who are humane enjoy the mountains'.
(*Rén* 'humane' refers to those who are humane through transferred designation.)

Rén   *zhě*   *rú*   *shè*
humane   marker   like   shoot (arrows)
'Being humane is like shooting arrows'.
(*Rén* 'humane' refers to the property of humaneness through self-designation.)

vii. *Qí*   *yù*   *lǚ*   *gù,*   *bú*   *zài*   *mǎ.*
His   drive   repeatedly   look back   not   on   horse
'His driver looked back repeatedly, and his attention is on the horses'.
(*Yù* 'drive' refers to the person who drives through transferred designation.)

Wú   *hé*   *zhí?*   *Zhí*   *yù*   *hū? Zhí*   *shè*   *hū?*
I   what   specialize   specialize   drive   MP   specialize   archery   MP

Wú   *zhí*   *yù*   *yǐ.*
I   specialize   drive   MP
'What should I specialize in? Driving? Or archery? I think I will specialize in driving'.
(*Yù* 'drive' refers to the activity of driving through self-designation.)

Both sentences in vi. are marked with *zhě*, while both sentences in vii. are unmarked. When it is transferred designation, the meaning shifts from actions to the persons or things associated with the actions, but this shift is predictable, regardless of language and context. For an intransitive predicative word like *rén* 'humane', its transferred designation must be its only argument; for a transitive verb like *yù* 'drive', its transferred designation must be one of its two arguments (see Zhu Dexi

194   *The asymmetry between nouns and verbs*

1983). In short, when words denoting actions function as subjects and objects, their meanings are always predictable, regardless of whether they are transferred designation or self-designation. This contrasts sharply with words denoting things that function as predicates.

Due to the invalidity of the first two criteria, the third criterion of exhaustiveness is by no means applicable. To conclude, Late Archaic Chinese is not a precategorial language, even by the standards established by Evans and Osada (2005).

5.5.2   *Chinese nouns are not classificatory verbs*

A key point Christoph Harbsmeier (1983) makes is that Classical Chinese nouns are verbal in nature and are essentially a type of classificatory verbs. In other words, Harbsmeier also proposes an inclusion framework for nouns and verbs in Classical Chinese. In his framework, Classical Chinese nouns are also not viewed as opposed to verbs. His framework differs from mine in that the verbs include the nouns and the nouns are a subclass of the verbs, known as classificatory verbs. These are the grounds on which he bases his argument:

Yě is generally considered to be a nominal predicate marker as in i.a., but it can also be used to mark verbal predicates as in i.b., and it can also appear after subjects and clauses as in i.c., i.d.:

i. a.   *Kuàng,   tàishī   yě.*
     Kuang   grand tutor   MP
     'Kuang is a grand tutor.'

  b.   *Wǒ   bì   bù   rén   yě.*
     I   must   not   humane   MP
     'I will not be humane.'

  c.   *Qiū   yě   cháng   shǐ   yú   chǔ   yǐ.*
     Qiu   MP   ever   ambassador   to   Chu   MP
     'Qiu have ever been an ambassador to Chu.'

  d.   *Wú   shào   yě   jiàn.*
     I   young   MP   humble
     'I was humble when I was young.'

Zhě can follow either a verb as in ii.a. or a noun as in ii.b.:

ii. a.   *Xián   zhě   zé   guì   ér   jìng   zhī.*
     virtuous   MP   then   valuable   and   respect   him
     'A virtuous man deserves to be valued and respected.'

  b.   *Mín   zhě   hào   lìlù   ér   wù   xíngfá.*
     people   MP   love   wealth-and-   but   hate   punishment
                       official-post
     'People love wealth and official post while hating punishment.'

The asymmetry between nouns and verbs 195

Zhě is both a nominalizer as in iii.a. and a clause-final marker as in iii.b.:

iii. a. | <u>*Rén*</u> | *zhě* | *lè* | *shān.* |
| --- | --- | --- | --- |
| humane | marker | enjoy | mountain |

'Those who are humane enjoy the mountains'.
(*Rén* 'humane' refers to those who are humane through transferred designation.)

b. | <u>*Rén*</u> | *zhě* | *rú* | *shè* |
| --- | --- | --- | --- |
| humane | marker | like | shoot (arrows) |

'Being humane is like shooting arrows'.
(*Rén* 'humane' refers to the property of humaneness through self-designation.)

In his view, both *yě* and *zhě* can be conflated in the three positions, namely, after a noun, after a verb, and after a clause, if nouns, like nominal predicates, are viewed as classificatory verbs. Additionally, *zhī* can be placed before a verb as in iv.a. or before a noun as in iv.b.:

iv. a. | *Běigong Yǒu* | <u>*zhī*</u> | *yǎng* | *yǒng* | *yě* |
| --- | --- | --- | --- | --- |
| Beigong You | zhī | cultivate | courage | MP |

'Beigong You cultivates his courage in this way.'

b. | *Cǐ* | *pǐfū* | <u>*zhī*</u> | *yǒng* | *yě.* |
| --- | --- | --- | --- | --- |
| this | ordinary-people | zhī | courage | MP |

'This is the courage of ordinary people.'

Ér, érhòu, and *zé* connect clauses, but they can also occur between subjects and predicates:

v. a. | *Rén* | <u>*ér*</u> | *wú* | *xìn,* | *bù* | *zhī* | *qí* | *kě* | *yě.* |
| --- | --- | --- | --- | --- | --- | --- | --- | --- |
| people | ér | not | faith | not | know | his | can | MP |

'Without faith, people don't know what they can do.'

b. | *Xián* | *zhě* | <u>*érhòu*</u> | *lè* | *cǐ.* |
| --- | --- | --- | --- | --- |
| virtuous | MP | érhòu | enjoy | this |

'Only the virtuous can enjoy this.'

c. | *Xián* | *zhě* | <u>*zé*</u> | *guì* | *ér* | *jìng* | *zhī.* |
| --- | --- | --- | --- | --- | --- | --- |
| virtuous | MP | then | valuable | ér | respect | him |

'A virtuous man deserves to be valued and respected.'

Suī, fán, and *měi* often precede verbs as in (6a), but they can also appear before nouns as in (6b):

vi. a. | <u>*Suī*</u> | *bó* | *bì* | *miù.* |
| --- | --- | --- | --- |
| although | knowledgeable | must | error |

'Although knowledgeable, (a man) will err.'

<u>*Fán*</u>	*lǜ*	*shì*	*yù*	*shú.*
every time	think	thing	want	mature

'The reckoning of things should be well thought out.'

196   *The asymmetry between nouns and verbs*

Bó Zōng	*měi*	*cháo,*	*qí*	*qī*	*bì*	*jiè*	*zhī.*
Bo Zong	every time	go-to-court	his	wife	must	warn	him

'Every time Bo Zong goes to court, his wife will warn him of it.'

b.
Suī	*dà*	*guó*	*bì*	*wèi*	*zhī*	*yǐ.*
although	big	country	must	fear	it	MP

'Even big countries must fear it.'

Fán	*dào*	*bú*	*yù*	*yōng.*
all	Tao	not	want	block

'All Tao should not be blocked.'

Zǐ	*rú*	*tàimiào,*	*měi*	*shì*	*wèn.*
Zi	enter	Imperial Ancestral Temple	every	thing	ask

'Zi (Confucius) asked everything whenever he entered the Imperial Ancestral Temple.'

According to him, if nouns, like nominal predicates, are viewed as classificatory verbs, the linking words *zhī*, *ér*, and *suī* in different syntactic positions can all be conflated, thereby providing a very succinct explanation of how to use these empty words.

Harbsmeier's reasoning mentioned earlier is not only based on the distribution of words but also on the principle of simplicity, both of which are what Zhu Dexi has always believed in. As a result, Harbsmeier's ideas must have caught Zhu's attention, as both of his articles (1988, 1990) respond to them.

To claim that nouns are classificatory verbs is essentially to assert that nouns are predicative. Zhu challenges this by highlighting the crucial fact that nominal constituents are predicative only in the subject position, not in the object or modifier positions. According to him, Yuen Ren Chao noted long ago that Chinese subject-predicate sentences consist of two minor sentences (see Chapter 3, Section 4). For example, the sentence *Fàn chī le* 'The meal has been finished' is composed of two minor sentences *fàn ne* 'How about the meal' and *chī le* 'It has been finished'. Since the subject *fàn (ne)* 'How about the meal' is a minor sentence, it is inherently predicative. Thus, Zhu contends that the subject's syntactic position determines a noun's predicativity rather than the noun itself. In other words, the predicativity of Chinese nouns does not follow from the predicativity of the subjects in Chinese sentences.

The structure "N *ér* V" is frequently used to demonstrate the predicative nature of nouns in Classical Chinese. For example, *rén* 'person' in *rén ér wú xìn* 'be a human, but break faith' is predicative. Yang Rongxiang (2008), however, asserts that the N is only judgmental when the whole structure serves as a predicate. Song Hongmin (2009) further argues that when the N's reference is definite, it is always an exclamatory judgment and that a full semantic understanding of the N depends heavily on the context and both interlocutors' real-life experiences. As explained in Section 3, the N here is a contextual, and the use of such N is still a particular phenomenon.

The asymmetry between nouns and verbs 197

In order to support his argument that "nouns are classificatory verbs", Harbsmeier (1983) interprets *rén zhě* in *Rén zhě lè shān* as "assuming someone is humane", which is predicative and *rén zhě* in *Rén zhě rú shè* as "presupposing that something is identical with being humane". Zhu criticizes that such an interpretation is very far-fetched and that it is better to divide *zhě* into the transferred designation ('those who are humane') and the self-designation ('humaneness'). Zhu's criticism is well-founded. Indeed, Harbsmeier's explanation is convoluted and farfetched in comparison to a simple and natural explanation based on a distinction between self-designation and transferred designation.

As Zhu argues, those who are influenced by Indo-European grammatical concepts tend to interpret verbs in the subject position as nouns rather than the other way around proposed by Harbsmeier; both arguments would negate the significance of the distinction between nouns and verbs. There is only part of this statement that we can agree with. As we have already stated in Section 1 of the Introduction, the inclusion of class A in class B does not imply that there is no difference between the two classes. To claim that nouns are classificatory verbs, a subclass of verbs, is not to deny the distinction between nouns and verbs or to render it meaningless.[10] Harbsmeier also argues that he does not deny the existence of a noun-verb distinction in Classical Chinese, since a relationship of class membership must be a mixture of similarities and differences. The problem with Harbsmeier's theory is not a denial of the significance of the noun-verb distinction, but it mistakes particular phenomena for common phenomena when it treats nouns as predicative classificatory verbs. This is equivalent to claiming that Chinese verbs are nominalized when they are used as subjects and objects, where the general is mistaken for the particular. If generality is confused with particularity, farfetchedness will surely follow. Moreover, Zhu asserts that nouns serving as predicates are predicative because the subject is a minor sentence, and the minor sentence is predicative. Such reasoning is also problematic because, as explained in Section 4 of Chapter 3 and will be discussed in Section 3 of Chapter 6, the minor sentence is essentially referential. The predicativity of Chinese nominal constituents in the predicate position is not because the noun is intrinsically predicative but because the predicate (minor sentence) is referential. If so, we can and should invert Harbsmeier's claim and assert that Classical Chinese verbs are essentially dynamic nouns; that is, nouns include verbs rather than vice versa.

Even in terms of quantity, nouns outnumber verbs by a wide margin. *The Contemporary Chinese Dictionary* contains more than 40,000 items, of which 56% are nouns and 36% are verbs and adjectives (Yin 1986). Dictionaries are actually very picky about the nouns they include, thus a lot of nouns, like from *xīngqīyī* 'Monday' to *xīngqīrì* 'Sunday', and *miányī* 'cotton coat', *mián'ǎo* 'cotton jacket', *miánkù* 'cotton trousers', *miánxié* 'cotton shoes', are not listed as entries. Only nouns, according to Yin (1986), belong to the typical open word class, whereas verbs and adjectives are semi-open word classes. It is therefore significantly more logical from all perspectives to assert that verbs are a subcategory of nouns rather than vice versa.

198 *The asymmetry between nouns and verbs*

5.6 Nominalism

It is the cognitive asymmetry between things and matters that determines the asymmetry between nouns and verbs. The skewed or favored direction of the asymmetry explains nominalism or the fundamental nature of nouns. In other words, when the distinction between nouns and verbs is neutralized, it is neutralized in favor of nouns.

Some scholars dispute this belief, arguing that a few languages, such as some aboriginal languages of North America, possess only verbs and no nouns and that nominal constituents are formed by verbal roots with affixes in these languages. For example, according to Jelinek (1995), in Strait Salish of North America, all content words are predicate words, and the sole class of predicate words is capable of representing features like actions, objects, and states, as well as serving as syntactic constituents such as subjects, objects, predicates, and modifiers. It is determined by their syntactic positions what features the predicate words represent. When the predicate words serve as predicates, the subjects and objects are attached as affixes; when the predicate words serve as subjects or objects, determiners need to be added. It is also frequently mentioned that most Sanskrit nouns are etymologically derived from verbal roots or verbs, such as *pādaḥ* 'foot' from the verbal root *pad* 'go', *sthāṇuḥ* 'post' from the verb *sthā* 'stand', and *rūpa* 'beauty' from the verb *rue* 'shine'.

These views regarding Sanskrit, however, are stated by Western scholars. As Duan (2001: V–XI) points out, Western scholars engaged in Oriental studies at that time were inevitably influenced by the consciousness that everything is judged by Western standards and is Western-oriented, which manifests itself in their habitual application of Western concepts to Eastern things and in their Westernization of Eastern expressions. For example, in *Elementarbuch der Sanskrit-Sprache* by A. F. Stenzler, the Sanskrit affix that expresses the meaning of *kāraka* is called "case" (*Kasus* in German), which is in fact a grammatical concept in Western languages. Stenzler's Westernized application makes explicit the variations of these affixes, but it also abstracts their original meanings into mere symbols, obliterating the features of traditional Indian grammars and casting a uniformed veil over all languages.

According to Duan (2001), in Sanskrit the roots without affixes are called *dhāhu* 'element', and the attached affixes are called *pratyaya* 'the cause of the root's sound change'. Although *dhāhu* primarily describes actions and behaviors, it can also include nouns that reflects actions and behaviors. The Chinese words *zhà* 'explode' and *sǐ* 'die' reflect actions and behaviors, but they correspond to not only English verbs *explode* and *die* but English nouns *explosion* and *death* as well. Similarly, the Sanskrit *dhāhu* is often referred to as a verbal root in Western scholarship, and this analogy is influenced by Western verb-centered grammatical views. So-called verbal roots are most likely nominal in nature. It is commonly believed that the basic formula for creating words in Sanskrit is "*dhāhu* + *pratyaya* = word", where *dhāhu* plus *pratyaya* exhibits the class characteristics of nouns, verbs, and so forth. If *dhāhu* is already verbal, why is it necessary to add *pratyaya* in order to exhibit

The *asymmetry between nouns and verbs* 199

the verbal characteristics? The *dhāhu* reflecting actions and behaviors does not necessarily have to be a verbal root, and whether it is verbal or not is more likely to remain unspecified (see Chapter 3, Section 3). It is also necessary to treat predicate words in Strait Salish as such.

As discussed in Section 7 of Chapter 3, many nouns in Tagalog were believed to be derived from verbal roots. For example, *b-um-ili* 'customer' is derived from the root *bili* 'buy' plus the infix *-um-*. However, Kaufman's (2009) analysis indicates all these roots are actually nominal. The Chinese *chī* 'eat' in *yī yā èr chī* 'two meals out of one duck', and the Tagalog *kuha* in *dalawa = ng kuha = ngà = lang nang = i~isang ibon* 'two takes (photos) of only one bird', exhibit a mixture of nominal and verbal characteristics. If we accept verb-centered grammatical views in their entirety, then we can also claim that all nouns in Chinese are verbs (so-called classificatory verbs) and that *hǔ* 'tiger' in *yī shān èr hǔ* 'two tigers in one mountain' and *chī* 'eat' in *yī yā èr chī* 'two meals out of one duck' are both verbs. This is blatantly absurd and clearly goes against the general laws of cognition. As part of verb-centeredness, there is also a stereotypical notion that the subject and object are the agent and patient of an action, respectively. Consider the following Chinese examples:

Táo   chántou,   chōng   hǎohàn.
escape   coward   charge   hero
'To escape is a coward and to charge is a hero.'

As a result of this stereotypical notion, one could say that the Chinese language uses the verb *táo* 'escape' to mean 'the person who escapes' and the verb *chōng* 'charge' to mean 'the person who charges'. In fact, as we have already explained in Section 3.3 of Chapter 4, what holds between subjects and predicates in Chinese is the relationship between topic and comment, and the connection can be rather loose, and it is very common for the subject not to be the agent and for the object to be diverse and not necessarily the patient as well. The words *táo* and *chōng* do not necessarily refer to the agent, and they refer to the actions instead. The *táo* and *chōng* in *Táo chántou, chōng hǎo hàn* 'To escape is a coward and to charge is a hero' is the same as the *táo* and *chōng* in *Táo róngyì, chōng hěn nán* 'To escape is easy and to charge is difficult'. If such expressions are completely used for subjects and objects in certain languages, it only indicates that these languages allow those words denoting actions to function as subjects and objects, but it cannot prove that those words denoting actions are real verbs instead of nouns.

According to some people, verbs are used in some languages to express what is expressed by nouns in other languages. We believe such languages should be re-examined. From a cognitive perspective, nouns are fundamental as a result of the asymmetry between nouns and verbs in all languages. The myth that certain languages have only verbs without nouns is merely a myth, since there has been no strong evidence that such languages exist (see Luuk 2010). It is probably simply a manifestation of word class typology (the polysynthetic type) in the verbs-as-nouns framework that nominal constituents consist of verbal roots and affixes, that is, all roots are nominal roots denoting actions.

Notes

1 Most of these examples are provided by Liu Dawei.
2 Wang Dongmei (2001) provides arguably the most detailed description of nouns used as verbs in modern Chinese, from which most of these examples are taken.
3 It may be argued that meaning is used as a judgment criterion when determining whether a change of word class is made based on original or non-original usage. In Zhu Dexi's (1985: 13–14) view, if identifying word classes must resort to meaning, regardless of the concrete lexical meaning, it is limited to judging whether the lexical meaning remains the same. In this case, meaning is also used to a limited extent, only to judge whether the lexical meaning is original or not, regardless of the change in concrete meaning.
4 The example was provided by Bernd Heine.
5 For the distinction between unaccusative and unergative verbs, see Chapter 4, Section 4.1. Baker (2009) speculates accordingly that there would not even be such a case as (a) in Tagalog, since the verbs in this language are actually nouns (See Chapter 3, Section 7).
6 The verb *boycott* is derived from the proper name C. C. Boycott (1832–1897), a British land lease manager in Ireland who was protested for refusing to reduce the rent of his tenant farmers in difficult times.
7 The verb *slate* is derived from the noun *slate*, a plate for writing on.
8 Section 1 of Chapter 1 in Volume II will explain how objects and complements in Chinese are of the same kind.
9 As well as explaining the asymmetry between nouns and verbs from a cognitive perspective, Tai (1997) asks a question: Since metaphors generally employ concrete concepts for expressing abstract ones, how is it that a concrete object, *a bottle*, represents an abstract action in a metaphor? This doubt is unnecessary as ontological metaphors and metonymies differ in nature and should be distinguished. Using the noun *bottle* as a verb is not an ontological metaphor but rather a metonymy.
10 This misconception is exactly what forces Zhu Dexi et al. (1961) to argue that verbs would become innately nouns if they were nominalized or referentialized.

References

Aitchison, J. (1994) *Words in the Mind: An Introduction to the Mental Lexicon*, 2nd ed., Oxford: Blackwell.
Anwood, J. (2000) 'A Dynamic Model of Part-of-Speech Differentiation', in P. M. Vogel and B. Comrie (eds) *Approaches to the Typology of Word Classes*, Berlin and New York: Mouton de Gruyter, 3–46.
Baker, M. C. (2009) 'On Some Ways to Test Tagalog Nominalism from a Crosslinguistic Perspective', *Theoretical Linguistics* 35(1): 63–71.
Bisang, W. (2008) 'Precategoriality and Syntax-Based Parts of Speech: The Case of Late Archaic Chinese', *Studies in Language* 32(3): 568–589.
Bisang, W. (2013) 'Late Archaic Chinese: An Lflexible Language Whose G Parameter Cannot Be Addressed', in J. Rijkhoff and E. van Lier (eds) *Flexible Word Classes*, Oxford: Oxford University Press, 278–287.
Chao, Yuen Ren (1968) *A Grammar of Spoken Chinese*, Berkeley and Los Angeles: University of California Press. Translated as *Hanyu Kouyu Yufa* by Lü Shuxiang in 1979, Beijing: The Commercial Press, and as *Zhongguohua de Wenfa* (Revised edition) by Pang-hsin Ting in 2002, Hong Kong: The Chinese University of Hong Kong Press.
Chen, Chengze (1922/1982) *Guowenfa Caochuang* (*Draft of Chinese Grammar*), Shanghai and Beijing: The Commercial Press.
Chen, Manhua (2008) *Tici Weiyu Ju Yanjiu* (*A Study of Sentences with Substantive Predicate*), Beijing: China Federation of Literary and Art Circles Publishing House.

The asymmetry between nouns and verbs 201

Chu, Zexiang (2001) 'Ming+shuliang yuxu yu zhuyi jiaodian' ('The Word Order of Name+Numeral-Classifier and the Focus of Attention'), *Studies of the Chinese Language* 5: 411–417.

Clark, E. V. and H. H. Clark (1979) 'When Nouns Surface as Verbs', *Language* 55(4): 767–811.

Duan, Qing (2001) *Bonini Yufa Rumen* (*Introduction to Pāṇini Grammar*), Beijing: Peking University Press.

Evans, N. and T. Osada (2005) 'Mundari: The Myth of a Language without Word Classes', *Linguistic Typology* 9(3): 351–390.

Green, G. M. (1974) *Semantics and Syntactic Regularity*, Bloomington: Indiana University Press.

Grice, H. P. (1975) 'Logic and Conversation', in P. Cole and J. L. Morgan (eds) *Syntax and Semantics 3: Speech Acts*, New York: Academic Press, 41–58.

Harbsmeier, Christoph (1983–1985) 'Where Do Classical Chinese Nouns Come From?', *Early China* 9–10: 77–163.

Hopper, P. J. and S. A. Thompson (1984) 'A Discourse Basis for Lexical Categories in Universal Grammar', *Language* 60: 703–752.

Jelinek, E. (1995) 'Quantification in Strait Salish', in E. Boch, E. Jenlinek, A. Kratzer and B. Partee (eds) *Quantification in Natural Languages*, Dordrecht: Kluwer, 487–540.

Jespersen, Otto (1924) *The Philosophy of Grammar*, London: George Allen & Unwin Ltd.

Kaufman, Daniel (2009) 'Austronesian Nominalism and Its Consequences: A Tagalog Case Study', *Theoretical Linguistics* 35(1): 1–49.

Lakoff, G. and M. Johnson (1980) *Metaphors We Live By*, Chicago and London: University of Chicago Press.

Langacker, R. (1987/1991) *Foundations of Cognitive Grammar*, vols. 1 & 2, Stanford: Stanford University Press.

Lü, Shuxiang (1979) *Hanyu Yufa Fenxi Wenti* (*Problems in Chinese Grammatical Analysis*), Beijing: The Commercial Press.

Luuk, E. (2010) 'Nouns, Verbs and Flexibles: Implications for Typologies of Word Classes', *Language Sciences* 32: 349–365.

McCawley, J. D. (1971) 'Prelexical Syntax', in R. J. O'Brien (ed) *Linguistic Developments of the Sixties: Viewpoints for the Seventies*, Monograph Series on Languages and Linguistics, Washington: Georgetown University, 24: 19–33.

Mithun, M. (2000) 'Noun and Verb in Iroquoian Languages: Multicategorisation from Multiple Criteria', in P. M. Vogel and B. Comrie (eds) *Approaches to the Typology of Word Classes*, Berlin and New York: Mouton de Gruyter, 397–420.

Pan, Shen et al. (1996) 'Gudai hanyu zhong wu cilei huoyong' ('No Flexible Use of Word Classes in Ancient Chinese'), in *Yuwen Xinlun* (*New Essays on Chinese Language*), Taiyuan: Shanxi Education Press, 69–76.

Song, Hongmin (2009) 'Yetan ming *er* dong jiegou' ('On the NP *er* VP Construction'), *Studies of the Chinese Language* 2: 184–187.

Tai, James H.-Y. (1997) 'Category Shifts and Word-Formation Redundancy', *Language and Linguistics in China* 3: 435–468.

Wang, Dongmei (2001) 'Xiandai hanyu dongming huzhuan de renzhi yanjiu' ('A Cognitive Study of the Categorial Shift Between Nouns and Verbs in Contemporary Chinese'), Doctoral Dissertation, Department of Linguistics, Graduate School of Chinese Academy of Social Sciences. Revised version, 2010, Beijing: China Social Sciences Press.

Wang, Kezhong (1989) *Guhanyu Cilei Huoyong* (*Active Use of Word Classes in Ancient Chinese*), Changsha: Hunan People's Publishing House.

202 *The asymmetry between nouns and verbs*

Xu, Denan (1984) 'Kouyu juzi zhong "tun" diao yufa chengfen de xianxiang' ('The Phenomenon of "Swallowing" Grammatical Constituents in Spoken Sentences'), *Linguistic Research* 4: 18–22.

Yang, Rongxiang (2008) 'Lun ming *er* dong jiegou de laiyuan jiqi yufa xingzhi' ('On the Origin and Grammatical Features of the NP *er* VP Construction'), *Studies of the Chinese Language* 3: 239–246.

Yin, Binyong (1986) 'Hanyu cilei de dingliang yanjiu' ('A Quantitative Study of Chinese Word Classes'), *Studies of the Chinese Language* 6: 428–436.

Yuan, Renlin (1989) *Xu Zi Shuo* (*Xie Huiquan zhu*) (*Empty Words* (*Annotated by Xie Huiquan*)), Beijing: Zhonghua Book Company.

Zhang, Jiangzhi (2013) 'Tici weiyu ju he hanyu cilei' ('Sentences with Substantive Predicate and Chinese Word Classes'), Doctoral Dissertation, Graduate School of Chinese Academy of Social Sciences.

Zhou, Ren (2012) 'N *de* V jiegou jiushi N *de* N jiegou' ('N *de* V Construction is N *de* N Construction'), *Studies of the Chinese Language* 5: 447–457.

Zhu, Dexi (1961) 'Shuo *de*' ('On *De*'), *Studies of the Chinese Language* 12: 1–15.

Zhu, Dexi (1982) *Yufa Jiangyi* (*Lectures on Chinese Grammar*), Beijing: The Commercial Press.

Zhu, Dexi (1983) 'Zizhi he zhuanzhi: hanyu mingcihua biaoji *de zhe zhi* de yufa gongneng he yuyi gongneng' ('Self-designation and Transferred Designation: The Grammatical and Semantic Functions of Chinese Nominalizers *De, Zhe, Zhi*'), *Dialect* 1: 16–31.

Zhu, Dexi (1985) *Yufa Dawen* (*Answering Questions about Chinese Grammar*), Beijing: The Commercial Press.

Zhu, Dexi (1988) 'Guanyu xianqin hanyu li mingci de dongcixing wenti' ('On the Verbal Characteristics of Nouns in Pre-Qin Chinese'), *Studies of the Chinese Language* 2: 81–86.

Zhu, Dexi (1990) 'Guanyu xianqin hanyu mingci he dongci de qufen de yize zhaji' ('A Note on the Distinction between Nouns and Verbs in Pre-Qin Chinese'), in *Wang Li Xiansheng Jinian Lunwen Ji* (*Collected Papers in Honor of Wang Li*), Beijing: The Commercial Press, 161–171.

Zhu, Dexi, Jiawen Lu and Zhen Ma (1961) 'Guanyu dongci xingrongci mingwuhua de wenti' ('On the Nominalization of Verbs and Adjectives'), *Journal of Peking University* (*Humanities and Social Sciences*) 4: 51–64, also in Dexi Zhu (1980) *Xiandai Hanyu Yufa Yanjiu* (*Studies in Modern Chinese Grammar*), Beijing: The Commercial Press, 193–224.

6   The referentiality of predicates

6.1   Nouns directly functioning as predicates

With respect to the phenomenon of nouns (i.e., stative nouns) in Chinese functioning as predicates, two points require discussion. It is necessary to look at what Chinese and other languages share and what is unique to Chinese. Otherwise, our understanding of Chinese will be one-sided. What Chinese and other languages share is the relatively special status of nouns when they function as predicates in contrast to verbs serving in that role and of verbs functioning as subjects or objects as opposed to nouns filling those two roles (see the previous chapter).

What is unique to Chinese is the ability of nouns and nominal constituents to directly function as predicates without the support of a copular verb. The sentences *tā Běijīngrén* 'he Pekingese' (he is Pekingese) and *jīntiān xīngqīsì* 'today Thursday' (today is Thursday) are examples of this. Nouns when directly functioning as predicates can also be modified by adverbs, as in *wǒ yě Běijīngrén* 'I also Pekingese' (I am also Pekingese) and *jīntiān cái xīngqīsì* 'today only Thursday' (It's only Thursday, today). Neither count as stylized rhetorical expressions.

The previous two points complement each other; they are in no way contradictory. The ability of nouns and nominal constituents to directly function as predicates is as important a linguistic feature of Chinese as verbs being able to function directly as sentential subjects and objects.

It is important to the contrast being argued for here that there are no derivational changes that English nouns can undergo that would permit them to function as predicates in sentences corresponding to the Chinese sentences *tā Běijīngrén* 'he Pekingese' (he is Pekingese) and *jīntiān xīngqīsì* 'today Thursday' (today is Thursday). They need the support of a copular verb. The sentences "*He a Pekingese" and "*Today Thursday" are ungrammatical.

Viewed from this perspective, the main difference between Chinese and English concerns predicate-hood (whether a noun can directly function as a predicate), and not subject-hood (whether a verb can directly function as a sentential subject or object).

The number and variety of sentences with nominal predicates is significantly greater than we had originally imagined. Yuen Ren Chao (1968), Chen Manhua (2008), and Zhang Jiangzhi (2013) discuss such sentences in detail. There is great

DOI: 10.4324/9781003385899-7

204   *The referentiality of predicates*

diversity in the kinds of nouns that function as predicates. Besides common nouns (*jīntiān qíngtiān* 'today sunny-day (today is a sunny day)), nouns denoting quantities (*xuèyā 140* 'blood pressure 140 ([the subject's] blood pressure is 140)), and attribute-head noun phrases (*Xiǎo Wáng huáng tóufa* 'Xiao Wang yellow hair' (Xiao Wang has blond hair)), there are also the following:

Proper nouns:	*Dīng*	*xiānsheng*	*ma?*	
	Ding	mister	MP	
	'(Are you) Mr. Ding?'			
	Wǒ	*Yuètíng.*		
	I	Yueting		
	'I am Yueting.'			

Pronouns:	*Wéi,*	*nǐ*	*nǎr?*	
	hello	you	where	
	'Hello, who are you?'[1]			
	Zhè	*ge*	*shénme*	*ya?*
	this	CL	what	MP
	'What is this?'			
	Nǐ	*shéi*	*a?*	
	you	who	MP	
	'Who are you?'			

De constructions:	*Zhè*	*běn*	*shū*	*tā*	*de.*
	this	CL	book	he	MM
	'This book is his.'				
	Tā	*yí*	*ge*	*mài cài*	*de.*
	he	one	CL	sell vegetables	MM
	'He's a vegetable seller.'				

There are many kinds of nominal predicate sentence patterns:

Parallel constructions:	*Nǐ*	*yi*	*yán,*	*wǒ*	*yi*	*yǔ.*
	you	one	word	I	one	speech
	'You have your say; I have mine.'					
	Chū	*yī*	*jiǎozi,*	*shíwǔ*	*tāngyuán.*	
	Begin	one	dumplings	fifteenth	soup-dumplings	
	'On the first day (of the lunar new year) we have dumplings; on the fifteenth we have sweet dumplings in soup.'					

N + *le* (current relevance):	*Tā*	*dōu*	*dàxuéshēng*	*le.*
	he	all	university-student	PSP
	'He's already a university student.'			

	Wŏmen	*lăo*	*péngyou*		*le.*	
	we	old	friend		PSP	
	'We're old friends.'					

N₁ *de* [relational marker] N₂:

Huìyì	*Lăo*	*Wáng*	*de*	*zhǔxí.*
meeting	Lao	Wang	MM	chair
'Lao Wang is the meeting's chair.'				

Jīnwǎn	*Mǎ*	*Liánliáng*	*de*	*Zhūgé*	*Liàng.*
today-evening	Ma	Lianliang	MM	Zhuge	Liang
'This evening Ma Lianliang is Zhuge Liang.'					

N then N:

Huài	*de*	*jiù*	*huài*	*de*	*ba.*
bad	MM	then	bad	MM	MP
'What's bad is bad.'					

Qī	*tiān*	*jiù*	*qī*	*tiān*	*bei.*
seven	day	then	seven	day	MP
'Clearly, seven days are seven days.'					

Distribution of a quantity:

Sān	*ge*	*rén*	*yī*	*jiān*	*fang.*
three	CL	people	one	CL	room
'Three people to a room.'					

Měi	*tiān*	*sān*	*tàng*	*bānchē.*
each	day	three	CL	scheduled vehicle
'Three buses a day.'				

All that is needed to see that there are several additional sentence types, especially sentences with *de* structures, is to break away from earlier approaches to grammatical analysis. These types are nominal predicate sentences or nominal minor sentences (see section 2.3). The following are examples of them:

Wŏ	*măi*	*de*	*piào.*
I	buy	MM	ticket
'I bought a ticket.'			

Tā	*qùnián*	*shēng*	*de*	*háizi.*
she	last-year	bear	MM	child
'She bore a child last year.'				

Shéi	*wèi*	*nǐ*	*zuò*	*de*	*jiàyī.*
who	for	you	make	MM	wedding-gown
'Who made your wedding gown for you?'					

Sentences in this pattern like *zhè běn shū de chūbǎn* 'this CL book MM publish (this book was published)' can function as predicates when in parallel constructions as in

206   *The referentiality of predicates*

Jīntiān zhè běn shū   de   chūbǎn, míngtiān nà běn shū   de   chūbǎn.
today   this CL book MM publish   tomorrow that CL book MM publish
'This book was published today; tomorrow, that book will be published.'

Although nominal predicate sentences function primarily to express judgments, there are other types. Chen Manhua (2008: 88) divides them into four types.

Judgment: *Nǐ   bèn   dàn.*
you   dumb   egg
'You're an idiot.'

Lǎo   Wáng   Shànghǎi   rén.
Lao   Wang   Shanghai   person
'Lao Wang is Shanghainese.'

Description: *Tā,   cháng   cháng   de   tóufa,   dà   dà   de   yǎnjīng.*
she   long   long   MM   hair   big   big   MM   eyes
'Her hair is very long; her eyes are very big.'

Explanation: *Lǎoshǔ   yǎnjīng   yī   cùn   guāng.*
mouse   eye   one   inch   light
'A mouse's eyes are short-sighted.'

Jiějie   Běidà,   mèimei   Qīnghuá.
elder-sister   Bei-da   younger-sister   Qinghua
'The elder sister is at Peking University; the younger sister is at Qinghua University.'

Narration: *Tā   yī   nián yī   běn shū, zhēn shì duō   chǎn*
he   one   year one CL book real   is   much produce
de   zuòjiā.
MM   author
'He writes a book a year. He is really a productive author'.

Nín zhè yàng huā   fǎ,   yī   bèizi   yě   huán bù   qīng.
you this way spend method one life-time also repay not clear
'If you keep spending like this, you won't be able to pay off your debts in your lifetime.'

There are many adverbs that can modify nominal predicates. Following are the three main types (Chen Manhua 2008: 66):

Range: *Quán* 'all', *zhǐ* 'only', *dōu* 'all', *zhěngzhěng* 'whole, entire', *zhěng gèr* 'whole, entire', *tǒngtǒng* 'whole, entire'
Temporal relations: *Cái* 'only then', *dōu* 'all', *jiù* 'then', *yǐjīng* 'already', *gāng* 'just (now)', *gānggāng* 'just (now)'
Mood: *Jiǎnzhí* 'simply', *jiūjìng* 'after all', *dàodǐ* 'after all'[2]

The particle *yě* often occurs at the end of nominal predicate sentences in Ancient Chinese. There are, however, many examples of such sentences without a sentence final *yě* as well. *Yě* functions to emphasize a judgment.

In poems and couplets, nouns and nominal phrases are often strung together to form sentences as in the following examples:

Gǔ	*téng*	*lǎo*	*shù*	*hūn*	*yā*
ancient	vines	old	trees	dark	crows
Xiǎo	*qiáo*	*liú*	*shuǐ*	*rén*	*jiā*
small	bridge	flowing	water	a person's	home
Gǔ	*dào*	*xī*	*fēng*	*shòu*	*mǎ*
ancient	road	west	wind	skinny	horse

(Ma Zhiyuan, "Autumn Reflections" in *Tiān Jìng Shā*)

Jī	*shēng*	*máo*	*diàn*	*yuè*
roost	crows	thatched	shop	moon
Rén	*jì*	*bǎn*	*qiáo*	*shuāng*
people	footprint	wooden	bridge	frost

(Wen Tingyun, "Early Morning Walk on Mount Shang")

Qiān	*duǒ*	*hóng*	*lián*	*sān*	*chǐ*	*shuǐ*
a	thousand	red	lotuses	3	feet of	water
Yī	*wān*	*míng*	*yuè*	*bàn*	*tíng*	*fēng*
one	curved	bright	moon	half	a pavilion	wind

(A couplet from Xingyin Pavilion in Suzhou)

There are many examples of juxtaposed nominal and verbal predicates in common sayings (Chen Manhua 2008: 193–201):

Guānjiā	*xiǎng*	*yì*	*xiǎng,*	*yínzi*	*yī*	*qiān*	*liǎng.*
an official	thinks	a	thought,	silver	a	thousand	ounces

'Money comes easy to officials.'

Bōxuē	*qián,*	*zài yǎn qián,*		*xuèhàn*	*qián,*	*wàn*
exploited	money is	before (your) eyes	blood-and-sweat	money	ten-thousand
wàn	*nián.*
ten-thousand	years

'The money expropriated through exploitation is there for all to see; it takes years to earn money through hard work'.

Dà	*chǎo*	*sān*	*liù*	*jiǔ,*	*xiǎo*	*chǎo*	*tiān*	*tiān*	*yǒu.*
big	arguments	three	six	nine	small	arguments	day	day	have

'Big arguments are relatively rare; small ones are a daily occurrence.'

208 *The referentiality of predicates*

Dōng   xuě   fēng   nián,   chūn   xuě   tǎoxián.
winter   snow   abundant   year   spring   snow   nuisance
'Snow in winter foretells a year with abundance; snow in spring is a nuisance.'

Dùlǐ   yī   liǎng   yóu,   mǎn   liǎn   fàngchū   guāng.
in-the-stomach   one   ounce   of oil   the whole   face   emits   a glow
'It shows in the face when somebody eats well.'

Fù   rén   qiān   tiáo   dào,   qióng rén   wú   lù   xíng.
rich   people   a thousand   CL   roads   poor   people   don't-have   a road   to walk
'The rich have many options; the poor have none.'

Rénqián   yī   xiào,   bèihòu   yī   dāo.
in-front-of-people   a   smile/laugh   behind-the-back   a   knife
'A friend to your face; a backstabber when you're not around.'

Shǐ   chòu   sān   fēn   xiāng,   rén   chòu   bùkě   dāng.
excrement   stink   three   tenths   fragrant   people   stink   can't   be-endured
'Excrement's stench has thirty percent fragrance (i.e., excrement can be used for things like fertilizer); a person's stench is unendurable.'

Yī   bèi   jī,   yi   bèi   míng.
one   generation   rooster   one   generation   crows(as a verb)
'If you keep a rooster for a lifetime, you'll have a lifetime of crowing.'

Tóu   fú   luóbo,   èr   fú   cài,   sān
head   9-day-hot-period   radishes   second   9-day-hot-period   vegetables   third
fú   zhòng   qiáomài.
9-day-hot-period   plant   buckwheat
'During the first 9-day-hot-period plant radishes; during the second 9-day-hot-period plant vegetables, and during the third 9-day-hot-period plant buckwheat'.

Zuǐlǐ   Yáo Shùn Yǔ Tāng, zuò shì   nán   dào nǔ   chāng.
in-the-mouth   Yao Shun Yu Tang   do   things   male   rob   female   prostitute
'They always talk about the ancient sage kings Yao, Shun, Yu, and Tang. But when they do things, the men rob, and the women are prostitutes.'

Shàngmiàn   yī   jùhuà,   xiàmiàn   máng   bù   tíng.
above   one   word   below   busy   not   stop
'A word from those on top, those below are busy without rest.'

  Guo Shaoyu (1979: 667, 709) holds that the claim that Chinese has only a few nominal constituents that function as predicates is not completely accurate. Yuen Ren Chao (1968: 53–57) states that there is no limit on the types of predicates in Chinese. (Also see Chen Chengze 1982: 53–57.)

The referentiality of predicates   209

In the traditional framework that distinguishes nouns from verbs, attempts to explain this unique feature found in Chinese encounter intractable difficulties. In practical terms, the theory of interchangeability that nouns can be used as verbs causes the characteristics of word classes to blur and for them to sometimes appear to be unnecessary verbosity. With respect to theory, it leads to the position that it is necessary to face the consequences that words do not belong to established word classes, that word classes lack set lexical members, and even that content words are not divisible into separate classes. See Lü Shuxiang (1954) and Chapter 2, Section 4.

Sentences composed of the constituent order VP + NP like *táo chántou* 'to escape is a coward' (Escape? You coward!) and *bù sǐ (jīnnián) yī bǎi suì* 'not die (this year) 100 years old' (If he hasn't died, he will be 100 years old this year) undermine generative grammar's sentence rewrite rule S→NP + VP, which is perplexing and embarrassing people committed to it.

The verbs-as-nouns theory resolves this difficulty (Chapter 3, Section 4). In this theory, NP is a referring expression. VP is a predicate-argument expression and a dynamic NP. The NP category includes the VP category. Not all sentences' predicates are predicate-argument expressions. However, a predicate-argument expression can always function as a sentence's predicate, making it possible to simply refer to predicate-argument expressions as predicates. If the notation NP (VP) is used to express "the NP category includes the VP category", then the class of referring expressions includes predicates. By using VP[NP] to express that "the VP category belongs to the NP category", all predicates are referring expressions. Following from this, the basic sentence rewrite rule can be stated as follows:

S→NP(VP) + VP[NP]

With the NP category including VPs, a VP can of course function as a subject. All VPs are NPs. All predicates are referring expressions. From this it follows that NPs are not excluded from functioning as predicates. To a certain extent, the verbs-as-nouns theory maintains the basic rewrite rule. Of course, this also shows that this rewrite rule has only a limited application in Chinese. By seeking alternative approaches when building generative rule systems for Chinese, computational linguists can have even better methodologies (see Bai Shuo 2014 and for new ideas Song Rou 2013 and others).

Some people find it hard to understand the claim that predicates are also referring expressions. They pose the question: Can predicates formed from verbal constituents also be referential? Do the predicates *shàng guo dàxué* 'have gone to college', *chī le dúyào* 'ate poison', and *zhèngzài chī fàn* 'is eating' in the sentences *wǒ shàng guo dàxué* 'I went to college', *tā chī le dúyào* 'he ate poison', and *tā zhèngzài chī fàn* 'she's eating' have referentiality and count as referring expressions? The answer is yes. Section 4 of Chapter 3 already argues for this based on minor sentences. This position can also be argued for based on the evidence discussed later. This discussion will begin by looking at the properties of *shì* 'be' (the copula).

210   *The referentiality of predicates*

6.2   *Shì* 'be' as a judgment verb

6.2.1   *The principle of "structural parallelism"*

Everyone recognizes that *shì* 'be' is a judgment verb in sentences like *tā shì mǎi fáng rén* 'he is buy house person' (he is a person buying a house), *mǎi fáng de shì Lǎo Lǐ* 'buy house de is Lao Li' (the one buying a house is Lao Li), and *mǎi fáng shì tóuzī* 'buy house is investment' (buying a house is an investment). However, there are disagreements whenever sentences like the following are encountered:

tā   shì   mǎi   fángzi.
he   be   buy   house
'He *is* buying a house.'

Zhè   ge   háizi   shì   tǐng   kě'ài.
this   CL   child   be   very   cute
'This child *is* very cute.'

Zhāng   Sān   shì   zuótian   qù   le   wàitān.
Zhang   San   be   yesterday   go   PSP   the Bund
'Zhang San did go to the Bund yesterday.'

In the previous examples, what follows *shì* 'be' is clearly a predicative constituent. There are those who claim that *shì* 'be' is not a judgment verb in these sentences. For them, it is an empty modal adverb or a marker of emphasis. Even while holding this position, they acknowledge that a constituent with predicate properties can act as a verb's object.

With respect to this point of contention, the principle of structural parallelism should be used to determine *shì*'s grammatical properties. Zhu Dexi (1985a: 31) puts forward this principle and attaches great importance to it. He claims that native-speaker linguistic intuitions are derived from structural parallelisms. To put it differently, structural parallelism is an expression of native-speaker linguistic intuitions. From this it follows that this principle should be adhered to when determining grammatical categories.

Given these considerations, it is easily demonstrated that *tā shì mǎi fángzi* 'he *is* buying a house', *tā shì mǎi fáng rén* 'He is a person buying a house', and *tā xiǎng mǎi fángzi,* 'he want buy house' (he wants to buy a house) share a structural parallelism. In contrast, *tā yěxǔ mǎi fángzi* 'he probably buy house' (he will probably buy a house) and *tā fǎnzhèng mǎi fángzi* 'he anyway buy house' (anyway, he's buying a house; *yěxǔ* and *fǎnzhèng* being modal adverbs) are not very similar to the previous three sentences.

A (Affirmative)	*Tā*	*shì*	*mǎi*	*fáng*	*rén*
	He	be	buy	house	person

'He is a person buying a house'

	Tā	*xiǎng*	*mǎi*	*fángzi*
	He	want	buy	house

'He wants to buy a house'

	Tā	*shì*	*mǎi*	*fángzi*
	He	be	buy	house

'He *is* buying a house'

B (Negative)	*Tā*	*bú*	*shì*	*mǎi*	*fáng*	*rén*
	He	not	be	buy	house	person

'He is not a person who is buying a house'

	Tā	*bù*	*xiǎng*	*mǎi*	*fángzi*
	He	not	want	buy	house

'He doesn't want to buy a house'

	Tā	*bú*	*shì*	*mǎi*	*fángzi*
	He	not	be	buy	house

'He *is not* buying a house'

C (Question)	*Tā*	*shì*	*bú*	*shì*	*mǎi*	*fáng*	*rén*
	He	be	not	be	buy	house	person

'Is he a person buying a house'

	Tā	*xiǎng*	*bù*	*xiǎng*	*mǎi*	*fángzi*
	He	want	not	want	buy	house

'Does he want to buy a house'

	Tā	*shì*	*bú*	*shì*	*mǎi*	*fángzi*
	He	be	not	be	buy	house

'*Is* he buying a house'

D (Question)	*Tā*	*shì*	*mǎi*	*fáng*	*rén*	*bú*	*shì*
	He	be	buy	house	person	not	be

'He is a person buying a house, isn't he?'

	Tā	*xiǎng*	*mǎi*	*fángzi*	*bù*	*xiǎng*
	He	want	buy	house	not	plan

'He wants to buy a house, doesn't he?'

	Tā	*shì*	*mǎi*	*fángzi*	*bú*	*shì*
	He	be	buy	house	not	be

'He *is* buying a house, isn't he?'

212 *The referentiality of predicates*

E (Answers to the questions)	*Shì* Be 'Yes or no'	*/búshì* /not be
	Xiǎng Want 'Yes or no'	*/bùxiǎng* /not want
	Shì Be 'Yes or no'	*/búshì* /not be

The sentence *tā yěxǔ mǎi fángzi*, 'he probably buy house' (he will probably buy a house) does not have corresponding negative and interrogative forms **tā bù yěxǔ mǎi fángzi* 'he not probably buy house', **tā yěxǔ bù yěxǔ mǎi fángzi?* 'he probably not probably buy house', and **tā yěxǔ mǎi fángzi bù yěxǔ?* 'he probably buy house not probably'. Even though it is possible for *yěxǔ* 'although' to stand alone when answering a question, the larger parallel pattern is unaffected because it is impossible to say the corresponding negative response **bù yěxǔ* 'not probably'.

Given the previous argument, it is reasonable to treat the *shì* in the sentence *tā shì mǎi fángzi* 'He *is* buying a house' as a judgment verb. The use of the principle of structural parallelism to determine the properties of syntactic constituents is in line with the principle of simplicity.

There are people who argue that judgment verbs can be distinguished from modal adverbs based on stress assignment. Modal adverbs can be stressed as can the *shì* 'be' in *tā shì mǎi fángzi* 'He *is* buying a house' showing that it is a modal adverb. This argument does not work because the *shì* in *tā shì mǎi fáng rén* 'he is a person buying a house' can also be stressed whereas the *shì* 'be' in *tā shì mǎi fángzi* is usually unstressed (Lü Shuxiang 1979: 80).

Some have used the following method to distinguish between judgment verbs and modal adverbs (Zhang Bin 2010: 596):

Zhè bĕn shū shì Xiǎo Zhāng de.   **Zhè bĕn shū Xiǎo Zhāng.*
this CL book be Xiao Zhang MM   this CL book Xiao Zhang
'This book is Xiao Zhang's.'

Tā shì sòng xìn de.   *Tā sòng xìn.*
he be send message MM   he send message
'He is a messenger.'   'He conveys messages.'

Shāmo shì kĕyǐ zhēngfú de.   *Shāmo kĕyǐ zhēngfú.*
desert be can conquer MM   desert can conquer
'The desert can be conquered.'   'The desert can be conquered.'

Tā   de   xuéshì   shì yuānbó   de.   Tā   de   xuéshì   yuānbó.
he   de   knowledge   be   deep-broad   MM   he   de   knowledge   deep-broad
'His knowledge is deep and broad.'   'His knowledge is deep and broad.'

They observe that the structures in the first two sentences either become ungrammatical or change after the deletion of *shì* and *de*. Their meanings either become uninterpretable or are changed significantly. From this it follows that the *shì* in these sentences is a judgment verb. In contrast, the structures and semantics of the last two sentences are unchanged by the deletion of *shì* and *de*. Since the only changes are pragmatic, it follows that *shì* in these sentences is a modal adverb.

This approach is not reasonable. The goal is to determine the properties of *shì*. However, the previous discussion links *shì* and *de* together. If only the word *shì* is considered or if a pause substitutes for *shì*, the resulting sentence *Zhè běn shū Xiǎo Zhāng de* 'This book is Xiao Zhang's' is acceptable. There are also no changes in structure or meaning in the sentence *tā, sòng xìn de* 'he is a messenger'. In fact, all of the *shì* that they treat as verbs (Zhang Bin 2010: 595) can be replaced by a pause:

Xiǎo   Lǐ   shì   zhè   ge   bān   de   bānzhǎng.
Xiao   Li   be   this   CL   class   MM   monitor
'Xiao Li is this class's monitor.'

Xiǎo   Lǐ,   zhè   ge   bān   de   bānzhǎng.
Xiao   Li   this   CL   class   MM   monitor
'Xiao Li is this class's monitor.'

Xiǎo   Wáng   zuótiān   shì   zuò   huǒchē   qù   de   Shànghǎi.
Xiao   Wang   yesterday   be   ride   train   go   MM   Shanghai
'Yesterday, Xiao Wang took a train to Shanghai.'

Xiǎo   Wáng   zuótiān,   zuò   huǒchē   qù   de   Shànghǎi.
Xiao   Wang   yesterday,   ride   train   go   MM   Shanghai
'Yesterday, Xiao Wang took a train to Shanghai.'

Shì in the second sentence is treated as a verb to express emphasis. However, in another place (Zhang Bin 2010: 161), it is claimed that a *shì* in a similar sentence is a modal adverb emphasizing the sentence's focus.

Shì   Zhāng   Sān   zuótian   qù   le   wàitān.
Be   Zhang   San   yesterday   go   PSP   the Bund
'It was Zhang San who went to the Bund yesterday.'

Zhāng   Sān   shì   zuótian   qù   le   wàitān.
Zhang   San   be   yesterday   go   PSP   the Bund
'It was yesterday that Zhang San went to the Bund.'

214 *The referentiality of predicates*

Zhāng   Sān   zuótian   shì   qù   le   wàitān.
Zhang   San   yesterday   be   go   PSP   the Bund
'Zhang San did go to the Bund yesterday.'

It is impossible to see what standard is being applied here to distinguish verbs from modal adverbs. However, if approached from the perspective of structural parallelism, *shì* in all three of the previous sentences is a judgment verb. This claim can be tested by negating these sentences with *bú shì*, forming questions from them with *shì bú shì* or *shì . . . bú shì* and answering those questions with *shì* and *bú shì*. In Chinese, subjectless sentences are well-formed sentences. *Shì Zhāng Sān zuótian qù le wàitān* 'it was Zhang San who went to the Bund yesterday', is such a sentence.

It has also been proposed that verbs can be distinguished for modal adverbs based on whether there is flexibility with respect to where a lexical item can occur in a sentence. In the previous three sentences, *shì* can occur before *Zhāng Sān* (a name) or *zuótiān* 'yesterday' or *qù wàitān* 'go to the Bund' depending on which of the three constituents is in focus. This variation is presented as evidence that *shì* is a modal adverb.

It should, however, be noted that without *shì*, stress assignment can be used to mark which of the three constituents is the sentence's main point of focus. Whichever constituent is assigned prominent stress is the one in focus.

The question arises as to whether the constituent after *shì* is always the one in focus whenever *shì* is added to a sentence. In fact, it is not always the case that *shì* occurs immediately before the focused constituent. What is true is that the constituent assigned prominent stress is the one in focus as can be seen from the following examples:

Shì   Zhāng   Sān   zuótian   qù   le   wàitān
be   **Zhang   San**   yesterday   go   PSP   the Bund
'It was **Zhang San** who went to the Bund yesterday'

Shì   Zhāng   Sān   zuótian   qù   le   wàitān
be   Zhang   San   **yesterday**   go   PSP   the Bund
'It was Zhang San who went to the Bund **yesterday**'

Shì   Zhāng   Sān   zuótian   qù   le   wàitān
be   Zhang   San   yesterday   **go**   PSP   the Bund
'It was Zhang San who **went** to the Bund yesterday'

Shì   Zhāng   Sān   zuótian   qù   le   wàitān
be   Zhang   San   yesterday   go   PSP   **the Bund**
'It was Zhang San who went to **the Bund** yesterday'

The referentiality of predicates 215

There are people who have also claimed that an unstressed constituent that occurs immediately after an added *shì* receives the main focus. In fact, this is not always the case as can be seen in the following examples:

Wǒ shì qùnián pōufù sheng de háizi.
I be last-year caesarian-section give-birth to MM child
'I gave birth to a child by caesarian section last year.'

Tā shì zuótiān dǎ dī qù de yīyuàn.
he be yesterday hit taxi go MM hospital
'He took a taxi to the hospital yesterday.'

In the previous examples, when there is no special stress assignment, *pōufù* 'caesarian section' and *dǎ dī* 'take a taxi' stand out as being in focus and not *qùnián* 'last year' and *zuótiān* 'yesterday', respectively.

Another frequently encountered approach maintains that *shì . . . de* 'be . . . de' frames what receives the main focus in a sentence. In this approach, independent of anything else that may be in play, *pōufù* 'caesarian section' and *dǎ dī* 'take a taxi' are within the *shì . . . de* frame. However, this frame is relevant to the type A sentences given later but not to the high frequency type B sentences where the main focus is assigned outside of the *shì . . . de* frame:

Type A   *Tā shì qùnián sheng de háizi.*
         she be last-year give-birth MM child
         'She gave birth to a child last year.'

         Tā shì zuótiān chū de yīyuàn
         she be yesterday leave MM hospital
         'She left the hospital yesterday.'

Type B   *Tā shì sheng de shuāngbāotāi.*
         she be give-birth MM twins
         'She gave birth to twins.'

         Tā shì jìn de fù chǎn yīyuàn.
         she be enter MM female give-birth hospital
         'She entered a maternity hospital.'

The previous examples demonstrate that the focus is not necessarily enclosed by *shì . . . de*. This is the same as the situation found in the following *shì* sentences that do not have *de*. Focus can fall on various post-*shì* positions:

Prominent focus on the attributes (*rìběn* and *měiguó*)

Lǎo Zhāng shì rìběn tàitài, Lǎo Wáng shì měiguó tàitài.
Lao Zhang be Japan wife Lao Wang be American wife
'Lao Zhang's wife is Japanese; Lao Wang's is American'

216 *The referentiality of predicates*

Prominent focus is on the heads (*fēngtián* 'Toyota' and *běntián* 'Honda')

Lǎo	*Zhāng*	*shì*	*rìběn*	*fēngtián,*	*Lǎo*	*wáng*	*shì*	*rìběn*	*běntián.*
Lao	Zhang	be	Japanese	Toyota	Lao	Wang	be	Japanese	Honda

'Lao Zhang has a Japanese Toyota; Lao Wang has a Japanese Honda.'

The claim that *shì . . . de* frames a sentence's prominent focus is modeled on the English pattern "It is . . . that. . . ." In fact, English also has situations in which "is . . . that" does not enclose what is in focus as in "It is hereby that I declare. . . .", though, admittedly, this kind of sentence is extremely rare in English.

6.2.2 *The Indo-European perspective 1*

One of the reasons some people categorize *shì* as a modal adverb that functions to single out a constituent for emphasis is that their approach is dominated by an Indo-European perspective on language. They incorrectly believe that Chinese is like Indo-European languages in allowing only nominal constituents to function as grammatical objects after verbs. For example, Fu Yu (2010) uses this kind of reasoning when arguing that *shì* is only an emphatic marker:

I like Syntax, and John *does* too.

Wǒ	*xǐhuān*	*jùfǎxué,*	*Xiǎo*	*Wáng*	*yě*	<u>*shì*</u>.
I	like	syntax	Xiao	Wang	also	<u>be</u>

'I like syntax and so does Xiao Wang.'

I *do* not like Syntax very much.

Wǒ	*bú*	<u>*shì*</u>	*hěn*	*xǐhuān*	*jùfǎxué.*
I	not	<u>be</u>	very	like	syntax

'I don't really like syntax.'

I *do* like Syntax.

Wǒ	<u>*shì*</u>	*hěn*	*xǐhuān*	*jùfǎxué.*
I	<u>be</u>	very	like	syntax

'I do like syntax.'

In the previous English sentences, *do* is treated as an emphatic marker. In the first sentence, it functions as a substitute for a verb phrase. It can be omitted. Its optional status shows that it functions to add emphasis. In the second sentence, *do* is an obligatory auxiliary verb in a construction that negates the predicate. Negation is a kind of emphasis. The third sentence's *do* is naturally understood as an emphatic marker.

Fu (2010) treats *shì* in Chinese as corresponding to *do* in English. From this it follows that *shì* should be classified as an emphatic marker. Fu's proposed approach only takes into account those situations where *shì* and *do* correspond to each other.

The referentiality of predicates 217

By leaving out those situations where *shì* and *do* do not correspond, significant differences between English and Chinese are obscured.

i. *I do not like syntax, and John does too.

> *Wǒ bù xǐhuān jùfǎxué, Xiǎo Wáng yě shì.*
> I   not like   syntax   Xiao Wang also be
> 'I do not like syntax, and Xiao Wang doesn't either.'

ii. I do not like syntax, and John doesn't either.

> **Wǒ bù xǐhuān jùfǎxué, Xiǎo Wáng yě bú shì.*
> *I   not like   syntax.   Xiao Wang also not be

iii. I like syntax, and John, too.

> **Wǒ xǐhuān jùfǎxué, Xiǎo Wáng yě.* (It is necessary to say, "Xiǎo Wáng yě shì")
> *I   like   syntax,   Xiao Wang also ("Xiao Wang also be" (And so does Xiao Wang))

When *do* in English functions as a verb, the only objects that can occur after it are nominal constituents or the form V-ing, which simultaneously possesses nominal properties, as in *do something, do my work, do a movie, do me a favor, do 80 miles an hour, do the shopping, do some reading, do a lot of running, do my washing and ironing*. If followed by a verbal constituent, *do* is an emphatic marker and not a verb.

This kind of a distinction for English is reasonable. It is, however, not reasonable for Chinese. This is because post-verbal objects in Chinese can be both nominal and verbal constituents.

If, in contrast to the previous proposal, *shì* in Chinese is uniformly treated as a judgment verb, it can occur when emphasis is marked; it can be omitted when nothing is emphasized; and it can occur before nominal and verbal constituents. This approach can successfully account for those cases where English and Chinese sentences correspond to each other. It can also provide a reasonable explanation for when there is no correspondence between them.

It is because *shì* is a judgment verb that the Chinese sentence in i. is acceptable and the one in ii. is not. In both examples, *shì* takes for the verbal constituent *bù xǐhuān jùfǎxué* 'not like syntax' as its understood object. In i., the entire object is omitted. In ii. the omission (which includes a constituent initial *bù* 'not') results in a semantic contradiction. The reason why the Chinese sentence in iii. is unacceptable is also because *shì* is a judgment verb. It is unlike English *do*, which can be easily omitted when it substitutes for an entire verbal constituent. Where the adverb *yě* 'also' occurs, *shì* cannot be omitted.

An object occurring after a verb can be a nominal constituent and it can be a verbal constituent. This is a general rule in Chinese. In reality, there is no need to treat *shì* as a modal adverb when a verbal constituent occurs after it. Zhu Dexi (1982: 105) observed that objects occurring after *shì* can be substantive constituents or

218   *The referentiality of predicates*

predicative constituents. If the object is a noun, *shì* is in neutral tone. It is also in neutral tone when its object is a predicative constituent. Compare the following pairs of sentences:

Tā	*shi*	*piànzi*	/	*Tā*	*shi*	*piàn*	*rén*
he	be	liar	/	he	be	deceive	people
'He is a liar'			/	'He deceives people'			

Tā	*shi*	*yǎnyuán*	/	*Tā*	*shi*	*yǎn*	*xì*
she	be	actress	/	she	be	act	drama
'She is an actress'			/	'She acts in plays'			

These facts demonstrate that it is not important in Chinese whether *shì* is followed by a nominal or a verbal constituent. In Ancient Chinese, *yě* sentences expressed judgments. Sentence-final *yě* can occur after nominal constituents (as in "Ānpíng jūn, xiǎo rén yě" 'Anping (a name) prince small person ye' (Prince Anping was a base person)) and after verbal constituents (Harbsmeier 1983; Li Zuofeng 2004: 378–393, and Zhang Yujin 2010) as in the following examples:

Kuàiyì	*ér*	*sàng*	*jūn,*	*fàn*	*xíng*	*yě.*
happy	and	mourn	ruler	commit	punishment	MP

'Being happy while mourning the ruler is a punishable offense'.
(Jin Discourses 3, *Discourses of the Kingdoms*)

Tiāndì	*shǐ*	*wǒ*	*zhǎng*[3]	*bǎi*	*shòu,*	*jīn*	*zǐ*	*shí wǒ,*	*shì*	*nì*
sky emperor	cause	me	to-be-leader	hundred	animal	now	you	eat me	this	violate
tiāndì		*mìng yě.*								
sky emperor		order MP								

'The Heavenly Emperor appointed me to be the leader of the multitude of animals. Now you want to eat me. This violates the Heavenly Emperor's order'.
(The Annals of Chu 1, *Annals of the Warring States*)

Wú	*bù*	*néng*	*zǎo*	*yòng zǐ,*	*jīn*	*jí*	*ér*	*qiú zǐ,*	*shì*	*guǎrén*[4]
I	not	able	early	use you	now	emergency	and	seek you	this	alone-person
zhī	*guò*	*yě.*								
MM	fault	MP								

'I could not appoint you to a position of responsibility before. Now in an emergency I turn to you. This is my fault'.
(The 30th year of the Duke of Xi, *Zuo Tradition*)

Shì was still a demonstrative pronoun in this period of Chinese. Only later did it change into a judgment word, taking on the judgment modality. After the sentence-final particle *yě* was lost through linguistic change, both the nominal *guǎrén zhī guò* and the verb phrase *nì tiān dì mìng* came to function as objects of *shì*. From this, it can be seen that what we have referred to as a general principle applies to both Ancient and Modern Chinese. Modern sentences with the lexical item *shì* systematically correspond to ancient sentences with the sentence-final particle *yě*.

Ancient Chinese				*Modern Chinese*			
Zhāng	*jūn,*	*piànzi*	*yě.*	*Lǎo*	*zhāng*	*shì*	*piànzi.*
Zhang	*a-title*	liar	MP	Lao	Zhang	be	liar
'Mr. Zhang is a liar.'				'Lao Zhang is a liar.'			

Zhāng	*jūn,*	*piàn*	*wǒ*	*yě.*	*Lǎo*	*Zhāng*	*shì*	*piàn*	*wǒ.*
Zhang	*a-title*	deceive	I	MP	Old	Zhang	be	deceive	I
'Mr. Zhang deceived me.'					'Lao Zhang deceived me.'				

When expressing a judgment, the verb *shì* can be added in front of a verbal constituent functioning as a predicate in Modern Chinese to strengthen the judgment. Following are examples of what were originally predicates being changed into referential objects of the verb *shì*: *wǒ (shì) chī guò fàn le* 'I (be) eat *past-exp* food *perf*' (I did finish eating) and *wǒ (shì) bù xǐhuān jùfǎxué* 'I (be) not like syntax' (I don't like syntax).

It is precisely because *shì* often occurs before predicates to strengthen a judgment and because it is optional that there are many conjunctions or adverbs + *shì* that underwent lexicalization. Examples of this phenomenon include *dànshì* 'but', *kěshì* 'but', *ruòshì* 'if', *zǒngshì* 'always', *háishì* 'still', *yuèshì* 'the more', *bùguǎn shì* 'whether', *huòzhě shì* 'or', *hǎoxiàng shì* 'seems', and *yóuqíshì* 'especially'. (See Dong Xiufang 2004.)

When *shì* functions to strengthen a judgment, it often co-occurs with sentence-final *de*. (For the ways in which *de* and *shì* are interconnected, see Section 5 of Chapter 3 in Volume II.) *Shì* can be added before almost all predicates and *de* (which can be pronounced *dì* when stressed) can be added after them. *De* also functions to strengthen an affirmation. For example, when analyzing the details of a case, one can say:

Fàn	*zuì*	*xiányí*	*rén*	*7*	*diǎn*	*zhōng*	*cóng*	*chūzūchē*	*xiàlái*	*dì,*
commit	crime	suspect	person	7	dot	clock	from	taxi	down-come	MP

'The criminal suspect got out of the taxi at 7 o'clock,

7	*diǎn*	*05*	*fēn*	*jìnrù*	*dàlóu*	*diàntī*	*dì.* . . .
7	dot	05	point	enter	building's	elevator	MP

entered the building's elevator at 7:05. . . .'

6.2.3 *The Indo-European perspective 2*

A second reason for why some people categorize *shì* as a modal adverb also arises from their approach being dominated by a perspective grounded in

220 *The referentiality of predicates*

Indo-European languages. They incorrectly believe that Chinese is the same as Indo-European languages in requiring a close semantic connection between subjects and predicates, as is found in English. With respect to judgment sentence, the English copula *be* mainly functions to express equivalency and attributions.

In Chinese the semantic connection between a subject and predicate can be extremely loose (Chapter 4, Section 3.3) as in *nǐ (de xié) yě pò le* 'you (de shoe) also broke asp' (your shoe is also worn out). With respect to judgment sentences with the word *shì*, although *shì* can express equivalence (as in <u>*Kuángrén Rìjì*</u> de *zuòzhě shì Lǔ Xùn* '*Madman Diary* de author be Lu Xun' (The author of *The Diary of a Madman* is Lu Xun)) and attributes (as in *jīngyú shì bǔrǔ dòngwù* 'whales be mammal animal' (whales are mammals)), a large number of judgment sentences express neither. According to native linguistic intuitions, sentences like the following are normal sentences.

Rénjiā   shì   fēng   nián
People   be   abundant   year
'People are having a prosperous year'

Tā   shì   liǎng   gè   nán   hár
he   be   two   CL   boy   child
'He has two sons'

Yī   ge   dòng   shì   húlí,   sān   ge   dòng   shì   yětù
one   CL   hole   be   fox   three   CL   hole   be   hare
'One hole has foxes; 3 holes have hares'

Moreover, because verbal constituents also occur after *shì*, Chinese has a great variety of judgment sentences that do not express equivalence or attributes. Being dominated by perspectives from Indo-European languages, in the past we could not imagine or did not wish to imagine what followed *shì* were in fact attributive constructions[5] in sentences like *Lǎo Wáng shì qùnián shēng de háizi* 'Lao Wang be last-year give-birth-to de child' (Lao Wang had a child last year) and *wǒ shì tóu de zànchéng piào* 'I be cast approve ballot' (I voted yes). After a brief comparison, it is easy to see that a parallelism exists between such structures and general attributive structures and that semantically both express a subjective identification or attribution (Shen Jiaxuan 2008).

i.   *Lǎo   Wáng   shì   rìběn   tàitài   (búshì měiguó tàitài)*
       Lao   Wang   be   **Japanese**   wife   (not an American wife)
       'Lao Wang has a Japanese wife'

       *Lǎo   Wáng   shì   rìběn   **tàitài**   (búshì rìběn mǔqīn)*
       Lao   Wang   be   Japanese   **wife**   (not a Japanese mother)
       'Lao Wang has a Japanese **wife**'

The referentiality of predicates   221

i. | *Wǒ* | *shì* | *rìběn* | | *qìchē* | *(búshì hánguó qìchē)* |
|---|---|---|---|---|---|
| I | be | **Japanese** | | car | (not a Korean car) |

'Mine is a **Japanese** car'

Wǒ	*shì*	*rìběn*		*qìchē*	*(búshì rìběn diànshì)*
I	be	Japanese		**car**	(not a Japanese television)

'Mine is a Japanese **car**'

ii. | *Lǎo* | *Wáng* | *shì* | *qùnián* | *shēng* | *de* | *háizi* |
|---|---|---|---|---|---|---|
| Lao | Wang | **be** | **last-year** | give-birth-to | MM | child |

'Last year, Lao Wang had a child'

Lǎo	*Wáng*	*shì*	*shēng*	*de*	*shuāngbāotāi*
Lao	Wang	be	give-birth-to	MM	**twins**

'Lao Wang had **twins**'

ii. | *Wǒ* | *shì* | *húluàn* | *tóu* | *de* | *piào* |
|---|---|---|---|---|---|
| I | be | random | cast | MM | ballot |

'I cast my ballot **randomly**'

Wǒ	*shì*	*tóu*	*de*	*zànchéng*	*piào*
I	be	cast	MM	affirmative	ballot

'I voted **yes**'

For the previous sentences, the forms used for negation, questions, and responses to questions demonstrate that there are structural parallelisms between the items in A and B.

Some people have given semantic incoherence as their reason for rejecting that *yī cì* 'one time' and *yī tiān* 'one day' are attributes for *tóu* 'head' and *lǚguǎn* 'hotel', respectively, in the sentences *yī cì tóu yě méi xǐ* 'one head also have-not wash' ([I] haven't washed my hair even once) and *yī tiān lǚguǎn yě méi zhù* 'one day hotel also have-not stay' (I haven't stayed in a hotel for even one day). Zhu Dexi (1985a: 53), however, has pointed out that it is not necessary for two structurally related constituents to have much of a semantic connection between them. It is also not necessary for semantically related constituents to be directly connected structurally.

Equally for the B sentences, how do you determine that *qùnián shēng de* 'last year gave birth to' is not an attribute for *háizi* 'child' and *shēng de* 'give birth to' is not an attribute for *shuāngbāotāi* 'twins'? Likewise, how is it determined that *húluàn tóu de* 'randomly cast' is not an attribute for *piào* 'ballot' or *tóu de* 'cast' for *zànchéng piào* 'yes vote'?

The only reason in support of the argument that these are not attributes is that Lao Wang is not in fact a child (*háizi*) or twins (*shuāngbāotāi*), and I am not in fact a cast ballot (*tóu de piào*) or a yes vote (*zànchéng piào*). If this kind of argument is reasonable, Japan (*rìběn*) is not an attribute in either *wǒ shì rìběn tàitài* (mine is a

222 *The referentiality of predicates*

Japanese wife) or *wǒ shì rìběn qìchē* (mine is a Japanese car) because I am neither a wife (*tàitài*) nor a car (*qìchē*). (Compare the analysis of related sentences in Tagalog in Chapter 3, Section 7.) An unstressed phrasal head modified by an attribute marked by *de* can be omitted under identity with a preceding constituent. This applies equally to B-type sentences as can be seen from the following comparisons:

i. *Dàjiā   dōu   shì   měiguó   de   bóshì,   wǒ   shì   déguó   de.*
   everyone   all   be   American   MM   PhD   I   be   German   MM
   'Everyone has an American PhD; mine is German.'

ii. *Tā   shì   qùnián   shēng   de   háizi, wǒ   shì   jīnnián   shēng   de.*
    she be   last-year give-birth-to MM   child   I   be   this-year give-birth-to MM
    'She had a child last year; I had one this year.'

Having demonstrated that both nominal and verbal constituents can occur after the verb *shì*, we should now establish the following relationship of structural parallelism between A (sentences with *de*) and B (sentences with *le*):

i. *Tā   shì   qùnián   shēng   de   háizi*
   she   be   last-year   give-birth-to   MM   child
   'Last year she gave birth to a child'

   Tā   shì   shēng   de   shuāngbāotāi
   she   be   give-birth-to   MM   twins
   'She gave birth to twins'

ii. *Tā   shì   qùnián   shēng   le   háizi*
    she   be   last year   give-birth-to   PSP   child
    'She gave birth to a child last year'

    Tā   shì   shēng   le   shuāngbāotāi
    she   be   give-birth-to   PSP   twins
    'She gave birth to twins'

By looking externally at the Chinese noun phrases and verb phrases in terms of the parallelisms found in the larger structure (*shì* judgment sentences), both types of phrases are the objects of the verb *shì*. Based on this parallelism, verb phrases and noun phrases can be assigned to the same category. According to the verbs-as-nouns theory, this category is the super-noun phrase. (Volume II, Chapter 3, Section 5.)

"The principle of structural parallelism" is an important principle in discussions of grammar and in constructing a grammatical system. It is not only Chinese, a language lacking in morphological markings, that needs to depend on this principle; languages with rich morphologies are equally dependent on it. English divides the uses of *do* into two types, verb and emphatic marker. The reason for this is the structural parallelism that exists between the verb *do* and verbs in general. Verbs

The referentiality of predicates   223

in general can only take nominal objects. It is this larger parallel pattern that determines this division in English.

Languages with inflection place great emphasis on the distinction between a verb's finite and nonfinite forms. This is because inflectional paradigms are the clearest and strictest expression of structural parallelisms.[6] A good grammar and a good grammatical system does not complicate what is in fact simple. Rather, it simplifies what appears to be complex. Only by adhering to the "principle of structural parallelism" can this be achieved.

Lü Shuxiang (1979: 41, 81) states that "it is entirely possible to unify the uses of the lexical item *shì*. It counts as its own subcategory of verbs". This chapter's conclusion is straightforward: Based on the principle of structural parallelism, the unified grammatical properties of *shì* define it as a judgment verb with an emphatic function and nothing else.

Judgments vary in strength. *Shì* is usually unstressed in a sentence. When it is not included (that is to say, when replaced by a pause) a sentence can still express a judgment. *Shì* is added to a sentence when it is necessary to strengthen the judgment. *Shì* is assigned prominent stress to express confirmation in the most emphatic way to state a judgment. Whether *shì* is followed by a nominal or verbal constituent is unimportant in Chinese. *Shì* can express objective judgments concerning equivalency or attributes and subjective judgments relating to identity or recognition.

6.3   The referentiality of Chinese predicates

6.3.1   Yǒu *'have/there be' is an existential verb*

Besides adding *shì*, the verb *yǒu* can be added before a predicate resulting in the predicate functioning as the referential object of *yǒu*. Zhu Dexi (1982: 71) once again used the principle of structural parallelism to establish that *méi* 'not[-have]' and *méi yǒu* 'not have' are verbs and not adverbs when they occur before Chinese predicative constituents. The following examples of the parallelism between *méi (yǒu) hái*zi 'not (have) children' and *méi (yǒu) qù* 'have not gone' illustrate this:

A (positive) *Yǒu*   *háizi*
      have   child
      'S/he has a child'

      Qù   *le*
      go   le
      'She has gone'

B (negative) *Méi*   *háizi*
      not-have child
      'He doesn't have a child'

      Méi   *qù*
      have-not go
      'She hasn't gone'

224 *The referentiality of predicates*

C (negative) *Méi yǒu háizi*
not have child
'He has no child'

Méi yǒu qù
not have go
'She hasn't gone'

D (question) *Yǒu háizi méi yǒu*
have child not have
'Do you have a child?'

Qù le méi yǒu
go PSP not have
'Did she go?'

E (answer
to a
question) *Yǒu or méi yǒu*
have or not have
'Yes or no'

Qù le or méi yǒu
go PSP or not have
'Yes or no'

Zhu explains the significance of the above distribution as follows:

> It is generally held that *méi* and *méi yǒu* are verbs when they occur before substantive constituents and adverbs when followed by predicative constituents. In fact, many aspects of the linguistic functions of *méi* and *méi yǒu* in these two positions run parallel to each other. The sentences in A are the only ones not to evidence parallel functions. (The affirmative forms in E are also not parallel to each other. But this involves the same phenomenon as in A.) However, in contrast to the above examples, the positive form corresponding to *méi yǒu* + Verb is precisely the form *yǒu* + Verb in some dialects (for example, Cantonese and Southern Min). Considering these grammatical aspects, it is reasonable to treat *méi* and *méi yǒu* as verbs when they occur before predicative constituents.

Due to the influence of southern dialects, combination of *yǒu* + VP is now frequently heard in Mandarin, for example, *yǒu fā shāo ma*? 'have emit fever' (Do you have a fever?), *wǒ yǒu zhuīguo nǚhái* 'I have chase-pass girl' (I have chased after girls). Wang Guoshuan and Ma Qingzhu (2008) state:

> Some people contend that *yǒu* + VP was "introduced" into Mandarin from Cantonese and Taiwan's variety of Southern Min. However, Cantonese and Southern Min have preserved many forms and usages from Ancient Chinese.

The referentiality of predicates   225

In the final analysis, Chinese originally permitted this kind of expression. In the Pre-Qin period there already appeared sentences like *chūnrì⁷ zài yáng, yǒu míng cāng gēng* 'spring-sun then warm, have call oriole' (The third month is warm, the oriole has called) ("Seventh Month," Airs of Bin section, Airs of the Domains, *Book of Songs*). From this it can be seen that the combination *yǒu* + VP is not a new phenomenon in Mandarin but rather the "resurrection" under a new era's conditions of a structure that had been lost historically.

Clearly, the previous structural parallels reflect the dominate situation in Chinese. The non-parallel structures are of lesser importance to the grammar. Discussions of structural parallelism should focus on the dominant situation and not be distracted by secondary phenomena. Only by placing the differences between *yǒu* and *le* in the context of the dominant situation is it possible to really see clearly what the relationship is between them (Wang Dongmei 2014). Zhu has demonstrated that *méi* and *méi yǒu* are verbs and not adverbs when they occur before predicative constituents. This is consistent with his long-held position that Chinese verbs like nouns can function as subjects and objects without undergoing nominalization.

Yǒu expresses the existence of "things" (in the sense of physical entities) and of "matters". To the Chinese mind, "matters" are "things". They are just abstract, dynamic things. From inscriptions on oracle bones to the *Book of Songs* to modern dialects, Chinese has always used *yǒu* to affirm the existence of "things" and "matters" (Yu Aiqin 2009). In the *Book of Songs yǒu lái* 'have come' is also rendered as *lái yě* 'come judgment-particle', *yǒu xíng* 'have walk', *xíng yǐ* 'walk perfective-particle' and *yǒu āi* 'have sad' as *āi zāi* 'sad emphatic-particle' (Guo Shaoyu 1979: 479). Li Zuofeng (1985) says: *Yǒu* expresses "to appear". It is not only people and things that can appear. Behaviors, changes, and the like can appear as well. Thus, *yǒu* can also take verbal words and phrases as its object as in i. and ii.:

i. *Xiǎo guó   wàng   shǒu   zé   wēi,   kuàng   yǒu   zāi   hū.*
    small country careless defend then dangerous let-alone have disaster MP
    'It is dangerous for a small country to be careless in matters related to defense, let alone disasters'.
    (Eighteenth Year of the Duke of Zhao, *Zuo Tradition*)

(2) *Qí   yǒu   luàn.*
    Qi   have   chaos
    'Qi is in chaos'.
    (Sixteenth Year of the Duke of Xi, *Zuo Tradition*)

Shí   nián   chūn,   wáng   zhēngyuè,   yǒu   xīng   chū   yú   Wù   Nǚ
tenth   year   spring   King   first-month   have   star   appear   in   Wu   Nü
'In spring of the tenth year, in the first month of the Zhou Royal calendar, there was a star that appeared in the Constellation Wu Nü'.
(Tenth Year of the Duke of Zhao, *Zuo Tradition*)

226   The referentiality of predicates

Li (1985) has also observed that *yǒu* was used in Pre-Qin Chinese to note the unusual, including unusual things and unusual happenings. Examples of the former include *yǒu fēi* 'have horsefly', *yǒu zāi* 'have disaster', *yǒu yāo* 'have demon', *yǒu huìxīng* 'have comet', *yǒu Sòng shī* 'have Song army (that is, to be attached by Song)', and *yǒu nián* 'have year/harvest'. Examples of the latter include *yǒu luàn* 'have chaos', *yǒu huò* 'have confusion, *yǒu shí zhī* 'have eat it', *yǒu shǐzhě chū* 'have envoy send'. This situation that existed from ancient times is preserved in a large number of typically 4-syllable idioms:

Yǒu   jiào   wú   lèi
have   teach   not-have kind
'To teach people without discriminating based on distinctions of rank or class'
(Duke Ling of Wei 15; 39, *Analects*)

Yǒu   sǐ   wú   èr
have   die   not-have two
'To die with undivided loyalty'

Yǒu   qù   wú   huí
have   go   not-have return
'There is only departure, never a return'

The X and Y of the structure "*yǒu* X *yǒu*/wú Y" includes items from the three word classes: Nouns, verbs, and adjectives:

(X and Y as   *Yǒu   shān   yǒu   shuǐ*
nouns)   have   mountain   have   water
               'There are mountains and water'

(X and Y as   *Yǒu   chī   yǒu   chuān*
verbs)   have   eat   have   wear
               'To have food and clothing'

(X and Y as   *Yǒu   féi   yǒu   shòu*
adjectives)   have   fat   have   thin
               'There are the fat, and there are the thin' or 'there are the fat and the lean'

The Great Chinese Dictionary and the fifth edition of *The Contemporary Chinese Dictionary* have entries for "*yǒu* + monosyllabic elemental motion" type verbs including:

Yǒu   chéng
have   become
'Achieve'

Yǒu   *rú*
have   like
'Resemble'

Yǒu   *dài*
have   wait
'Await'

Yǒu   *dé*
have   obtain
'Gained' (from experiences of various kinds)

Yǒu   *guān*
have   relate
'Be related to'

Yǒu   *shòu*
have   sell
'Available for sale'

Among these examples, some were already current in ancient times (*yǒu chéng* and *yǒu rú*). Some were created only recently (*yǒu guān* and *yǒu shòu*). In some of the examples, the lexical item *yǒu* has already undergone a process of semantic emptying to become a prefix with little meaning. However, the majority of examples of *yǒu* are verbs that have retained their original meaning (Diao Yanbin & Li Yanyan 2010). The forms "*yǒu* + monosyllabic verb" and "monosyllabic verb + le" coexist in colloquial Mandarin:

Yǒu   *dé*   *jiù*   *yǒu*   *shī*
have   gain   then   have   loss
'With gain there is loss'

Yǒu   *huán*   *cái*   *yǒu*   *jiè*
have   return   only-then   have   borrow
'Only with reimbursement is there borrowing'

Dé   *le*   *jiù*   *shī*   *le*
gain   PSP   then   lose   PSP
'With gain there is loss'

Huán   *le*   *cái*   *jiè*   *le*
return   PSP   only-then   borrow   PSP
'Only with reimbursement is there borrowing'

228 *The referentiality of predicates*

Adverbial modifiers can occur before *yǒu*, for example:

Yīzhí   dōu yǒu zài shàng wǎng ma?
uninterruptedly all   have at   go   net   MP
'Have you been online all this time?'

Céngjīng yǒu jiàn guò yī zhǐ yī tiáo tuǐ de hépíng gē.
once   have see pass one CL one CL leg MM peace dove
'I once saw a one-legged peace dove.'

There are also *yǒu*—V combinations where the verbal nature of *yǒu* is even clearer, for example:

Èr zhě   yǒu yī bǐ.
two particle have one compare
'The two are comparable.'

Zhǎng de gēn Déguó rén   yǒu yī pīn.
grow   de with German person have one join-together
'(S/he) looks like a German.'

When people define *shì* as a modal adverb or *yǒu* as a perfective aspect marker,[8] they are being dominated by an Indo-European way of looking at language. However, the reality for Chinese is that *yǒu* is always the *yǒu* that expresses 'have' in the pair "*yǒu* and *wú*" (have and not-have). It expresses nothing else.

With regard to "aspect", Chinese has its own *yǒu*-aspect. This is most clearly observable in southern dialects. For example, in Cantonese, *yǒu* and *wú* are used to express whether a matter exists or not. What is expressed is conceptually different from whether or not an action has been completed.

Keui5 gam1yat6 yau5 mou4   sik6   yin1?
he   today   have not-have ingest smoke
'Did he smoke today?'

Keui5 bat1 lau1 dou1 yau5 mou4   sik6   yin1?
he   not   slide all   have not-have ingest smoke
'Does he usually smoke?'

Such usages have been most extensively retained in Southern Min and southern varieties of the Wu dialects. Chen Zeping (1998: 174–175) and Zheng Minhui (2009) give examples from the Fuzhou dialect to illustrate this:

Mén zhǐ   xíng yǒu   kāi.[9]
door only do   have Open
'The door is open at this time.'

Hòurì   yǒu   shàngtáng.
after-day   have   go hall
'The day after tomorrow (he) has class.'

Míng   dàn   yī   yǒu   qù,   wǒ   wú   qù.
bright day   he   have go   I   have-not go
'Tomorrow, he will go; I won't.'

These examples with *yǒu* all express that some action appeared or some state of affairs existed in contrast to their non-appearance or nonexistence when *wú* is used. Li Rulong (1986) observes that the pattern *yǒu* + VP can express that something has happened no matter the time in Southern Min dialects (including the dialects of Fuzhou, Shantou, and Puxian). For this pattern, it is irrelevant whether an action is completed or not as exemplified here:

Yī   zuó   fāng   yǒu   xiě   hǎo   a.[10]
he   yesterday   space   have   write   good   MP
'He finished writing yesterday.'

Yī   zuó   fāng   yǒu   liě   yī   xiě.
he   yesterday   just   have   MP   one   write
'Yesterday, he was writing.'

Yī   jí   jiǔ   yǒu   liě   xiě.
he   immediately   long-time   have   MP   write
'He is writing now.'

Yī   xiàbǔ   yǒu   pāi   suàn   yào   xiě.
he   afternoon   have   hit   plan   want   write
'He plans to write this afternoon.'

Tīnghòu   yī   yǒu   liě   xiě   rǔ   zé   lái   kàn.
hear time   he   have   MP   write   you   then   come   see
'Wait for him to be writing before coming to see him.'

It is even the case that an isolated sentence (an interrogative sentence) can express many meanings:

(Fuzhou dialect with characters transcribed into Mandarin)

Rǔ   yǒu   kàn   diànyǐng   wú
you   have   see   movie   not-have
'Have you seen the movie?' or 'Are you going to see the movie?'

(Ningde dialect with characters transcribed into Mandarin)

Rǔ   yǒu   wú   mǎi   shū
you   have   not-have   buy   book
'Are you buying a book?' or 'Have you bought books?' or 'Have you bought the books?'

230   *The referentiality of predicates*

Here are examples of *yǒu* expressing that something is ongoing or yet to begin from the Shantou dialect (a variety of Southern Min spoken in eastern Guangdong Province; Shi Qisheng 1996):

(Shantou dialect with characters transcribed into Mandarin)

Āxiōng   yǒu   [lo5324] zuò   zuòyè.
prefix-elder-brother have   MP   do   homework
'The elder brother is doing homework.'

(Also transcribed into Mandarin)

Nǐ   ā   shì   yǒu   yùzhe   yī   lī   qǐng yī   lái   wǒ
you   MP   be   have   encounter-touch   him   MP   ask   he   come   I
nèi   zuò   yīxià.
home   sit   one   down
'If you run into him, ask him to come to my home to chat'.

Lü Shuxiang (1942/1982: 238) stated that wèi 'not-yet' and méi (yǒu) 'not (have)' are not restricted to negating already realized facts. Their uses are actually much broader than English negative sentences in the perfect. This statement refers to the phenomenon that either the Chinese sentence *tā wèi qù* 'he not-yet go' or *tā méi (yǒu) qù* 'he not (have) go' corresponds to both the English sentence *he didn't go* (present tense) and *he hasn't gone* (perfective). To express the latter (perfective) meaning, Chinese can optionally add words like *hái* 'still or yet' or *shàng* 'still or yet'.

Chinese will not feel that the way the word *wèi* corresponds to each of the two English tenses is in any way ambiguous. Moreover, the previous dialect examples demonstrate clearly that *yǒu* not only encompasses English past tense but also its present tense, progressive tense, and future tense. Provided that what is expressed is that an action or state exists, *yǒu* can be used.

Some people have said that the *le* in Mandarin marks the perfective aspect and that *yǒu* and *le* are the same in this respect. Actually, *le* should not be treated the same as the English perfective aspect, for example:

Mén   kǒu   zhàn   le   yī   gè   jǐngwèi.
door   opening   stand   PSP   one   CL   guard
'A guard stood at the doorway.'

Tāmen   dǎ   le   qǐlái.
they   hit   PSP   up-come
'They started fighting.'

Shān   shàng   de   yèzi   hóng   le   dàbàn.
hill   top   MM   leaves   red   PSP   big-half
'More than half the leaves on the hill have turned red.'

Xiǎo	*Wáng*	*xiànzài*	*yǒu*	*(le)*	*hěn*	*dà*	*de*	*gǎibiàn.*
Xiao	Wang	now	have	(PSP)	very	big	MM	change

'Xiao Wang has changed a lot.'

The first example can be said as *mén kǒu zhànzhe yī gè jǐngwèi* 'a guard stand-aspect-marker one classifier guard' without there being a change in its basic meaning. What the second example asserts is the beginning of the action of hitting rather than its completion. The third example does not so much state the attainment of the property of being red as its appearance. In the final example, *le* is optional. (See Wang Wei 2010.) From this discussion, it follows that *le* expresses existence with the caveat that it tends to mark what is "present", appears, or is realized.

Since the predicates in the sentences *wǒ chīguò yěcài* 'I eat-pass wild-vegetable' (I have eaten wild vegetables), *wǒ xiǎng kǎo yánjiūshēng* 'I want test graduate-student' (I want to take the post-graduate entrance exam), and *xiǎo jiǎn là dúshū*[11] 'small kid spicy read book' (Shànghǎi dialect *for háizi zài dú shū* 'child at read book' (The child is studying)) can be emphasized by adding *yǒu* before them to yield *wǒ yǒu chīguò yěcài* 'I have eat-pass wild-vegetable' (I have eaten wild vegetables), *wǒ yǒu xiǎng kǎo yánjiūshēng* 'I have want test graduate-student' (I want to take the post-graduate entrance exam), 'small kid have spicy read book' (Shànghǎi dialect *for háizi yǒu zài dú shū* 'child have at read book' (The child is studying)), this demonstrates that the predicates are also referential.[12]

There is more to say about the word *zài* 'be-in'. Popular grammar books treat *zài* as a verb when a noun occurs after it as its object as in *tā zài chúfáng* 'he be-in kitchen' and as an adverb or an auxiliary verb when it is followed by a verb as in *tā zài zuò fàn* 'he be-in cook food'. This is yet another consequence of being led by Indo-European views of language that hold that a verb's object can only be a nominal constituent. If Chinese is looked at through a simpler lens, one *zài* should be posited according to structural parallelism. It would be a verb that expresses the meaning "be-in". *Tā zài chúfáng* means *tā chǔ zài chúfáng de kōngjiān lǐ* 'he is in the space of the kitchen' and *tā zài zuò fàn* means *tā chǔ zài zuò fàn de guòchéng (shíjiān duàn) lǐ* 'He is in process (time segment) of cooking food'. *Zài* like verbs in general can be modified by many different adverbs, for example, <u>*shàng*</u> *zài chényín* 'still be-in intone' (to still be intoning), <u>*yòu*</u> *zài xià yǔ* 'again be-in fall rain' (it's raining again), <u>*yě*</u> *zài nàmèn* 'also be-in puzzle' (to also be puzzled; Zhang Jie 2011)

If *shì*, *yǒu*, and *zài* are looked at together, the referentiality of Chinese predicates is clearly illustrated:

Tā	*(shì)*	*shā*	*le*	*yī*	*tiáo*	*gēng*	*niú.*
he	(be)	kill	PSP	one	CL	plow	cow

'He killed an ox.'

Tā	*(yǒu)*	*shāguò*	*yī*	*tiáo*	*gēng*	*niú.*
he	(have)	kill-pass	one	CL	plow	cow

'He killed an ox.'

232   *The referentiality of predicates*

Tā	*(zài)*	*shāzhe*	*yī*	*tiáo*	*gēng*	*niú*	*ne.*
he	(be-in)	kill-zhe	one	CL	plow	cow	MP

'He is/was killing an ox.'

The *shì*, *yǒu*, and *zài* in these three sentences are optional. However, when there is a need for emphasis they can appear. When they do not occur, the sentence's final part is its predicate. In these cases, the predicate's referentiality is not apparent. In contrast, when one of the three words *shì*, *yǒu*, or *zài* occurs, the predicate's referentiality is obvious. What is called "emphasis" is the causing of the referentiality of the target of emphasis to become prominent (see Section 4). Following from this, the demonstratives *zhè ge* 'this' and *nà ge* 'that' can also be added before a predicate to express the emphatic mood; see Chen Xiao (2009).

Èr	*gūniáng*	*xīnlǐ*	*zhè*	*ge*	*bièniu*	*wa!*
Two	daughter	mind-inside	this	CL	awkward	MP

'The second daughter felt so awkward'.
("The Fool Learns to Be Well Behaved" by Liu Baorui)

Shàn	*dàyé*	*zhè*	*ge*	*qì,*	*jiù*	*bú*	*yòng*	*tí*	*la!*
Shan	uncle	this	CL	angry	then	no	use	raise	MP

'With Uncle Shan so angry, it isn't necessary to bring it up'.
("Small Amount" by Song Youmei from the late Qing dynastic period)

The same effect can be achieved without *zhè ge* and *nà ge* through either stress assignment or intonation. Although the *zhè ge* and *nà ge* here have already undergone emptying, the premise underlying emptying is that before emptying, *zhè ge* and *nà ge* were already frequently occurring in front of predicates. Because of this, Chen believes that the verb phrases in these structures implicitly possess the properties of noun phrases.

In summary, predicates made up of verbal constituents possess two properties. They have the property of being a predicate-argument structure and the property of referentiality. Returning to the initial question concerning the sentences *wǒ shàng guo dàxué* 'I went to college', *tā chīle dúyào* 'he took poison', and *tā zhèngzài zuò fàn* 'he's cooking', the predicate *shàng guo dàxué* 'go to college' as with the rest of the predicates in these sentences simultaneously possesses the two properties mentioned earlier. When negating one of these predicate's predicate-argument structure, *tā <u>méi yǒu</u> shàng guo dàxué* 'he has not gone to college' is used; when negating its referential property, *tā <u>bú shì</u> shàng guo dàxué* 'it *is not* that he has gone to college' is said.

In English, a negative verb phrase is used to negate the former (that is, a predicate-argument structure) as in *he has never done it*. To negate the latter (the referential property) a negative clause is used: *It's not (the case) that he has done it*. The distinction between verb phases and clauses in English has a language-internal motivation: Clauses have subjects; verb phrases do not.

The referentiality of predicates   233

In Chinese, clauses can be subjectless. Phrases and clauses are constructed using the same principles (Chapter 2, Section 2.2). All a verb phrase requires is a complete intonational pattern and a pause to be a clause. In the same way, when in the affirmative, to emphasize the predicate-argument properties, *yǒu* is used as in *tā yǒu chīguò le* 'he has eat-pass le' (he has eaten). To emphasize the predicate's referential properties, *shì* is used as in *tā shì chīguò le* 'he be eat-pass le' (it is the case that he has eaten). Because the predicate is also a referring expression, in the final analysis emphasis gives prominence to its referential properties.

6.3.2   A "comment" is the next "topic"

Besides what has been discussed so far, predicate referentiality can also be looked at in terms of conversation and discourse structure. In a conversation a speech act frequently has the two functions "replying" and "eliciting" as in the following excerpt from *Dragon Beard Gully*:

$Ji\check{a}_1$:	$N\check{i}$	$q\grave{u}$	$zh\check{a}o$	$Xi\check{a}o$	$L\check{i}.$
A_1:	You	go	look-for	Xiao	Li
	'Go look for Xiao Li'.				

$Y\check{i}_1$:	$T\bar{a}$	$z\check{o}u$	le	$ba?$
B_1:	He	leave	PSP	MP
	'Has he gone?'			

$Ji\check{a}_2$:	$H\acute{a}i$	$m\acute{e}i$	$z\check{o}u$	$ba!$
A_2:	Still	not	leave	MP
	'Not yet'.			

$Y\check{i}_2$:	$H\check{a}oxi\grave{a}ng$	$z\check{o}u$	$le.$
B_2:	seems	leave	PSP
	'It seems like he has'.		

The question and answer B_1 and A_2, respectively, are situated between doubt and belief. The question has more doubt than belief; in the answer, belief is greater than doubt. Some people have referred to *ba* as a semi-question particle. This is completely appropriate. B_1 elicits the response in A_2. It is also the answer to A_1. A_2 is the response to B_1. It is also what elicits the response in B_2.

It is precisely because a speech act in actual conversation frequently has both the function of eliciting and of responding that scholars who engage in conversational analysis like Goffman (1976) and Coulthard (1977) hold that the basic unit of conversational structure should not be "replies". Rather, a conversation should be seen as a succession of responses with each response being both the consequence of an elicitation and what elicits the next response.

Elicitation and response are connected by relevance. The specific way in which a contribution is relevant is determined by the context, the interlocutors' cognitive

234 *The referentiality of predicates*

states, and reasoning. According to Sperber and Wilson (1986), regardless of how loose the connection appears to be between the eliciting utterance and the response, the interlocutors always consider it relevant. This kind of relevance is also the connection between a topic and a comment in a discourse. No matter what the comment's content is, it can always be understood as relevant to the topic in some way as in the following examples:

A. *Shuō qǐ yú, wǔchāng yú zuì hào chī.*
   say   rise fish Wuchang fish most good eat
   'Talking about fish, the most delicious fish are in Wuchang.'

B. *Shuō qǐ yú, wǒ nǚ'ér zuótiān sòng yīyuàn le.*
   say   rise fish I   daughter yesterday send hospital PSP
   'Talking about fish, my daughter was sent to the hospital yesterday.'

A. *Zhè chǎng huǒ ya, xìngkuī xiāofáng duì lái de zǎo.*
   this CL   fire MP fortunately fire-defense team come CSC early
   'As for the fire, it's fortunate that the fire department got here quickly.'

B. *Zhè chǎng huǒ ya, xìngkuī qìwēn méi zài língxià.*
   This CL   fire MP fortunately temperature not at zero-under
   'As for the fire, it's fortunate that the temperature wasn't below zero.'

The connections between the topics and comments in the B sentences appear to be quite loose but are always understood as relevant. There is a correspondence between elicitation-response patterns in conversations and topic-comment patterns in texts, the structure of texts being based on conversation. In Chinese two minor sentences consisting of a question and an answer combine to form a complete sentence. In daily life minor sentences are the norm. Complete sentences are the main sentence type only in continuous intentionally planned discourses (Chapter 3, Section 4). The play *Dragon Beard Gully* has a monologue by a member of the People's Police. In what follows, it is possible to observe the monologue's intentional planning:

> *Zhè huí shèr hái suàn hǎo, méi yǒu shāng le rén. Dàjiā de dōngxī ne, lái-déjí de wǒmen dōu gěi bān dào kàng shàng qù le. Xiànzài, yǔ zhù le, tiān yě liàng le, dàjiā yuànyì huí jiā kàn kàn qù ne, jiù qù; yuànyì xiān xiē huèr zài qù ne, xībian zánmen bāo le liǎng suǒ xiǎo diàr, dàjiā suíbiàn yòng.*

'This whole situation has to count as turning out OK. Nobody got hurt. As for everybody's stuff, we had enough time to move everything onto the kangs.[13] Now, it's stopped raining, and the sun is out. Everyone who wants to return home and take a look can go. For anyone who wants to first rest awhile and then go home, we've reserved two small hostels to the west that you can go to if you want'.

The referentiality of predicates   235

This passage can be worked into the following dialogue:

Jǐngchá: *Zhè   huí shèr   hái suàn hǎo,   méi yǒu shāng le   rén.*
Police: this   CL matter still count good, not have hurt   PSP people
                'This situation counts as having turned out OK. Nobody got hurt.'

Zhòngrén: *Dàjiā   de   dōngxī ne?*
Everybody: everyone MM stuff   MP
                'Our stuff?'

Jǐngchá: *Láidéjí   de   wǒmen dōu gěi bān   dào kàng shàng qù   le.*
Police: come-in-time MM we   all give move to   kang up-go PSP
                'We had enough time to move everything onto the kangs.'

Zhòngrén: *Xiànzài, yǔ   zhù   le,   tiān yě   liàng le,   dàjiā   yuànyì*
Everybody: now   rain stop   PSP, sky also bright PSP, everyone wish
                huí   jiā   kàn   kàn qù   ne?
                return   home look look go   MP
                'The rain has now stopped. The sun is out. What if we want to go
                home to take a look?'

Jǐngchá: *Nà   jiù   qù   ba!*
Police: that   then   go   MP
                'In that case, feel free to go'.
Zhòngrén: *Yuànyì xiān xiē   huèr   zài   qù   ne?*
Everybody: wish   first rest awhile again go   MP
                'What about those of us who want to first rest awhile before going?'

Jǐngchá: *Xībian   zánmen   bāo   le   liǎng suǒ xiǎo*
Police: westside   we   reserve   le   two   CL small

                diàr,   dàjiā   suíbiàn   yòng.
                hostel,   everyone as-you-please use
                'We've reserved two small hostels to the west that you can go to if
                you want'.

These kinds of examples demonstrate that a monologue employs the "make
the first move" strategy (Edmondson 1981) by anticipating what questions or
responses a listener or reader may raise and then raises them beforehand as topics
that moreover are comments. Because of this, rather than saying that discourse
structure is constructed from a series of "topic-comment" pairs, it is better to
say that it is a succession of comments. Every comment is the follow-up to the
previous elicitation and can itself elicit the next comment. Or to put it differently,

236 *The referentiality of predicates*

every comment (or part of a comment) becomes the topic (or part of the topic) of the next comment (or part of that comment). The prior monologue can be analyzed in this way:

Topic 1:	*Zhè huí shèr hái suàn hǎo,* *méi yǒu shāng le rén.* This whole situation has to Nobody got hurt. count as turning out OK.
Topic 2/Comment 1:	*Dàjiā de dōngxī ne,* As for everybody's stuff,
Comment 2/Topic 3:	*láidéjí de wǒmen dōu gěi bān dào kàng shàng qù le.* we had enough time to move everything onto the kangs.
Comment 3/Topic 4:	*Xiànzài, yǔ zhù le, tiān yě liàng le, dàjiā yuànyì huí jiā kàn kàn qù ne,* Now, it's stopped raining, and the sun is out. Everyone who wants to return home and take a look can go.
Comment 4/Topic 5:	*jiù qù;* Then go;
Comment 5/Topic 6:	*yuànyì xiān xiē huèr zài qù ne,* (For anyone who) wants to first rest awhile and then go (home),
Comment 6:	*xībian zánmen bāo le liǎng suǒ xiǎo diàr, dàjiā suíbiàn yòng.* we've reserved two small hostels to the west that you can go to if you want.

There is no follow-up comment after Comment$_6$. However, it is nevertheless a potential topic. For example, it is possible for a comment like "[now if] the small hostels can't accommodate everyone" to occur after it.

Generally speaking, if a section XY or YZ is abstracted from a larger passage XYZ and analyzed in isolation as a static pair, the division into a topic and a comment is easily determined. The topic comes first. The comment follows. Looking at the passage as a continuous dynamic sequence, there is no clear dividing line between topics and comments. All comments are either actual or potential topics[14] (see Shen Jiaxuan 1989 for details).

A characteristic of Chinese is that both subjects and predicates can occur as independent minor sentences. Subjects are topics; predicates are comments. When comments function as the following topic they undergo no formal changes. The modal particles *a*, *ba*, *ne*, and *ma* that occur after comments are also markers that can be added to topics (Chapter 3, Section 4). Following is another example from *Dragon*

Beard Gully, one in which the dialogue between Er Chun and the chief inspector can be changed into a monologue spoken by Er Chun as she talks to herself:

Zhuā	*yào*	*chī*	*ba,*	*yǒu*	*wǒ*	*cìhòu*	*tā*	*ne,*	*nà*
grab	medicine	eat	MP	have	I	take-care-of	he	MP	that

yě	*dānwù*	*zuòhuó*	*ya*
also	delay	work	MP

'Have the prescription for the medicine filled and take it. I'm here to take care of him. That will also delay my going to work'.

The single form *yǒu wǒ cìhòu tā ne* 'I'm here to take care of him' is the previous topic's comment and the following comment's topic. Because of this, it can be said that Chinese does not have a topicalization process. The comment is in fact a topic. Dong Xiufang (2012) discovered that there are many topic chain structures in Chinese. In a sequence of topic structures, the topic of a following topic structure is the same as the comment of the previous topic structure as in the following:

Yì	*zé*	*yín,*	*yín*	*zé*	*wàng*	*shàn,*
Leisure	then	wantonness,	wantonness	then	forget	good

wàng	*shàn*	*zé*	*ě*	*xīn*	*shēng*
forget	good	then	evil	mind	arise

'With leisure comes wantonness; wantonness leads to forgetting the good; forgetting the good leads to an evil mind arising'.
("Lu Discourses, Part 2", *Discourses of the Kingdoms*)

Guó	*jūn*	*bù*	*kěyǐ*	*qīng,*	*qīng*	*zé*	*shī*	*qīn;*
Country	ruler	not	can	light	light	then	lose	(those)-close

shī	*qīn,*	*huàn*	*bì*	*zhì.*
lose	close	danger	certain	arrive

'A country's ruler cannot treat matters lightly. If he does, he'll lose those close to him. If he loses those close to him, danger will certainly arrive'.
("Fifth Year of Duke Xi", *Zuo Tradition*)

Similar examples are frequently seen in modern Chinese, for example, wǒ qù, qù bùnéng kōngshǒu qù, kōngshǒu qù bù lǐmào 'If I go, I cannot go empty-handed. To go empty-handed is impolite'. There are also examples from Fang Mei (2011) (involving *zhè* 'this' being added to a following topic):

Nǐ	*shuō tā*	*yīshǒutuōtiān,*[15]	*nǐ*	*kě*	*zhīdào*	*tā*	*zhè* *yīshǒutuōtiān*
you	say he	one-hand-hold-in-palm-sky	you	indeed	know	he	<u>this</u> one-hand-hold-in-palm-sky

cái	*yǒu*	*shuō*	*bu*	*chūlái*	*de*	*kǔzhōng*
only	have	say	not	out	de	hardship

'You say he's doing impossible tasks. You should know that this doing of impossible tasks is loaded with inexpressible hardships'.

238 *The referentiality of predicates*

Since comments are actual or potential referential topics, it follows that predicates also possess referentiality.

6.3.3 *Juxtaposition and referentiality in flowing sentences*

By understanding that predicates possess referentiality, it becomes easy to understand the phenomenon of there being a very large number of flowing sentences in Chinese. Lü Shuxiang (1979: 27) used the term "flowing sentence". He said:

> Using clauses as the basic unit rather than sentences is more appropriate for the situation in Chinese. Because there are an especially large number of flowing sentences in spoken Chinese with one clause following another, there are many places where it is possible to either introduce a break between two constituents or connect them. To see this, try comparing the different punctuations for an old novel. It is often the case that one version has a period where another has a comma or the other way around where the first version has a comma where the second one has a period.[16]

Hu Mingyang and Jin Song (1989) conducted a phonetic experiment to study pauses in flowing sentences. They proved that when different people orally read a passage, they do not pause in the same places nor are the lengths of their pauses the same. The reason why there are so many flowing sentences in Chinese is because minor sentences dominate the language. Relational conjunctions are often not used between sentences, making it necessary to infer semantic connections from context.

In the 1960s, Lü first proposed the idea of using a new framework involving segment structure to analyze Chinese grammar to break away from the established practices of traditional Western grammar. Segments are minor sentences and complete sentences marked off by pauses and intonation.[17] Fan Jiyan (1985) built on this work by proposing a tentative analytic framework classifying segments into different categories. This study proposed that the two basic units for sentence formation in Chinese are segments that can independently serve as sentences (single segment sentences) and segments connected together to form sentences (multisegment sentences). Besides a few scattered articles (Hu Mingyang & Jin Song 1989; Shen & Gu 1997; Wang Hongjun 2011; Wang Hongjun & Li Rong 2014), it is rare to see research and thinking that continues this line of analysis.

An important reason for why research in this area has not moved forward is well expressed by what Hu Mingyang has said, "It involves basic questions about syntax". However,

> our grammatical theories, methods of analysis, and patterns of analysis are originally from the West. It will be a long process to develop a conception of language compatible with the facts of the Chinese language . . . I am afraid that only after several generations of arduous effort will it be possible to achieve this.

The referentiality of predicates   239

Shen Jiaxuan (2012a) observes that a prominent "basic syntactic question" concerns the fact that flowing sentences are not just a series of juxtaposed minor sentences. These juxtaposed minor sentences include verbal segments and nominal segments as in the following:

Lǎo   Wáng   ne?
Lao   Wang   MP
"What's up with Lao Wang?"

Yòu   shēng   bìng   le   ba!
again   arise   sick   PSP   MP
'He's sick again.'

Yě   gāi   qǐng   ge   jià   ya!
also   should   ask   CL   leave   MP
'He should ask for leave.'

Zǒu   bú   dòng   le   me!
walk   not   move   PSP   MP
'He cannot walk.'

Érzi   nǚ'ér   ne?
son   daughter   MP
'What about your son and daughter?'

Shàng   bān   máng   ba?
go   work   busy   MP
'I suppose they're busy with work?'

Qǐng   ge   bǎomǔ   me!
ask   CL   caregiver   MP
'Hire a caregiver.'

Gōngzī   dī   ya!
wages   low   MP
'My wages are low.'

Xiān   jiè   diǎn   ne?
first   borrow   a little   MP
'How about borrowing a little first?'

Jiàng   píqì   yī   ge   ya!
stubborn   temperament   one   CL   MP
'He's headstrong.'

240   *The referentiality of predicates*

We can combine any two consecutive minor sentences into a complete sentence. All that is necessary is to remove any complete pauses or sentence-final intonations from within the resulting utterance. Following are examples of this:

Lǎo Wáng ne yòu shēng bìng le
'Lao Wang is sick again'.

Qǐng gè bǎomǔ me gōngzī dī.
'As for hiring a caregiver, my wages are low'.

Xiān jiè diǎn ne jiàng píqì yī gè
'As for first borrowing a little, he's strongheaded'. (He is too proud to borrow.)

Of course it is difficult to resolve this question in a traditional approach that separates nouns from verbs. According to the verbs-as-nouns framework, verbs belong to the category nouns, and predicates are essentially referring expressions; the surprising but obvious conclusion is that the composition of flowing sentences in Chinese is:

$$S_{flowing} \rightarrow S'_{NP} + S'_{NP} + S'_{NP} \cdots$$

Juxtaposed structures are more basic than subject-verb structures. It is possible to infer subject-predicate relations (topic-comment) from relations of juxtaposition. Many idioms in Chinese have an expressiveness and liveliness that people love to see and hear like

Yī	*cùn*	*guāngyīn*	*yī*	*cùn*	*jīn*
one	inch	time	one	inch	gold

'A moment in time is worth an inch of gold'

Yī	*fēn*	*gēng*	*yún,*	*yī*	*fēn*	*shōuhuò*
one	minute	plow	weed	one	cent	harvest

'A minute plowing and weeding is worth a cent from the harvest'
That is, what somebody earns depends on how much they work.

Idioms like these all consist of the juxtaposition of referring expressions. It is also possible to infer subject-predicate relations as well.

Yuen Ren Chao (1970) said that the grammar for spoken Chinese is more or less the same whether comparing dialects with each other or even classical literary Chinese with vernacular Chinese. Subjects always occur before predicates, objects always occur after verbs, and modifiers always occur before what they modify. In Cantonese it "seems a little bit as if" adverbs are placed after verbs in sentences like *bei2 di1 seui2 ngo5 tim1* 'give water I increase' (Give me a little more water) and *nei5 heui3 sin1* 'you go first'. But in Chinese grammar, adverbs cannot occur after verbs. Given this consideration, it would be best to treat this use of *tim1* and *sin1*

The referentiality of predicates 241

syntactically as their being the second items in juxtaposed structures. *Nei5 heui3 sin1* can be analyzed as *nei5 heoi3 dik1 si6 sin1 (jat1 gin6 si6)* 'you go Nom be first (one classifier matter)' (Your going is first). In Chao's view, *nei5 heui3 sin1* is made of syntactically juxtaposed structures. The minor sentences *nei5 heui3* 'you go' and *sin1* 'first' are juxtaposed. However, it is possible to understand this as a subject-predicate relation as well.

Yuen Ren Chao (1955) also said that Chinese does not have a conjunction corresponding to the English *and*. Chinese expresses coordination through juxtaposition. What appears to be similar to *and* like *gēn* 'with, and', *tong* 'with, and', *hé* 'with, and', and the classical literary forms *jí* 'and', *yǔ* 'and', and the forms *yòu . . . yòu . . .* 'again . . . again . . .' *bìngqiě* 'moreover', *érqiě* 'moreover', *yě* 'also' and the classical literary form *ér* 'and, but' function primarily as resumptive words. In addition, all of these forms are optional as in *xiānshēng tàitài bú zàijiā* 'The mister [and] mistress are not home', *tā lǎo dǎ rén mà rén* 'he always hits people, curses people' (He's always hitting and cursing people.) Moreover, juxtaposition is a simplified expression of conjunction in logic.

The categories of Chinese question sentences also reflect the Chinese characteristic that it depends on juxtaposition. English choice questions use the same syntactic means (subject-auxiliary inversion) as yes-no questions. The only difference between these two question types is that the choices offered by a choice question are not limited to one. From this it follows that choice questions are a subcategory of yes-no questions.

The situation in Chinese is different. Yes-no questions are marked by a sentence-final *ma*. Choice questions cannot use *ma*. They can, however, like special questions, use *ne* as in *nǐ chī mǐfàn háishì miàntiáo ne?* 'you eat rice or noodles' (Do you want rice or noodles?) and *nǐ chī shénme ne?* 'you eat what ne-particle' (What do you want to eat?). This shows that choice questions are an independent category. Chinese also has reduplication questions (also referred to as positive-negative questions). These are a subcategory of choice questions, specifically positive-negative choice questions (Liu Danqing 2008: 2–3).

Choice questions (including reduplication questions) have a very important status in Chinese, forming as they do their own category. This is because choice questions are intrinsically juxtaposition questions as in *nǐ chī fàn chī miàn?* 'you eat rice eat noodles?' (Do you want to eat rice or noodles?). This question is formed from the juxtaposition of *chī fàn* 'eat rice' and *chī miàn* 'eat noodles'. *Nǐ chī bù chī?* 'You eat not eat?' (Are you eating?) is formed by the juxtaposition of *chī* 'eat' and *bù chī* 'not eat'. Once again, it can be seen that juxtaposition has an extremely important status in Chinese.

From a historical perspective, Chinese yes-no questions also developed from juxtaposed reduplication questions: *nǐ qù bú qù > nǐ qù bù > nǐ qù ma* 'you go not go > you go not > you go question-particle'.

Due to the feature of unidirectional linearity in language, two constituents juxtaposed immediately before and after each other are naturally in a continuity relation. These continuity connections can be realized in one of three domains, a behavioral

242 *The referentiality of predicates*

domain, a logical domain, and a spoken domain. Continuity connections marked by the word *ér* are used here to illustrate these possibilities:

Behavioral continuity connections (continuity of "what was done")

Jié   zé   ér   yú
drain   swamp   ér   fish
'To drain a swamp to get the fish'

Wáng   yáng   ér   bǔ   láo
loss   sheep   ér   repair   pen
'Close the barn door after the horse gets out'

Logical continuity connections (continuity based on "what is thought")

Purpose

Hǔ   qiú   bǎi   shòu   ér   shí   zhī
tiger seek   hundred   animals   ér   eat   them
'Tigers seek animals (in general) to eat them'

Concession

Pǐfū   ér   wéi   bǎi   shì   shī
ordinary person   ér   act-as   hundred   generation   teacher
'To be an ordinary person who becomes the teacher for one-hundred generations'

Adversative

chū   wūní   ér   bù   rǎn
come-out-of   mire   ér   not   contaminated
'To maintain one's integrity despite being in a corrupt environment'

Spoken continuity connections (continuity of "what is said")

Rén   ér   wú   xìn
person ér   have-not   trust
'An untrustworthy person'

Zǐchǎn   ér   sǐ
Zichan (a name)   ér   die
'Zichan died'

The behavioral continuity connection is the connection between "things that are done". We can often see the previous action as the way in which the subsequent action is carried out as in *gǔ zào ér jìn* 'drum shout ér advance' ("To advance beating a drum and shouting"). "Beating the drum and shouting" become manner adverbials for "advance". This is a modifier-head relation that is inferred from the continuity connection.

The referentiality of predicates   243

Logical continuity connections are continuities based on "what is thought". In fact, all of the constituents that express reasons, concessions, suppositions, and the like are topics.[18]

Spoken continuity connections are based on "what is said". *Rén ér wú xìn* actually means "They are said to be people but they are not honest" and *Zǐ Chǎn ér sǐ* actually means "talking about Zi Chan (such a sagacious person), that he should die". Both involve the following constituent being a continuation of "what was said" in the previous constituent. There is an adversative meaning between the two. There is also a subject-predicate relation between the former and latter constituents. The "what is said" continuity connection has the greatest dependency on context of the three types of connections (See section 3.4).

The coordination condition requires that the juxtaposed constituents possess the same properties (Chapter 2, Section 3.2). It is certain that a predicative constituent has referentiality when it and a substantive constituent are juxtaposed. Juxtaposed forms imply subject-predicate relations. Thus, predicates originally possess referentiality.

Li Zhanbing and Jin Lixin (2012) working from the perspective of typology infer that it is possible that human language first had markers for connecting juxtaposed substantives and only later extended their functions to connecting predicates. Their article cites statistical data from Zheng Wenping and Cao Wei (2007) showing that *bìng* 'and, moreover' in the novel *The Water Margins* (first published in the early 16th century) primarily connected juxtaposed substantive phrases. Examples of this include:

Shòu   le   mián'ǎozi   bìng   féi   yáng   jiǔ   lǐ
receive PSP cotton jacket bìng fattened sheep wine gifts
'He received a cotton jacket, a fattened sheep, wine, and gifts.'

Dāngxià   shōushí   le huǒ dāo, huǒshí bìng yǐn   huǒ méitǒng
immediately put-in-order le fire knife flint   bìng ignite fire coal-canaster
'They immediately put in order the fire knife, flint, and coal cannister used for igniting fires.'

Less than 1% of the occurrences of *bìng* involve connecting predicates in *The Water Margins*. Only after the May Fourth Movement did *bìng* begin to connect juxtaposed verbs and verbal phrases and cease to connect juxtaposed substantive constituents. In the following section, the Ancient Chinese structure "N ér V" is reexamined from this perspective.

6.3.4   *Reexamining the structure "noun* ér *verb" in Ancient Chinese*

The "N *ér* V" structure has received a lot of attention in academic circles since the publication of *Ma's Grammar*. The main reason why this structure has given rise to so much discussion is that one of the two constituents connected by the coordinating conjunction *ér* is a nominal and the other is a verbal constituent. Together

244 *The referentiality of predicates*

they form what looks like a "subject *ér* predicate" structure. This clearly violates the condition on coordination that coordinated constituents should be of the same grammatical type.

Most earlier treatments have used an approach that introduces additional expressions to the structure. They expand N into a predicate-argument constituent. For example, Yang Rongxiang (2008) expands *wáng rén ér guó jiàn zhī* 'exile person ér country treated-with-ruler's-courtesy him' (he was an exile yet treated with ceremonial courtesy by the ruler) into *gōng zǐ wáng rén ér guó jiàn zhī* 'duke son exile person ér country treated-with-ruler's-courtesy him' (The duke's son was an exiled person yet treated with ceremonial courtesy by the ruler). The topic *gōng zǐ* is added before *wáng rén* making *wáng rén* into a comment on *gōng zǐ*. The original structure becomes two comments.

Wu Chunsheng and Ma Beijia (2014) expand *Guǎn Shì ér zhī lǐ* 'Guan Shi ér know ritual' (Guan Shi knows rituals) into *Guǎn Shì huài rén yě ér zhī lǐ* 'Guan Shi bad person particle ér know ritual/propriety' (Guan Shi is a bad person and yet knows ritual/propriety) adding the predicate *huài rén yě* 'bad person particle' (is a bad person) after *Guǎn Shì* and *shéi ér jí zhī zhě* 'who ér attain it nominalizing particle' (Who is one who has reached it?) into *(zhèlǐ) yǒu shéi ér jí zhī zhě* '(here) has who ér attain it nominalizing-particle' (Who is here who has reached it?) by adding the existential verb *yǒu* 'have/there be' before *shéi* 'who'. Xue Fengsheng (1991) expanded the *rén* of *rén ér wú yí* 'person ér not-have propriety' into *zuòwéi yīgè rén* 'to be a person', the *Guǎn Shì* of *Guǎn Shì ér zhī lǐ* 'Guan Shi knows rituals' into *shuō dào Guǎn Shì nàyàng de rén* 'speaking of Guan Shi', and the Zǐ Chǎn of *Zǐ Chǎn ér sǐ* 'Zi Chan died' into *yǒu Zǐ Chǎn zhèyàng de guān* 'have Zi Chan this kind of official' (There was Zi Chan, this kind of official).

Adding implied and omitted constituents is probably useful in helping to interpret Ancient Chinese. However, it is quite problematic when dealing with grammatical theory. It is uncertain what words should be added to fill in omitted items. Everyone has his or her own approach to such expansions. Some people add a topic before a noun. Some add a predicate after the N. Some add the verb *yǒu* 'have/there be' before the N or *zuòwéi* 'to act as, to be' or *shuō qǐ* 'speaking of'. Consider the *example rén ér wú yí* 'a person ér lack propriety'. Some have expanded this sentence into *tāmen zuòwéi rén què méiyǒu lǐyí* 'they are people and yet lack propriety'. Others have expanded it into *zhèlǐ yǒu rén què méi yǒu lǐyí* 'Here there are people, however, who lack propriety'. Still others expand it into *rén yǒu liǎnmiàn què méiyǒu lǐyí* 'People have face but lack propriety'. In some cases, it is unknown what should be added. Contrary to intent, after elaborations are introduced, the resulting sentences have superfluous elements and an unnatural quality.

A sentence from Song Hongmin (2009) completely captures the situation: 'It is necessary to depend on context and the actual lived experiences of listeners and speakers to fill out the meaning of these nominal constituents'. Section 5.2 of Chapter 5 has already explained that when nouns act as predicates, their interpretations are context dependent. This kind of interpretation changes with context. Given that the number of contexts is limitless, the number of interpretations is limitless as well.

The referentiality of predicates   245

Consider the interpretation of the *Zǐ Chǎn* (a name) in *Zǐ Chǎn ér sǐ* as "to be wise like *Zǐ Chǎn*" and of *Guǎn Shì* (a way to refer to *Guǎn Zhòng*, a person) in *Guǎn Shì ér zhī lǐ* as "to be a bad person like Guan Zhong". These interpretations involving good and bad people are not the lexical meanings of the names *Zǐ Chǎn* and *Guǎn Zhòng* but rather are the interactive understandings of listeners and speakers in a context. Each of the following three examples seems to allow for only one interpretive elaboration (Chen Zhuqin 2009):

Qín zhàn ér shèng sān guó,   Qín bì   guò Zhōu, Hán ér yǒu   Liáng.
Qin war ér win   three kingdom Qin must pass Zhou Han ér possess Liang

Sān   guó   (zhàn) ér shèng Qín, sān   guó   zhī   lì,
three   kingdom (war)   ér win   Qin three   kingdom particle strength

suī   bù zú   yǐ gōng Qín, zú   yǐ bá   Zhèng.
although no enough use attack Qin enough to seize Zheng

'If Qin goes to war and defeats the three kingdoms, it must pass through Zhou and Han to possess Liang. Although the three kingdom's strength is inadequate to attach Qin (that is, its territory), it is enough to seize Zheng'.
("Zhao 1", *Annals of the Warring States*).

Guì   pìn   ér jiàn nì   zhī, jūn (zhī) ér bēi   zhī,
respect betroth ér base go-against her ennoble her   ér humble her

lì   ér fèi   zhī, qì   xìn ér huài qí   zhǔ,
establish ér depose her discard trust ér bad her master

zài guò   bì luàn, zài jiā bì wáng.
in kingdom must chaos in clan must perish

'If you betroth her showing great respect and then treat her disrespectfully and then ennoble her only to depose her and then establish her (as your spouse) only to discard her, you will have abandoned trust and treated her master badly. Your kingdom will definitely fall into chaos, and your clan will certainly perish'.
("Tenth Year of Duke Wen", *Zuo Tradition*)

Dà fū   wéi zhèng   yóu yǐ zhòng kè,   kuàng míng   jūn
big person do government still use masses conquer moreover enlightened ruler

(wéi zhèng)   ér shàn yòng qí zhòng hū?
(do government) ér good use his masses MP

'If a high official serving in government can use the people to defeat [an enemy], how much will be done by a wise ruler do who is good at employing his people?'
("Second Year of Duke Cheng", *Zuo Tradition*)

246 *The referentiality of predicates*

However, it is clear that these unique lexical and phrasal elaborations were determined based on what occurs earlier in the texts. We can in fact replace "verb ér verb" structures with "noun ér verb" ones in situations where the listener understands the context as in the following:[19]

Kuàng ān zhái   ér fú jū, shě   zhèng lù ér bù yóu, āi zāi!
desolate safe residenct ér not live abandon correct road ér not follow sad MP
'It is sad indeed if a safe residence in the wilderness is not lived in or the correct road is not followed'.
(Li Lou part 1, *Mencius*)

Ān   zhái   ér fú jū,   zhèng lù   ér bù   yóu,   āi   zāi!
safe residence ér not live correct road ér not follow sad MP
'It is sad indeed if a safe house is not lived in or the correct road not followed'.

Bīng fǎ   bù yuē xiàn zhī sǐ   dì   ér hòu shēng,
army method not say trap part death place ér after live

zhì   zhī wáng dì   ér hòu cún?
place part perish place ér after survive

'Doesn't Sun Zi's *Way of War* say: trap them in a deadly place and they will live, place them in a place where they may perish and they will survive?'
("Biography of the Marquis of Huailin", *Historical Records*)

Bīng fǎ   bù yuē sǐ dì   ér hòu shēng, wáng dì   ér hòu cún?
army method not say die place ér after live perish place ér then survive
'Doesn't Sun Zi's *Way of War* say: in a deadly place and they will live, in a place where they may perish and they will survive?'

In summary, according to the principle that "only if there is only one word or phrase that can serve as an elaboration can an omission be identified", it is worthwhile to discuss this method of adding material to a sentence.

In an article, Wu and Ma (2014) point out the important fact that Ancient Chinese also has cases of the structure "N (yě) ér N (yě)" where ér connects two noun phrases:

Dìzǐ   yuē: "Shì hēi   niú   yě ér bái   tí."
disciple say be   black cow   yě ér white hooves
'The disciple said that this is a black cow with white hooves'.
("Jie Lao", *Han Fei Zi*)

Cǐ   jūn zhī xiànlìng, ér xiǎo guó   zhī wàng yě.
this ruler MM decree   ér small kingdom MM hope   MP
'This ruler's decree is a small kingdom's hope'.
("Twenty-eighth Year of Duke Xiang", *Zuo Tradition*).

The referentiality of predicates 247

In addition to there being examples of "N ér V", there are also examples of "N yě ér V yě", as in *sī rén yě ér yǒu sī jí yě* 'this person *yě* ér this illness *yě*" (How can it be that such a good person comes down with such an illness?) ("Yong Ye", *Analects*); *jí yǒu qǔ zhě, shì shānggǔ zhī shì yě, ér lián bùrěn wèi yě* 'if have take particle, this merchant particle matter, ér Lian (a name) not bear do yě' (If I (Lian) were to accept compensation, that would be acting like a merchant, and that is something too unbearable for me to do.; "Biographies of Lu Zhonglian and Zou Yang", *Historical Records*). Moreover, it is almost always possible to add *yě* after a N as in *wú yī fù rén (yě), ér shì èr fū, zòng fú néng sǐ, qí yǒu xī yán*? 'I one female person (yě), ér serve two men, even-if not can die, it have what say' (If I am one woman who serves two husbands, even if I cannot die, what can I say?; "Fourteenth Year of the Duke of Zhuang", *Zuo Tradition*).

In view of this, we should change our thinking. Instead of expanding the noun before *ér* into a declarative constituent, we should analyze the verb following *ér* as a referential constituent. That is to say *ér* connects two juxtaposed referring expressions. The entire structure includes "two degrees of reference". It is possible to infer from context continuity relations and subject-predicate relations for them just like for regular patterns of juxtaposed referring expressions in general. The following are two examples, one from Ancient Chinese and one from modern Chinese. The items have corresponding structures. Both are made up of two juxtaposed referential constituents.

Sī   rén   yě,   ér   yǒu   sī   jí   yě.
this   person   MP   ér   have   this   illness MP
'How can it be that such a good person comes down with such an illness?'
("Yong Ye", *Analects*)

Zhè   ge   rén!   (Tā)   yě   bù   gēn   péngyǒu   dǎ   zhāohū!
this   CL   person   (He)   also   not   with   friend   hit   greeting
'What's up with this guy? He doesn't even say "hi" to his friends.'

These examples are from Yuen Ren Chao (1968: 61). They are used to illustrate structurally that two juxtaposed minor sentences can be combined into a complete sentence. Moreover, minor sentences like these, according to the previous argument, always possess juxtapositionality and referentiality. Conjunctions are not needed with juxtaposition. Further, *ér* is not a real conjunction but rather a resumptive demonstrative pronoun that refers to the preceding topic while possessing the functions of a conjunction (also see the arguments in the two articles Simon 1951, 1952, 1954; Lan Ying (1990) observes that *ér* and the demonstrative pronoun for "that" in Zhuang-Dong display many parallel phenomena).

6.3.5 *Antithesis in Tang poetry's word classes*

Antithesis in regulated verse refers to the following: i. in sound, level and oblique tones must contrast with each other; ii. in meaning, items from the same word classes must contrast with each other (Zhang Zhongxing 1992: 115). Depending

248   *The referentiality of predicates*

on the degree of attention paid to antithesis, contrasts can be divided into "strict/ working contrasts", "close contrasts", and "lenient/wide contrasts". "For 'wide contrasts', which involve the lowest degree of attention paid to contrast, all that is necessary is that lexical features be the same for it to be possible for two items to be in contrast" (Wang Li 2005: 180). So-called identical lexical properties here mean that "the only permitted contrasts are a noun with a noun, a verb with a verb, an adjective with an adjective, and an adverb with an adverb for an antithesis to be acceptable" (Wang Li 2005: 146). The following are examples of this requirement. (The assignment of lexical properties in the examples follows Wang Li 2005).

Xiá   yún   lóng   shù   xiǎo,   hú   rì   luò   chuán   míng[20]
gorge   clouds   envelop   tree   small   lake   sun   descend   boat   bright
'Clouds envelop the gorge, small trees/The sun sets on the lake, dazzling boats'.
(Du Fu, "Seeing Assistant Governor Duan Off on His Return to Canton")

However, an antithesis between words from different word classes is not a rare phenomenon in Tang poetry. Wang Li (2005) and Tsao Feng-fu (2004a) both discuss and give examples of their occurrence. One, adjectives often contrast with verbs:

Jìn   lèi   wú   <u>gān</u>   tǔ,   dī   kōng   yǒu   <u>duàn</u>   yún
near   tear   have-not   *dry*   ground   low   space   have   *break*   cloud
'Approaching, my tears leave no ground dry,/Low in the sky are broken clouds'.
(Du Fu, "Departing from the Tomb of the Grand Commandant Fang")

This example shows that adjectives can be considered to be intransitive verbs.
Two, situations where intransitive verbs and transitive verbs contrast are also commonly encountered:

Tā   xiāng   <u>shēng</u>   bái   fà,   jiù   guó   <u>jiàn</u>   qīng   shān
other   region   *bring-forth*   white   hair   old   country   *see*   green   mountain
'In a distant place, our hair turned white,/In our home region
you will see green mountains'.
(Lu Lun, "Seeing People Off on Their Return to the North after Pacifying Bandits")

This example shows that Chinese does not put much emphasis on the distinction between transitive and intransitive verbs.
The third point is closely related to the main topic of this chapter. The verb *yǒu* 'have/there be' not only contrasts with *wú* 'not have' and other verbs but also with *bù* 'not' and *wèi* 'still-not', two items that are adverbs:

<u>*Bù*</u>   *yǔ   shān   cháng   rùn,*   <u>*wú*</u>   *yún   shuǐ   zì   yīn.*
not   rain   mountain   constant   moist,   *have-not*   cloud   water   self   dark
'It hasn't rained; the mountain is always moist./There are no clouds; the water darkens on its own'.
(Zhang Hu, "About Gushan Temple in Hangzhou")

_Wú_   fēng yún   chū   sāi,   _bú_ yè   yuè   lín guān.
have-not wind clouds come-out-of strategic-pass _not_ night moon near pass
'There is no wind; the clouds move out of the strategic pass./It is not night; the
moon nears the pass'.
(Du Fu, "Miscellaneous Poems on Qinzhou" number 7)

_Xì_ yǔ shī yī   kàn _bú_ jiàn, xián huā   luò dì   tīng _wú_   shēng.
fine rain soak clothes look _not_ see idle flowers fall ground hear _not-have_ sound
'A fine drizzle soaks the clothes unseen./Idle flowers fall to the ground
unheard'.
(Liu Changqing, "Seeing Yan Shiyuan Off")

Shēn shān   qí _wèi_   zhǎn, yīn qì   gǔ _wú_   shēng.
deep mountain flag _still-not_ display dark moraine drum _not-have_ sound
'In the deep mountains, the flags have yet to unfurl;/in the moraine, the
drums have yet to sound'.
(Zhang Ji, "The General of a Western Expedition")

The questions this phenomenon raises are very difficult to explain within the traditional conceptual framework that "separates nouns and verbs". First, _yǔ_ 'rain'
and _yè_ 'night' are modified by the adverb _bù_ 'not'. This is usually explained as an
example of nouns "being used as verbs". The words _zhào_ 'edict', _chūn_ 'spring',
qiū 'autumn', and _huā_ 'flower' in the following examples all seem interpretable in
this way:

_Bú_   dài   jīn   mén _zhào,_   kōng   chí   bǎo   jiàn   _yóu._
not   wait gold door _decree_ empty hold precious sword _travel_
'Not waiting for an imperial decree,/I roam holding aloft my precious sword'.
(Li Bai, "Sent to a Friend on Hainan Island")

Yún   xiá   chū   hǎi _shǔ,_   méi   liǔ   dù   jiāng _chūn._
cloud glow come-out sea _light-at-dawn_ plums willows cross river _spring_
'From the glowing clouds out over the sea, I know it's dawn./The plums and
willows across the long river tell me it's spring'.
(Du Shenyan, "Reply to Lu Cheng's 'Early Spring Sight-Seeing in Nanjing'")

Yuǎn   xún   hán jiàn _bì,_   shēn rù   luàn   shān   _qiū._
distant search cold stream _blue_ deep enter chaotic mountain _autumn_
'Searching afar for a cold blue mountain stream,/going deep into the autumn
chaos of mountains'.
(Li Xianyong, "Seeking with Friends on a Spring Day")

250 *The referentiality of predicates*

Zhūquè   *qiáo biān yě cǎo <u>huā,</u>*   *wūyī*   *xiàng kǒu*
Zhuque (name) bridge side   wild grass *flowers* Wuyi (name) alley   mouth
xī   *yáng <u>xié.</u>*
evening   sun   *slant*
'Wild grass is in bloom by Zhuque Bridge./The evening sun slants across Wuyi Alley's entrance'.
(Liu Yuxi, "Wuyi Alley")

Using nouns as predicates is "using them as verbs". However, it is common in Tang poetry for nouns and noun groupings to function as predicates and for consecutive sentences with such predicates to be in contrast with each other.

Bái huā yán wài <u>duǒ,</u>   *qīng liǔ kǎn*   *qián <u>shāo.</u>*
white flower eave out *drooping* green willow threshold before *tip-of-branch*
'White flowers droop beyond the eaves;/the tips of green willows extend before the threshold'.
(Du Fu, "On the North Bridge Tower in Xinjin [Rhyming] to the Provided-Word Jiāo")[21]

Xì   *cǎo wéi fēng <u>àn,</u> wēi qiáng dú yè <u>zhōu.</u>*
fine   grass slight wind *shore* danger mast alone night *boat*
'A slight wind blows the fine grass by the shore./The tall mast of a lone boat at night'.
(Du Fu, "Writing Thoughts while Traveling at Night")

Xiāng dào   *zhuó yú <u>yīngwǔ lì,</u> bì wú*   *qī*
fragrant rice   peck excess *parrot grain* green parasol-tree perch
lǎo   *<u>fènghuáng zhī</u>*
old   *phoenix branch*
'Parrots peck at leftover grains of fragrant rice./Old phoenixes perch on a green parasol's branch'.
(Du Fu, the eighth of eight poems on "Autumn Activity")[22]

Is it tenable to say that these nouns are being "used" as verb? According to people's intuitions, these kinds of nouns originally were able to function as predicates.

There is yet another issue in need of attention. In the phrases (*tīng*) *wú shēng* 'hear without sound' and (*kàn*) *bú jiàn* '(look) not see' and *wú shēng* 'without sound' and *wèi zhǎn* 'still-not unfurled', not only is *wú* 'not-have' in contrast with *bù* 'not' and *wèi* 'still-not', but also the noun *shēng* 'sound' contrasts with the verbs *jiàn* 'see' and *zhǎn* 'unfurl'. It is in fact common for nouns and verbs (including adjectives) to be in contrast. This situation is not restricted to where *wú* 'not-have' and *bù* 'not' or *wèi* 'still-not' contrast with each other, as can be seen in the following:

The referentiality of predicates   251

Wú   *biān* *luò* *mù*   *xiāoxiāo*   *xià,*
have-not *side*   fall   tree   xiaoxiao (onomatopoeia)   down

bú *jìn*   *chángjiāng* *gǔngǔn* *lái.*
not   *exhausted*   Long River   roll-roll come
'Over an endless expanse fallen leaves rustling below./Endlessly, the Long River
comes rolling along'
(Du Fu, "Climbing High").

Qiān   *shān*   *niǎo* *fēi* *jué,* *wàn*   *jìng* *rén*   *zōng* *miè.*
thousand mountain bird *fly* end ten-thousand paths human *traces* disappear
'Birds fly away over the thousands of mountains./All traces of humans along the
tens of thousands of paths are obliterated'.
(Liu Zongyuan, "Snow on the River").

Wǔ   *hú*   *sān*   *mǔ* *zhái,*   *wànlǐ*   *yī*   *guī*   *rén.*
five   lakes three   *mu* abode   10,000 li   one   *return* person
'Your abode by Lake Tai has three *mu* of land./You return over 10,000 li[23] alone'.
(Wang Wei, "Seeing Qiu Wei Off").

   In all of the following examples, nouns contrast with verbs, whether looked at
in terms of monosyllabic words or disyllabic compound words:

Báidì   *kōng* *cí*   *miào,*   *gū* *yún* *zì* *wǎng* *lái.*
Baidi (Place name) empty *ancestral-halls* *temples* lone cloud self *go*   come
'The ancestral halls and temples stand empty in Baidi Town./Solitary clouds
come and go on their own'.
(Du Fu "Going to Baidi Town")

Xīng *wáng* *liú* *bái* *rì,* *jīn*   *gǔ*   *gòng* *hóng* *chén.*
rise   fall   leave white sun   *present* *past* share red   dust
'Kingdoms rise and fall; the white sun remains./Present times and ancient times
share in the vanity of the world'.
(Sima Li "Climb Stork Tower on an Island in a River")

Xié *nìng* *měi* *sī*   *dāngmiàn* *tuò,* *qīng* *pín* *zhǎng* *qiàn* *yī* *bēi* *qián.*
evil flattery each thought *to-the-face spit* clear poor long owe *one cup money*
'Every thought, evil flattery, cursed him to his face,/cold and poor owing money
for a cup of wine'.
(Du Mu, "Post Station for Merchant Mountains and Rich Waters")

252   *The referentiality of predicates*

In the final example, *yī bēi qián* (literally 'one cup money') contrasts with *dāngmiàn tuò* (literally 'to-the-face spit'). Although both are modifier-head constructions in what counts as a case of structural parallelism, one of them is a nominal attribute-head structure, and the other is a verbal adverbial-head structure.

This kind of situation exists in so-called borrowed contrasts. "Borrowed pairs" can be divided into two types, "borrowed meanings" and "borrowed sounds". Tsao (2004a) gives the following examples:

Jiǔ	*zhài*	*xúncháng*			*xíng*	*chǔ*	*yǒu,*
wine	Debt	*8-foot unit (and) 16-foot unit*			walk	place	have

rén	*shēng*	*qīshí*	*gǔ*	*lái*	*xī.*
person	life	*70*	ancient	come	rare

'Owing money for wine is common everywhere./Since ancient times, it's been rare to live to 70'

(Du Fu, "Qu River").

Shì	*zhí*	*huáng*	*tiān*	*zài,*	*guī*	*chí*	*bái*	*fà*	*shēng.*
matter	straight	*emperor*	heaven	be-at	return	late	*white*	hair	grow

'The matter is correct; Heaven is your witness./Your return was delayed; your hair has gone white'.

(Liu Changqing, "Xin An Bestowed on Mu Yude").

The contrast between *xúncháng* '8-foot unit [and] 16-foot unit' and *qīshí* '70' is superficially a contrasting of two numbers (8 feet is 1 *xún*; 2 *xún* is 1 *cháng*). However, within the poem, *xúncháng* has a different meaning, 'often, usual'. This is an example of "borrowed meaning". The poet borrowed *huáng* 'emperor' for *huáng* 'yellow' to contrast with *bái* 'white' in order to put the pair of colors in what counts as a strict contrast. This is an example of "borrowed sound".

Jiang Shaoyu (1990: 75) said that "borrowed contrasts" are an ingenious way to make use of the complex relationship between characters and compound words. It is a case of "characters being in contrast but not the compound words". What we would like to add to the explanation is that "compound words are not in contrast" refers to differences in word meaning or in word classes. The premise underlying this kind of borrowing is that nouns and number words can contrast with adjectives.

The issue we now face is that later generations of poetry critics did not feel that nouns contrasting with verbs (including adjectives) were "incorrect" or "not strict". They went so far as to use such contrasts as examples of "strict contrasts". This contradicts Wang Li's explanation of "wide contrasts". If it is accepted that this situation belongs to "wide contrasts", does the term "wide contrasts" actually have a boundary? Within a conceptual framework that distinguishes nouns from verbs, it is not clear whether "noun contrasts with verbs" count as cases of "close contrasts".

Tsao Feng-fu (2004a) also said that "antitheses involving word classes" have long been a major problem perplexing researchers". He tends to interpret "wide

The referentiality of predicates   253

contrasts" as being "idioms contrasting with idioms" as in the following Du Fu poem:

Gùrén   jù   búlì,   zhé   huàn   liǎng   yōurán
old friends   all   not-profit (unfavorable)   demoted   officials   both   leisurely
'None of old friends lived in favorable circumstances;/both demoted officials are leisurely.'

Búlì 'literally: not-profit; unfavorable' and *yōurán* 'leisurely' originally could not contrast with each other. However, the two items were already idioms (and had already lexicalized into disyllabic forms). The individual constituents internal to the idioms do not have to contrast with each other.

Having idioms contrast with idioms is not unreasonable given that the tendency in Chinese to form disyllabic lexical items was already quite clear by the Tang period. However, we believe that it is not appropriate to put excessive emphasis on this point when discussing antitheses involving word classes. First, this cannot explain the majority of cases that involve the question of why monosyllabic words do not contrast with each. Second, in talking about the couplet it is possible to say that *qiūfān* 'autumn sail' and *gǔmù* 'ancient trees' have already lexicalized. (The actual degree of lexicalization is not the same.) It is not important whether the idiom-internal constituents *qiū* 'autumn' and *gǔ* 'ancient' are in contrast. However, *Qīngfēngjiāng* and *Baidi-Town* are both place names. They are even more like idioms and their internal constituents are in strict contrast with each other.

Qīngfēng jiāngshàng qiūfān   yuǎn, báidìchéng biān gǔmù   shū.
Qingfeng River-on   autumn-sail distant Baidi-Town side ancient-tree sparse
'On an autumn, a distant sail on Qingfeng River,/few are the ancient trees surrounding Baidi Town.'

Tsao has also said that the personal name Sūn Xíngzhě cannot freely contrast with Zhào Shǒuchéng but could contrast with Hú Shìzhī.[24] Contrast between consecutive words[25] also should consider whether they belong to the same word class. *Huāngtáng* 'absurd' can only contrast with *cēncī* 'uneven' and not with *yīngwǔ* "parrot'. Third, *xíng zhōu* 'sailing boat' contrasts with *kè lù* 'traveler's road'. It is possible to say that *xíng zhōu* is an idiom. It is difficult to say that *kè lù* is one too. It is actually difficult to clearly determine when a combination has lexicalized.

Yuen Ren Chao (Chao 1975) said that every character has the same length and loudness in Chinese. As a result, an utterance's rhythm progresses in an even, equally spaced monosyllabic tune. To this is added the fact that each character has a meaning. Thus, in writing poetry or prose, a composition's conception depends on the number of characters to be used. Regardless of whether the lines are five or seven characters long, the poet always must thoroughly consider how to put characters in contrast with each other. *Yōurán* 'leisurely' is in opposition to *búlì* 'unfavorable'. Although *rán* had doubtlessly already lexicalized into a bound suffix by the

254   *The referentiality of predicates*

Tang period, it still preserved its meaning of "like or similar shape". It can be said that structurally *yōurán* and *bùlì* maintain a parallelism (both being modifier-head structures). Consequently, explanations of "idioms in contrast with idioms" as "wide contrast" is not entirely convincing.

Jiang Shaoyu (1990: 168) when discussing that antithesis requires that words in the same word class be in contrast with each other said that "that which is called 'identical word classes' cannot completely be according to contemporary grammatical concepts". We believe that "contemporary grammatical concepts" are under the influence and domination of Indo-European grammatical concepts, "the separation of nouns from verbs" being one of them. The previous problem receives a reasonable solution in the verbs-as-nouns framework; nouns include verbs, verbs belong to nouns, and predicate argument expressions possess referentiality.

Nominal constituents can function as predicates not because they possess in themselves predicate-argument properties but because predicate-argument expressions originally possess referentiality. What is referred to as "wide contrasts" involves nouns and verbs. This is a contrast between dynamic nouns (verbs) and stative nouns. Although there is a distinction between dynamic and stative, the items that possess these properties are all nouns. Moreover, dynamic nouns are only in "strict contrast" with dynamic nouns, and stative nouns are only in "strict contrast" with stative nouns.

Word-class antithesis in Tang poetry provides evidence that in Chinese the noun category includes verbs. Or to put it differently, the verbs-as-nouns framework provides a reasonable explanation for word-class antithesis in Tang poetry.

6.4   An examination of predicate referentiality informed by dummy verbs

Dummy verbs[26] are also referred to as empty verbs. According to Zhu Dexi (1985b), the term refers to a small number of transitive verbs that developed in modern written Chinese including *jìnxíng* 'carry out', *jiāyǐ* 'add to', *gěiyǐ* 'give', *yǔyǐ* 'give', and *zuò* 'make', It is clear that the original lexical meanings of these verbs have already weakened. Zhu uses dummy verbs to define "nominal verbs" like *diàochá* 'investigate', *yánjiū* 'research', *pīpíng* 'criticize', and *chéngbàn* 'punish'. These items possess properties of nouns and verbs and can serve as the objects of dummy verbs. Section 2 of Chapter 2 has already provided an analysis of the issues related to "nominal verbs". This section discusses questions related to the grammatical functions of dummy verbs.

Zhu has identified three functions that dummy verbs have. One function is to convert nominal constituents into predicates as in **duì xīnzàng bìng huànzhě shǒushù* 'for someone suffering from heart disease an operation' → *duì xīnzàng bìng huànzhě **jìnxíng** shǒushù* 'for someone suffering from heart disease to carry out an operation'. A second function is to add complexity to a nominal verb to satisfy structural requirements as in **jīnhòu hái yào búduàn zǒngjié* *jīngyàn, gǎijìn* 'from now on, we will constantly summarize [our] experiences improve' → *jīnhòu hái yào búduàn zǒngjié jīngyàn, **jiāyǐgǎijìn*** 'from now on, we will constantly summarize [our] experiences to make improvements'. The third function arises from semantic and rhetorical considerations and marks how the object of a dummy verb relates to what precedes it as in *tāmen duì zhè pī xìngzhì hé láiyuán dōu bù xiāngtóng de zīliào bùdé bù **jiāyǐzhěnglǐ*** 'The quality and origins of this consignment's material are all different. It is necessary to straighten things out'.

Because there are no inherent connections among these three functions, Diao Yanbin (2004) and Jiang Zixia and Ding Chongming (2011) want to create a generalization that leads to a single unified function. They believe that the function of dummy verbs is to activate the following nominal verbs' nominal properties and to remove their grammatical verb features. This produces a logical contradiction. Nominal verbs were originally defined based on their cooccurrence with dummy verbs. They possess both nominal and verb properties. How is it possible for them to lose their verb properties after adding a dummy verb? Besides, there is also the noun *shǒushù* 'operation'. It has no verb properties to lose.

Previous research would also have difficulty explaining the following three facts:

i. | **Duì* | *zhè* | *zhǒng* | *xiànxiàng* | *pīpíng* | |
    |---|---|---|---|---|---|
    | toward | this | CL | phenomenon | criticize | |

Duì	*zhè*	*zhǒng*	*xiànxiàng*	*jiāyǐ*	*pīpíng*
toward	this	CL	phenomenon	add	criticize
    'To criticize this kind of phenomena'

*Duì	*zhè*	*zhǒng*	*xiànxiàng*	*pī*	
towards	this	CL	phenomenon	criticize	
*Duì	*zhè*	*zhǒng*	*xiànxiàng*	*jiāyǐ*	*pī*
towards	this	CL	phenomenon	add	criticize

ii. | **Jìnxíng* | *gānggāng* | *pínggū* | *Jìnxíng* | *chóngxīn* | *pínggū* |
    |---|---|---|---|---|---|
    | carry-out | just | assess | carry-out | anew | assess |

                                                             'To carry out a reassessment'

*Jiāyǐ	*yīzài*	*gōngjí*	*Jiāyǐ*	*sìyì*	*gōngjí*
add	repeated	attack	add	wanton	attack

                                                             'to attack wantonly'

iii. | **Jìnxíng* | *chǎojià* | *Jìnxíng* | *zhēngchǎo* |
     |---|---|---|---|
     | carry-out | quarrel | carry-out | quarrel |

                                                         'To quarrel'

*Jìnxíng	*bānjiā*	*Jìnxíng*	*bānqiān*
carry-out	move home	carry-out	move

                                                         'To move'

256 *The referentiality of predicates*

i. With respect to the contrast in grammaticality between the left and right examples in the first row, in the past it was held that because the verb properties of the nominal verb *pīpíng* 'criticize' were too weak; it was necessary for it to be supported by a dummy verb before it could serve as a predicate. The problem with this explanation is that the verb properties of *pī* 'criticize' are quite strong, and yet as the following line shows, it cannot function as a predicate regardless of whether it is supported by a dummy verb. ii. If all the objects of dummy verbs are nominal verbs, why do differences in adverbial modification (*gānggāng/chóngxīn* 'just/anew', *yīzài/sìyì* 'repeatedly/wantonly') create the contrast in grammaticality between the left and right items? iii. It is also necessary to explain why written forms like *zhēngchǎo* 'quarrel' and *bānqiān* 'move' can be the objects of dummy verbs but not spoken forms like *chǎojià* 'quarrel' and *bānjiā* 'move'. It is not possible to explain this by saying that the former items are nominal verbs while the latter are not. This is a circular argument because the only reason the latter are not classified as nominal predicates is because they cannot occur as the objects or dummy verbs. In addition, the contrast in grammaticality between *jìnxíng dì sān cì chǎojià* 'to carry out the third quarrel' and **jìnxíng dì sān cì chǎo* 'to carry out the third quarrel' needs to be accounted for as well.

It is necessary to have a unified theoretical foundation to provide a simple account of the functions of dummy verbs without introducing contradictions and to explain the three facts discussed earlier. This theoretical foundation posits that predicate expressions and predicate phrases all possess referentiality; they are all referring expressions; moreover, the degree of referential strength varies among them. The function of dummy verbs is to strengthen the referentiality of predicate words and phrases and increase their degree of deicticity. The contrast in grammaticality for the items on the left and right and upper and lower in example i. is accounted for in this way: The end of a sentence is the natural position for information that is focused on. *Pī/pīpíng* 'criticize' is placed in sentence final position to highlight and emphasize the action of criticizing. The addition of a dummy verb to strengthen their referentiality can serve this emphatic function. Although the referentiality of *pīpíng* is fairly strong, it is not strong enough and so depends on *jiāyǐ* 'add' to strengthen its referentiality. *Pī*'s referentiality is not as strong as *pīpíng*'s. Even with *jiāyǐ*, its strength is still not enough to emphasize the action of criticizing.

Strengthening referentiality is a kind of emphasis. What is "strengthening referentiality"? Strengthening referentiality involves increasing a referent's deictic definiteness (or simply definiteness). Essentially, it involves the speaker trying to make it easier for the hearer to identify the referent, differentiating it from other entities. There are many ways to strengthen referentiality, as can be seen in the following examples:

Bǎ[27] *bēizi* *dì*   *gěi*   *wǒ!*
ba   cup   pass   give   me!
'Pass me the cup!'

Bǎ 'bēizi [zhòngdú]   dì   gěi   wǒ!
ba   'cup [assigned stress]   pass   give   me!
'Pass me **the cup**!'

Bǎ   zhè   zhī   bēizi   dì   gěi   wǒ!
ba   this   CL   cup   pass   give   me!
'Pass me this cup!'

Bǎ   zhè   zhī   bēizi   [tóngshíyòngshǒuzhǐ]   dì   gěi   wǒ!
ba   this   CL   cup   (accompanied by pointing)   pass   give   me
'Pass me this cup!' (accompanied by pointing)

Dì   gěi   wǒ   zhè   yī   zhī   bēizi!
pass   give   me   this   one   CL   cup!
'Pass me this cup!'

Stress assignment and the addition of one of the demonstrative words *zhè* 'this' or *nà* 'that' are frequently used ways to raise the degree of deicticity for a word like *bēizi* 'cup'. If it is felt that this approach is inadequate, it is possible to add pointing with a finger. A change in word order is also an option. The sentence final position is the position used to focus on information. The difference between the two expressions *pīpíng zhè zhǒng xiànxiàng* 'criticize this kind of phenomenon' and *duì zhè zhǒng xiànxiàng jìnxíng pīpíng* 'this kind of phenomenon engage in criticism' (engage in criticism of this kind of phenomenon) rests in the latter *pīpíng* 'criticize' becoming the object of the preceding dummy verb *jìnxíng* 'carry out'. The action of criticizing is treated as a referent and is emphasized.

The link between emphasis and strengthening referentiality is universal. For example, in English it is possible to emphasize an action by adding the dummy verb *do* before a verb:

He wrote a letter.
He *did* write a letter.

Although the dummy verb *do* has lost its lexical meaning, its dynamic properties are extremely strong. After adding *do*, the tense marker on the verb *wrote* is shifted to *do*. The verb's base form *write* can be considered to be the object of *did*. The action of writing a letter is emphasized as an independent referent.

In Korean a similar situation is even more obvious. According to Jo (2000), *ha* in Korean is more or less equivalent to the dummy verb *do* in English. Korean is an SOV language. By adding *ha* after a verb, the preceding OV or SOV becomes

258   *The referentiality of predicates*

a referent. Not only does it occur with the nominalization marker—*ki*, but it also takes the topic marker—*nun* as in the following examples:

i.   Chelsu-ka   maykewu-lul   mai-ess-ta
      Chelsu-nominative case   beer-object case   drink-past-tense comment-marker
      'Chelsu drank beer.'

ii.   [Chelsu-ka   maykewu-lul   masi]-**ki-nun**   ha-ess-ta
      Chelsu-   beer-   drink]-nominalizer-   do-past-
      nominative case   object case   topic marker   comment
      'Yes, it is the case that Chelsu drank beer.'

iii. Chelsu-ka   [maykewu-lul   masi]-**ki-nun**   ha-ess-ta
      Chelsu-nominative   [beer-object   drink]-nominalizer-   do-past-
      case   case   topic marker   comment
      'Chelsu did drink beer.'

In ii., the example is a sentence with event focus. In iii., the sentence has a VP-focus. It should be noted that the nominalization marker—*ki* and the topic marker—*num* range over the same domains. A topic is a constituent with strong nominal or referential properties. Along these lines, consider the following Chinese examples:

Běi   fēng   nà   gè   chuī,   xuěhuā   nà   gè   piāo.
north   wind   that CL   blow   snowflake that CL   float
'The north wind did blow and snowflakes did float.'

Wǒ   dāngshí   nà   gè   hàipà!
I   at-that-time that CL   fear
'I was that scarred.'

Wǒ   nà   jiào   yī   gè   jǐnzhāng   ó!
I   that call   one   CL   nervous   MP
'I was then so very nervous.'

In the past, it was said that *nà ge* 'that' emphasized the high degree of blowing, fear, or nervousness. Now it is possible to say that it is precisely because of the high degree of blowing, fear, and nervousness that it is necessary to raise their deicticity (by adding *nà ge*) to cause the hearer to pay greater attention to them.

An explanation for the contrasts in grammaticality displayed in iii. follows from this understanding of the links between emphasis and strengthening referentiality. Zhēngchǎo 'quarrel' is used in writing. Chǎojià 'quarrel' is used in the spoken language. Both of these words were originally referring expressions referring to the same action. Because they have been frequently used as predicates, they have

The referentiality of predicates   259

gradually moved from being referring expressions to predicate expressions with an accompanying emptying of referentiality, this also being the semantic emptying found when nouns move in the direction of verbs (see Section 2 of Chapter 3 in Volume II for details).

This kind of emptying occurs more rapidly in the spoken language than in its written form both in Chinese and in other languages. Because of this, the degree of emptying in the direction of verbs is deep for the colloquial dynamic nouns *chǎo* 'quarrel' and *chǎojià* 'quarrel'. Their dynamic or predicate properties are strong. In contrast, the emptying in the direction of verbs is shallow for the written form *zhēngchǎo* 'quarrel'. Its nominal properties or referentiality are strong.

The majority of colloquial dynamic nouns are monosyllabic. Most written dynamic nouns are disyllabic. From this it follows that the emptying of *chǎo* in the direction of verbs is deeper than *chǎojià*'s, and its referentiality is weaker. An examination of actual linguistic corpora reveals that *jìnxíng chǎojià* 'carry-out quarrel', *jìnxíng bānjiā* 'carry-out move', and *jìnxíng dúshū* 'read' are not absolutely unacceptable. It is even easier for them to co-occur with dummy verbs when a numeral-classifier compound occurs before them.

jìnxíng zhēngchǎo	*? jìnxíng chǎojià (Jìnxíng dì-sān cì chǎojià)*	**Jìnxíng chǎo*
carry-out quarrel	carry-out quarrel (carry-out third time quarrel	carry-out quarrel
'To quarrel'	To quarrel (to quarrel a third time)	
jìnxíng bānqiān	*?jìnxíng bānjiā (jìnxíng dì-sān cì bānjiā)*	** jìnxíng bān*
carry-out move	carry-out move home (carry-out third time move home)	carry-out move
'To move'	'To move home' (to move a third time)	
jìnxíng yuèdú	*?jìnxíng dúshū (jìnxíng dì-sān huí dúshū)*	** jìnxíng bān*
carry-out read	carry-out read (carry-out third time read)	carry-out read
'To read'	'To read' (to read a third time)	

From left to right, the degree of nominal emptying in the direction of verbs deepens with each item. In general, the objects of dummy verbs belong to a relatively formal register of written language. They cannot occur in too colloquial a context. It is for this reason that the degree of their emptying is shallow. Shen Jiaxuan (2011) also explains the advantages to this kind of explanation based on the brevity maxim.

260 *The referentiality of predicates*

Finally, the contrasts in grammaticality in ii. brought about by different adverbs are in need of explanation. To account for this fact, all that is needed is to understand one principle: The tighter the bonds within words and phrases, the stronger their nominal properties and referentiality. The following examples can be used to illustrate this.

Tā   xǐhuān   mǎi   hóng   bāo₁.
she   like   buy   red   envelope
'She likes to buy red envelopes.'

Lǎobǎn   méi   fā   hóngbāo₂
boss   not-have issue red-envelope
'The boss has not issued red envelopes.'

For *hóngbāo₂* X can only be used to refer to it as a unit as in *lǎobǎn méi fā X* 'the boss did not issue X'. For *hóng bāo₁*, X can be used to refer to *X bāo* as in *tā xǐhuān mǎi X bāo* 'she likes to buy X envelopes' (with X taking as values *hóng* 'red', *bái* 'white', *hēi* 'black', and *lán* 'blue' and the like). In this sense, with respect to their being referents, the individuality of *hóngbāo₂*'s referent is stronger than the individuality of *hóngbāo₁*'s. The link between the two morphemes in *hóngbāo₂* is very tight merging them into a single "word" that is like a "name". However, the link between the two morphemes in *hóngbāo₁* is loose. They do not form a "word". They do not seem like a "name". Or to put it differently, the more something becomes like an individual entity, the more we feel the need to give it a name.

According to Zhang Hongnian (1972) and Zhang Risheng (1959), in Cantonese, *hóngbāo₁* is *hungbaau,*[35] while *hóngbāo₂* is *hungbaau:*[55] Moreover, 55 is the yinping[28] tonal contour characteristic of nouns in Cantonese.

This is to say that in the Chinese mind, a "word" is a "name". If something is not like a "word", it is not like a "name". To become a "word" is naturally to become a "name". Chinese "words" or "content words" naturally possess nominal properties. (Chapter 4, Section 3.1) Shen Jiaxuan (2012b) demonstrates the principle of "density iconicity" that the tighter the internal relations of a combination are, the more it seems like a noun. Lu Bingfu (2012) argues that the richer a word's connotations are the more it seems like a noun. Because the morphemes in *hóngbāo₂* are more tightly related to each other than those of *hóngbāo₁*, and *hóngbāo₂* has many more connotations, it has a dictionary entry where its connotations are explained.

The same is the case for names that refer to actions. Because the referents for *sùhuá* 'speed skating' and *tiàomǎ* 'horse-vaulting' (both being sports) are "individuals", while those for *kuài huá* 'fast skating' and *qí mǎ* 'ride horse' are not, *sùhuá* 'speed skating' and *tiàomǎ* 'horse-vaulting' are "names", whereas *kuài huá* 'fast skating' and *qí mǎ* 'ride horse' do not seem like names. For the same reason, because there is a tighter link between manner (*chóngxīn* 'anew') and an action than time (*gānggāng* 'just now') and an action in expressions referring to individuated referents, relations between the morphemes in *chóngxīn pínggū* 'reassessment' are closer than those in *gānggāng pínggū* 'just assessed'. This is illustrated in the following example:

Gānggāng, wǒmen pínggū le nà fèn jìhuà.
just-now we assess PSP that CL plan
'We just assessed that plan.'

?Chóngxīn, wǒmen pínggū le nà fèn jìhuà.
?anew we assess PSP that CL plan
'We assessed that plan anew.'

Wǒmen gānggāng chóngxīn pínggū le nà fèn jìhuà.
we just-now anew assess PSP that CL plan
'We just reassessed that plan.'

*Wǒmen chóngxīn gānggāng pínggū le nà fèn jìhuà
we anew just-now assess PSP that CL plan

For cognitive reasons, we often classify actions according to the manner in which they are performed. However, it is very improbable that an action's classification would be based on the time when it occurs. Because of this, the individual properties of the referent for *gānggāng pínggū* 'just assessed' are not as strong as those for *chóngxīn pínggū* 'reassessment'. As a consequence, its nominal properties or referentiality are not sufficiently strong. Even with the support of a dummy verb, its strength is not enough to emphasize reference to that action. For details on what this section discusses, see the article (Shen Jiaxuan & Zhang Jiangzhi 2013).

6.5 Viewing English predicates from another angle

6.5.1 The V-ing form is a quasi-referring expression

In Section 6 of Chapter 3, it is said that it is impossible to see Chinese clearly if only looked at in terms of Chinese. Likewise, English cannot be seen clearly if looked at only in terms of English. After discovering that Chinese predicates have referentiality, we can reexamine English in terms of Chinese to develop an even deeper understanding of English predicates.[29] In the past, under the domination of an Indo-European perspective, the starting point for looking at Chinese was always English and other like languages. Unexpectedly, it is possible to reverse the starting point. To begin, consider *killing* in the following three sentences:

i. His job is killing people mercilessly.
ii. Killing people mercilessly is unimaginable.
iii. He is killing people mercilessly.

The difference between *killing people mercilessly* in the two sentences i. and ii. is that the former functions as an object (complement) while the latter is a subject.

262 *The referentiality of predicates*

Both manifest referentiality and are referring expressions. However, the identical form in sentence iii. is part of a predicate. It is generally held that it possesses only predicate-argument properties and lacks referentiality. If, however, English is reexamined in terms of Chinese, it is possible to analyze *killing people mercilessly* in sentence iii. as a quasi-referring expression. This is consistent with the position taken in Jespersen (1924: 277–281) that *be V-ing* expresses an "expanded tense" rather than a "progressive tense". If characterized as a "progressive tense", the focus is on V-ing and on the progress or continuation of the action. If characterized as an "expanded tense", the focus is on *be*, which is marked for tense. V-ing is just the expanded time frame surrounding *be*. The difference between the two characterizations is illustrated in the following figure:

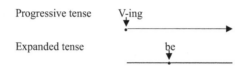

Figure 6.1 The difference between progressive tense and expanded tense

For example, the meaning of *he is hunting* is 'he is in (the middle of) the action of hunting'. The action denoted by the word *hunting* is expanded to encompass the times before and after the moment denoted by *is*. The focus of the "expanded tense" is not on the progression or continuation of an action. Rather, it is on the time of a given action being relatively short when compared to that of another action. For example, in *Methuselah lived to be more than nine hundred years old*, the verb *lived* is marked with a 'unexpanded tense' denoting that Methuselah lived an extremely long time. In *he was raising his hand to strike her, when he stopped short*, the form *was raising* is in an "expanded tense". It denotes that the action of raising a hand to strike someone was of very short duration.

The expanded tense characterization helps us in understanding the exact meaning of the modern English form *be V-ing*. For example, this form often denotes a state of short duration in contrast to the states of long duration denoted by an unexpanded tense. Consider the following comparisons:

He is staying at the Savoy Hotel.
He lives in London.
What are you doing for a living? I am writing for the papers.
What do you do for a living? I write for the papers.

For another example consider that habitual actions are generally expressed using a non-expanded tense.

  A great awe seemed to have fallen upon her, and she <u>was behaving</u> as she <u>behaved</u> in church.

Thanks, I *don't smoke*.
Compare the previous statement with "I am not smoking".

The referentiality of predicates   263

However, if a habitual action is treated as another action's time frame, the expanded tense must be used:

I realize my own stupidity when I *am playing* chess with him.
(Wǒ **yī** gēn tā xià qí jiù yìshí dào wǒ de yúbèn (fairly literally, 'I **one** with him play chess, then realize my stupidity'))

Every morning when he *was having breakfast* his wife asked him for money.[30]
(Měitiān zǎoshang tā **yī** chī zǎofàn, tā qīzi jiù wèn tā yào qián (fairly literally, 'Every day in the morning, he **one** eat breakfast, his wife then asks him for money').)

The expanded tense characterization helps explain the following series of facts:

i.   From the perspective of the history of English, the *be V-ing* structure primarily derives from the loss of the word initial vowel of the preposition *on* in *on* prepositional structures: *Is on hunting→is a-hunting→is hunting* (the evolutionary process being the same as with *burst out on weeping→ . . . a weeping→ . . . weeping* and *set the clock on going→ . . . a going→ . . . going*). It was precisely when a more general phenomenon of the loss of [unstressed] word-initial vowels became very common (as in *on bæc→a back→back*) that the modern V-ing structure started to become frequently used.

ii. The original way to express the passive meaning for *the house was building* was *the house was on building*. The same way of speaking is still often used in examples like *while the tea was brewing* and *my MS is now copying*.

iii. Verbs denoting psychological states and feelings do not use the expanded tense generally. Thus, it is impossible to say *he is on* (*engaged in, occupied in*) *liking fish*. Exceptions to this occur when talking about a state of brief duration like *I am feeling cold*.

iv. When an auctioneer says *going, going, gone, going* denotes an exceedingly brief state. So, it is not difficult to understand why *be coming* and *be going* denote imminent time:

I *am going* to Birmingham next week.
Christmas *is coming*; the geese are getting fat.

Jespersen believed that the time frame denoted by *on V-ing* is essentially a nominal structure. He calls it "[a] construction of the verbal substantive [noun] with the preposition *on*" (Jespersen 1924: 278). It is very easy to understand this structure by comparing it to Chinese. The Chinese sentence *tā zài dǎliè (zhī zhōng)* 'He is-at hunting('s middle)' ("He is in the middle of hunting") is the natural way to express the meaning of the English sentence *he is (in the middle of) hunting*. In the Chinese, the copula is hidden and not visible. This is the same as in the Chinese sentence *tā zài shānshàng* 'he is-at the mountain-top' (He is on the mountain). Both *shānshàng* 'mountain-top' and *dǎliè* 'hunting' are nominals. This means that it is unnecessary to see *V-ing* as the predication of an action when it functions as a predicate in

264   *The referentiality of predicates*

English. Rather, it can be seen as referring to the action. If *killing* in the previous three sentences i., ii., and iii. are to be given a unified account, iii. should move in the direction of i. and ii. with the result that all of them would be considered referring expressions. It is not possible to move i. and ii. closer to iii. (and call all three of them predicate expressions). This is determined by the favored direction of the asymmetry between reference and predication (see Chapter 5).

That said, there are three reasons for why English does not usually treat the *killing* in iii. as a referring expression. One, for verbs there is the difference between finite and non-finite forms. Two, the relation between subjects and predicates is very close. With respect to sentences with the copula, the subject-predicate relation generally expresses equivalence and attributes. Three, an ontological metaphor like KILLING IS AN ENTITY is realizational and not constitutive in English (see Chapter 4, Section 2.1). All the same, it is not unwarranted to follow Jespersen in seeing *killing* in iii. as a quasi-referential phrase.

6.5.2   *The V-ed form is a potential referring expression*

Consider "kill" in the following four sentences:

| i. | He | killed | a | man. |
| | *Tā* | *shāle* | *yīgè* | *rén.* |

| ii. | He | did | kill | a | man. |
| | *Tā* | ***shì*** | *shāle* | *yīgè* | *rén.* |

| iii. | He | has | killed | a | man. |
| | *Tā* | ***yǒu*** | *shāguò* | *yīgè* | *rén.* |

| iv. | That | he | killed | a | man | is | a fact |
| | | *Tā* | *shāle* | *yīgè* | *rén* | *shì* | *shìshí.* |

Examining English from an alternative Chinese perspective, the V-ed part of English predicates possess potential referentiality. In i., this potential referentiality is not at all apparent. In the sentence in ii., this referentiality is partially visible but in part remains hidden. The phrase *killed a man* is equivalent to *something. He did kill a man* asserts *he did something.* In the previous Chinese translation for ii., *shā le yī gè rén* 'killed a person' (underlined in the previous example) is the referential object of *shì* 'be' (in bold in the previous example). The phrase *killed a man* in the iii. sentence can be treated as the referential object of *has.* It is exactly the same as in the Chinese where *shāguò yī gè rén* 'killed a person' is the referential object of the verb *yǒu* 'have/there be'. In the sentence in iv., *that* is added before the clause *he killed a man* so that it can be realized as a referring expression. Chinese has no need to for this realization process.

The characterization of V-ed as a referring expression is compatible with Jespersen's (1924: 269–271) position that *have V-ed* indicates tense and not aspect.

The referentiality of predicates 265

When Jespersen discusses aspect (286–289), he treats the "perfective aspect" in English as a "perfect tense". Moreover, this "perfect tense" belongs to the "present tense". It is a kind of "permansive present tense" since it represents the result produced by a past action as a stable state. This kind of characterization receives empirical support from the following facts:

i.   *Have V-ed* can occur with the adverb *now* but not with words and phrases that denote past time as in the following examples:

Now I have eaten enough.
*I have eaten enough yesterday.[31]

ii.   The meaning it denotes is very different from the meaning of the past tense as in the following examples:

He has become mad ("[being] mad" is the present state)
He became mad (not relevant to the present state)
Have you written the letter? (a question raised concerning the present moment)
Did you write the letter? (not relevant to the current moment)

iii. When the main clause is in the perfect tense, the dependent clause must use the present tense. Compare the following examples:

He has given orders that all spies are to be shot at once.
He gave orders that all spies were to be shot at once.

iv.   In Old Aryan the perfective aspect was originally a kind of emphatic permansive present tense. It denoted a state as in *odi* 'I hate', *memini* 'I remember', *hestēka* 'I stand', *kektēmai* 'I possess', *kekeutha* 'contain hidden in my heart', *heimai* 'I wear', and *oida* 'I have before my eyes'. In Anglo-Irish there is a perfective aspect that is expressed as *He is after drinking*. "He is in the after-drinking state" is used to express the meaning that "He has already drunk".

These facts show that there is an inferential relationship between a "present state" and the "results of a past event". For example, "he who possesses has acquired" and "he who wears a garment has put it on".

Jespersen also said that by considering *have V-ed* as a perfective aspect, the focus is on completion, on the *V-ed* (-*ed* being a past participle suffix), and on whether an action has been completed or not. On the other hand, by treating *have V-ed* as a perfect tense, the focus is on time, on *have* (-*ed* being a past tense suffix), and on the relation between what happened in the past and the present. This means that from Jespersen's perspective, the V-ed in *have V-ed* can be treated as the referential object of the verb *have* (present tense). The sentence *he has killed a man* is formed by seeing *he* who did something in the past, *killed a man*, as *he* who consistently maintains a result state from this action in the present. Thus, it can be said that it is no accident that the *V-ed* of the English past tense has the same form as the *V-ed* of the past participle. This convergence has a reasonable basis. The reasonable basis is that the predicate *killed a man* has potential referentiality.

266   *The referentiality of predicates*

Thus, since V-ed of the past tense (finite form) and the V-ed of the past participle (non-finite form) are the same and moreover not accidentally so, why do English grammars in general distinguish the two from each other? The answer remains that there are structural parallelisms in the conjugations of finite verbs that form conjugation paradigms.

Finally, this section will briefly discuss how English bare infinitives also have potential referentiality. Huddleston and Pullum (2002: 1184) point out that the *to* of the *to* + V infinitive derives from the homophonous preposition *to*. This is still reflected in contemporary English grammar. First, looking at distributional constraints, neither the infinitive phrase *to* + V nor the prepositional phrase *to* + N can serve as the object of a preposition:

*We are thinking of *to London*.
*We are thinking of *to travel by bus*.

Second, there are antonymous verbs that form pairs (like *persuade* and *dissuade*, *encourage* and *discourage*, and the like) for which the *to* of the infinitive form and the prepositions *from* and *against* have corresponding distributions:

I persuaded her to go.	*I dissuaded her from buying it.*
I encouraged her *to* try it.	I discouraged her *from* trying it.
I warned her *to* stay indoors.	I warned her *against* staying indoors.

However, in the final analysis, English nouns and verbs are distinct from each other. Although it is currently grammatical to say *I agree to it* and *I agree to go*, *it* and *go* cannot be juxtaposed (*I agreed to it and go). The *to* of the infinitive and the preposition *against* also cannot be juxtaposed (*I don't want you warning her to or against). Because of this, the *to* of the infinitive should still be characterized as an additional marker of the V and remain distinct from prepositions. Although this is the case, it is also true that the bare infinitive possesses potential referentiality.

6.6   Chinese is a "nouny" language

Is Chinese a language that puts greater importance on nouns or verbs? Different research orientations lead to different conclusions. Guo Shaoyu (1979: 667, 709) begins with a primary focus on the existence in Chinese of an independent grammatical category for classifiers/measure words and holds that Chinese puts greater importance on nouns. However, unlike Chinese, Indo-European languages generally have morphological "gender" and "number", which moreover are obligatory. Verbs also need to agree with nouns in gender and number. Research in linguistic typology has discovered that "classifiers/measure words" and "number" are complementary forms that embody the same functions. Both conceptually distinguish things that are bound from those that are unbound (Lyons 1977: 277; Shen Jiaxuan 1995).

In addition, Ancient Chinese did not have classifiers. On the other hand, nouns in modern Chinese not only have "noun classifiers", but also verbs also have "verb classifiers"

The referentiality of predicates 267

like *cì* 'time', *biàn* 'time', *huí* 'time', *xià* 'down', *tàng* 'trip', *zhèn* 'short-period', *zāo* 'time', and the like. In general, nouns cannot use these verb classifiers. Zhu Dexi (1985a: 16) clearly states that being able to be modified by a classifier is not a linguistic feature that distinguishes nouns from verbs. Thus, having classifiers is insufficient to prove that Chinese is a language that places greater importance on nouns.

Taking a position that is the opposite of Guo's, Liu Danqing (2010) offers many facts to demonstrate that there are many situations where English uses nouns to express what Chinese expresses with verbs and so holds that Chinese is a language that puts greater importance on verbs. However, Chen admits to having no way to explain the important fact that Chinese nouns can function as predicates. It is explained in Section 1 that nouns functioning as predicates is a much more important feature of the language than verbs functioning as subjects and objects.

According to the verbs-as-nouns framework, Chinese verbs are nouns. They are a subcategory of a super-noun category. From this perspective, Chinese assigns greater importance to nouns. From another perspective, verbs are a special category within the super-noun category. Besides having referentiality, verbs also have predicative properties, something ordinary nouns do not have. From this other perspective, Chinese assigns greater importance to verbs. However, a key point of the verbs-as-nouns theory is that verbs are also nouns and that predicate expressions have referentiality. There is a similar situation in other languages like Tagalog and Tongan (Section 7 of Chapter 3 in this volume and Chapter 2 in Volume II). These languages are consistently classified as nominalism in linguistic typology literature. This is the opposite of the verb-centered orientation of Indo-European languages. For Chinese, the significance of nouns being a language's foundation is that it is a "nouny" language. It gives greater importance to nouns. The verbs-as-nouns theory can explain the important fact that nouns can function as predicates and it can also explain why there are many situations where English uses nouns where Chinese uses verbs. Each of these facts will be explained in the following examples.

Exclamatory cheer:	*Obama! Obama!* *Huānyíng àobāmǎ! (Welcome Obama!)*
Curses and insults:	Death to the invaders! *Ràng qīnlüè zhě qù sǐ ba!* (Let the invaders die!)
Petitions and exhortations:	Shorter working time! *Suōduǎn gōngzuò shíjiān!* (Shorten working time!)
Prohibitions and dissuasion:	No smoking! *Jìnzhǐ xīyān* (Don't smoke!; *Jìnzhǐ* 'prohibit' occurs before an action to mark that action as being prohibited.)
Reminders and warnings:	Wet paint. *Yóuqī wèi gān* (The paint isn't dry yet.)

This shows quite precisely that it is normal to use verbs in English and that the use of nouns is exceptional. Consider prohibitions for example. The strength of the prohibition *No smoking* is obviously greater than *Don't smoke*.

268 *The referentiality of predicates*

Where English has the noun determiner *all*, Chinese must use the adverb *dōu* 'all':

All the students are gone.

(*Suǒyǒu*)	*xuéshēng*	*dōu*	*zǒu*	*le.*
(all)	students	all	leave	PSP

*Suǒyǒu	*xuéshēng*	*zǒu*	*le.*
*all	students	leave	PSP

Where English can omit a predicate's verb, Chinese cannot, as shown in the following:

I ate noodles, and he rice.

Wǒ	*chī*	*le*	*miàntiáo,*	*tā*	** (chī*	*le)*	*mǐfàn.*
I	eat	PSP	noodles	he	* (eat	PSP)	rice.

However, as already explained before, *chī le miàntiáo* 'eat le noodles' can serve as the object of the verb *shì* 'be' as in *Wǒ shì chīle miàntiáo* 'it is the case that I am eating noodles'. Thus, *chī le miàntiáo* has referentiality. In addition, Chinese can say *wǒ miàntiáo, tā mǐfàn* 'I noodles, he rice' or *chū yī jiǎozi, shíwǔ tāngyuán* 'On the first, dumplings, on the 15th, glutinous rice balls'. English cannot say 'I noodles and he rice'. English allows for the omission of a verb based on identity with a preceding verb precisely because English independent clauses must have a verb in the predicate.

Where English uses attributes, Chinese must use complements or adverbial modifiers as in the following:

To marry the wrong man

jià	cuò	le	rén
marry	wrong	PSP	person

To make a pot of thick soup

nóng	nóng	de	zhǔ	le	yī	guō	tāng
thick	thick	MM	cook	PSP	one	pot	soup

Chapter 1 in Volume II will explain that it is precisely because Chinese verbs are a subgroup of nouns that Chinese complements are a kind of object, a "dynamic resultative object" and Chinese adverbials a kind of attribute, "dynamic attributes".

English has a greater variety and larger number of nouns that can be used as verbs than Chinese has. English nouns are relatively dynamic in this regard while it is rare in Chinese. For example, English can say *to pie the demonstrators*. Chinese cannot say *xiànbǐng le shìwēi zhě* 'pie le demonstrators'. However, Section 2 of Chapter 5 has already shown that Classical Chinese has as

The referentiality of predicates   269

great a variety and as large a number of monosyllabic nouns that can be used as verbs as English.

The reason why modern Chinese disyllabic nouns are rarely used as verbs (*duǎnxìn wǒ* 'short message me;' *shìdiǎn Xiǎojìnzhuāng* (place name) 'experimental unit Xiaojinzhuang') is because disyllabic nouns' emptying in the direction of verbs is still not very great in the verbs-as-nouns framework (Section 2 of Chapter 4 in Volume II). With respect to occurring with an object, all Chinese verbs can take an object (with the qualification that the type of object is often different depending on the verb). Objects in Chinese can be dropped. The objects of transitive verbs in English cannot be dropped. This clearly shows that Chinese has no "pure" predicate verbs.

In summary, all of the characteristics that Liu (2010) says show Chinese to be a verby language can be explained by the verbs-as-nouns theory: i. verbal predicates lack the finite-nonfinite distinction. This shows precisely that verbs, that is to say, "dynamic nouns", have yet to divide off from the super-noun category. ii. The morpho-syntactic link between subjects and predicates is fairly loose. This actually shows that Chinese does not have pure predicates. Predicates are comments on topics and are referring expressions. iii. Verbs can directly serve as subjects, objects, and modifiers. This is precisely because verbs are themselves nouns. As for adjectives being classified as verbs in a broad sense and not as nouns, this does not show that Chinese puts more importance on verbs since verbs are a type of nouns. The verbs-as-nouns theory can also help to explain the "noun bias" in children's acquisition of nouns and verbs.

From the perspective of nominalism, Chinese puts greater importance on nouns. It is a nouny language. The so-called dynamic qualities of verbs can all be explained based on nominalism. From the perspective of dynamic evolution, Chinese nouns that express actions are transforming into verbs. However, they have yet to completely separate from nouns to become an independent verb category. Because of this, there is no nominalization in Chinese. Regarding the nominalism of Chinese, the reader can also consult Xu Tongqiang (2008: 73–77) as well as Wang Wenbin (2013) and Wang Wenbin and He Qingqiang (2014) for arguments based on spatiality.

This chapter's discussion can be summarized as follows. The main feature that differentiates Chinese from Indo-European languages is not that "Chinese verbs can act as subjects and objects". Rather, it is that "Chinese nouns can act as predicates". The reason why Chinese nouns can act as predicates is not because nouns have predicative properties but because Chinese predicates have referentiality. Chinese does not have pure predicates. What is called a predicate is a comment on a topic, which, moreover possesses referentiality.

In the past, studies of Chinese had English as their starting point. The focus was on verbs, how they acted as predicates and subjects and objects. It was believed that Chinese verbs underwent nominalization and that there was a difference in form between finite and nonfinite verbs. None of this corresponded to the realities of the Chinese language.

By having a Chinese starting point in the investigation of English, the focus turns to nouns, how they act as subjects and objects or predicates. This approach

270 *The referentiality of predicates*

notices that English nouns cannot directly act as referring expressions and that predicates are quasi-referring expressions or potential referring expressions.

From the dynamic perspective of linguistic evolution, grammatical characteristics develop as the result of the emptying of pragmatic categories (Chapter 4, Section 4.3). The category of verbs is an offshoot of the super-noun category (Volume II, Chapter 2, Section 5). Thus, taking Chinese as the starting point in the investigation of other languages has great significance for linguistic typology and evolutionary linguistics, which can at least offset the biases of previous investigations.

The recognition that Chinese predicates have referentiality can also explain the phenomenon of nouns being modified by adverbs as in *Xiǎo Wáng yě huáng tóufǎ* 'Xiao Wang (a name) also yellow hair' and *wǒ yǐjīng dàxuéshēng le* 'I already university student' as well as the phenomenon of nouns acting as adverbial modifiers as in *diànhuà liánxì* 'telephone connect' and *xiàoliǎn xiāng yíng* 'smiling face welcome each other'. This will be explained in the next chapter when the question of adverbials is discussed.

In the sense that for Chinese usage includes grammar and grammar is based on usage, Chinese is a usage-type language (see Chapter 4, Section 4.3). Likewise, in the sense that for Chinese the noun category includes verbs and verbs are based on nouns, Chinese is a "nouny" language. Taken as a whole, the two claims are compatible with each other.

Notes

1 This would have been used in the past by a caller or a call receiver to confirm that the intended party was reached by phone (trs).
2 According to Su Xiaoqing and Wan Lianzeng (2011: 335), in Jiangsu's Ganyu dialect it is possible to say sentences like the following: *hélǐ hěn yú le* 'river-inside very fish particle' (There are a lot of fish in the river), *tā jiā hěn qián le* 'his home very money particle' (His family has a lot of money), and *jīntiān hěn rén le* 'today very people particle' (there are a lot of people today). This kind of use for the degree adverb *hěn* 'very' is different from how the modifier is used in Mandarin sentences like *tā hěn shūnǚ* 'she very lady' (she is very ladylike).
3 Zhǎng is functioning here as a verb that means 'to be a leader'. Its basic meaning is 'elder' or 'leader' (trs).
4 *Guǎrén* was used in self reference by rulers in Ancient China (trs).
5 Zhu Dexi (1982: 146) refers to this kind of attribute as a quasi-attribute. Given that the loose semantic relationship between subjects and predicates in Chinese is a general phenomenon, it also can be acknowledged that this kind of attribute is a general attribute.
6 The lexical item "tead" in the English sentence "We tead at the vicarage" is indisputably an authentic verb for this reason. (See Chapter 5, Section 2.1.)
7 *Chūnrì* is the name of the third month in the Xia calendar, a calendar used in ancient China (trs).
8 C.-T. James Huang (1988) calls *tā yǒu méi yǒu qù?* 'he have not have go' (did he go?) a perfective sentence. However, perfective sentences are actually a kind of existential sentence. The difference is that existential sentences' sentential meaning refers to the existence of a person or thing while a perfective sentence's sentential meaning refers to the existence of a matter or action.
9 The Chinese characters are transliterated into Mandarin. The translators did not have access to transliterations of the Fuzhou dialect (trs).

The referentiality of predicates   271

10 The characters here are also transliterated into Mandarin (trs).
11 The characters representing the Shanghai dialect sentence are transliterated into Mandarin (trs).
12 There is an example from Wang Shuo: Nǐ pěng tā, tā <u>yǒu</u> bù ài tīng yě bù huì xiàng nǐ mà tā nàyàng yǐnchū shēnchóudàhèn 'you flatter he, he <u>have</u> not love hear also not will like you curse he that manner arouse deep-hatred' (If you flatter him, he won't like to hear it and he won't curse him arousing deep hatreds like you.)
13 A kang is a brick structure with an internal oven that was commonly found in northern Chinese homes before the introduction of modern heating. Its top was often covered with mats and provided a place to sit and eat during the day and a place to sleep at night (trs).
14 This kind of analysis helps in picking out contrastive topics. Some people doubt that contrastive topics are topics because they convey new information. Actually, all that is going on is that contrastive topics have as their stronger of two roles that of comment as with *tā ne* 'she particle' (as for her) in *nǐ bù qù; tā ne, gèng bù huì qù* 'you not go, she particle, even not will go' (If you don't go, it is even more likely she won't.)
15 An idiom meaning to do the impossible (trs).
16 Clause here clearly does not refer to clause as used in English where a clause has a complete subject and predicate. The majority of clauses in Chinese are minor sentences.
17 Wang Hongjun (2011) advocates replacing "segment" with "pause".
18 Li Zuofeng (2004: 455–482) agrees with Chao's position. He contends that all Ancient Chinese clauses that express concessions, reasons, conditions, and the like "are juxtaposed sentences from a formal point of view". Moreover, he divides complex sentences into two types: Compound sentences for which no topic-comment relation exists and modifier-head relations, which have a topic-comment relation.
19 This example was pointed out and provided by Xu Liqun.
20 This shows that the position that considers Ancient Chinese to be a precategorial language (Section 5.1, Chapter 5) is untenable.
21 Xu Peiyuan's explanation (in a personal correspondence) of the social conventions surrounding writing poetry to a set rhyme was helpful in translating this title (trs).
22 There has been a lot of discussion of this couplet's structure. It would be awkward to analyze it according to a "subject-verb-object" argument structure. The natural analysis would be as a "topic-comment" structure. "Parrot grain" and "phoenix branch" are the comments on the earlier topics. (See Tsao Feng-fu 2004b.)
23 A *li* was about a third of a mile (trs).
24 The final syllables in the names Sūn Xíngzhě and Hú Shìzhī are grammatical particles. The final syllable in Zhào Shǒuchéng is a verb (trs).
25 Disyllabic words that have a non-compositional meanings (trs).
26 Literally formal verbs (trs).
27 *Bǎ* is a form that historically was a full verb meaning 'take'. It now occurs before a nominal constituent that is often understood to correspond to what would be the following verb's grammatical object in sentences with a verb-object word order (trs).
28 Yīnpíng is a high level tone. It is one of the phonemic tones in Cantonese (trs).
29 This section's content is the result of in-depth discussions with Wang Wei. See Wang Wei and Shen Jiaxuan (2011).
30 Note that in the Chinese translations, the quantity word *yī* 'one' occurs before the verbal constituents *gēn tā xià qí* and *chī zǎofàn* 'eat breakfast'. This shows that the duration of the active behavior is short and that the verbal phrase has referentiality.
31 English *have V-ed* cannot co-occur with a word or phrase denoting a past time. German does not have this restriction.

   *I have seen her yesterday.
   Ich habeihngesterngesehen. (yesterday, I saw her)

272 *The referentiality of predicates*

Why is this? Jespersen states that the perfect tense has two sides—an event that occurred in the past and the resulting state in the present; it is hard to maintain a stable balance between the two sides. The perfect tense often evolves into a pure past tense as with English *drove, sang, held* and like forms that have already undergone this evolution. For these forms, to express the meaning of the perfect, it is now necessary to add *have* in the present tense as in *have driven* and the like. The addition of *have* is a complex roundable way to denote the prefect tense found in many languages (see Mallet *Linguistique historique et linguistique générale*). The perfect tense's evolution towards a past tense is gradual because of the great difficulties in distinguishing the present results of a past action from the past action itself. Because the extent of this evolution is still fairly limited in English, its perfect tense cannot cooccur with words and phrases denoting a past event. This change's evolution is further along in German than in English. The reason for why it is possible to say *wǒ zuótiān yǒu jiànguò tā* 'I yesterday have see-past her yesterday' or *wǒ zuótiān jiàn dào le tā* 'I yesterday see to le her' is because Chinese verbs do not have tense. The *yǒu* for the present and the *yǒu* for the past are both *yǒu*.

References

Bai, Shuo (2014) 'Lun *zhe ben shu de chuban* yu X-bar lilun de jianrongxing' ('On the Compatibility of *Zhe Ben Shu de Chuban* with X-bar Theory'), http://blog.sina.com.cn/s/blog-729574a00102uzf6.html.

Chao, Yuen Ren (1955) 'Notes on Chinese Grammar and Logic', *Philosophy East and West* V(1): 31–41, also in A. S. Dil (ed) *Aspects of Chinese Sociolinguistics: Essays by Yuen Ren Chao*, Stanford: Stanford University Press, 237–249. Translated as 'Hanyu Yufa yu Luoji Zatan' by Bai Shuo, in *Essays in Linguistics by Yuen Ren Chao*, 2002, Beijing: The Commercial Press, 796–808.

Chao, Yuen Ren (1968) *A Grammar of Spoken Chinese*, Berkeley and Los Angeles: University of California Press. Translated as *Hanyu Kouyu Yufa* by Lü Shuxiang in 1979, Beijing: The Commercial Press, and as *Zhongguohua de Wenfa* (Revised edition) by Pang-hsin Ting in 2002, Hong Kong: The Chinese University of Hong Kong Press.

Chao, Yuen Ren (1970) 'Guoyu tongyi zhong fangyan duibi de ge fangmian' ('Aspects of Contrasting Dialects in the National Language Unity'), *Bulletin of the Institute of Ethnology, Academia Sinica* 29: 37–42.

Chao, Yuen Ren (1975) 'Rhythm and Structure in Chinese Word Conceptions', *Journal of Archeology and Anthropology* XXXVII and XXXVIII, also in A. S. Dil (ed) *Aspects of Chinese Sociolinguistics: Essays by Yuen Ren Chao*, Stanford: Stanford University Press, 275–292. Translated as 'Hanyu Ci de Gainian Jiqi Jiegou he Jiezou' by Wang Hongjun, in *Essays in Linguistics by Yuen Ren Chao*, 2002, Beijing: The Commercial Press, 890–908.

Chen, Chengze (1922/1982) *Guowenfa Caochuang* (*Draft of Chinese Grammar*), Shanghai and Beijing: The Commercial Press.

Chen, Manhua (2008) *Tici Weiyu Ju Yanjiu* (*A Study of Sentences with Substantive Predicate*), Beijing: China Federation of Literary and Art Circles Publishing House.

Chen, Xiao (2009) 'Lun zhege/nage+VP teshu jiegou' ('A Study of the Special Structure of This/That+VP'), *Nankai Linguistics* 2: 97–107.

Chen, Zeping (1998) *Fuzhou Fangyan Yanjiu* (*A Study of Fuzhou Dialect*), Fuzhou: Fujian People's Publishing House.

The referentiality of predicates 273

Chen, Zhuqin (2009) '"Zichan er si" "fu er ke qiu" lei juzi de yuyi wenti' ('Semantic Issues in the Sentences Like *Zichan Er Si* and *Fu Er Ke Qiu*'), *Journal of School of Chinese Language and Culture Nanjing Normal University* 2: 159–165.

Coulthard, M. (1977) *An Introduction to Discourse Analysis*, London: Longman.

Diao, Yanbin (2004) 'Shilun xiandai hanyu xingshi dongci de gongneng' ('On the Function of Dummy Verbs in Modern Chinese'), *Journal of Ningxia University* (*Social Science Edition*) 3: 33–38.

Diao, Yanbin and Yanyan Li (2010) 'Shilun *you*+danyinjie dongsu shi dongci' ('A Discussion of the Verb Structure of *You*+Monosyllabic Morpheme'), *Language Teaching and Linguistic Studies* 1: 38–43.

Dong, Xiufang (2004) '*Shi* de jinyibu yufahua: you xuci dao cinei chengfen' ('Further Grammaticalization of *Shi*: From Functional Word to Word-Internal Element'), *Contemporary Linguistics* 1: 35–44.

Dong, Xiufang (2012) 'Shanggu hanyu yilun yupian de jiegou tedian: jianlun lianxi yupian jiegou fenxi xuci de gongneng' ('Structures and Features of the Argumentative Texts in Archaic Chinese: A Discourse Analysis of *Fu* and *Jin*'), *Studies of the Chinese Language* 4: 356–366.

Edmondson, W. (1981) *Spoken Discourse: A Model for Analysis*, London: Longman.

Fan, Jiyan (1985) 'Hanyu juduan jiegou' ('The Structure of Sentence Segments in Chinese'), *Studies of the Chinese Language* 1: 52–61.

Fang, Mei (2011) 'Beijinghua de liangzhong xingwei zhicheng xingshi' ('Two Patterns of Action Reference in Colloquial Beijing Mandarin'), *Dialect* 4: 368–377.

Fu, Yu (2010) 'Zuijian jufa kuangjia xia de weici shenglüe yanjiu' ('A Study of the VP-ellipsis in the Framework of the Minimalist Syntax'), *Journal of Foreign Languages* 4: 253–267.

Goffman, E. (1976) 'Replies and Responses', *Language in Society* 5: 257–313.

Guo, Shaoyu (1979) *Hanyu Yufa Xiuci Xintan* (*New Explorations of Chinese Grammar and Rhetoric*), Beijing: The Commercial Press.

Harbsmeier, Christoph (1983–1985) 'Where Do Classical Chinese Nouns Come From?', *Early China* 9–10: 77–163.

Hu, Mingyang and Song Jin (1989) 'Liushuiju chutan' ('A Preliminary Study of Flowing Sentences'), *Language Teaching and Linguistic Studies* 4: 42–54.

Huang, C. T. James (1988) 'Shuo *shi* he *you*' ('On *Be* and *Have* in Chinese'), *Zhongyanyuan Lishi Yuyan Yanjiusuo Jikan* (*Bulletin of the Institute of History and Philology, Academia Sinica*) 59(1): 43–64.

Huddleston, R. and G. K. Pullum (2002) *The Cambridge Grammar of the English Language*, Cambridge: Cambridge University Press.

Jespersen, Otto (1924) *The Philosophy of Grammar*, London: George Allen & Unwin Ltd.

Jiang, Shaoyu (1990) *Tangshi Yuyan Yanjiu* (*A Linguistic Study of Tang Poetry*), Zhengzhou: Zhongzhou Guji Press.

Jiang, Zixia and Chongming Ding (2011) 'Xuyi dongci de wanju gongneng ji tedian: yi *jinxing* weili' ('On the Sentence-Completing Function of Delexical Verb: A Case Analysis of *Jinxing*'), *Chinese Language Learning* 2: 83–88.

Jo, Jung-Min (2000) 'Morphosyntax of a Dummy Verb *ha-* in Korean', *Studies in the Linguistic Sciences* 30(2): 77–100.

Lan, Ying (1990) 'Cong shaoshu minzu yuyan kan *er* de xuhua yanbian' ('The Delexicalization of *Er* as Seen from Minority Languages'), *Research in Ancient Chinese Language* 1: 64–70.

274 *The referentiality of predicates*

Li, Rulong (1986) 'Minnanhua de *you* he *wu*' ('*You* and *Wu* in Minnan Dialect'), *Journal of Fujian Normal University* (*Philosophy and Social Sciences Edition*) 2: 76–83.

Li, Zhanbing and Lixin Jin (2012) 'Binglie biaozhi de leixingxue kaocha' ('A Typological Study of Coordinate Markers'), *Minority Languages of China* 4: 23–31.

Li, Zuofeng (1985) 'Zuozhuan *riyoushizhi* zhong de *you*' ('The *You* in *Ri You Shi Zhi* in *Zuo Tradition*'), *Journal of Inner Mongolia University* 2: 111–119.

Li, Zuofeng (2004) *Gudai Hanyu Yufaxue* (*A Grammar of Ancient Chinese*), Beijing: The Commercial Press.

Liu, Danqing (ed) (2008) *Yufa Diaocha Yanjiu Shouce* (*A Handbook for Grammatical Investigation and Research*), Shanghai: Shanghai Educational Publishing House.

Liu, Danqing (2010) 'Hanyu shi yizhong dongcixing yuyan' ('Chinese as a Verby Language'), *Chinese Teaching in the World* 1: 3–17.

Lu, Bingfu (2012) 'Hanying zhuyao shijian mingci de yuyi tezheng' ('The Semantic Characteristics of Event Nouns in Chinese and English'), *Contemporary Linguistics* 1: 1–11.

Lü, Shuxiang (1942/1982) *Zhongguo Wenfa Yaolüe* (*Essentials of Chinese Grammar*), Shanghai and Beijing: The Commercial Press.

Lü, Shuxiang (1954) 'Guanyu hanyu cilei de yixie yuanzexing wenti' ('Some Fundamental Problems about Chinese Word Classes'), *Studies of the Chinese Language* 9: 6–14, 10: 16–22.

Lü, Shuxiang (1979) *Hanyu Yufa Fenxi Wenti* (*Problems in Chinese Grammatical Analysis*), Beijing: The Commercial Press.

Lyons, J. (1977) *Semantics*, vol. 2, Cambridge: Cambridge University Press.

Shen, Jiaxuan (1989) 'Budai shuoming de huati' ('Topics without Comments'), *Studies of the Chinese Language* 5: 326–333.

Shen, Jiaxuan (1995) 'Youjie yu wujie' ('Boundedness and Unboundedness'), *Studies of the Chinese Language* 5: 367–380.

Shen, Jiaxuan (2008) 'Yiwei haishi yiqing: xi *ta shi qunian sheng de haizi*' ('Moving What? On Emotional Movement in *Ta Shi Qunian Sheng de Haizi*'), *Studies of the Chinese Language* 5: 387–395.

Shen, Jiaxuan (2011) 'Cong youya zhunze kan liangzhong dongdan mingshuang shuo' ('Two Views on Monosyllabic Verbs and Disyllabic Nouns as Seen from the Principle of Elegance'), Paper presented at the Third Cross-Strait Mini-Symposium on Modern Chinese Syntax and Semantics for the Mainland, Taiwan, Hong Kong and Macau.

Shen, Jiaxuan (2012a) 'Lingju he liushuiju: wei Zhao Yuanren xiansheng danchen 120 zhounian erzuo' ('On Minor Sentences and Flowing Sentences in Chinese: In Commemoration of the 120th Anniversary of the Birth of Yuen Ren Chao'), *Studies of the Chinese Language* 5: 403–415.

Shen, Jiaxuan (2012b) 'Lun xushi xiangsi yuanli: yunlü he yufa zhijian de niuqu duiying' ('On the Principle of Fullness Iconicity: The Skewed Correspondence Between Prosody and Grammar'), *CASLAR* (*Chinese as a Second Language and Research*) 1(1): 89–103, Berlin: De Gruyter Mouton.

Shen, Jiaxuan and Y. Gu (1997) 'Conversation and Sentence-hood', *Text* 17–4: 477–490.

Shen, Jiaxuan and Jiangzhi Zhang (2013) 'Yetan xingshi dongci de gongneng' ('On the Grammatical Function of Dummy Verbs in Chinese'), *TCSOL Studies* 2: 8–17.

Shi, Qisheng (1996) 'Lun *you* zi ju' ('On Sentences with *You*'), *Studies in Language and Linguistics* 1: 26–31.

Simon, Walter (1951) '*Der erl jiann* and *der jiann* in *Luenyeu* (VII, 25)', *Asia Major* 2(1): 46–67.

Simon, Walter (1952 & 1954) 'Functions and Meanings of *erl* (I-IV)', *Asia Major* 2(2): 179–202, 3(1): 7–18, 3(2): 117–131, 4(1): 20–35.

Song, Hongmin (2009) 'Yetan ming *er* dong jiegou' ('On the NP *er* VP Construction'), *Studies of the Chinese Language* 2: 184–187.

Song, Rou (2013) 'Hanyu pianzhang guangyi huati jiegou de liushui moxing' ('A Stream Model of Generalized Topic Structure in Chinese Text'), *Studies of the Chinese Language* 6: 483–494.

Sperber, D. and D. Wilson (1986) *Relevance: Communication and Cognition*, Oxford: Basil Blackwell.

Su, Xiaoqing and Lianzeng Wan (2011) *Ganyu Fangyan Yanjiu* (*Studies on the Ganyu Dialect*), Beijing: Zhonghua Book Company.

Tsao, Feng-fu (2004a) 'Tangshi dui'ouju de xingshi tiaojian yu pianzhang xiuci gongneng' ('Formal Conditions and Discourse Rhetorical Functions of Couplets in the Tang Poetry'), in *Cong Yuyanxue Kan Wenxue: Tang Song Jintishi San Lun* (*Literature as Seen from Linguistics: Three Topics on Modern-Style Poetry in the Tang and Song Dynasties*), Taipei: Institute of Linguistics, Academia Sinica, 97–173.

Tsao, Feng-fu (2004b) 'Cong zhuti-pinglun de guandian kan tongsongshi de jufa yu shangxi' ('Syntax and Appreciation of the Tang and Song Poetry from a Theme-Comment Perspective'), in *Cong Yuyanxue Kan Wenxue: Tang Song Jintishi San Lun* (*Literature as Seen from Linguistics: Three Topics on Modern-Style Poetry in the Tang and Song Dynasties*), Taipei: Institute of Linguistics, Academia Sinica, 49–96.

Wang, Dongmei (2014) 'Cong *shi* he *de you* he *le* kan kending he xushu' ('Distinction between Assertion and Narration: With Reference to the Contrast of *Shi* vs. *You* and *De* vs. *Le*'), *Studies of the Chinese Language* 1: 22–34.

Wang, Guoshuan and Qingzhu Ma (2008) 'Putonghua zhong zouxiang duicheng de *you*+VP+(*le*) jiegou' ('The Grammatical Symmetry of the *you*+VP+(*le*) Structure in Putonghua'), *Nankai Linguistics* 2: 87–91.

Wang, Hongjun (2011) 'Hanyu yufa de jiben danwei yu yanjiu celüe (zuozhe buji)' ('The Eseential Units of Chinese Grammar and Research Strategies (Author's Addendum)'), in *Jiben Danwei de Xiandai Hanyu Cifa Yanjiu* (*A Study of Morphology of Basic Units in Modern Chinese*), Beijing: The Commercial Press, 414–420.

Wang, Hongjun and Rong Li (2014) 'Lun hanyu yupian de jiben danwei he liushuiju de chengyin' ('On the Basic Units of Chinese Texts and the Causes of the Flowing Sentence'), *Essays on Linguistics* 49: 11–40.

Wang, Li (2005) *Hanyu Shilüxue* (*Chinese Poetics*), 2nd ed., Shanghai: Shanghai Educational Publishing House.

Wang, Wei (2010) '*Le*$_1$ biao *you* lun: hanying duibi chutan' ('On *Le*$_1$ Denoting *You*: A Preliminary Contrastive Study between Chinese and English'), Paper presented at The 18th Annual Conference of the International Association of Chinese Linguistics (IACL-18) and the 22nd North American Conference on Chinese Linguistics (NACCL-22), Harvard University.

Wang, Wei and Jiaxuan Shen (2011) 'Hanyu weishenme meiyou zhenzheng de weiyu: mingdong de zhicheng/shuwei buduicheng' ('Why There Is No Real Predicate in Chinese: The Reference/Predication Asymmetry of Nouns and Verbs'), Paper presented at the Third Cross-Strait Mini-Symposium on Modern Chinese Syntax and Semantics for the Mainland, Taiwan, Hong Kong and Macau.

Wang, Wenbin (2013) 'Lun yingyu de shijianxing tezhi yu hanyu de kongjianxing tezhi' ('On the Trait of Temporality in English and that of Spatiality in Chinese'), *Foreign Language Teaching and Research* 3: 163–173.

276 *The referentiality of predicates*

Wang, Wenbin and Qingqiang He (2014) 'Lun yingyu *be* yu hanyu *shi/you/zai*' ('An Analysis of English *Be* and Chinese *Shi/You/Zai*'), *Journal of Foreign Languages* 5: 2–10.

Wu, Chunsheng and Beijia Ma (2014) 'Ming *er* dong jiegou bushuo' ('A Supplement to the NP+*er*+VP Construction'), *Studies of the Chinese Language* 2: 116–126.

Xu, Tongqiang (2008) *Hanyu Zibenwei Yufa Daolun* (*An Introduction to Character-Based Grammar of Chinese*), Jinan: Shandong Education Press.

Xue, Fengsheng (1991) 'Shilun lianci *er* de yuyi yu yufa gongneng' ('On the Semantic and Syntactic Functions of the Conjunction *Er*'), *Linguistic Research* 1: 55–62.

Yang, Rongxiang (2008) 'Lun ming *er* dong jiegou de laiyuan jiqi yufa xingzhi' ('On the Origin and Grammatical Features of the NP *er* VP Construction'), *Studies of the Chinese Language* 3: 239–246.

Yu, Aiqin (2009) 'Ruhe jiehe fangyan he gudai wenxian yanjiu hanyu de lishi: yi *you* de yongfa weili' ('How to Study the History of Chinese in Combination with Dialects and Ancient Documents: The Case of the Usage of *You*'), Lecture at the Institute of Linguistics, Chinese Academy of Social Sciences.

Zhang, Bin (ed) (2010) *Xiandai Hanyu Miaoxie Yufa* (*A Descriptive Grammar of Modern Chinese*), Beijing: The Commercial Press.

Zhang, Hongnian (1972) *Xianggang Yueyu Yufa de Yanjiu* (*A Study of Hong Kong Cantonese Grammar*), Hong Kong: The Chinese University of Hong Kong Press.

Zhang, Jiangzhi (2013) 'Tici weiyu ju he hanyu cilei' ('Sentences with Substantive Predicate and Chinese Word Classes'), Doctoral Dissertation, Graduate School of Chinese Academy of Social Sciences.

Zhang, Jie (2011) 'Putonghua fuci *zai* yuanliu kaobian' ('An Investigation of the Origin and Evolvement of the Adverb *Zai* in Mandarin'), *Language Teaching and Linguistic Studies* 1: 76–81.

Zhang, Risheng (1959) 'Xianggang yueyu yinpingdiao ji biantiao wenti' ('Dark Level Tone in Hong Kong Cantonese and the Problem of Tone Sandhi'), *Journal of Chinese Studies* 2(1): 81–107.

Zhang, Yujin (2010) 'Chutu zhanguo wenxian zhong de yuqici *ye*' ('*Ye* in the Unearthed Literatures from Warring States Period'), in Xiancheng Zhang (ed) *Jianbo Yuyan Wenzi Yanjiu* (*Studies on the Language of Bamboo Slips and Silk Manuscripts*), vol. 5, Chengdu: Bashu Press, 197–252.

Zhang, Zhongxing (1992) *Shici Duxie Conghua* (*Talks on Poetry Reading and Writing*), Beijing: People's Education Press.

Zheng, Minhui (2009) 'Fuzhou fangyan *you*+VP jushi de yuyi he yuyong gongneng' ('On Semantic and Pragmatic Function of *You* +VP Construction in Fuzhou Dialect'), *Journal of Fujian Normal University* (*Philosophy and Social Sciences Edition*) 6: 92–98.

Zheng, Wenping and Wei Cao (2007) 'Shuihu Zhuan zhong binglie lianci yongfa fenbu jiliang kaocha' ('A Quantitative Study of the Coordinate Conjunctions in *The Marshes of Mount Liang*'), *Journal of Changshu Institute of Technology* (*Philosophy and Social Sciences*) 5: 94–98.

Zhu, Dexi (1982) *Yufa Jiangyi* (*Lectures on Chinese Grammar*), Beijing: The Commercial Press.

Zhu, Dexi (1985a) *Yufa Dawen* (*Answering Questions about Chinese Grammar*), Beijing: The Commercial Press.

Zhu, Dexi (1985b) 'Xiandai shumian hanyu li de xuhua dongci he mingdongci' ('Delexicalized Verbs and Nouny Verbs in Modern Written Chinese'), *Journal of Peking University* (*Philosophy and Social Sciences*) 5: 1–6.

Subject index

abstract noun 24, 57, 62, 146
abstract verb 22
adjective 8–10, 12, 16–19, 27, 41–42, 44, 47, 51–52, 55, 71, 73, 75–77, 79–83, 85, 95–96, 100, 106, 113, 115–119, 121–126, 134, 151, 158, 164, 182, 197, 226, 248, 250, 252, 269; adjectival predicate 47, 151; non-predicative adjective 81; participial adjective 47
adjunct 71
adverbial-*de* 96–97, 132
adversative 242–243
affirmation 168, 219; affirmative 2, 145, 167–169, 186, 211, 221, 224, 233
affix 182, 198–199; infix 199; prefix 227, 230; suffix 18, 26, 32, 37, 39, 51, 121, 146–147, 182, 253, 265
agent 47, 73, 75, 126–127, 129, 134, 166, 179, 199
agentive object 186
agreement 4, 33–34, 154, 156–157, 167–168, 171; agreement property 33–34; disagreement 11, 167–168, 210
ambiguity 105; ambiguous 37, 64, 230
ambitransitive alternation 166
analogy 65, 75, 134, 171, 198
answer-positioning type 167–168
antithesis 247–248, 252–254
argument 9, 18, 26, 41–43, 91, 94, 126, 132–134, 139, 154, 156–159, 166, 170, 176, 182–183, 193–194, 197, 207, 209, 212, 221, 232–233, 244, 247, 254, 256, 262, 269, 271
article 9, 37, 39, 51, 53, 67, 92–94, 123, 132–133, 145, 167, 186, 196, 238, 243, 246–247, 261
aspect 31, 91, 224, 228, 230, 264–265

assertion 11, 30, 65–66, 70, 83, 132–133, 159, 163, 169
assertive sentence 24, 47
asymmetry 10, 45, 176–200, 264; asymmetry between nouns and verbs 45, 176–200
attribute-head 8, 76, 79, 84, 125, 204, 252
attributive-*de* 96–98, 132
atypical function 77
auxiliary verb 33, 40, 216, 231

base form 91, 257
bidirectionality 192–193
The Book of Poetry 134
borrowed meaning 252
borrowed pair 252
borrowed sound 252
borrowed Spanish nouns 130
bound 4, 81, 131, 166, 253, 266; unbound 266

case concord 125
Case theory 123
Chinese logic 152–153, 167–168
Chinese words that enter Japanese 131
Chinese words that enter Korean 131
choice question 166, 241
classificatory verb 194–197, 199
classifier 31, 41, 57, 92–94, 97, 132, 181, 187, 190, 231, 241, 259, 266–267; temporal classifier 187; verbal classifier 181, 190
class overlap 60, 80–81, 83, 85; words classed as nouns and verbs 44, 60, 80, 84; words classed as verbs and adjectives 80
clause 17, 22, 40–41, 109–112, 126–127, 133, 153, 191–192, 194–195, 232–233, 238, 264–265, 268, 271;

278 *Subject index*

causal 110; concessive 109–110; conditional 40, 109–110, 133, 153; spatial 110, 153, 169; temporal 109–110, 153, 187, 206
clause subject 111
close contrast 248, 252
cognitive reason 182, 189, 191, 261
cognitive state 139
colloquial 20, 22, 74, 171, 187, 227, 259
comment 128–129, 139, 150–151, 154, 159, 167–169, 199, 233–238, 240, 244, 258, 269, 271
comparative sentence 153
complementarity principle 31
compositionality 191–192
conceptual integration 160–161
condensed form 82
conjunction 98–100, 109–110, 133, 219, 238, 241, 243, 247; conjunctive 59
connotation 59, 81, 160, 189, 260
consistency 4, 7, 28, 45, 47, 51, 71, 171
constitutive 8, 10, 138–172, 264; constitutive relation 10, 138–172; constitutive rule 142–144
The Contemporary Chinese Dictionary 43, 81, 141, 146, 171, 197, 226
content word 14, 42, 76, 102–103, 106–107, 148, 198, 209, 260
contextual 188–189, 193, 196; contextual expression 188–189
continuity connection 241–243
continuum 30, 34, 141, 184
contrastive topic 271
Cooperative Principle 183, 189
coordinate 27, 45, 72, 74, 102
coordination condition 66, 71–72, 75, 166–167, 243
coordination test 11, 71, 166
correlated markedness pattern 47, 77

declarative sentence 150
de construction 8, 204
deep structure 71, 189
default concept 145
definiteness 92–93, 256
deictic expression 188
demonstrative 95, 218, 232, 247, 257; demonstrative pronoun 95, 218, 247
denominal verb 180, 183–185, 188–189
denotation 44, 81, 138, 160, 188; denotational expression 188
depictive 11, 113, 119, 122–123, 134; depictive word 123, 134; non-depictive 11

derivation 27, 160; derivative 134; derive 4, 108, 263, 266
determiner phrase 67–68, 127, 132
deverbal noun 35–37, 39
dhāhu 198–199
diachronic 127
differentiating word 40
direct integration 161
discreteness 31, 47, 77, 98, 170
disjunctive 59
distinguishing word 81–83, 85
distorted relation 132
distribution 27, 32, 36, 76–77, 81, 95–96, 98, 101–102, 106, 138, 140, 162, 176, 196, 205, 224, 266
disyllabification 84–85
DP analysis 68–69
dummy verb 11, 41, 60–63, 85, 254–257, 259, 261
dynamic attribute 268
dynamic noun 1–3, 37, 80, 90–91, 106, 197, 254, 259, 269
dynamic resultative object 268

economy of expression 183–184
eliciting 233–234
ellipsis 149–151, 154; elliptical 82
emotional component 122
emphasis 27–28, 80, 107, 132, 141, 210, 213, 216–217, 223, 232–233, 248, 253, 256–258; marker of emphasis 210
empty verb 254
empty word 59, 188, 196
entity 5, 69, 94, 106, 123, 132, 139, 147–148, 179, 190, 225, 256, 260, 264
exhaustiveness 192, 194
existential verb 223, 244
explanatory 6, 11, 141–142
extraction 127
Ezafe 10, 123–124

finite form 6, 17, 19, 125, 264, 266; non-finite form 19, 125, 264, 266
flexibility 179, 214
flowing sentence 11, 113, 238–240
focus 9, 16, 37, 47, 76, 92, 95, 153, 162, 167, 213–216, 225, 257–258, 262, 265–266, 269
formal feature 107, 109, 133
form class 32–34, 37, 39, 42–43, 45, 47
full sentence 8, 17, 27–30, 79, 107–110, 112–113

Subject index 279

full word 59, 188
functional category 68–69, 85
functional head 182
function word 27, 81, 107, 260

gender 51, 266
generality 34, 105, 191, 197
generalized morphology 76–77
general noun 3
generative grammar 10, 12, 15, 26, 66–68,
  71, 80, 111, 123, 125–127, 131,
  134, 164, 170–171, 182, 189, 209
generic 92–93, 134, 138–139
genitive 35–36, 39, 122, 127–129; genitive
  case marker 127
gerund 16, 33, 35–40, 85, 91, 131; gerund-
  participle 33, 36
grammar 1, 3–4, 6–8, 10–12, 14–21, 26–27,
  30–37, 40, 42–45, 47, 51, 58–61,
  66–68, 71, 75–76, 80–81, 83–85,
  90, 94, 97, 100, 111, 123, 125–127,
  131, 134, 148, 151, 154, 159, 161,
  163–164, 166–172, 177–179, 182–
  183, 185, 189, 198, 209, 222–223,
  225, 231, 238, 240, 243, 266, 270
grammar-type language 168
grammatical category 1, 9, 15, 47, 83,
  140, 146, 151, 154, 164,
  167–168, 210, 266
grammatical class 164, 166
grammatical feature 32, 51–52, 58–60, 102
grammaticalization 151, 154, 168, 170,
  185; grammaticalized 83, 132, 151,
  154, 158, 168, 170–171
grammatical meaning 151–152, 154
grammatical property 16–17, 31, 39, 52,
  102, 210, 223
grammatical system 5–7, 11, 16, 18, 27–28,
  30, 32–33, 45–46, 51, 61, 64–65,
  123, 132, 159, 191, 222–223

head 6, 8, 11, 21, 25, 27, 42, 65–69,
  71, 75–76, 79, 84–85, 105, 117,
  123–125, 160–161, 169–170, 176,
  182, 204, 216, 222, 242, 252, 271;
  adverbial-head 85, 252; attribute-
  head 8, 76, 79, 84, 125, 204,
  252; modifier-head 27, 84,
  242, 252, 271
head feature convention 11, 66–67, 71,
  75, 85, 160–161; head feature
  extension 65–66
historical linguistics 126
homonym 104–105

icon 138
identifiability 47, 126, 133, 170
imperative 33–34, 167; imperative
  sentence 167
implicit copula 126
inclusion 1–3, 7, 11, 80, 83, 91, 102–106,
  123, 133, 140, 158–159, 169–171,
  194, 197; inclusion of predicative
  expressions in referring expressions
  2–3; inclusion of structure in use 1;
  inclusion of verbs in nouns 2–3, 7,
  11, 102, 140
inclusion pattern 1–3, 11, 80, 83, 103–106,
  123, 169–170
inclusive 83, 102, 141
indefiniteness 92
indeterminate syntactic functions of word
  classes 11, 75
index 138–139
indicative mood 11; non-indicative
  11, 123
indirect integration 161
individuality 51–52, 260
infinitive 6, 17–19, 33, 35, 47, 133, 179,
  181, 266
inflection 91, 223; inflectional paradigm 33,
  223; inflectional phrase 68
information structure 129, 169
informative 169
innovative denominal verb 180, 184–185,
  188–189
interface 1, 157, 169
Interpreting Names 146
intonation 112–113, 133, 149–150, 232,
  238, 240
intransitive verb 83, 162, 164, 166,
  182–183, 186, 248

jìngzì 'stative' 134
judgment modality 218
judgment verb 210, 212–214, 217, 223
juxtaposed sentence 113, 271
juxtaposed structure 240–241
juxtaposition 85, 190, 238, 240–241, 247
juxtaposition question 241

kāraka 198

Larson's Shell Hypothesis 123
lenient/wide contrast 248
level of integration 161
lexicalization 219, 253
location word 133
logical domain 242

280 *Subject index*

logical fallacy 81
logical-historical consistency 171

main subject 111
"make the first move" strategy 235
marked 10–11, 18, 27, 34, 77, 92, 102–104, 132, 163, 193, 217, 222, 238, 241–242, 262; non-marked 10; unmarked 10, 77, 102–103, 168, 193
marked combination 77
markedness 10, 47, 77, 102–103, 107; markedness reversal 10, 107; markedness theory 10, 103, 107
Ma's Grammar 14–15, 43, 134, 243
maximal projection 182
maxim of quantity 183
metaphor 139–144, 146–148, 191, 200, 264; constitutive metaphor 139–142, 144, 146; ontological metaphor 147–148, 191, 200, 264; realizational metaphor 139–140, 142, 144, 146
metonymy 200
minor sentence 8, 107, 109–113, 149, 196–197, 205, 209, 234, 236, 238–241, 247, 271; minor sentence theory 107, 149
modal 20, 36, 210, 212–214, 216–217, 219, 228, 236; modal adverb 210, 212–214, 216–217, 219, 228; modal verb 20
modifier 19, 25, 27, 36, 40–41, 84, 96, 166, 169–170, 176, 196, 198, 228, 240, 242, 252, 268–271; modifier-head 27, 84, 242, 252, 271
monosyllabic 8, 12, 20–22, 24, 27, 42, 52, 61, 63, 65, 72, 74, 84, 98, 113, 116, 121–122, 131, 146, 226–227, 251, 253, 259, 269; monosyllabic noun 84, 116, 269; monosyllabic verb 20–21, 24, 61, 63, 65, 84, 116, 122, 227
mood 11, 116, 206, 232
morphology 9, 15, 33, 43, 47, 51, 76–77, 103, 113, 123, 126–128, 130, 222; morphological change 6, 19, 43, 47, 76, 91–92, 179, 181; morphological marker 18, 34, 42, 51, 76–77, 91, 129
morphosyntactic 12, 34
multi-class word 11, 80–81, 83, 85

N + *le* 204
narration 11, 206

narrative sentence 8, 24
narrow morphological standard 76
natural sign language 169
N *de* V 20–21, 27, 75
negation 8, 98, 123, 168, 216, 221; negative 2, 4–5, 7, 15, 60, 75, 102–103, 110, 167–169, 186, 211–212, 223–224, 230, 232, 241
negatively defined 8, 46, 59–60, 75, 85
N (*yě*) *ér* N (*yě*) 246
N *ér* V 11, 196, 243, 247
neutralization 176; neutralized word 176
nominal emptying 259
nominalism 198, 267, 269
nominalization 6–8, 19, 26–27, 32, 42, 45–46, 48, 65, 69–70, 76, 90–91, 102, 125, 133–134, 140, 147, 159, 225, 258, 269; nominalized 16, 18–21, 26–27, 31, 39, 41, 43, 45–46, 65, 69, 84, 182, 197, 200
nominal predicate 11, 110, 150, 182–183, 185–188, 194–196, 203–207, 256
nominative case marker 127
noun bias 269
noun determiner 268
noun-verb 2, 7–9, 11–12, 30, 47, 51, 60, 65, 83, 95, 103, 131, 140, 191, 197; noun-verb confusion 83; noun-verb continuum 30; noun-verb covariation 47; noun-verb distinction 3, 7–9, 11–12, 51, 60, 80–81, 84, 95, 99–100, 103, 131, 140, 191, 197–198
nouny 11, 37, 60–66, 72–73, 75, 80, 84, 266–267, 269–270; nouny adjective 73; nouny verb 11, 60–66, 72, 75, 80, 84
N then N 205
numeral-classifier 41, 259
N *yě ér* V *yě* 247

object 5–9, 14–22, 24–27, 31–32, 37, 39–41, 43–47, 51–52, 59–61, 63–65, 69–70, 72, 74–77, 80, 82–85, 90–91, 94–95, 102, 106, 126, 133–134, 138–140, 146, 157, 162, 165–166, 169–170, 172, 176, 179, 182–183, 186–187, 190–194, 196–200, 203, 210, 216–219, 222–223, 225, 231, 240, 254–259, 261, 264–269, 271
objective judgment 223
obligatory 67, 91, 132, 163, 216, 266
Occam's razor 5, 7, 65, 69

Subject index 281

omission 171, 217, 246, 268
one-to-one correspondence 16, 76–77, 81, 95, 98, 104
oppositional pattern 1, 3, 11, 103–105
optional 91, 132, 216, 219, 231–232, 241
organization of composition 151
original usage 179, 200; non-original usage 179, 200

paradox of material implication 152
parallel construction 205
parameter 10
participle 6, 17–19, 33, 35–36, 39–40, 91, 265–266; past participle 6, 33, 91, 265–266; present participle 6, 33
particularity 185, 188, 191, 197
part and whole 2, 30
pause 107–109, 112–113, 149–150, 213, 223, 233, 238, 240, 271; pause particle 107–109
perfective 110, 228, 230, 265, 270; perfective aspect marker 228
phrasal "fusion" 6
phrase-based 5–7, 18, 27–28, 46
place word 133
polysemy 105; polysemous word 105
positive-negative question 241
possessive relation 155
potential 85, 107, 129, 236, 238, 264–266, 270; potential object 85; potential referring expression 264, 270; potential subject 85; potential topic 236
pragmatics 10, 12, 157, 170; pragmatic category 1, 140, 146, 154, 156, 158, 161, 164, 167–168, 270; pragmatic structure 170
pratyaya 198
precategorial language 191, 194, 271
predicate 6, 8, 11, 16–20, 23–25, 27, 39, 45, 47, 52, 59–60, 69–70, 75–77, 80, 83–84, 90–92, 94–95, 102, 105–113, 123, 126–133, 138–139, 149–151, 153–154, 156–160, 162, 168–169, 171, 182–183, 185–199, 203–272
predicate-complement 27
predicate function 94
predicate logic 139
predicate-object 27, 76, 84, 162
predicate verb 3, 20, 26, 158, 171, 182, 187, 189–191, 269
predicative expression 1–3, 44, 91, 138, 140, 146, 161, 168, 172, 191

predict 120, 191–192; predictable 193–194; unpredictability 193; unpredictable 193
preposition 124–126, 133, 153–154, 263, 266; prepositional 27, 110, 125–126, 263, 266
primary 44–45
primary concept 138
principle of simplicity 3, 5–7, 12, 19, 37, 39, 44–45, 65–66, 69, 123, 125, 131–132, 159, 196, 212
pronoun 95, 122, 154, 169–170, 204, 218, 247
pronoun object 169–170
proper noun 204
proposition 8, 25, 112, 151–153, 168–169, 171
propositional content 168

Q&A-relationship type 167–168
quantifier 39–40, 51–53, 57–60, 63, 95
quasi-attribute 270
quasi-referring expression 261–262, 270

realizational 8, 10, 30, 138–172, 264; realizational relation 138–172
recursion 66–67
reduplication 12, 59, 97, 113–119, 121–123, 241; AABB 117; reduplication question 241; reduplicative 117–118
reference 3, 9, 12, 24, 26, 42, 44, 47, 59, 93, 126, 132, 138–139, 149, 159–160, 177, 188, 196, 247, 261, 264, 270
referential 44, 69, 95, 106, 112–113, 128, 133, 138–140, 169, 197, 209, 219, 223, 231–233, 238, 247, 256, 258, 264–265
referentiality 106–107, 126, 129, 168, 203–272; referentiality of predicates 203–272; strengthening referentiality 256–258
referentialization 91, 133, 140
referentially saturated 139, 148
referentially unsaturated 139
referentially unspecified 95
referring expression 1–3, 44, 91–92, 94, 113, 132–133, 138–139, 148, 161, 167, 172, 191, 209, 233, 240, 247, 256, 258–259, 261–262, 264, 269–270
regulative rule 142–143

282 Subject index

relativization 125, 127
relevance 204, 233–234
reply 56, 163, 167, 233, 249
resumptive word 241
rewrite rule 15, 111, 209
rhetorical use 130, 176, 185
root 10, 18, 84, 121, 124, 126, 129–131, 134, 168, 182, 198–199

secondary 44–45
segment 107, 149, 231, 238–239, 271; segment structure 238
self-designation 193–195, 197
semantics 10, 12, 47, 68, 170, 213; semantic indeterminacy 105; semantic proximity principle 170; semantic role 166; semantic type shift 94
sentence 6–8, 11, 14–21, 24, 26–30, 34, 36, 41–45, 47, 55, 64, 67, 70, 74, 76–77, 79–81, 84–85, 91–94, 104–105, 107–113, 116, 126–131, 134, 139, 145, 148–171, 177–180, 183–184, 186–187, 189, 192–193, 196–197, 203–207, 209–210, 212–225, 229–232, 234, 236, 238–241, 244, 246–247, 250, 256–258, 261–265, 270–271; sentence with event focus 258; sentence pattern 34, 55, 157, 204; sentence type 11, 104–105, 154, 167, 205, 234
sentence-based 6–7, 18
sentence-final intonation 113, 240
serial verb 18, 27
shénme 27–29, 101–102, 106, 111, 129, 176, 179, 187, 204, 241
shì 'be' 8, 11, 22, 144–145, 150–151, 186, 209–210, 212, 264, 268
skewed 80, 95–96, 98, 101–102, 104, 132, 140, 176, 198; skewed correspondence 104; skewed distribution 95–96, 98, 101–102, 140, 176; skewed relation 95, 132
solidification 82
spatial order 169
special 2, 17, 24, 45, 51, 54, 68, 74–75, 83, 95, 125, 131–132, 155, 158, 177–180, 203, 215, 241, 267
specialized 155, 185
specific 7, 9, 11, 28, 31, 37, 41, 43, 58, 92–93, 126, 138–139, 150, 183, 187, 189, 191, 233
speech act 168, 233

split 105, 169–170
static noun 3, 106
stress 212, 214–215, 223, 232, 257
structural parallelism 68, 181, 187, 210, 212, 214, 221–223, 225, 231, 252, 266
structure 1, 8, 11, 14–20, 25–28, 30, 45, 64–66, 68–72, 74–75, 79, 82, 84, 93, 102, 111–112, 123, 125–126, 129, 134, 154, 156, 161–163, 166, 169–170, 186, 189, 196, 205, 213, 220, 222, 225–226, 232–235, 237–238, 240–241, 243–244, 246–247, 252, 254, 263, 271
subject 6–9, 14–25, 27, 31, 34–35, 40, 43–47, 51, 59, 65, 69–70, 72, 74–77, 80, 82–83, 85, 90–92, 94–95, 102, 106–113, 123, 126–127, 129, 133–134, 139–140, 149–160, 162, 168–169, 171, 176, 179, 182–183, 186, 190–199, 203–204, 209, 220, 225, 232, 236, 240–241, 243–244, 247, 261, 264, 267, 269–271
subjective comment 93
subjective meaning 187
subjectivity marker 94
subjectless sentence 18, 149, 214
subject-predicate 8, 17–19, 27, 69–70, 76, 110–113, 123, 126, 149, 151, 154, 156–157, 162, 171, 240–241, 243, 247, 264; subject-predicate construction 8; subject-predicate phrase 8, 69, 162
subject-prominent 159
subjects and/or objects 6–8, 15–22, 25, 27, 43–46, 51, 65, 74–77, 82–83, 90–91, 94–95, 106, 133, 139–140, 176, 182, 190, 192–194, 197–199, 203, 225, 267, 269
subjunctive 33–34
subordinate clause 110
subordinate conjunction 109, 133
substantive 58, 83, 110, 181, 217, 224, 243, 263
super-noun 3, 10, 59–60, 113, 123, 125, 222, 267, 269–270; small noun 3, 60
surface structure 71, 186
symbol 67, 138, 198
synchronic 127
syncretism 32–34, 36
syntax 4, 10, 113, 151, 157, 216–217, 219, 238; syntactic 11, 14–19,

Subject index   283

21, 26–27, 30–34, 36, 42–47, 71, 75–77, 83–84, 130, 134, 138, 151, 154, 156–158, 162, 170, 183, 191–192, 196, 198, 212, 239, 241, 269; syntactic category 71, 154, 157–158; syntactic constituent 14–16, 42, 44–45, 47, 76–77, 83–84, 157, 183, 198, 212; syntactic structure 14, 16–17, 19, 26, 30, 45, 156, 162, 170; syntactic topic 156–158

temporal relation 206
temporary nominal quantifier 57
temporary verbal quantifier 57–58
tense 33–34, 68, 91, 131, 160, 176, 181, 190, 230, 257–258, 262–266, 272; expanded tense 262–263; future tense 230; permansive present tense 265; present tense 33, 230, 265, 272; progressive tense 230, 262
tense marker 257
tertiary 44
theory of endocentric constructions 66
theory of ranks 44–45
three-plane analysis 15
three-tier system 42, 44–45
time word 133
topic 8, 24, 40, 112–113, 128–129, 133, 139, 151–159, 162, 167–169, 171, 199, 233–238, 240, 243–244, 247–248, 258, 269, 271
topicalization 127, 157, 159, 237
topic marker 113, 156, 258
topic-prominent 159
transferred designation 193–195, 197
transitive verb 31, 162, 166, 182–183, 186, 193, 248, 254, 269
truth value 168–169, 171
two comments 244
two degrees of reference 247
type/token 10, 47, 148
typology 9–11, 85, 126, 131, 170, 199, 243, 266–267, 270; linguistic typology 9–11, 126, 131, 266–267, 270

unaccusative verb 164, 183
unbalanced relation 132
unergative verb 164, 183, 200
universality 142, 179; language universal 77; universal 2–3, 10, 51, 59, 77, 80, 105, 127, 138, 171, 183, 189, 257
usage class 161, 164

usage-type language 168, 171, 270
use 1, 3, 8–9, 20–21, 24, 26–27, 29, 37, 44, 47, 65–66, 71, 76, 82, 85, 92, 94–95, 97–98, 100, 103, 105, 107, 110, 112, 121, 124–126, 128, 130–132, 134, 138–143, 146–148, 150–151, 154, 160, 164, 166–168, 170, 176–177, 179–181, 184–185, 188–193, 196, 199, 212, 216, 218, 222–223, 230, 232, 235, 240–241, 245, 252, 254, 263, 265, 267–268, 270; flexible use 179, 188–190; temporary use 181
utterance 24, 28–31, 43, 93, 105, 110, 113, 130, 148–151, 159, 161, 168–169, 176, 188, 234, 240, 253

vagueness 105; vague 142, 181
verb-adverbial 18
verbal noun 35–37, 39
verbal predicate 126, 154, 156, 185, 187, 194, 207, 269
verb-centered 126, 176, 198–199, 267; verb-centered grammatical view 126, 176, 198–199
verb-complement 31
verb-object 8, 162, 271
verbs functioning as subjects and objects 6, 16, 19, 21–22, 27, 45, 133, 267
verbs-as-nouns 1–3, 7–12, 46, 48, 59–60, 66, 75, 83–84, 90–134, 138, 140, 161, 176, 199, 209, 240, 254, 267, 269; verbs-as-nouns framework 3, 8–12, 46, 59–60, 66, 83, 90–134, 138, 176, 199, 240, 254, 267, 269; verbs-as-nouns theory 1–3, 7–8, 10–11, 46, 48, 75, 83–84, 107, 113, 133, 140, 161, 209, 267, 269
verbs used as nouns 176, 178–179, 181, 190–191; nouns used as verbs 176–181, 184, 190–191, 200; used as nouns 47, 91, 176, 178–179, 181, 185, 190–191; used as verbs 84, 176–181, 184, 188, 190–191, 200, 209, 249, 268–269
view of categories 12
V-ing form 32, 34–35, 37, 39, 42, 47, 64–66, 261
voice morphology 126–128, 130

word class 2–4, 6, 8–12, 14–19, 30–31, 42–47, 51–52, 63, 71, 75–77, 81, 83–85, 105–106, 113, 117, 131, 134, 177, 179, 183, 190–191, 197,

284 *Subject index*

199–200, 209, 226, 247–248, 252–254; open word class 197; word class conversion 6; word class system 3–4, 9–12, 30, 47, 51, 76, 83; word class typology 10, 199
word order 9, 47, 71, 92, 129, 133, 161–162, 169–170, 257, 271; inverted word order 133; word order typology 9, 170
words belonging to no definite classes 75–76
written 20, 60, 74, 254, 256, 259

X-bar theory 66–67

yes-no question 8, 11, 167–168, 241
yǒu-aspect 228
yǒu 'have/there be' 8, 11, 22, 60, 73, 132, 144–145, 150, 223, 244, 248, 264
yǒu and *le* 225, 230
yǒu X *yǒu/wú* Y 226

zěnmeyàng 23–24, 101–102, 106, 150
zero derivation 27

Index of languages and dialects

Anglo-Irish 265
Austronesian 126–128, 182

Chinese 1–3, 5–12, 14–22, 24, 26–30,
32, 37–40, 42–48, 51–53, 58–61,
64–72, 74–77, 79–81, 83–85, 90–
134, 138–139, 141–172, 176–177,
179–181, 183–187, 189–194,
196–200, 203, 207–209, 214,
216–220, 222–226, 228, 230–231,
233–234, 236–238, 240–241, 243–
244, 246–248, 253–254, 258–264,
266–272; Ancient Chinese 145,
169, 179, 207, 218, 224, 243–244,
246–247, 266, 271; Classical
Chinese 21, 24, 98–99, 133, 179–
180, 189–190, 193–194, 196–197,
268; early modern Chinese 53;
early vernacular literature 97;
inscriptions on oracle bones 225;
Pre-Qin Chinese 149, 225–226

dialect 64, 92–93, 117, 119, 121–122,
132, 153, 224–225, 228–231, 240,
270–271; Cantonese 224, 228, 240,
260, 271; Daye 121; Fuling 122;
Fuzhou 228–229, 270; Gan 121;
Ganyu 270; Lianjiang 120; Ningde
229; Northern Jin 122; Puxian 229;
Shanghai 72, 75, 78–79, 83, 117,
206, 213, 271; Shantou 120–121,
229–230; Shaoxing 153; Southern
Min 224, 228–230; Wu 153, 228;
Xiamen 120; Zhangzhou 120

English 1, 6, 8, 10–12, 17–18, 20, 26–27,
29, 32–40, 42, 45–48, 51, 61,
64–66, 71, 74, 76, 91–95, 98, 100,
103, 112, 126–134, 139, 145–154,
156–157, 159–161, 163, 166–169,
171, 177, 179–182, 184–185, 188,
190, 193, 198, 203, 216–217, 220,
222–223, 230, 232, 241, 257, 261–
272; Pidgin English 130–131, 134

Farsi 124, 126

German 110, 198, 222, 228, 271–272
Gilaki 124, 126

Hebrew 182

Indo-European 1–3, 6–11, 14–18, 30,
42, 45–47, 51, 75, 77, 83, 90–91,
95–96, 123, 126, 132–133, 142,
145–146, 151, 157, 159–161,
167, 169–171, 186, 197, 216,
219–220, 228, 231, 254, 261,
266–267, 269
Iranian 10, 123, 125–126
Iroquoian 182
Italian 182

Japanese 7, 131, 134, 152, 155, 168, 182,
215–216, 220–222

Khoisan 182
Korean 131, 221, 257

Latin 33, 161–162, 169

Manipuri 182
Maori 182
Mohawk 182, 187

Old Aryan 265

286 Index of languages and dialects

Polynesian 10

Russian 168, 182

Sanskrit 198
sign language 169
Spanish 130

Tagalog 10, 126–131, 134, 199–200, 222, 267
Tibetan-Burmese 182
Tongan 10, 47, 129, 267

!Xun 182